EcCentric Visions

This book is part of a series of semio-ethnographic studies of English-speaking post-frontier cultures. In its challenge to uniformitarianism, it is also a test case in ethnographic theory. Its aims, in other words, involve both description and (albeit implicitly) interpretation. Multifaceted, formally recursive, using methods ranging from the hermeneutic through the structuralist to the psychoanalytic, it deploys the self-evidence of communal life and language to establish not only that all cultural phenomena, manifest or propaedeutic, are "patterned," but that this patterning is unique to and consistent across the entire system. As such, it is also generative with respect to individual responses, whether public or private. Imprinting every aspect of the social fabric from soap operas to political behaviour, lurking behind or within both folk tales and "official" histories, it not only influences but constrains the way the Australian conceptualizes, codifies, and *expresses* his/her existential position. The result is a kind of omnipresent structuredness that cumulatively signals being-in-the-world. Particularly notable in this regard is the national predilection for icons of intermediacy: the verandah in architecture, the bush in literature, the beach in folk culture, the middleground in landscape painting, the pub in everyday life. The concatenation is not accidental. The identification with buffer zones between inside and outside not only mimics the Australian's real bracketing between desert and ocean, but more importantly embodies his/her sense of disablement vis-à-vis both culture and nature, art and techne, superego and id, *all* of which are coded as "feminine."

Gaile McGregor is an itinerant scholar whose research falls somewhere near the juncture of Cultural and Communication Studies, Sociology of Culture, and Cultural Anthropology. Following on graduate degrees in both Literature and Sociology, her recent appointments include a Canada Research Fellowship at York University in Toronto and a Fulbright Fellowship at Rice University in Houston. Now affiliated with the Anthropology Department at the University of Western Ontario, she is currently completing a book on North American culture and society entitled *Signs of Difference: Cycles, Markers and Mythos.*

D1554946

EcCentric Visions

RE CONSTRUCTING AUSTRALIA

Gaile McGregor

Wilfrid Laurier University Press

Canadian Cataloguing in Publication Data

McGregor, Gaile, [date]
  Eccentric visions : re constructing Australia

Includes bibliographical references and index.
ISBN 0-88920-229-X

1. Australia – Civilization.   2. Australian
literature – History and criticism.   I. Title.

DU107.M34 1994   994   C94-930356-9

A version of Chapter 2 appeared as "Marker Traits in Australian Literature" in *Australian and New Zealand Studies in Canada* 1, 1 (1989). Some of the material in Chapter 3, subsection entitled "Television: Copping It," appeared in "Imitation and Resistance: The Differential Assimilation of American Popular Culture," *Australian-Canadian Studies* 8, 2 (1991).

Copyright © 1994

WILFRID LAURIER UNIVERSITY PRESS
Waterloo, Ontario, Canada
N2L 3C5

Cover design by Jose Martucci,
Design Communications
Cover photograph by the author

Typeset by Adams & Hamilton, Toronto
Printed in Canada

EcCentric Visions: Re Constructing Australia has been produced from camera-ready pages supplied by the author.

CONTENTS

v

Theoretical space replaces geographical space. We write now of the inversion in the European mind represented by the antipodes long before their actual discovery, the myths of disappearance linked to the journey "inward" from the safe coast "surface" on which we cluster – for example, the myths of Burke and Wills, Voss and Azaria Chamberlain, the dominant role of the cinematographer in figuring the landscape and other flirtatious nihilisms which could have been uttered by a Joseph Conrad or a Jean Baudrillard. Perhaps our greatest paradox, indeed, is that while Australia is so patently an artificial culture, so continuously recolonised and so ambivalent about its past and present, its culture maintains an imaginative purchase on the future, a potential for storytelling and stock-in-trade of . . . self-images.

Paul Taylor, "A Culture of Temporary Culture"

PREFACE

What this book represents is, quite literally, a "slice" of (white) Australian life. Though broad-ranging, that is, it makes no claims to inclusiveness. All first-hand observations were made during one four-month stint in mid-1986. Even those historical reconstructions which draw significantly upon secondary sources are time-specific, since they depend entirely on the texts available during that period and on the opinions of the scholars who provided me with my "leads." This isn't to say that the portrait I am proffering here is necessarily any less representative than the kind of compilation one might come up with using "hard" (statistical or archival) data. It's merely arrived at differently. Instead of exhaustively documenting "key" aspects of national culture (which would mean prejudging the importance of given factors), I have constructed a model by noting the patterns and parallels that emerge when one randomly samples social phenomena of widely varying types. Though this process may *appear* to be somewhat impressionistic, the validity of my conclusions can easily be gauged by the extent to which all the different pieces of the puzzle "fit."

The evidence per se is presented for the most part in Chapter 3. This section is made up of two different texts – a journal or memoir recounting my own experiences in Australia plus a series of mini-essays on different topics which were prepared later from books and other research materials collected during my trip. I have not, on the other hand, made any attempt to maintain a strict division between these contrapuntal strands along categorical lines. Some books, for instance, especially in the areas of art and architecture, were read during my stay, and as such were instrumental in guiding my responses to more immediate kinds of phenomena. Discussion of these thus forms part of the journal narrative. Complementarily, it is obvious that my first-hand experience would have influenced the way I selected and assessed and interpreted my secondary sources once I returned. So why choose such an unwieldy format? My primary purpose was to make visible the normally tacit process of negotiating a balance or compromise between objective and subjective viewpoints which *always* characterizes the critical act. Secondarily, though, by reconstructing the mental along with the physical "trip," I hoped also to enable the reader to share the process as well as the results of my research. For those who may be puzzled or bothered by the unconventionality of this approach, I have provided a brief explanation of my methodology in Chapter 1.

This brings up another point. Not all aspects of this book will be equally interesting to all readers. For those who are neither familiar with nor concerned about recent issues of ethnographic theory – particularly the debate over representation – the introduction, for instance, may seem both obscure and tangential. This shouldn't be a problem. The main text speaks for itself in any case. Australian readers, similarly, may be bored by the survey of Australian fiction in Chapter 2. While it is true that the conclusions I draw from this body of material are significantly different from those put forth by their compeers, it is equally true that most of the individual features discussed here have been discussed previously by indigenous critics. The main thing in both of these cases is to avoid getting hung up. While it's quite natural for authors to treasure their every word, when it comes down to druthers I'd much prefer that my readers treat me irreverently than not at all. But that's not quite right either. Reverence doesn't have anything to do with it; receptivity *does*. What should be understood right from the start is that this book is not intended as a "scientific" tract. By design as well as by necessity, it is, rather, what James Clifford calls a "serious fiction" (1988: 10). As such it demands to be approached both less and more solemnly. But note that *and*. While quite openly inviting its auditors to skip, skim, dabble, argue, even disbelieve, my text cannot ultimately be abstracted from itself. To make its point properly, in fact, it is best swallowed whole, like a novel or a poem. This invocation of literariness should not be taken to imply that my intentions are any the less scholarly. It just means – again – that I come at things from a slightly different angle than most of my colleagues. Where most social scientists extract social particulars from the world in which they are generated, the backbone of my thesis is that cultures are rational in the same way that fictions are. I hold it as axiomatic, in other words, that all facets and aspects and phases and kinds of social experience within any given "community," far from circumstantial, are both consonant with and diagnostic of a single pervading mythos. As such, the only way they can be understood is holistically.

The same can be said of my reconstruction.

This project was not carried out without the accumulation of a significant number of debts. I am particularly grateful to the Australians, too numerous to name, who gave so generously of advice, information, and hospitality during my sojourn in the country. On a different level, I also owe much to my colleagues in the Sociology Department at York University, especially Ioan Davies, Christopher Nichols, and Ray Morris, all of whom contributed in different ways to the development of the ideas which came to fruition first in a dissertation and then in this book. I would like to thank the Social Sciences and Humanities Research Council of Canada for providing me with the Postdoctoral Research Fellowship (1987-89) which allowed me the leisure to finalize this work. I would like to thank my women's dinner network in Toronto for keeping me sane during my endeavours. I would like to thank Sandra Woolfrey of Wilfrid Laurier University Press, my publisher, colleague, and very good friend, without whose faith, perseverance, and adroitness in overcoming practical and especially (considering the current economic climate) financial obstacles, the book would not have appeared at all. (In Sandra's case, in fact, a simple thank you doesn't seem enough.) Finally, I owe my greatest debt to my husband, Norman Duke, who has not only been of immeasurable practical help during the preparation of this manuscript, but who also, still, comprises my "ideal reader."

I

INTRODUCTION

THIS BOOK is part of a series of semio-ethnographic studies focusing on the three grossly similar (in language, in derivation, in geohistorical terms) post-frontier cultures of the United States, Canada, and Australia. This series, collectively entitled "Voice in the Wilderness," was originally designed as a means of elucidating that fugitive entity which has been termed the *Weltanschauung*. In the course of the research, however, the focus was deflected perforce from Culture to cultures. It was not an entirely happy development. Considering the now almost consensual entrenchment of assumptions about the ideological homogenization of postmodern society (the world according to Coke!), for a researcher to postulate significant and basic cross-cultural differences entails both conceptual and methodological problems. Before I could even begin to speculate on the reasons for deviation, it was necessary to determine what it was that made a given culture cohere. This meant finding a way to isolate and explain the mechanics of cultural change. It meant rationalizing the relations between culture-at-large and various kinds of cultural expression. Most important of all, it meant devising a portable methodology for "mapping" culture which had the capacity to cut through the accidents to the essential. Since the approach to these tasks was cumulative rather than simply additive, the present study should be viewed not as one of a number of discrete parallel cases, but as the culmination of a progressive unravelling.

Two volumes have already been published.[1] In addition to its "hard" data, each illuminates a different aspect of the problem of

---

1. By an accident of history, the first work written was actually the second volume to be published (see G. McGregor, 1988). Since it remains *logically* prior to the Canadian study (G. McGregor, 1985) by which it was temporally preceded, however, I have referred to the American book throughout this introduction as the first of the series.

decipherment. At the same time, each also lays the ground for its successor, not by establishing answers but by posing new questions. The first, focusing on the United States, demonstrates how overt patterning in literature changes directly with changes in the socio-political environment. Singling out the emblematic convention of the noble savage, this book reveals not only that a quasi-cyclical alternation between primitivism and progressivism is historically characteristic of American culture, but that key features of both literary and sub-literary usage during any given period can be used to identify and plot the complex phases of this progression. The second volume, on Canada, probes a little deeper. Now simply assuming what the American study set out to demonstrate, that there is indeed an orderly reciprocity between different kinds and levels of cultural activity, this book goes on to establish that an even more fundamental – and largely covert – kind of patterning provides a consistent substratum to *all* social phenomena such that it not merely reflects but actually controls the mode of communal response, structuring both the form and the content of expression in any given cultural ambience in precise accordance with what we might call the "syntactic signature" of that ambience.[2] The present study extends the investigation to Australia with the dual aim of testing the theoretical assumptions about the structured nature of culture derived from the American and Canadian examples and of collecting more evidence about the impact of the environment on the socio-historical development of a transplanted people.

Apart from its substantive contribution, *EcCentric Visions* was also intended to provide a kind of methodological control to the series as a whole. Whereas my personal experience of and preconceptions about North American culture may be expected to have guided and coloured the analytic process to a greater or lesser extent in both earlier studies, Australia offered what was almost entirely fresh ground. In order to take best advantage of this circumstance – in order to minimize the prejudicial potential of even theoretical expectations – the approach this time (like the postmodern multivocal novel) utilizes the interreflective potential of serial viewpoints. Although the

---

2. For a better sense of the findings and implications of these earlier volumes, see Appendix A, " 'Voice in the Wilderness': A Note on Grounds and Precedents," p. 287.

specific mode of presentation has been determined at least as much by formal as by functional considerations (in both of the initial studies an attempt is made not merely to explain but to express the object of analysis such that the style of each book broadly mimics the style of the culture under consideration), the goal has been to balance intensive with extensive, general with particular, and inductive with deductive modes of analysis. To offset the effects, or at least the appearance, of authorial intervention, the coherence of the text is achieved by implicit rather than explicit means. Rather than simply documenting findings post facto, for example, there is an attempt to enlist the reader as a participant in the act of elucidation by reproducing the temporal/incremental dimensions of the quest.

Explicit theorizing is kept to a minimum. Insofar as intellectual strategies are as wholly a product of culture as films and fashions (see G. McGregor, 1986), the a priori privileging of a theoretical stance, even of a specific vocabulary, necessarily imports a bias to a study of this type. To my mind, indeed, the only way to produce a truly objective ethnography would be in the form of a totally decentred discourse.[3] Since this is in practice impossible, I have at least made an effort to ensure that the centre resolves itself within the spoken, and not the speaking, subject. Most important of the strategies employed to this end is the construction of a narrative persona whose obtrusiveness underlines rather than, as is more normal in "scholarly" writing, obscuring the gap between the observer and the observed. As far as the risk to its "scientific" credibility is concerned, the poetic licence is, I think, more than adequately offset by the range and variety of materials considered, the range and variety of modelling techniques, and, especially, the self-correcting nature of the multivocal narrative. Unmediated except by its own subject(s), the text generates its own rules. Terms are defined by their use. Evidence is tacitly adjudicated with respect to its consonance. "Meaning" emerges gradually, as part of the process of reconstitution. And the agent of all this is not the invisible theorist in the wings, but the reader.

---

3. Though these discussions are extrinsic to the documentary project per se, for a fuller discussion both of the problems entailed by traditional "realist" approaches to ethnographic representation and of potential narrative/strategic remedies, the reader is referred to Clifford and Marcus, 1986; Marcus and Fischer, 1986; and Clifford, 1988.

The text itself, apart from its framing, comprises three complementary sections corresponding to four phases of research. The first of these is propaedeutic. Establishing a substantive pre-view of the country in question, it also lays the ground for the aforementioned methodological control. If social phenomena really are "patterned" in the way that I claim, then the essence of a culture, as of a holograph, should be carried at least vestigially by every small "piece" one might detach from it. As a kind of test case, I hence chose to begin my investigation not with the kind of search-and-review process that would supply me with a readymade informing context, but with a comprehensive (structural, semiotic, and psychoanalytic) analysis of a limited number of "representative" works of literature. The psycho-typology inferred from this data – written up in Chapter 2, *Image / Self-Image* – provided me with a testable model to be carried into the field. By pointing up systematic discrepancies between what is articulated in, and what is betrayed by, Australian cultural production, it also provided me with some important clues to the critical nexi around which cultural tensions could be expected to gather.

Chapter 3 is called *Coming into the Country* – and that's exactly what it does. Its burden is at least in one sense the recapitulation of a physical journey from the coast of Australia to its interior, and thence to the big cities of the south. In another and more critical sense, this journey is merely an analogue for the process by which the Australian "langscape"[4] became constituted in the observer's mind. In recognition of its iconic character, the linear narrative, with its emphasis on the immediately seen and heard and thought, is both supplemented and offset by a series of short, interpolated essays on a variety of both directly relevant and tangential topics. Text and intertext thus mimic in form as well as in content the interplay of subject and object. Far from pure documentation, however, *both* strands take as their

---

4. "The coinage 'langscape,' far from adventitious, is meant to underline the extent to which nature, like other aspects of reality, is not simply perceived but socially constructed. By mythicizing our environment we convert it into a body of symbols, a kind of code which – like all language – reveals the ability both to reflect *and* to coerce our experience of the world. Where the landscape is passive, morally neutral, and ultimately inaccessible, 'langscape' suggests a kind of accommodation or complicity between self and other" (G. McGregor, 1985: vii).

primary objective an attempt to "get at" the structures of consciousness that underlie and inform the surficial diversity of manifest culture. In line with this objective, special attention has been paid to the "markers" that proved significant in the North American cases: communal images of self and other, past and future, good and evil, hero and villain, nature and technology, art and science, country and city, house and garden, male and female, love and sex and families.

Chapter 4, *Alternative Readings*, attempts to resolve the problematic implied by Chapter 2. Turning to the critical corpus, it sets Australian self-assessments against a range of "hard" data yielded by the historical record. It then tackles the task of reconciling both of these realities with the sur-reality that emerges covertly from the communal imagination. Underlining what may have been obscured by the "occasional" style of the preceding sections, it brings the question of cultural determinism out of the closet. The characterizing features and anomalies uncovered by field and library research are now related as far and as systematically as possible to specific, local, geo-social factors – and to each other. The final step is a retrospective reassessment of the whole picture from an international perspective. Having by now established, I hope beyond cavil, the extent to which manifest culture, like myth, not only expresses but mediates communal tensions, I conclude by considering whether recent shifts in public policy and national self-imaging are likely to presage "real" changes in Australian social psychology.

2

IMAGE/SELF-IMAGE

Methods and Models

Actually, that summary makes the exercise sound a lot simpler than it was in practice. I began, as I said, with the assumption that there was something to be gained by approaching the data, at least initially, with an "innocent" eye. Even in the preliminary study, however, I also wanted to make use of the informative context provided by the North American studies. This presented something of a problem when it came to determining the specifics of approach. My solution, as it turned out, was neither a relinquishment of, nor a compromise between, two ostensibly conflicting goals, but a serial alternation of different instrumentalities that allowed me to shift my vantage on the problem through a full three hundred and sixty degrees.

Step one was purely inductive. It involved, as mentioned, a close reading (not yet a reading into) of sixty Australian novels. In order to select a sample without "boning up" on the subject, it was, of course, necessary to employ rather arbitrary criteria. In this case a list of works by forty-five novelists, spanning the period from the mid-nineteenth century to the mid-sixties, was compiled by culling the tables of contents, prefaces, and bibliographies of a variety of survey-type Australian literary-critical and literary-historical texts. This was then both updated and modified on the basis of what was available in the Canadian libraries to which I had ready access. If the resulting selection is either incomplete or unbalanced,[1] given my postulate of structural homogeneity the fact should not prejudice the analysis – and indeed should serve as a more stringent test of my thesis.

---

1. I was surprised but pleased to discover, once I had the opportunity to familiarize myself with the broader context, how "representative," even in conventional terms, my random culling actually turned out to be. Though it is true that a significant number (because of the difficulty of evaluative categorizations, I will not attempt to be more exact than this) of the writers listed would

On completion of the reading, I proceeded to work backwards from fact to ground in an attempt to elucidate the syntactic characteristics of the entire oeuvre. It was at this point that extrinsic considerations were brought into the picture. My work on Canada and the United States has yielded ample evidence that under conditions of physical and psychological vulnerability the unmediated confrontation with the wilderness has the power literally to re-imprint the communal imagination (see G. McGregor, 1985, Chapters 1-4; also 1987a, 1988). Assuming that the Australian experience must have been at least as traumatic as the North American one, I looked for evidence of such imprinting in the covert content of the novels in my sample, and particularly in transforms of the human/nature (self/other) relation.

On an intuitive level at least, the results of this scrutiny were gratifying. Keeping in mind the fact that the Canadian's recoil from the northern wilderness perpetuated itself as a kind of ubiquitous centripetal impulse underlaying all levels and aspects of communal expression (see Appendix A; also G. McGregor, 1985, especially Chapter 4), one might predict that the initial disposition of the Australians around the edges of an alien and seemingly impenetrable island continent would produce exactly the opposite effect: extraversion rather than introversion, fear of the "inside" rather than fear of the "outside," a masculine rather than a feminine orientation to the world. And this was exactly what the literature seemed to suggest. Note, though, that qualifier, "seemed." If the generalities proved quite consonant with my earlier expectations, the particulars of these novels, and especially the meta-meanings one may infer from the play of and spaces between constituent significants, map a pattern of response both more subtle and more complex than the simple inversion model would tend to suggest. Though space prohibits detailed treatment of either the texts or the strategies that document this syntax, its salient features are summarized in the following section.

----

be considered as "minor" or "popular" – indeed, there are even a couple of total unknowns – the sample as a whole contains a remarkable proportion of what would consensually be considered the county's most important writers and/or novels.

Marker Traits in
Australian Literature[2]

Nature/The Land

If the landscape is the key formative factor in the colonist's psycho-social environment, then it is no wonder that the Australian should turn out to be a somewhat ambivalent character. In novel after novel, the aspect emphasized in descriptions of the land, quite apart from any specific features that might be invoked, is its alienness. In early fictions and historical reconstructions alike, the continent is depicted as not merely coincidentally inimical to human survival (Tucker, Clarke, Herbert), but somehow *essentially* impervious to human efforts and intentions. In Dark's *The Timeless Land*, for instance, a recurrent motif is the explorers' failure, after repeated attempts, to penetrate beyond the mountains that guard the coastline. A similar sense of impenetrability is conveyed in Drake-Brockman's *The Wicked and the Fair*. Recent novels perpetuate the impression of estrangement by underlining the reactions of newcomers (Sydney, McCullough, Wilson), or by setting their protagonists in unfamiliar and mind- if not life-threatening settings (Stow, Cook, Carey). Australia, it is often suggested, is separated from the civilized world not just by space but by an impassable chasm in time.

Along with and perhaps even concomitant upon this irremediable foreignness, the second most strenuously insisted upon feature of the Australian literary landscape is its duplicity. If, in purely quantitative terms, it is the negative image that predominates (see especially Penton, Herbert), this is far from implying that there is no other side to the picture. When Tennant's itinerant "battlers" are struck dumb by

---

2. The following overview deals with generalities rather than particulars. For further details on individual works, see the capsule summaries included in Appendix B. Note that the lists of novels cited in brackets as exemplary with respect to given features are meant to be representative rather than exhaustive.

their sudden transition from a bleak, wind-swept plain to a lush green river valley, with its masses of blossoms and flocks of brightly coloured birds, their awe as much as their pleasure gives us a trenchant glimpse of the Australians' sense of their country's infinite variability. The relief is short-lived, of course. In this case as in almost all similar cases throughout the oeuvre, paradise soon turns back into the familiar inferno. The feelings of insecurity spawned by the inevitable transience of these tantalizing flashes of beauty perhaps explain why natural menace is so often bodied forth in terms of sudden, all-encompassing disasters like flood and fire (Franklin, Cleary, White, McCullough). Even more sinister, on the other hand, are those occasions when it is the beauty itself that turns out to be a deadly snare. In Kingsley's *Geoffrey Hamlyn*, for instance, a child is lured into the wilderness – and death – by fantasies of pixies living across the river among the trees.

Alienness and duplicity, then, are the key elements in Australian views of the land. Given the physical realities, this is perhaps no more than one might expect. Slightly less predictable, however, and all the more interesting because of that fact, is the psycho-sexual symbolism that seems to underlie more direct responses. In marked contrast to Canada, where the wilderness becomes masculinized in opposition to a strongly "feminine" sense of self (G. McGregor, 1985: 133ff.), in Australia nature in both its negative and its positive aspects is more often than not associated with feminine iconography. In Glaskin's *Flight to Landfall*, for instance, the gorge and garden discovered by the band of plane-crashed refugees near two breast-like mountains in the middle of the desert are clearly meant to represent the malevolent and beneficent aspects of the feminine. In Carey's *Bliss*, the dark, fecund rainforest, home of the natural woman, combines both aspects in one. Apart from such more or less idiosyncratic usages as these, the strongest evidence for a feminized nature may perhaps be inferred from the significant number of novels that make explicit connections between anima figures and ocean imagery. The frequency with which this motif recurs, as well as its ambivalence – its capacity to carry both positive (Forrest, Palmer, Cook) and negative implications (Stead, Charlwood) – signals its importance in the Australian psycho-symbology. It also signals a complication that my previous comments about a communal bent for centrifugality did not take into consideration. If it is true that the alienness *of* the inside has led to an alienation *from* "insideness" in Australia, it is equally true that the association of the inaccessible but desirable "outside" (not just ocean, but home, mother, gentility, and civilization) with feminine images as well, renders the emotional concomitants of the self/other opposition less clear-cut than they are in Canada. This is undoubtedly why, as we shall see, the iconic female in Australian literature stands for both all-too-immanent destructiveness *and* all-too-inaccessible goodness – and why the masculine protagonist, whether man or woman, tends, for all his/her vestigial extraversion, to be incapacitated by ambivalence.

The Aborigines

If the American westering myth reinforces primitivistic clichés about the mediating function of the noble savage, the Canadian corpus, with its Indian alter egos, gives clear evidence that even the most traditional of symbolic alignments are far from immutable. The Australian example reinforces such a conclusion. Like the Canadian native, the literary aborigine is commonly bodied forth as an victim of history rather than a symbol of freedom. Like the American savage, he is more allegorical than real. Unlike both, however, this figure invites neither positive nor negative identification. Far from invoking some hidden or neglected aspect or fragment of self, the Australian aborigine in fact represents all that is *un*mediatable in the world-as-given – the most absolute and irreconcilable aspects of otherness.

This peculiarity is, of course, related to and rooted in the features discussed in the last section. For the early colonists, the alienness of the land not only exacerbated the alienness of the people who lived there, but also underlined the links between the two. The imputed nature connection, reinforced no doubt by the high value placed on ritual femininization in the aborigines' own mythology (see G. McGregor, 1987a), triggered an association between savagery and femaleness that served in the long run to further ambiguate both elements in the equation. It also served to codify and conventionalize literary treatments of the native. With very few exceptions, aborigines in Australian novels tend to be limned in exactly – and only – the same terms as the landscape itself. Sometimes they are made to epitomize nature's irrationality and destructiveness (Penton), sometimes they embody natural wisdom (Glaskin), but most often they exhibit the same duplicity, the same ambivalent combination of threat and promise, that the land does (Tucker, Boldrewood, Dark). The symbolic associations add considerably to their usefulness, if not their verisimilitude. Pre-mythicized to such an extent, the individual aborigine can easily be used as a foil (Stow) or a touchstone against which the reader may gauge a protagonist's moral worth or emotional health (Herbert, McLean). This latter function is most striking in books where the aborigine is also an anima figure. Prichard's *Coonardoo* provides what is perhaps one of the most moving and apposite fables in the oeuvre, insofar as the white hero's rejection/destruction of the native woman whom he secretly loves clearly represents a denial of his own inner – that is, inward – self. It is significant that after Coonardoo departs, the land itself is overtaken by blight.

Social Existence

One of the things that "everyone knows" about Australia is the "shocking truth" about its brutal beginnings as a penal colony. It is not merely in novels of the bad old days (Tucker, Clarke, Penton, Dark, Porter) that we find an infelicitous image of the Australian public world, however. Furphy, Stone, Herbert, Tennant, Marshall, Cusack and James, Park, Hardy, Astley, and Ireland all in their different ways depict a society in which the powerful are corrupt and the weak dishonest, where self-interest reigns supreme and every man's hand is turned against every other. History cannot be blamed for more than a fraction of this pervasive negativity. Of equal or perhaps even more importance for explaining the Australian's suspicions of transpersonal institutions and mechanisms is the fact that this realm is associated with the feminine, whether it is Britannia across the sea or the henpecking wife at home.

One must, on the other hand, be careful not to oversimplify this matter. To mention henpecking, for instance, is perhaps to invite misleading assessments of the situation. Although it is certainly one element, it is clear from the covert content of the oeuvre that the natural "masculine" dislike for regulation is only part of the reason why Australians take such a dim view of the social world per se. More invidious, because more deeply rooted, is the fear that this world is simply beyond their talents and their control. In no national literature that I can think of is there so much insistence on the fragility of civilization. At least one implication of the decline and fall story so beloved of Australian novelists is that man, deprived of his civilized supports, will quickly lose his polish, his morals, his health, and eventually – in many cases – his life. Richardson's chronicle of Richard Mahoney (see next section) is the prototype for this genre, but deteriorating heroes abound throughout the entire corpus, right from Clarke's *For the Term of His Natural Life* through Penton's *Landtakers* to Sydney's *The Return* and Wilson's *The Mulga Trees*. Religion, art, love: *anything* that depends upon "feminine" intuition and sensitivity tends to be treated ambivalently in Australian literature not simply because it is undervalued but because, like the anima herself, it is both desirable and intimidatingly alien.

This inherent asociability perhaps explains some of the more ambiguous aspects of the mateship myth that plays so great a part in the popular Australian imagination. The fact is, judging at least by their literature, Australians themselves don't seem to believe in it. Not as a real possibility at least. The reason? A society of two is still a society of sorts. As such it requires at least a modicum of social talents. This, of course, explains why, despite numerous paeans to the solidarity of the trail (Furphy, Niland), and despite even more numerous and enthusiastic disquisitions on the issue of class solidarity (Tennant, Waten, McLean), in virtually every novel that deals with real, one-on-one relationships the result of any sort of interpersonal dependency is disappointment if not destruction. Boldrewood, Penton, Herbert, Stow, Charlwood, Turner, McDonald: each of these in his own way confirms the message that Koch conveys so saliently in *The Boys in the Island* – real mates ruin your life; "good" mates exist only in dreams. This pessimism about the possible does not, to be sure, mean that the *idea* of mateship is not important to the Australian. Indeed, the fact that most of the betrayals in these books are entirely inadvertent ones testifies vividly to the good intentions of the individuals involved. It also, however, testifies to the fact that, if only because of the malevolence of Lady Luck, the Australian feels just as much trepidation about "relation" on a private as on a public level.

Male Characters

Predictably enough considering the asocial bias of the entire oeuvre, the type protagonist of the Australian novel is the outsider. Restless, rootless, and chronically bewildered, this character spends his life trying to escape from the dangerous world of his own emotions by projecting the inward outward. His typical response to mental confusion is physical activity. His need for love, similarly, is replaced by the self-validating fantasy of male camaraderie or translated into dreams of the big strike over the next hill. The conditioned obliviousness makes him both vulnerable and dangerous. If at best the centrifugal man is White's Stan Parker – obtuse, inarticulate, groping half-consciously for comprehension – at worst he is Turner's vicious drunk or Harrower's sadistic bully or Hardy's and Stone's totally amoral men-on-the-make. Often we find goodness and badness schizophrenically juxtaposed in the same persona (Stow, Mass, Ireland, Carey). "Good" or "bad," however, in virtually all cases the keynote to the characterization is emotional ineptness. The Australian proto-protagonist simply doesn't understand how emotions "work."

This perhaps explains why, no matter how benign his intentions, he so often ends up hurting himself or others. If he maintains his distance, his sense of isolation undermines not just his ability to function publicly but even at times his will to live (Stead, Cook, Sydney). If he opts for commitment, on the other hand, his restlessness undermines the happiness and well-being of his family (Cleary, Niland, Williamson). Richard Mahoney's fate is in a very real sense exemplary. Increasingly torn between ambition and caprice, self-pity and self-hatred, uxoriousness and misogyny, the good doctor simply reacts by withdrawing from reality. His fate is exemplary, too – not just because his madness represents the ultimate isolation, but because the metamorphosis from gentleman to bully that he undergoes on the way to that madness is an exact analogue for the physical and moral deterioration we see in "frontier" types like Penton's Cabell. The point is clear. It is not the land itself that the Australian blames for the decay of civilization, but the seeds of violence and irrationality that every man carries within himself. The land only releases what is already there.

The half-conscious conviction of immanent inner rot is detectable in the tension set up in novel after novel between the author's obvious belief that the protagonist is responsible for his own downfall and the latter's equally obvious sense of being a pawn of fate or luck or simply "bad blood." Boldrewood's *Robbery under Arms* offers a particularly striking example of this phenomenon, but a dissonance of objective and subjective viewpoints (modelling, no doubt, the felt tension between self and other) might almost be considered a diagnostic feature of the oeuvre. Like most critical nexi, moreover, this particular dissonance generates both a variety of "symptoms" and a variety of complementary stress management strategies. With respect to the characterization of the males, in the first category (apart from the protagonist's own personality problems) would be the biased disposition of supporting personae. Judging by the predominance of negative male role models – villains rather than heroes – among the ranks of secondary characters (Tucker, Clarke, Eldershaw, Prichard, Penton, Timms, Anderson, Drake-Brockman, Williamson, Charlwood, especially Keneally), the Australian writer has a hard time imaging an active role model who is both positive (that is, good) *and* successful (that is, not punished for the sins that he *doesn't* evince). In the second category is the propensity to idealize war, not – as is usually supposed – because it provides a proving ground for the macho male, but because, on the contrary, it first strips the individual of his freedom of choice, thus rationalizing his impotence, and then "punishes" him, thus assuaging his guilt. It is interesting but not surprising that Hungerford's *The Ridge and the River* and Forrest's *The Last Blue Sea*, both participant-observer World War II novels, offer not only the most harrowing pictures of human suffering in the sample, but also the most unequivocally positive endings.

Female Characters

Establishing beyond cavil that the symbolic ego is a cultural rather than a biological phenomenon, the female protagonist of Australian literature demonstrates many of the same character traits and confronts many of the same problems as her masculine counterparts. She is an outsider, though perhaps not in such obvious ways or for such obvious reasons (Drake-Brockman, Astley). She is self-centred (Elliott). She is restless and dissatisfied, forever groping after some half-imagined outlet or opportunity (Eldershaw). Though less absolutely obtuse than her brothers (her awareness usually extends at least to the recognition that there is a realm of experience beyond her grasp), she is equally at sea when it comes to dealing with real emotions (Harrower). The implication of all this is clear: in literature at least, the type Australian female, just like the type Australian male, is self-perceived to suffer from an excess of "masculinity."

What happens when we get a cross-sexual ego image like this? Actually, the Australian case is strongly reminiscent of, if exactly inverse to, the situation in Canada, where it is a feminine symbolic ego that dominates the communal sense of self. It is predictable, therefore, that just as in Canada it is the inappropriately modelled male protagonist who evinces the most marked signs of psychic stress, in Australian literature it is the female who goes through the most profound identity crises. This is not always apparent on the surface. Given the endemic lack of self-consciousness among both writers and their characters, it is often unclear that what's going on *is* a search for identity. The theme shows up strikingly, though, in the recurrent emphasis on sex role confusion. Not only do Australian heroines have trouble dealing with sex itself (I will be returning to this later), but they commonly display an awkward and unwonted masculinity of demeanour that impedes their ability to play the roles that either they themselves or others expect of them. Admittedly, this assertiveness is often inadvertent, a defensive reaction to male ineptitude (Richardson, Waten, Sydney). Lest we be tempted to conclude that the phenomenon is simply fallout from the problems touched upon in the last section, however, it is important to note that even in the relatively conventional cases already mentioned the *propensity* for role reversal pre-exists any particular stimulus. And in the few books that focus directly on the experience of the female, the sexual ambivalence of the heroine – the irresolvable conflict between her need for love and her obsessive independence – often emerges as a key theme (Eagle, Langley).

One thing that must be stressed is that this typology normally only applies when the female in question functions as a centre of consciousness in a given novel. When the female is "other," a figment of the male imagination, whatever confusions one may infer to exist beneath the surface of her frequently inexplicable behaviour, from the outside she appears very much a seamless whole. She is also, as one might expect in a culture disconcerted by "inwardness," portrayed as the ultimate alien. There are two versions: the wicked wife or predatory manhunter (faithless, unloving, unfeminine) and the good but inaccessible anima figure. Often these are paired in a single novel (Boldrewood, Timms, Williamson, Palmer, Turner). Often, too, the pairing is a structurally important element in the working out of the protagonist's destiny. One must be careful, on the other hand, not to mistake the function that this element fulfils. Unlike the masculine role models mentioned in the last section, neither the good nor the bad woman in any sense represents a potential mode of action for the protagonist, but merely some aspect of his (rarely, her) field of operation. In the second place, both the bad *and* the good woman represent threats. The bad woman – associated with sex, violence, and the city – threatens his physical and emotional well-being. The good woman, however, by enticing him into the dangerous worlds of art and spirit and emotion, threatens his psychic survival. Martin's *The Young Wife* is exemplary. The eponymous ingenue here, despite or perhaps even because of her natural, innocent "womanliness," becomes an unwitting catalyst for catastrophe when misplaced jealousy leads to violence.

Gender Relations

It is hardly surprising, considering the bias in character types noted above, that relations *between* the sexes are generally depicted in Australian literature in very equivocal terms. Individual men and women may in themselves suffer from the same kind of personality defects, but once the focus shifts from one to two the portrait is less likely to reflect this particular fact than it is to underline the absolute disparity between femaleness and maleness in the abstract. It also underlines the fact that attempts to resolve this disparity are almost inevitably difficult, and often even dangerous.

The residual uneasiness signalled by this last feature shows up with particular vividness in the treatment of sex – perhaps because lovemaking represents the ultimate coming together with otherness. In Langley's *The Pea Pickers* physical intimacy is rendered problematic insofar as it is set in ambivalent opposition to an ideal of purity. In other books, like McDonald's *1915*, it is made to seem risky by its (largely coincidental) results. Going far beyond such gentle adumbrations as these, however, in many matings throughout the oeuvre there is an explicit association made between sex and violence, sex and pain, perhaps even – if we accept as cautionary the large number of pregnancy/childbirth disasters that crop up – between sex and death (Clarke, Drake-Brockman, Martin, Harrower, McCullough, Jessica Anderson). Why the unallayed negativity? My thesis would hold that the ambiguation of sex is simply a byproduct of the obsessive asociability mentioned above. In Astley's *A Descant for Gossips* – a book redolent with subtle sexual disgust – the abortive love affair is not only set *against* a background of community-wide backbiting and maliciousness, but, given the emotional incapacities of the protagonists, and particularly the self-obsession that makes each oblivious to any pain except his/her own, in the end seems only to represent a privatization of, rather than a foil to, the endemic distemper.

With such generalized antipathy lurking around the fringes of their stories, it is predictable that Australian writers would find it difficult to depict "real" heterosexual relations in a positive light. Scanning the sample one notes that even before the fact there tend to be a great many barriers to romance in Australian novels. One common problem, popularly attributed to male incorrigibility, is a reluctance or inability on the part of one or both protagonists to commit themselves. Marshall's *How Beautiful Are Thy Feet*, provides multiple examples. Another is the choice of an inappropriate or unworthy or unreciprocating object (Timms, Cusack & James). Even when the participants do manage to reach a mutually satisfactory agreement, the author more often than not interposes some kind of physical obstacle like accident, enforced separation, or death (Clarke, Boldrewood, Kingsley, Eldershaw, Capricornia, McLean, Drake-Brockman, Sydney, McDonald). Brent of Bin Bin's[3] *Up the Country* provides an interesting early illustration of this propensity. Despite its generic resemblance to Victorian romantic comedy, in fact, this novel, more than practically any other in the sample, exemplifies the dictum that love just doesn't work. Consider the following outline: Bert loves Rachel, who is married to Simon. Emily loves Bert, and eventually he is talked into proposing to her, but she dies before the match is consummated. Tim loves Emily, but is rebuffed. Jessie proposes to Bert at the Leap Ball, and when he refuses she engages herself to Hugh. Later she

---

3. One of Miles Franklin's masculine pseudonyms. See *Women Writing, Women Written*, pp. 85-89 below.

backs out, and Hugh marries Louisa on the rebound. Mary loves Bert but becomes a nun. After Emily dies Bert proposes to Jessie, but she has too much pride to accept. After Simon dies Bert proposes to Rachel, but she too turns him down for no other reason than the fact that she has had enough of marriage. If *Up the Country* is eminently conventional in its catalogue of romantic mismatches, it is definitely *not* conventional in its failure to provide even a token number of happy unravellings.

Portraits of "marriages" are marked by the same radical pessimism. If they last, just as one might expect in a culture that associates femininity with "civilization," the anomaly is usually attributable to the strength, or perhaps just the stubbornness of the wife (Richardson, Penton, Cleary, Waten, Williamson). If they *don't* last, on the other hand – and it should be noted that there is at least one major example of marital breakdown in over half the novels in the sample – the fault, though ostensibly evenly divided between the sexes, is attributable to the excess "masculinity" of one *or* the other party. The bad husband is brutal, restless, or obtuse (Clarke, Stone, Tennant, Hardy, Turner); the bad wife – underlining her lack of femininity by her propensity to disregard and even damage her children – is faithless, greedy, or selfish (Mann, Prichard, Niland, Palmer, Carey). The message is clear: though women are in an *ideal* sense better suited to marriage than men (and here it is interesting that in two of the few unequivocally positive marriages in the corpus, Stuart's *Walk, Trot, Canter and Die* and Glaskin's *Flight to Landfall*, the wife is, or is associated with, an aboriginal anima figure), in practice their symbolic masculinization tends to make them, just as much as their male counterparts, constitutionally incapable of healthy interpersonal relations.

This doesn't mean, to be sure, that love is not possible at all in the Australian fictional universe. Interestingly enough, though, love is shown to have the best chance when sex, or at least sexual *difference*, is eliminated from the picture. In the original version of Clarke's *For the Term of His Natural Life* the long-separated lovers are finally allowed to come together in an orgy of happiness at the moment when consummation is no longer possible, the moment of death. If this seems a little too morbid to be considered affirmative there are numerous less traumatic cases in the oeuvre that convey the same essential message. It is significant, for instance, that among all possible varieties of male persona it is the "feminine" type – the fool/saint (Elliott) or the artist (Lindsay) or the priest (McCullough) or the homosexual (Jessica Anderson) – with whom women are most likely to be able to relate in a non-self-destructive fashion. The risk of damage is minimized, it would seem, if and only if the "other" can be symbolically assimilated to "self." This is not, of course, an altogether healthy kind of resolution to the problem. As is made quite clear in Stead's tale of incest and angst, *Seven Poor Men of Sydney*, to desire the "other self" is in the end to desire annihilation. That Michael drowns himself on the rebound from a love affair with his sister seems only appropriate when we remember that anima equals ocean.

Familial Relations

If horizontal relations are problematic in Australian literature, vertical ones are equally so. Within families, discord is almost a norm. Children disappoint or betray their parents (Eldershaw, White, Carey). Siblings are alienated or antagonistic (Herbert, Timms, McLean, Keneally). Even those relationships which begin in mutual support end up being corroded by divergent visions, by self-interest, or simply by fate (Malouf). Johnston's *My Brother Jack* is a key text here, not simply because of its poignant and exemplary demonstration of the active role model's defeat by a world that is too complex, too irrational, for his simple, old-fashioned virtues, but because of what it reflects, albeit covertly, about the Australian myth of brotherly solidarity. The fact that Davy only has time for his big brother as long as the latter is ascendant underlines the ephemerality of even the strongest and most positive fraternal bonds. Even more telling: the fact that his rise is temporally coincident upon the latter's fall hints that success of one sibling is always bought at the expense of another. The book coincidentally provides an interesting sidelight on the war. Supporting what I suggested earlier, that military experience is important to the Australian less for its positive (heroic) associations than for its negative ones, it is interesting that in this book it is the "born" soldier who loses out in wartime and the reluctant civilian who prospers.

Siblings apart, it is the ubiquitousness of parental failings throughout the oeuvre that really documents the Australian's pessimism about the possibility of wholesome familial relations. Particularly significant are those cases that deal not with overt venality on the part of a parent but with good intentions that somehow produce bad results (Eldershaw, Cleary, Waten). In most books, for good or ill, it is the father who stands forth as the most problematic presence for the child. Mothers, if hardly unequivocal, tend to be rendered irrelevant by impotence or absence (Boldrewood, Hardy, Elliot). Even in those instances where a mother exerts an actively detrimental influence on her children, it is likely to be for negative reasons rather than positive ones, because she is unmotherly or antipathetic or simply remote (the grandmother in Malouf). This doesn't mean, of course, that the damage done by the mother is any less considerable – indeed there is a significant number of cases where children are killed as a direct or indirect result of maternal neglect (Palmer, Mass, Stuart) – but insofar as she has already symbolically defined herself as un-mother by her disinterest in and resentment of her offspring, there is a sense in which her destructiveness seems almost inadvertent, part and parcel of her mysterious female nature. Fathers are quite different. The father is someone to grapple with, to react against. The father is very much there.

Perhaps, though, this is to simplify somewhat. Certainly the father tends, from the child's point of view at least, to be the most important of the two parents. There are, however, at least two distinct types. And judging by the current sample, their distribution is not quite what folk wisdom would lead one to expect. The aggressive masculinity self-attributed to Australians theoretically implies some version of the "old bull" syndrome. In fact, the conventionally brutish patriarch, though hardly absent, is in a minority (Charlwood, Johnston). Much more common is the father who is either sympathetic but weak or charismatic but absent (Stead, Langley, Waten, Keneally, Langley). Remote, in other words. Lest we be tempted to draw the wrong conclusions from this, though, it must be noted that what we have here is quite a different kind of remoteness from that of the mother. For one thing, far from signalling alienation it typically documents strength of affect. As we see clearly from the experience of the several bastards that turn up in our sample, the more remote the father is, the more numinous he becomes (Tucker, Stead, Ireland). More to the point, it also contributes considerably to his psycho-symbolic significance. Naturalistic effects aside, in other words, the real importance of the father's remoteness is the role it plays on the mythic level of the oeuvre. In fact, the father's remoteness serves the same kind of critical offsetting function as the active role model's requisite failure.

Why is such a function necessary? In a culture that makes an almost automatic association between relation and threat, the idea of parental benevolence is almost a contradiction in terms. To evince even a symbolic faith in the possibility of such benevolence is thus viewed as not merely foolish but risky. In order not to invite such faith, the "good" father, even more than the "bad" father, has to be neutralized in some way. At the same time, because he is alter ego rather than other, he cannot simply be dismissed like the inherently alien mother. This is why, in novel after novel, though the father himself rarely proves to be of much use, the ideal of masculinity he represents is a significant emotional focus for the growing child. It is also why, even when it is *abstractly* positive, this lurking presence tends to have distinctly detrimental effects on those who fall under its influence. Langley's *The Pea Pickers* – a book in which the family legend of the father's wanderlust is so enticing that his daughters actually attempt to turn themselves into imitation males – is perhaps an extreme example, but over and over again throughout the oeuvre we see young protagonists being emotionally, morally, even physically damaged, as a byproduct of their fathers' exemplary "masculinity" (Boldrewood, Kingsley, Eldershaw, Cleary, Waten, Wilson). Given the profundity of these problems, it is hardly surprising that by far the most common fate for a family in Australian literature is to fragment, deteriorate, or die out entirely (Kingsley, Eldershaw, White, Malouf).

Artist Figures

In Canadian literature, where the idea of transcendence generates just as much anxiety as it does in Australia, the artist, archetypal mediator between human and inhuman, plays a particularly prominent role. At least in quantitative terms this would not seem to be the case in Australia, perhaps because the association between art and the archetypal feminine tends to discourage identification. Such artist figures as do turn up, however, are interesting for the extent to which they not merely point up but interweave many of the themes and propensities we have already observed. As might be expected, the most important of these themes concern, or relate to, the question of psycho-sexual association. From the point of view of everyman [sic], the artist (whether as painter or writer) in a very real sense epitomizes the absolutely alien. In books like White's *The Tree of Man* and Malouf's *Harland's Half Acre* the auditor's sense of his otherness emerges quite blatantly. Even in cases where he plays the role of protagonist or narrator, however, despite his *ostensible* accessibility the artist's apartness is underlined by an emphasis on the emotional barriers that exist between him and his natural peers. At the very least he is one who dissociates himself from his own middle class roots to take up the cause of the disaffected and the stigmatized (Tennant, McLean). Or he turns his back on his emotional roots (Johnston). More telling, the artist frequently has a much profounder kind of isolation thrust upon him willy-nilly. We need not look far for an explanation of this phenomenon. It is both typical and significant, for example, that in Porter's *The Tilted Cross* and Turner's *A Waste of Shame* the artist figures are victimized by "unwomanly" women. This fact does not in itself distinguish them from a vast number of their fellows, to be sure. What *does* set them apart is that rather than repudiating their domestic ties in retaliation, as is more normally the case (Niland, Palmer, Stuart), these men remain faithful to their spouses. By doing so – and this is the key point – they tacitly accept a kind of symbolic role reversal. The subsequent social ostracization they suffer is thus clearly implied to comprise a punishment not for anti-social behaviour (the brutality Arthur evinced during his drinking days is far less of a stigma than his later association with a known "poofter"), but simply for unmanliness.

The "femininity" of the artist comprises much more than an abstraction, then. Nearly every artist in the corpus, despite the fact that they are virtually all biologically masculine, displays clear evidence of alignment with the feminine. In some cases, as mentioned above, they are identifiable by their anomalous capacity to love (Cowan, Mass). In others there is an association with an explicit anima figure (Lindsay, Martin). Allied with this, they are also likely to evince some kind of connection with, or unusual sympathy for, nature (Carey, Malouf). Here is the rub, of course. I have already noted that for the Australian nature is not just ambivalent but frequently outright deadly. This is why, no doubt, so many of the artist fables in Australian literature turn out to be cautionary tales. To create art – to give oneself over to the dangerous and alien realm of the anima – is almost invariably to risk psychic, perhaps even physical disfigurement. In Ireland's *The Flesheaters* the artist – with obvious and rather gruesome significance – is self-castrated. And even this is far from the worst that can befall him. The artist in White's *The Tree of Man* is driven to commit suicide. In Martin's *The Young Wife* he is murdered as a byproduct of his liaison with the anima herself. In Glaskin's *Flight to Landfall* he dies young, it is implied, simply because he is too "good." And in Malouf's *Harland's Half Acre*, most provocatively of all, having elected to live an almost animal existence out in the bush, he is so badly brutalized by the elements that he dies of exposure.

The intimations of doom carried by such negative exempla do not, to be sure, necessarily detract from either the charisma or the authority of the artist figure. In Canadian literature the artist is all the more highly regarded because his hubristic assumption of godlike efficacy does invite retribution. Insofar as the Australian variant seems far less manipulator than victim, however, the impression we bring away from the oeuvre is that art, as a wilful activity, is not so much taboo as simply logically impossible. Feminine by definition, it requires powers beyond the reach – or at least the understanding – of a "normal" man.

Formal Characteristics

In line with the apparent helplessness of individual artists, the Australian oeuvre as a whole conveys an impression of accident. Most of the novels in the sample are strikingly artless. As if the writer were unwilling or unable to take responsibility for the story he/she tells, the bulk of the oeuvre comprises pseudo-biographies, where the only structure is provided by the structure of the imitation "life" (Tucker, Boldrewood, Stone, Prichard, Richardson, Penton, Hardy, Johnston, Harrower, Stuart, McCullough, McDonald, Wilson), or pseudo-documentaries, which simulate primitive sociology in their naive martialling of social facts (Furphy, Marshall, Cusack & James, Park), or loosely focused slices of life exhibiting features of both (Herbert, Tennant, Mann). At least until the seventies (when there was a minor and not entirely successful vestigial shift into a more self-consciously postmodern mode), even those few books – like White's *The Tree of Man* – which bespoke a more than fortuitous degree of skill and control on the part of the author tended to mimic the shapelessness of "real" human experience. Missing almost entirely from the corpus, in fact, are both the densely populated, wide-ranging novels of political and social intrigue so beloved of the American (it is interesting that the one notable exception here, Hardy's *Power Without Glory*, is the thinly disguised biography of a "real" historical personage) and the artful, introspective, broadly allegorical prose poems by means of which the Canadians preferentially convey their somewhat claustrophobic sense of self.

The one thing uncovered by my survey that might be considered as a purely "literary" feature is a kind of recurrent symbology revolving around the ambiguities of, or conflicts between, feminine and masculine modes of action. At times the picture that emerges on this level is both complex and resonant. We have already discussed the problematic anima/ocean association. More often the vehicles chosen are both simple and traditional. Throughout the oeuvre, for instance, there is a persistent sounding on the theme of horses versus houses. Often the two polarities are explicitly paired within a single novel (Bolderwood, Cleary, McCullough). At other times writers may choose to explore the concomitants of one or the other.

The horse, of course, is usually taken to represent an exemplification of male energy. It is hardly surprisingly, therefore, considering the patterns of response we have been documenting throughout this section, that the books which most blatantly idealize the animal are also the books in which we find the strongest counter-symbolism. In Boldrewood's *Robbery under Arms*, for instance, the gentleman bandit Starlight is in the end self-betrayed through his exemplary attachment to his legendary steed. In Stuart's *Walk, Trot, Canter and Die*, though the betrayal is more subtle, the health and even the life of the protagonist are clearly endangered by the lingering effects of the horsebreaking that earned him his reputation.

The symbolic houses that appear throughout the corpus are even more equivocal than the horses. Almost always, as one might expect, they are – for good or ill – identified explicitly with some aspect of the feminine (Prichard, Elliott, McCullough). What is more interesting, though, is the fact that (with one notable exception, to be discussed below) their psycho-symbolic associations are brought out most pointedly in relation to the men who identify *against* them. This is not to say that the house is viewed by these men in an entirely negative light. Often, indeed, it comes to represent for them all the things in life that elude their grasp. It is precisely because the house, in its archetypal sense, is both desirable *and* inaccessible, however, that it exerts such a baleful influence over so many Australian protagonists. Richard Mahoney is typical in that it is his lifelong obsession with grand mansions which, in leading to financial recklessness, precipitates his downfall. On a very different level but with entirely similar implications, the exemplary deserter of Sydney's *The Return* is brought almost to his death by his attempt to master the hut in the wilderness. Insofar as one's frustration and despair can only be exacerbated by visions of unattainable safety and security, it seems wholly appropriate that when Turner's protagonist finally goes all the way off the rails, it is his wife's house that he turns on and destroys with an axe.

The one exception to this pattern is Elizabeth Harrower's *The Watchtower*, where the house, as a literally concrete manifestation of the constricting social role imposed upon women by patriarchy, is clearly meant to be taken as a male-generated ideological construct. Inasmuch as it is not an arbitrary but a natural symbol, however, *qua* construct it carries a number of divergent subtexts that undermine or at least ambiguate Harrower's iconography. Particularly troublesome is the question of affiliation. Patriarchy notwithstanding (and in this regard we must remember that in Australia the entire realm of "social roles" is itself construed as feminine), insideness is not only an appropriate but an almost unavoidable metaphoric correlative for a woman. Such adumbrations make it exceedingly difficult to interpret *The Watchtower* as it would itself seem to demand: that is, as a conventional feminist tract. Given the undertones, in fact, it seems impossible *not* to conclude that the reason Harrower's house proves so deadly for its mistress's emotional health is less that it represents a male "plot" – and here, I think, we have to set aside the red herring of the domineering husband, if only because he seems an even more severely damaged personality than his wife – than because she, as evinced by her early confusions, is simply not womanly enough to "fit" the traditional female image it provides. Analogously, it is neither surprising nor coincidental that when the younger sister escapes in the end, it is not, as convention would dictate, into a relationship –

indeed, as an initial step she has to work her way through, and prove her immunity to, that particular stereotypic solution – but, like Langley's pea-pickers, into an open-ended journey.

From this viewpoint, Harrower's *Watchtower* isn't really an exception at all. If we are predisposed to "see" the house in this book as exerting a more baleful influence on the female protagonist than on her male counterpart, it is perhaps only because, as a same-sex symbol, it appears on conventional grounds to pose a more profound or at least more immediate psychological threat to the former than the latter. Conventional expectations aside, it is in fact equally alien to both.

Comments

One obvious conclusion to draw from the foregoing overview is that Australian literature is overwhelmingly and irredeemably negative. Oddly enough, this simply wouldn't be true. Granted, there are almost twice as many "unhappy" endings in the sample as there are happy ones, but the statistic is misleading: the fact that so many of the novels amble along aimlessly from youth to old age biases the distribution. What *is* the bottom line to the Australian world view, then? One thing is certain, it is likely to be something quite different from, or at least more complex than, what is offered explicitly in the oeuvre. Even apart from their notably naive approach to plot and characterization, it is clear from the frequent, apparently non-purposive violations of convention we find throughout the oeuvre (see especially Franklin, Ethel Anderson), not to mention the mixed messages and radically ambiguous denouements, that a good many of these writers are just as lacking in self-awareness as their characters. Take Eagle's *Who Could Love the Nightingale?*, for instance. Although the destabilization of viewpoint in this novel presumably echoes the search for identity, it also intimates that the author himself has trouble "seeing" his characters, especially the woman, who is inconsistent, evasive, and in the end perhaps even hypocritical. Eagle, it will be noted, is far from anomalous. Cook, Ireland, Sydney, Jessica Anderson, McDonald, Jolley – all have produced novels about which it is difficult to say with certainty not merely what particular moral vision is being conveyed, but whether the author is trying to convey that kind of "message" at all. Didactic elements are undercut by irony. Irony, on the other hand, is undercut by the ofttimes impression of fortuitousness.

Does this simply mean that Australians produce "bad" literature? I would say not. This isn't the place to tackle any extended textual explication. I would suggest, though, that the peculiarities of individual novels appear less peculiar – less individual – when they are read systematically as part of a single, unique, self-consistent oeuvre. They also appear far less incidental. If the Australian oeuvre lacks the conscious sophistication of other contemporary literatures, this is perhaps only because its power resides not on the literary but on the mythic level. It is here, therefore, that we should be looking for our key to interpretation, the common denominator that "makes sense" of all the idiosyncracies. And it is here that we find it. Once we take note of the psycho-sexual bias that seems a ubiquitous feature of the Australian imagination it is easy, for instance, to see the likelihood that Eagle's confusion simply signals his covert anxiety about the role reversal that his characters enact but never quite recognize. It is easy to recognize the cultural significance of Langley's heroines' penchant for masculine clothing. It is even easy to extract the complex and ambiguous "family drama" that lurks behind the grotesqueries of Ireland's *The Flesheaters*. To what extent is the model a useful one for "explaining" Australian culture *outside of* literature? Based on my North American findings I would predict a significant degree of inter-systemic homology. Even in the United States, where one finds significant differences not merely between the stylistic conventions but even more between the ideological subtexts carried respectively by "high" and popular fiction, once one has extracted the appropriate markers it is a simple task to detect the structural underpinnings that are propaedeutic to *both* bodies of material (G. McGregor, 1988). Will it be the same in Australia? The proof of the pudding, as they say, is in the eating. In the next section I will address myself to the smorgasbord.

3

COMING INTO THE COUNTRY

BRISBANE

From Darwin to the region of Bourke in central New South Wales [the air traveller] crosses over country which is burnt brown and patchy, like a tender sunburnt skin, with sections of darker brown and blood red and blisters of lighter ochre . . . It is not treeless; the shadows of trees can be seen, but they are dry . . . spare, blue-grey, hanging limply, vertically, with no real intention of providing shade . . .

Unlike most countries, this red backland of Australia looks from the air satisfyingly like its own maps . . . Near the rare settlements a white road darts zigzagging in long straight draftsmanly lines. Every element stands out clearly: a tiny black square of water, a spidery track, twenty or so buildings at a station headquarters, their iron roofs dazzling white.

This is the Australian Never-Never, the back of beyond; hard, raw, barren, and blazing. Yet it is not malevolent in appearance . . . [I]t is a subtle desert, insinuating itself into the background of Australian life, even to the life of the factory worker in a southern city . . . Its presence can never be forgotten for long.

Robin Boyd, *The Australian Ugliness*

Our arrival in Australia has been marked by a subtle disorientation attributable only in part to the fact of having been en route so long that we lost an entire day. The crux of the problem, I think, was an unassimilable juxtaposition of familiarity and strangeness. In the airport I tried to make a telephone call, a procedure I have been conditioned to consider as invariant. After several unsuccessful experiments, however, I was forced to give up, unable either to guess at the procedure or to decipher the, to me, utterly inexplicable printed directions. Later I discovered that there are three kinds of public telephones in Australia: green ones for local calls, red ones for local and continental long distance, gold ones (which are rare) for local, continental, and overseas calls. I also discovered that international credit cards are accepted only for the latter. For calls inside Australia, one must have enormous amounts of change in the right denominations with which to feed the machines.

I dwell on this "initializing" incident not because I mean to imply that Australian telephone norms are abnormal in some way (although I suspect that the complexity and inefficiency of this system relative to North America is not entirely coincidental, being strikingly consonant with other aspects of the national psyche). What I want to convey, rather, is the extent to which, right from the beginning, I was made aware of the problematic nature of my stance as outsider-observer. What that telephone episode brought home to me, in fact, is that a culture so close to one's own is likely to be all the more inaccessible simply because one is *not* constantly reminded that what one is dealing with is "foreign." The shock of confronting left-side driving, because it was obviously and self-announcingly different, was in some ways much easier to come to terms with than many of the subtler discriminations that the newcomer is forced to make in conceptualizing the reality of this country.

Brisbane itself has done nothing to dispel that initial reaction. One's first impression is of its Americanness. Here are all the familiar icons of suburbia: McDonald's, Burger King, Kentucky Fried Chicken. Only gradually does one become aware of the unAmericanness of the background against which these are set. The commercial strip development, for one thing, which at first seems interchangeable with the garishly flagged and neoned shopping-centre/car dealership/fast food franchise/discount outlet-lined highways that garland western cities from Phoenix to Calgary reveals itself at closer sight to lack both the plastic homogeneity and the cheerfully vulgar self-confidence which invariably characterize the latter. Not that there is any lack of vulgarity in the Australian version. It is, however, a more amateurish, less commercial kind of vulgarity. Signs are more likely than not to be hand-painted. Shop decor, inside and out, has a kind of anxious fussiness to it that fights against the obvious desire to be slick and progressive. This tension between uncertainty and bravado seems well-nigh endemic. Between the parapets, the pillars, the ostentatious verandahs and awnings and arcades, the gaudy paintwork, and the relentless clutter of signs, the keynote to Brisbane's commercial areas is neither American pop-culture casualness nor British understatement but a kind of overassertion one might call "front."

The city itself seems to suffer from the same kind of ambivalence. One must, of course, make allowances for one's own divergent conditioning, but the sheer irrationality of Brisbane's layout strikes me as disfunctional for resident and visitor alike. For the first few days we were here we got lost every time we tried to go anywhere. The only maps locally available seem designed deliberately to misrepresent the terrain. Route marking is erratic and often ambiguous. Many streets have no signs. The difficulties are not simply those of unfamiliarity, however. The real problem is the fragmentation of the city – every section and suburb seems a world unto itself – and the failure of its designers to allow for or even, it would seem, to consider the possibility of anyone wanting to drive from one part of it to another. To get from the southern suburbs to the northern ones, for instance, one has to go right through the heart of downtown, a tightly gridded, roughly triangular core made even more labyrinthine than necessary by its not-quite-systematic system of one-way streets and its absolutely *unsystematic* connections with contiguous areas. To get from the south-central suburbs to the southwestern ones right across the river, one again has to traverse the downtown, travelling many times the crow-flight distance simply because of the scarcity of bridges. Quite apart from the frustration of having to literally learn each route by rote, one can't help wondering about the effects such a layout must have on the conceptualizing propensities of its residents.

Despite these obvious drawbacks, it would be misleading to imply that Brisbane is not, on the whole, an exceptionally attractive city. The sunshine makes up for a lot, of course. The bright tropical flora helps too. More interesting to the ethnographer, however, is the fact that the public disorder, at least on the face of it, seems to be balanced by an almost neurotic private tidiness. One hears of the low density of Australian cities. Certainly this one seems to consist almost entirely of separate single-family dwellings, mostly bungalows, each on its own small, neatly fenced or hedged plot of land, and each with its own small, neatly landscaped front yard. The overall effect is wholesome, slightly old-fashioned, and almost smugly domestic. Given that Queensland is supposed to be the most primitive of Australian states – falling somewhere between the wild west and the deep south – this already argues that the Australian self-characterization as rough-and-ready falls somewhat askance of the truth.

The inhabitants seem just as domesticated as their city. Casual clothing is the norm – women in cotton dresses; men sporting short-sleeved shirts and shorts. Seldom, however, does this informality slide over into slovenliness. Virtually everyone in this city looks well fed, well pressed, and extremely clean. This hint of a nurturing "mum" in the background is reinforced, moreover, by the appearance and behaviour of young people. In marked contrast to the strikingly individualistic self-presentation of North American teenagers, Australian schoolchildren – public or private – more often than not wear uniforms. More telling, their street behaviour, again in contrast with North American norms, suggests that here there is far less emphasis on "self-expression" and far more on observing the perquisites of rank and age.

As far as demeanour is concerned, the average Australian, as advertised, is extremely friendly. The task of organizing for our trek into the outback has not been without its problems. The bank draft on our Canadian bank turned out not to be immediately negotiable. Car-leasing rates are about twice what we anticipated. And so on. But every time we have felt ourselves on the brink of disaster, a friendly Aussie has stepped in and saved the day. The cut-rate car rental man, on hearing that we are Canadians, not only rented us a van at car prices, but threw in a useful assortment of camping equipment. The bank accountant arranged for a short-term loan. Is this helpfulness, this cavalier cutting-through of red tape, an Australian universal? Or is it something to do with the "frontier" self-image of Queensland?

It has its underside, of course. Forewarned, I have been on the alert for any signs of the much-mythicized Australian misogyny. And they *are* there. When we first approached the bank, the same helpful officer already mentioned had a hard time coming to terms with the fact that we wanted our account to be in my name, not that of my male partner. He wasn't rude. He was, however, visibly taken aback. And although he recovered quite slickly, his re-cognition of the situation clearly involved a rather ponderous shifting of mental gears. The fact is, though, they *did* shift. Contra the more horrifying stories one hears in North America, this episode pretty well characterizes my experience thus far of Australian men. They are, indeed, male chauvinists, but they are not by any means male chauvinist pigs.

Apart from commercial encounters I haven't, to be sure, actually had the chance to interact with many Australians, male *or* female. Since the primary raison d'être for our stay here is the semi-annual meeting of the

Australia-New Zealand Association for Canadian Studies, virtually all my one-on-one encounters have been with academics. *These* men seem almost without exception to be nicer, more civilized, and more "enlightened" than their North American counterparts. This could have something to do with class differences. Australian academics seem to be singularly well-bred, while the "ocker" – the protagonist of choice for Australian sexist jokes – is always an uneducated, working class boor.

Class notwithstanding, on the other hand, there are clear signs that prejudice against women, if not as offensively paraded, is in fact just as firmly entrenched among the intelligentsia as it is among the proletariat. At least among those I have met so far, female academics are very much in the minority. They are also in general junior to their male colleagues. And judging by their priorities, their unquestioning acceptance that a career does not and should not constitute an excuse for shirking more traditional marital and maternal responsibilities (if husbands help out around the house at all, it is generally viewed as a "favour"), most of those I talked to seem to suffer a certain amount of ambivalence about their professional roles.

One of the most interesting things I picked up at the conference, apart from some good contacts, was an image. An Adelaide academic named Russell McDougall, I am told, has a paper in the works right now on an aspect of Australian culture that he calls "sprawl." I'm not sure what McDougall himself makes of it, but it strikes me as a perfect term to describe/evoke the quality of slovenly male meander that characterizes Australian literature. If my psychotyping is borne out, it wouldn't be surprising to find sprawl playing as central and summarizing a role in the Australian iconography as the box does for Canada.

Class, Education, and Self-Image

Central to the Australian communal self-image is the idea of egalitarianism. Despite the obvious and broadly acknowledged socio-economic disparities that can be seen to exist in this country ("the wealthiest 1 per cent of Australians own about 20 per cent of the total wealth held by individuals and the wealthiest 5 per cent about 45 per cent of the total wealth" [Parkin, 1980: 274]), there is a general disinclination to admit that these document any *essential* difference in status. "Australians like to think they live in a community blessedly free from the social snobberies and caste categories of older, more corrupt civilizations," says Craig McGregor. "When two Melbourne academics set out to analyse class distinctions in Australia, they found that almost one in every ten people they interviewed had no clear idea of social classes or denied they existed. And a smaller survey by some New South Wales university students unearthed several people who simply replied 'No classes, only income groups,' 'Everyone has equal rights'" (1981: 60).

McGregor himself, while rhetorically acknowledging the fictiveness of the egalitarian myth, at the same time tacitly augments its authority by focusing his own discussion of class on the recent growth, in terms both of subjective alignment and of objective economic indicators, of a new "middle" class. Surveys show that "twice as many Australians now regard themselves as middle class than consider themselves as working class," he says. "The contrast with other countries such as Britain and the United States is enormous, because there the majority of people think of themselves as working class. In a 1964 election study ... 56 per cent of the Americans said they were working class and 39 per cent said they were middle class; in a 1963 British election study twice as many people regarded themselves as working class than as middle class – whereas in Australia it is precisely the other way around" (64). McGregor accepts this apparent burgeoning as a real and significant feature of post-war Australia. Other commentators, however, deny vehemently that it is supported by the observable levels of material living standards (Connell, 1977; Rowse, 1978; Connell and Goot, 1979; Dwyer et al., 1984). If the latter are right – and their arguments, at least on the face of it, seem plausible enough – the question then becomes, why should Australians be so eager to mis-identify themselves in this fashion?

Dwyer et al. invoke the notion of a self-fulfilling prophecy. "[B]ecause most Australians are said to be middle class," they claim, "most Australians . . . describe themselves as middle class, regardless of their family background, home address, type of employment, or personal wealth" (1984: 32). Others see the phenomenon as somewhat more sinister. Borrowing Gramsci's concept of hegemony, Sydney sociologist R.W. Connell, for instance, suggests that the middle class self-designation is founded in a kind of "false consciousness" deliberately fostered by the country's rulers (see Connell and Goot, 1979). Tim Rowse takes a similar line. "By examining . . . documents from the post-war period," he says, it becomes clear "that 'middle class' refer[s] to political values and social attitudes defined as desirable within the traditions of Australian liberalism" (1978: 198). Both these critiques are marred, unfortunately, by exactly the same weakness its authors impute to their opponents: an insufficiently rigorous use of class terminology. "There are . . . gaping holes in Connell and Irving's treatment of the ruling class and the state," says John Herouvim in a review of *Class Structure in Australian History*. They "avoid similar problems with the middle class by simply ignoring it" (1983: 87; see also C. McGregor, 1981: 103ff.).

What of the "hard" facts of the matter? At least part of the problem, as Austin points out, is that much of the available evidence lends itself to almost diametrically opposed interpretations. Where Broom and Jones, for instance, take their studies of intergenerational and career mobility to demonstrate the "openness" of Australian society, Connell uses the same data to show how *little* movement there is "from the bottom to the top of the class structure" (Austin, 1984: 49ff. and 84ff.). A lot depends on how one defines class, of course. If a "class" is deemed to be a closed, hereditary grouping, then Broom and Jones must be seen as having mounted a strong argument that Australia doesn't have any. If exclusiveness counts for less than does the structural entrenchment of economic disparities, on the other hand, they haven't. As Austin summarizes, while their data do "illustrate that . . . European Australia does not exhibit the most radical inequalities," they also make clear that "there are patterned and enduring inequalities that sociologists with a different theory would be happier to characterize as a class system" (73).

Other ways of approaching the stratification issue are equally problematic. Noting the extent to which power in Australia is divorced from wealth, John Higley and his associates attribute the ruling function not to a "class" per se, but to an interlocking system of "elites." The distinguishing feature of such individuals, they explain, "is their strategic decision-making locations in organizations. *Elites are . . . persons with power to affect organizational outcomes individually, regularly and seriously"* (Higley et al., 1979: 3). Even leaving aside the question of whether the money issue in itself is enough to debar the use of class terminology (Austin, for instance, points out that if wealth doesn't distinguish the professional and managerial strata, family background, and particularly father's occupation, certainly does), the individualistic bias of Higley's – as, indeed, of Broom's and Jones's – approach makes it difficult to relate status in any meaningful way to what Austin calls "the real process of economic and political life in Australia" (89). There is also a problem (which Austin does not note) with using "power" as an indicator in the first place. *Having* power is quite a different thing from *wielding* it. Although this is not the place to go into the matter (see Chapter 4, *"National Fictions"*), there is considerable evidence that the elite member of Australian society is just as timid, as reactive, and as pessimistic about his ability to manipulate events as the non-elite one is. Under such circumstances it is perhaps foolish to talk about a "ruling" anything, whether class or agglomerate.

If neither wealth nor power nor inherited status provide an adequate basis for elucidation of social differences in Australia, we are still left with the fact that, the myth of an egalitarian myth notwithstanding, according to almost every serious commentator such differences do exist, on a broad and fairly systematic basis. Perhaps rather than relying on "hard" indicators, social strata are explicable in terms of differential group consciousness. How, given the much-touted homogeneity of Australian culture, does such differentiation occur? Connell points to the ideological functions of class-related discrepancies in the education of Australian children. Working class children, he says, are not only disadvantaged in terms of facilities, but also intellectually disabled by the lack of viable models – with respect, that is, to both goals and *modes* of work – in their home environment (1977, Chapter 8; see also Dwyer et al., 1984, Chapter 3). The problem, he continues, is in at least one sense more serious for the male. Where female children are relatively more ill served across the board (M.J. Poole, 1986), lower class boys are additionally handicapped in that, for them, unlike their upper class compatriots, gender is defined almost exclusively in physical rather than intellectual terms. For the working class youth, says Austin, "Masculinity mainly involves being 'tough' and physically aggressive, both socially and sexually. By contrast notions of masculinity among the ruling class involve an emphasis on . . . the power to control other people, to make significant decisions, and to accumulate wealth" (1984: 9-10).

A corollary to this thesis is, of course, that the disadvantagement is deliberate. Just as the state inculcates passivity in the populace through its manipulation of media imagery (see "A Quick History of Australian Film," pp. 209-15 below), it also "educates" the working class in such a way as to keep it both quiescent and ignorant. Retrospective examination of the education system reveals much to support such a claim. Even apart from such obvious factors as the historic reluctance to establish a free secondary system as an alternative to the private schools (as late as 1900 there were no state secondary schools in Victoria), the curriculum in the state schools, as Richard Selleck points out, was from the beginning narrow, utilitarian, and vocationally oriented. Particularly telling, moreover, is the extent to which class was invoked *explicitly*, at least during the early years, as a justification for the deliberate impoverishment of public programs. During the nineteenth century, says Selleck, public school teachers "were constantly watched to ensure that they walked the narrow path of social and cultural propriety. State schools . . . were permitted to offer for a fee, and out of school hours, some 'extra subjects' which included the 'secondary school' subjects – French, algebra, Euclid, the classics. These subjects were not very popular, but both the state and the Common schools were made to feel uneasy about offering them. There was a fear that through them the poor might be educated above their station" (1982: 32). Such statements are obviously no longer publicly palatable. They nevertheless cast a provocative light on the recurrence of complaints, from the twenties up to the present day, about the public schools' "neglect of the three Rs in favour of 'fads' or 'frills'" (Selleck: 35).

With respect at least to education, then, the Connell faction would seem to have ample support for their classist interpretation of Australian society. Accepting the conspiracy theory would, moreover, provide ample explanation for the persistence of the egalitarian myth itself. The working class believes it because it has been conditioned to do so. The upper class fosters it – and here it is interesting to note the finding of H.G. Oxley's study of mateship in small-town New South Wales that the upper stratum males tended to be more egalitarian in their behaviour and attitudes than the lower stratum ones (1978: 204ff.) – because it defuses the tensions that might arise if the working class were allowed to develop a collective consciousness. Despite all this, there are other, more ambiguous elements in the communal text to suggest that the picture is not quite so simple. For one thing, as mentioned above, there is the fact that close examination of the so-called elite strata simply doesn't reveal the kind of self-confidence or manipulative skills that Marxist and other Left commentators tend to assume as part of the ruling class stock-in-trade. Austin, for instance, comments gloomily on the "uniform and depressing opacity" exhibited by Higley's elite respondents when they were questioned on "their vision of the future for Australian society" (72). She betrays traces of the same kind of uncertainty herself when, invoking the spectre of the transnational corporation, she notes that the "notion of an elite or even a ruling class in Australia which entirely determines our future is . . . quite out of the question" (92). This may be no more than common sense, but it is striking nevertheless how widely it is repeated, believed, and used as an excuse for failure or inaction by the Australian leadership (see Chapter 4, "National Fictions").

Political ineptness aside, on the other hand, an even greater stumbling block to accepting Connell's thesis is that the Australian ruling class, so called, exhibits even less of a sense of self-consciousness than its supposed subordinates. As is demonstrated amply throughout the following discussion, no matter that the majority has now come to call itself "middle class," Australia's most cherished myths of identity enshrine working class values and its folk heroes are drawn from the margins, not the top, of the social heap. Even its national "style" – its preference for casualness, its disdain for pretension – is self-consciously working class. How do we explain this? If we were just talking about popular culture productions, the glorification of "ordinariness" could be interpreted as yet another instance of hegemonic chicanery, a means of keeping the subordinate masses satisfied with their lot – and this is exactly what cultural critics like Graeme Turner *do* claim. The fact is, though, that it is *not* merely those artifacts destined for "popular" consumption that carry the ideological subtext. Australian "literature," as D.R. Burns points out, has celebrated "the virtues, the toils and the tribulations of basic Australian man" as enthusiastically as specifically folk forms like ballads (1975: 16). And this is only the least of it. Even in those relatively rarefied media, like painting and poetry, where subject matter is ostensibly more elevated, the sense that emerges of being-in-the-world is, as discussed below, almost identical to the sense that emerges from the B movie and the television "cereal."

From this it would seem clear that the upper class in Australia simply does not have a distinct and distinctive self-image. One might suggest some reasons for this. If, as I have intimated, self-uncertainty is a national rather than a class-specific trait, then the emphasis on power wielding and decision making in upper class education could actually be *disfunctional* with respect to identity formation. Although this is to get somewhat ahead of my argument, it is notable that sports heroes – whose achievements rely neither on wit nor will but on god-given physical attributes – are the *only* heroes in the Australian pantheon who are construed as "winners." From this we might speculate that the working class modes so deplored by Connell are in fact far less productive of anxiety than the kind of criteria their "betters" are asked to measure themselves against. Under such circumstances it is hardly surprising that even – or perhaps *particularly* – upper stratum individuals should prefer a working class image. This doesn't, of course, mean that they don't have and even use relatively more "real" power than the true (that is, economically constructed) working class. Given the negative implications of the out-group reference, though, it is highly unlikely they would be capable of successfully playing the self-consciously manipulative roles that Connell imputes to them. So who *is* in charge in Australia? Who is responsible for the patent differences that mar the would-be picture of mass affluence? According to the national mythos, no one. It's all a matter of luck.

TOWNSVILLE

[Contra the myth] of a relaxed Deep North . . . it is difficult to find proof that the average northerner is less tense, more contented and suffers from fewer of the illnesses produced by anxiety than his southern counterpart. The streets of Cairns, Mt Isa, Townsville and Mackay, for example, flow with a more leisurely motor and pedestrian traffic . . . but the northerner does not noticeably smile more as he walks along. One might even say that he looks less alert and less amiable than a pedestrian in Albury or Launceston. There is no doubt that the tropical climate is enervating and wearing, even for those who enjoy it and prefer it to any other, and it leaves a physical mark on those who live here for any length of time.

Elizabeth Perkins, "Living in the Deep North"

The trip north was quite an eye-opener. I don't think I'd be foraging this far afield if I were on my own. As an urban-oriented Canadian, I tend to think that the view from the fort is the true one. Inasmuch as my travelling companion is a geologist whose interests are very much *anti*-urban, however, I have been lured significantly beyond my usual ambit. And judging from what I have already seen, it is a fortunate accident. I don't think one can really understand the ambivalence Australians evince toward their own country unless one confronts the reality of the landscape that so inexorably backdrops their sense of self.

Re that landscape: there is surprisingly little evidence of appropriation. Away from the populated centres (which in this part of the country are relatively few and scattered) there are few signs of the human. This effect is no doubt exacerbated by the fact that the scenery itself – if I may be excused a cliché that has sprung to the lips of every visitor since Captain Cook – is utterly and completely alien. Although it's difficult to put one's finger on the reasons, this landscape seems stranger, less spiritually akin to the Western

46

consciousness, than even the most fantastic and inimical of North American environments. Perhaps it's because there really is no continuity with what we identify, unconsciously, as "normal." The stunted willows of the northern tundra are still recognizable relatives of the graceful trees that line our southern Ontario rivers. The trees here, however, look "wrong" somehow. The colours, the smells, the quality of light are all – like the cultural differences mentioned in the previous section – subtly disorienting.

Actually, there are two landscapes in the stretch of territory north of Brisbane. Near the coast are canefields and patches of tropical forest not unlike Hawaii. Further inland, along the main north-south highway, are drylands which, at least from a distance, remind me of movie versions of the African veldt. This unconscious association no doubt adds to the sense of estrangement. Even without exotic comparisons, though, I think I would find this terrain unsettling. It's not a question of being overwhelmed by space. Indeed, the region is much less intimidating in that respect than the Canadian prairies. There are mountains. Often they are even picturesque. They are also, however, disconcertingly abrupt: unnatural wall-like extrusions from the dominant horizontal.

The forested areas are similarly ambivalent. Unlike North American woodlands, these are simply open stretches punctuated more or less densely with ragged, fragile-looking, sparsely-leaved trees. There is no underbrush, no variation in species or (locally) in concentration. The effect is much less claustrophobic than our northern landscapes, but the very monotony is daunting. Something else that daunts are the constant reminders of the immanence of disaster. Wind, flood, particularly fire. Time and again we found ourselves passing through large tracts where (old or recent) grass fires had left acre after acre of charred trees. Aesthetics quite aside, I can't help thinking that the omnipresence of these arboreal graveyards must exert a somewhat unwholesome influence on long-time inhabitants.

Apart from the landscape, the two-day drive has afforded me a number of other interesting insights into Australian social praxis. Three points in particular might be mentioned. First, there are lots of pubs, often two or three in one tiny town. There are also many race tracks even in relatively small centres. Second, well beyond those coastal villages catering to the tourist trade there are enormous numbers of motels, caravan parks, and campgrounds. This culture is obviously geared to the itinerant to a far greater degree than (outside, perhaps, of the Sun Belt) North America. Third, and perhaps most socially significant, everything – public offices, retail outlets, businesses of all sorts – closes up tight at five each evening and from Saturday noon to Monday morning. This phenomenon would seem not only to attest to the truth of the myth of the "lazy" Australian who is more interested in leisure than in "getting ahead," but to confirm as well that in Australia the woman's place is indeed assumed to be in the home. This raises a number of troubling questions. Despite the fact that almost half the married women in Australia are now in the work force, the ideological construction of "normal" female roles would seem to be so rigid, at least in these fringe areas, as to prevent any practical accommodation to the change. One wonders how a working woman manages to get even the necessary minimum of shopping and erranding done.

Townsville – our destination for this leg – is a small, thriving port city which serves as the main outlet for the timber, mining, and agricultural (sugar, beef, wool) products constituting the economic base to this region. *Qua* city, its layout is even more chaotic than Brisbane's. One gets the impression of a hodge-podge of unrationalized low density residential, industrial, and commercial development spreading aimlessly across the dusty landscape in patterns utterly devoid of rhyme or reason. Outside the central core the commercial architecture, perhaps due to its relative newness, seems blandly middle American. The domestic architecture, on the other hand, is classic Queensland. As in Brisbane it is characterized by surficiality: lots of detail, trim, colour, and textural features.

Very few homes have more than one storey. In the new suburbs there is a smattering of California or ranch-style bungalows. In the older areas the most common style is the verandahed bungalow on stilts. Although at the moment the temperature here is around 32°C, the high, hipped roofs and small-paned windows of these old-fashioned cottages remind one vividly that this is only the barest aftertaste of summer heat. Oddly enough, one sees very few trees in residential areas. I am informed that the old-timers in particular insist on removing every trace of foliage from the vicinity of their houses. Why? They *say* it's because of the insects. Thinking about that glaring January sun, though, I can't help but suspect that there is a more than a hint of nature paranoia involved in this violent antipathy to trees.

One final feature of Townsville that seems worth mentioning is that it is the home of James Cook University, the only Australian university in the tropics. This institution is a center for research in the veterinary and marine sciences. It also hosts a rather unique geological research institute which (in contrast to North America where the practical and the academic are usually kept well segregated) is funded and administered co-operatively by government and industry. This, of course, is why we are here. Unlike my partner, who has been off poring over rocks for the last two days, I am, however, more interested in the cultural than the natural setting. Like Griffith University in Brisbane, this is a new, modern campus landscaped in the formerly unfashionable "native" style. Also like Griffith it is in an enclave of its own, separated both symbolically and in fact from the rest of the city. Both campuses, moreover, are designed in such a way that the main buildings are contained within a womb-like ring road or loop. I have to wonder whether this is a common pattern throughout the country. If so it would clearly seem to indicate that the university, the centre of "learning," is identified as both symbolically "feminine" and definitively "other."

Sprawl, Urban and Otherwise

Despite all efforts by Governor Phillip and his engineer, Lieutenant Edward Dawes, to impose a semblance of military order on the urban landscape, early settlement at Sydney Cove was characterized by what J.M. Powell calls an "anarchical mode of expansion" (1986: 28). The rudimentary plan, he says, "reflected [the] broken topography. Firstly, there was a clear demarcation of the main convict, military and civil establishment at Sydney Cove from the government reserves on more favoured soils at the adjacent Farm Cove . . . Secondly, there was a strong linear development southwards from the Cove following the western ridge and the actual valley of the Tank Stream. By the 1820s similar developments had sketched out a rough rectangular grid in which topography, not government edict, was . . . the prime control." The recalcitrance of the landscape invoked here was exacerbated by the recalcitrance of the colonial mentality. By the early 1790s, says J.R. Freeland, "the self-interest and avarice that were to plague the colony for a century were already stirring. Following Phillip's departure . . . the plan broke down completely. Buildings crept towards the centre of the streets or ignored them altogether according to the personal convenience and greed of the land-owners" (1972a: 100).

As they began, so they continued. "The stories of Australia's first two attempts to plan its towns are a capsulated version of the stories of nearly all town and city development in Australia," Freeland notes disapprovingly (100-101). The result? Evincing a spirit almost absurdly opposed to Governor Darling's 1829 universal survey regulations (a code whose very rigidity attests to the tenacious unruliness of the Australian popular imagination), urban Australia became and remained a stubborn, striking, concrete expression of private wilfulness. "The most remarkable thing about Australian cities," says Craig McGregor, "is not the size of their populations but their sheer sprawl . . . Australians have always shown a penchant for living in a bungalow of their own surrounded by their own lawn and garden, so that as the land near the centre of the city was taken up they moved farther and farther out . . . Melbourne, with a quarter of the population of London, covers an area twice the size. The continuously developed area of Sydney extends over an incredible six hundred miles" (1981: 125-26).

Given our own external stance on this matter, one thing to note about the propensity for spreading, apart from its existence, is that it is not, despite both aesthetic and practical drawbacks ("Shortages of water, sanitary primitiveness, paying-one's-own-way, and long travelling time over extensive distances," to mention only a few [Freeland, 1972a: 113]), perceived as negative by the general population. Even apart from its facilitation of privacy, the sprawl of Australia's cities evidently expresses something central to the Australian sense of self. Russell MacDougall, in a fascinating essay entitled "Sprawl and the Vertical" (1986), goes so far as to identify the quality as the key to both Australian art and Australian character. Sprawl, he says, is the tendency of poets (like Les Murray, from whom he borrowed the term in the first place) to fill up the page. It is the aggressive shapelessness of Australian novels. It is the triumph of kinesis over form. It is the pioneer's expropriation of the land. It is the bush yarn. It is the verandah. It is the beach, and the "democracy of the body." It is the devaluation of the vertical in painting: "In many different ways, in the landscape art of many different artists, the vertical line is made conditional, transforming space to possess (even within a frame) the quality of sprawl" (223). Sprawl is the way the Australian inhabits the world. As such it is also, MacDougall points out, less an objective, rejectable "possibility" than a taken-for-granted *norm* for world habitation. "Australian readers will often respond initially to Canadian literature, in some ill-defined way, as lacking substance; Canadian readers, conversely, may at first find Australian literature not sufficiently crafted, unpolished, limited in its sense of style. Such responses are instinctively right, yet naive. In Australia, it might be argued, substance *is* style . . . [A]rtfulness is defined, positively, as having the appearance of lacking art, keeping to the truth of the *matter*" (205, 211).

Normalization notwithstanding, on the other hand, the idea and even more the fact of sprawl does not seem to play quite so unequivocal a role in the Australian consciousness as McDougall implies. Despite the approving notation of freedom and self-sufficiency ("Sprawl . . . makes its own laws" [207]), despite the invocation of such respectable literary precursors as Whitman – or perhaps because of it – McDougall's own essay has a tangible undertone of defensiveness to it. Nor does he seem quite confident in his grasp of his subject. One area of uncertainty is his attempt to explicate gender associations. Mistakenly identifying the Canadian self/other-image as a masculine "tower" in the midst of a formless feminine landscape (in fact, nature being both masculine and threatening for the Canadian, the tower actually represents the feminine interior, whether house on the prairie or fort in the wilderness [G. McGregor, 1985]), he also misreads the Australian symbology as a reversal of what is "normal" elsewhere. "'Sprawl leans on things. It is loose-limbed in its mind,'" he quotes Murray as saying. "At the same time, it should be [noted] that 'one boot up on the rail' is a male posture, and if it is central to the dominant discourse of cultural iconology this says much about the gendered nature of that discourse. Yet the stereotype of sprawl is more often female, with the vertical as a phallus. The maleness of Murray's version of sprawl is an unexpected gendering of the metaphor" (212, 214).

The invocation here of the phallus makes clear that what is wrong with McDougall's conceptualization is the initial tension he sets up in his title between the (purportedly) feminine horizontal and masculine vertical. What one realizes if one discards one's preconceptions about the conventionality of genderization (see G. McGregor, 1986) is that both horizontal sprawl *and* phallic verticality are icons of masculinity inasmuch as they both code an impulse toward exteriority. This doesn't mean that McDougall's polarity is not a critical one. The pertinent comparison here is not Canadian literature but American landscape painting, with its recurrent images of "penetration" (see Appendix A). The Australian version of masculinity, precisely because it is *not* phallic, bespeaks vividly a sense of manly aggressiveness "deflated" by the sheer impenetrability of its erstwhile object.

"THE OASIS"

Where the Queensland "outback" begins is a question to which there are innumerable answers. For the average tourist, it may begin past Cairns on the seashore, somewhere beyond Toowoomba inland. Hence the outback includes an enormous area, most of it untamed land, with rich and semi-arid pastures, artificial oases of pleasant mining towns, and deserts in between. It has its special fascination, especially for people who enjoy nature in the raw and don't mind occasional discomfort.

. . . A tour of the Outback is not a lightly taken drive but an expedition that needs careful preparation and execution. Such a tour does not present insurmountable difficulties, provided one has sufficient time, money, and, above all, the necessary expertise. But, for the overwhelming majority of tourists, it will be simpler, more pleasant, and probably far cheaper to join one of the many tours organized by experts.

Fodor's Australia, New Zealand, and the South Pacific

As of this minute we comprise a full 50 per cent of the customers at a small, remote service station/campground about 200 kilometres northwest of Townsville. This is cattle country. Animals of all shapes and sizes range freely through the bush. One wonders how they survive. To the outside eye there would seem to be little forage for even the hardiest beast. Parched and monotonous, this landscape is an even bleaker version of the parched, monotonous drylands we traversed coming north from Brisbane. There are few signs of human habitation.

One interesting feature – we noticed this on the previous leg, but it is now more pronounced – is the poor and uneven quality of the roads. Long stretches in this area are roughly paved single-laners; if one meets an oncoming car, both parties have to get off onto the shoulder. Flying stones are a real hazard, particularly when one's opposite number is a three-trailer road train barrelling along at 100 km/hour. Now I know why the people we leased the van from seemed to take it for granted that we would need to replace the windshield at least once. There are (for no apparent rational reason) intermittent short stretches of better quality two-lane paving, but these are both infrequent and brief. We are not all that far off the beaten track yet. To find such bad roads in (according to popular myth) a nation of inveterate travellers would seem to be something of an anomaly.

Another peculiarity: the locals here think we are crazy for tenting at this time of year with the weather getting so cold. A mere 25°C in the daytime and 15°C at night apparently strikes them as almost beyond human endurance. Is this symptomatic of a general fear of climatic extremes (unexpected in a people so renowned for their toughness), or is it only the cold that triggers their paranoia? It is interesting in this regard that in Colleen McCullough's new novel, *A Creed for the Third Millennium,* a near-future fantasy set in the United States, the requisite disaster is the onset of a new ice age. In the present of the book, despite the fact that the climate of the northern states would seem to be no worse than the currently fully-habitable regions of northern Canada and Alaska, virtually the whole population has packed up and moved south.

This book is interesting in other regards, too. For all its superficial and obviously deliberate similarities to popular American genres, it is actually very unAmerican. For one thing, it mixes modes. The base fable would seem to derive from an eighties-style progressivistic world vision (nature as enemy), but the proffered solution (grow plants and love your brother) smacks of the primitivistic sixties. Second, the social psychology is all wrong. We are to believe that under pressure from the combined Third World countries, the United States has signed a treaty agreeing to limit its population growth to one-child families for four generations. On the criteria of both fact and fiction, this premise is nonsensical. There is no way that America would allow external elements to dictate how it should conduct its domestic affairs. Conditioned by an absolutely impervious ideology of independence, the country would fight such intervention to the last gasp, even if the war were unwinnable. Individual Americans would fight equally hard before allowing their own government to tell them where and how to live. The "hero" of this book – bewildered, housebound, and easily manipulated – is also all wrong. The fact that he ends up not just mad but *unmanned,* while perhaps admissible in the self-consciously existentialist mainstream novel of the fifties and sixties, is entirely inconsistent with the conventions of Reagan-era popular fiction.

This is the key point as far as I'm concerned. Where Joshua Christian does fit, pre-eminently, is in the *Australian* oeuvre. Although the frameworks are strikingly different, here is the classic deteriorating hero of Clarke and Penton. Here too are the rest of the typical Australian personae: the charismatic but absent father, the inadvertently destructive mother, the ambivalent siblings, the masculine-woman-as-villain. In his lack of self-awareness, his inability to articulate ("write down") his ideas, his mystical (and "feminine") vision of universal love, Christian is clearly a variant on the Australian artist figure. It is notable that it is his mysterious and unwonted power that contains the seeds of his doom. From all this it would seem that the Australian can't escape his/her conditioning even when the terms of reference are changed.

Carrying implications quite counter to this, on the other hand, is another book I have been reading in the last few days. John Hooker's *The Bush Soldiers* is a peculiarly Australian version of *Heart of Darkness*. This time the genre is alternate-history fantasy — although the verisimilitude is such that it's almost difficult to believe that the author is not dealing with real events. The time is World War II. The Japanese have successfully invaded Australia; the civilian population has fled westward, and the remnants of the defending forces are pursuing a scorched earth policy, rendering the countryside uninhabitable in their wake. The focal protagonist is the classic Australian type: dynamic, pragmatic, a doer rather than a thinker, and so emotionally inept (unselfconscious, obtuse, and inarticulate) that his wife (another classic type: the unwomanly woman who prefers independence to maternity) is literally driven into another man's arms. There is a sense, therefore, in which the anarchy and violence of the post-invasion world is actually better suited to his skills and temperament than the "normal" world before the war. Opposed to this, and in quite marked contrast to the American post-atomsmash fantasy, is the fact that, far from establishing a new community close to nature, this man and his comrades are defeated not by their human enemies but by their own land.

The book follows the bush soldiers on their flight to "the centre" — a mysterious realm that the protagonist early defines as the place where god is. Judging by the hardships they suffer, however, if this bleak and barren desert is home to any deity, it can only be the god of death. What is more significant, "he" must in all probability be a "she." The climax of the journey, juxtaposing the group's arrival at a (deceptively) lush river valley, a deadly showdown with a hostile aborigine, and the protagonist's visions of his lost/faithless wife, obviously signals confrontation with the archetypal feminine in its most malevolent guise. Shortly after this, the deterioration of the man-adrift ends, as in so many Australian fables, with physical decrepitude, madness, and death.

What is intriguing about this book is not, on the other hand, the extent to which it mirrors – in some ways exemplifies – patterns already observed throughout the oeuvre, but the fact that its author was born and raised in New Zealand. If McCullough can't escape her native imprinting, why should this man so clearly have escaped from his? Unless we assume that the New Zealand psychotype is the *same* as the Australian one (which I do not believe [see McGregor, 1987c]), the difference between the two cases must have something to do with either the intensity of the transplanting experience or the presence/absence of some kind of psychological predisposition on the part of the transplantee. One might speculate that it would be easier for a man to self-identify at a rather profound level with a centrifugal culture like Australia than for a woman to assimilate America during the progressivist (masculine) phase of its cycle.

Two brief notes on Australian wildlife before closing this section.

First, it has been my impression so far that Australian birds, while hardly the "songless" creatures invoked a century ago by the renowned colonial poet, Adam Lindsay Gordon, do not in general produce anything resembling music. They shriek. They squawk. They cackle, coo, gibber, honk, whistle, mutter, squeak, giggle, and caw. They do all this, moreover, in a disconcertingly obtrusive manner. At our campsite today, for instance, even in the drowsy midday the muted bickering of the galahs and lorikeets serves as a constant reminder of the omnipresence of otherness.

Second and finally, though I have not yet in fact seen any live kangaroos, we have passed literally dozens of dead ones at the side of the road. I can't help thinking that there is a moral here for Canadians and Australians alike. Whether one goes to ground like a groundhog (see G. McGregor, 1985, Chapter 8, on the Canadian's propensity to self-identify with small, furry, burrowing animals) or spends one's life jumping frenetically around the landscape, one is likely to end up the same way: squashed by some heedless passing juggernaut.

SF and Fantasy[1]

For Britain, SF has traditionally served as a tool of social analysis and a vehicle for radical thought. For the United States, the connections are less with the outer world of social forms than with the inner one of social psychology. Bodying forth in a direct and almost unmediated fashion the community's favourite wishful fantasies, SF reveals not only the asocial underside to the collective unconscious but also, like the dreams of private individuals, the mechanisms by which both logical and moral inconsistencies are hidden from the subject. For Australia, its functions are less clear. For one thing, it remains, even after the "boom" of the late seventies, a very minor genre in the antipodes. More important it also remains a very derivative one. Australian writers have been content for the most part merely to use conventions generated elsewhere – though whether this is a cause or a symptom of its weaker appeal is a moot point. Despite this, I felt it worth looking a little closer at the genre if only to discover how it adapts, or fails to adapt, its borrowed ideas.

The task was not an easy one. Even after culling a sample list of names from an historical collection put together by the University of Queensland Press (Ikin, 1982), I was unable to find many, or indeed any, of the books in question in regular bookstores. Fortunately I came across an SF specialty bookstore in Melbourne where, while failing notably to fill out my checklist (SF has as short a shelf life in Australia as elsewhere), I was able to put together what seemed at the time to be a reasonable sample of local writing. By taking one book or set of books from each author represented in the "Australian" section of the store, I ended up with twenty-five items. When I had the leisure to look more closely at the material, I was unfortunately forced to discard eleven out of the twenty-five. The proprietors were obviously so hard-pressed to fill out a respectable collection of indigenous SF that they had been

---

1. In categorizing material for this section, I have used the "loose" (conventional-cum-consensual) definitions of SF and fantasy put forth in G. McGregor, 1988, chapter 5.

forced to take considerable liberties with their classifications. One book was
an Australian reissue of an American novel by an American author set in the
United States. One book, though set in Australia, was by an American who
had merely visited the country to collect background material. Two books I
eliminated because I felt they belonged elsewhere on the spectrum of literary
kinds. Gerald Murnan's *The Plains* is a psychosymbolic fantasy of the Australian inscape. Peter Carey's *Illywacker*, alternately, is a picaresque black
comedy with only minor fantasy elements. Three more I eliminated because,
although in at least two of the cases striking use was made of traditional SF
themes – Lee Harding's *Displaced Person*, an interdimensional adventure,
and Ruth Park's *Playing Beatie Bow*, with its time travel motif (of Helen
Frances' *The Devil's Stone* I will have more to say later) – they also, and more
importantly, belonged to the differentially conventioned subgroup of children's literature. The final four – Jack Wodham's *Ryn*, A. Bertam Chandler's
The Wild Ones, David Lake's *Ring of Truth*, and Victor Kelleher's *The Beast
of Heaven* – I struck off because the authors (including, significantly enough,
two of the country's best-known long-time SF writers), though technically
Australian, having immigrated as adults were, I thought, unlikely to reflect a
specifically Australian world view in any consistent or trustworthy fashion.
This left me with fourteen.

The first thing I noticed in reading this material was that, though certainly variable with respect to literary quality, it was even more variable with
respect to its semiology. In marked contrast to the American oeuvre, no clear
mythos – indeed, very little "mythic" element at all – emerges from Australian SF. Where in the United States the central conventions tend both to
reflect and to energize the psychological subtext (see G. McGregor, 1988,
Chapter 5), the most successfully "conventional" of the Australian books
were the least interesting and least numinous of the sample. Wynne White-
ford's *Thor's Hammer* is an old-fashioned (forties- and fifties-style) space
adventure; Keith Taylor's *The Lances of Nengesdul* is a slightly less old-
fashioned but equally formulaic variant on the American heroic-barbaric
romance. Both feature clear-cut, predictable moral/emotional alignments,
and both have happy endings. Conversely, the better and more original novels
in the sample tend to be both flawed *and*, from the point of view of their read-
ability, strengthened by a much muddier moral vision. This may be the crux
of the whole problem. The encoded ideological messages carried by the
imported conventions are incompatible with the Australian world view. The
complexity and, especially, the covert subversiveness of the latter (to be
forced to question, perhaps even deny, the Briton's humaneness and even

more the American's optimism must, one suspects, be all the more painful for those who have originally been attracted to the genre for the positivism of its mythopoesis) make it difficult for the writer to generate more appropriate forms of his/her own. Australian SF, says Van Ikin, "has mirrored the nation's apprehensive fascination with its own unexplored emptiness, and its fear of forfeiting its never-too-clear racial identity" (1982: xxxvii). If this is the case – and certainly my own sampling would tend to support it – then it is no wonder that the self/other images that emerge from the oeuvre are also "never-too-clear."

In earlier periods, according to Van Ikin, the "apprehension" tended to revolve around literal questions of race. In the late eighteenth and early twentieth centuries, for instance, there appeared a notable spate of didactic romances in which were made concrete the national "fears of the Asian hordes" (xxi). More recent production, in contrast, tends to focus not on race but on gender. It seems significant that two out of my small sample of novels take sex role inversion as a central theme. It is even more important that both of them betray considerable ambivalence on the issue. On the surface at least, Rick Kennett's A Warrior's Star is the most idiosyncratic of these. Plot complications aside, what this story hinges on is the discovery that a young girl who has been genetically engineered to be a superior spacecraft captain is actually – on a cellular rather than a somatic level – sexually coded as "male." This could be an interesting premise. In practice, it is so poorly developed as to seem no more than a gimmick. Since the ambiguation of gender is presented as both a particular advantage (her resistance to the villain's super-aphrodisiac facilitates the successful accomplishment of her mission) and a general mistake ("MALE SEXUAL INSTINCTS WERE ACCIDENTALLY INTRO-DUCED . . . WE REGRET ANY INCONVENIENCE OR EMBARRASSMENT THIS MAY CAUSE" [217]), we are not only offended by the flimsy plotline but left completely unsure in the end as to how we are meant to regard the masculinized woman. Such confusions are not, as we have seen, unusual in the Australian corpus. Lest we be tempted to write off the book's peculiarities as "just" bad writing, however, it is important to note that the covert message it carries bears strong similarities to the one that emerges quite blatantly from David Ireland's much slicker and better known City of Women. This near-futuristic fantasy of an Australia in which all men are banished to the wilderness, in striking contrast to the American version of this theme in Philip Wylie's classic The Disappearance, implies on the one hand that Australian women are exactly the same under the skin as their masculine counterparts ("Paradoxically," says P.K. Elkin, "in [a] book related by a woman about women in a metropolis of women, Ireland has produced his most limitingly masculine novel . . . Although the characters have female names . . . and although they are given female parts . . . their behaviour is unmistakably male – their conversation is Australian male pub conversation, and their interests and opinions are those that characterize the drinkers in an Australian public bar . . . They drink beer and tell stories, many of them dirty, and occasionally bash one another up . . . just like ordinary male ockers" [1983: 174]), and on the other, through almost obsessively recurrent images of deformity and disease (see Elkin: 175), that the situation is a decidedly unwholesome one.

In other books the ambiguity tends to be somewhat more diffuse. Apart from the problem of sex roles – though not entirely unconnected in a psychological sense – there is really only one feature that recurs widely enough to be considered to reflect on the corpus as a whole. Even more than their uncertainty about "identity" (and it is interesting here that the ego-image in Linda Macken's quasi-allegorical epic animal fable, *And Brothers All*, is a big-hearted but physically feeble rabbit overshadowed equally by the aristocratic hauteur of the ancient British lion and the adolescent arrogance of the American eagle), the Australians, judging by their fantasy fiction, are both bewildered by and apprehensive about *power*. Given that this is what SF, in a world sense, is really at bottom "about," authorial uncertainty in the area tends to undercut not merely the "morals" of given books but the ideology of the entire oeuvre. It is not a matter of political "slant." Whatever a writer's *personal* alignment, established authority is rarely depicted as unequivocally bad in better quality Australian SF. Indeed, even outright oppression, insofar as it regulates private greed and violence, is often shown to have its good side. Political solutions of *any* stripe hence tend to be imaged very ambiguously. The only thing that does come through clearly (and here is where the difference from the American pattern really becomes striking) is the *sub voce* message that the individual him(her)self is *normally* neither free nor capable. Among the current sample, two very different novels, M. Barnard Eldershaw's *Tomorrow and Tomorrow and Tomorrow* and Barnes' and Broderick's *Valencies*, take as their common theme the futility of revolution – or at least the unreliability of the public will and the weakness of revolutionaries. The former, a 1940s publication reissued in 1983 for the first time in uncensored form, is particularly poignant in that the technocratic regime which seems so repressive to the exceptional minority is clearly shown to have been the salvation of the nation as a whole.

The same issues of public good versus individual freedom, of commendable intentions with ambivalent consequences, is approached differently but with equally problematic results in George Turner's *Yesterday's Men*. By contrasting the vigour of the title personae (relict bushmen-turned-soldier culled from the Australian outback) with the effeteness of their ultracivilized twenty-first-century compeers, this novel shows how world pacifism, for all its obvious benefits, has enfeebled the population at large without diminishing one whit its venality. While the American version of such a theme would end with the digger hero coming into his own, however, Turner's book concludes with a Machiavellian scene in which the political puppetmaster schemes with the immortal who is the book's most convincing image of "otherness" to train a cadre of adventurers in the image of the diggers who will then be deployed to serve the interests of the state. Even apart from questions of "control," on the other hand, the thing that really undermines Turner's vision – as, to an even greater extent, Eldershaw's – is an uncertainty about the relative value and/or efficacy of both nature (vigour versus violence) *and* culture (peace versus passivity).

It is this single factor, indeed, that provides our best clue to the ambiguous treatment of power throughout the entire oeuvre. The root problem is a conflict between psychology and convention. Since the nineteenth century, says Sneja Gunew, SF has demonstrated a special affinity for the theme of "Earth-Mother-Nature versus Science-Father-Culture" (1982: 281). The observation, though quite right, is hardly original. Of particular significance for the present topic, however, is the qualifying corollary Gunew does *not* point out, that is, that unlike its British precursors (Gunew cites in particular Mary Shelley's *Frankenstein*), the American version of the nature/culture theme – which has been the most influential model for Australians – comes in two variants, the progressivistic pioneer fable, which celebrates human power *over* nature, and the primivistic noble savage fable, celebrating human assimilation of nature's power (G. McGregor, 1988, Chapter 5). While utilizing many of the conventional forms in which this dual myth expresses itself, the Australian – accustomed to code both nature *and* culture as feminine, and therefore *un*assimilable – is unable to ratify the underlying psycho-symbology. The result is, at best, a somewhat scrambled message ("the real villain in this novel," says Gunew of one of Turner's other books, "is in fact a woman . . . who absolves culture, the male mother, by being the archetypal bad mother, nature" [282]), and at worst, an a priori discrediting of the happy ending. John Baxter's *The Hermes Fall* is typical in this regard. Quite unlike the invincible American-style world saviour, astronauts sent to destroy a giant meteor heading for earth in this book manage only to make matters worse by deflecting it into the ocean. The story ends with the entire planet devastated by volcanoes, tidal waves, and titanic storms. The message seems clear. If the

Australian is quite ready to believe in nature's malevolence, as per the pioneer myth, he/she seems substantially *less* prepared to credit human capacity to counter it by means of either technological expertise or force of will.

This brings me to my last point. Considering its entrenched ambivalence about both nature and women, it is interesting to note the attitudes evinced in Australian SF toward the aborigine. If we include Helen Frances' children's book, four of our sample texts revolve around or extrapolate from aboriginal mythology or "magic." In every case, the source of power/danger in the story is connected with caves or water or both. Reinforcing the symbolic implications on the level of plot, taken together the endings to these four novels seem clearly to imply that the white *man*, no matter how exceptional, is helpless to defend himself against the feminine threat. Despite his supernatural foreknowledge, for instance, the protagonist of Petru Popescu's *The Last Wave* is unable to avert, or even save his family from, a cataclysmic flood. The half-aboriginal questor of Damien Broderick's *The Dreaming Dragons* and the girl-children of Frances' *The Devil's Stone* survive their subterranean confrontations, though not without considerable concomitant trauma (see "BROKEN HILL," pp. 131-36). The only one in the entire sample who – like the American in his noble savage mode – is able to control, rather than being controlled by, the power of the earth-mother, is the full-blood aboriginal hero of Patricia Wrightson's fantasy trilogy, *The Book of Wirrun*. Although it would be rash to generalize too broadly from such a limited number of examples, taken in context the implications of this pattern are at least provocative.

CAIRS

[N]ineteenth-century Queensland was a . . . dangerous place. Firstly, there was the climate. Droughts, cyclones, and floods were – and still are – an uncomfortable fact of life . . . Then there were the grave natural dangers to life and limb of colonial conditions. There are numerous reports of death by violent accident . . . adults killed by falls from horses, or by being thrown from buggies; children killed from falling down mineshafts or by falling timber. The incidence of fire was also very great . . . But granted that life in the country was rigorous and often threatening, what of the towns? They seem to have been seen as bastions of order . . . Violence was encapsulated . . . and . . . kept at a latent and manageable level by the strength of authoritarian attitudes in the communities at large.

Glen Lewis, "Violence in Australian History: The Queensland Experience"

If we had for a moment considered what outback roads were going to be like, we would never have set ourselves such a demanding itinerary. This too, of course, is a symptom of ethnocentrism – extrapolating from red lines on a map to North American-style highways. Scarcely a week out of Brisbane, and we are already running a full day behind schedule. The result, unfortunately, is to leave us less than twenty-four hours in Cairns. Since this is not enough time to take in such obligatory tourist attractions as a crocodile farm, a tour of the rainforest, or a daytrip to the Great Barrier Reef, I decided to take the opportunity to soak up some indigenous popular culture.

It was easier said than done. Every single movie playing in town is American. The television lineup is only slightly better, offering a choice between American imports and British ones. A browse through a newsagent's quickly convinced me that in the magazine field, too, imports – or thinly disguised "Australian" editions of British and American standards – far outnumber native products. There was a fair showing of Australian

63

specialty magazines (guns, cars, sailing, etc.), but very little in the way of general publications, and certainly nothing in the category of medium-brow issues-oriented magazines like *Harper's* in the United States or *Saturday Night* in Canada. The overall impression was of a fairly blatant anti-intellectualism. The only areas in which an indigenous product dominated were paperback romances and, to a slightly lesser extent, pulp westerns. It struck me as significant, moreover, that both these bodies of material included a substantial number of "picture books" – only a short step up from children's comics in North America.

How representative is this selection? Obviously one would get a different impression from a university bookstore, but is a lowbrow general public a common denominator? Certainly in Cairns such would seem to be the case. Even in "real" bookstores which give at least a token nod to more intellectual categories of writing – history, literature, religion, science, and so on – the selection tends to be both scant and "soft." Nor are Australian authors any better represented than in the paperback racks at the newsagents. The only exception to this rule was, in one bookstore, a three-shelf section labelled "Australiana." Oddly enough, however, literature does not seem to be included under this designation. Apart from such practical items as maps and tourist guides, the offerings were all humour, folklore, and popular and natural history. The one thing that did surprise me about this selection was the fact that it included a significant number of studies of aboriginal history and culture. Even allowing for the desire of the proprietors to cash in on every possible source of exotica – Cairns is, after all, a tourist town catering largely to overseas visitors – it does seem a little odd, in the most notoriously racist part of a notoriously racist country, to find what seems to be evidence of a burgeoning interest in a subject traditionally considered below contempt. Perhaps it is an anomaly. Certainly beyond this tiny cache there was little to be found apart from British and American bestsellers and genre fiction.

The town itself, on the other hand, has a physical presence that seems to me quite distinct from either of its extra-national referents. How to describe it? Ice cream Victoriana? Brighton crossed with Virginia Beach? Again there is the notable emphasis on *surface*. Particularly striking are the numbers of pastel, particoloured buildings in the downtown area. Again, too, there is the beautiful landscaping that struck me so forcefully in

Brisbane. Both here and in Townsville the potentially unruly ocean is framed (denied?) by a carefully manicured esplanade. The public square in the centre of downtown is full of trees and birds. (The uncharacteristic touch of wildness is permissible, perhaps, because this particular patch is "officially" contained.) Even more striking than such displays of civic pride, however, are the elaborate, lovingly tended, largely "English-style" gardens that one sees in the residential section.

This is not a feature peculiar to Cairns, to be sure. Throughout Queensland, in large and small communities alike, we have been singularly impressed by the consistent kemptness of both public and private grounds. There is even, one gathers, an annual contest for the "tidiest" town in the north. The values one infers from such an emphasis seem at first sight to run completely counter to the social psychology that emerges from the literary oeuvre. One would hardly expect a country in which domestication in general and the "city" in particular are viewed very much askance to dote on its gardens to the extent that this one obviously does. If one reads the phenomenon in context, though, it is perhaps not as inconsistent as it seems. I said above (pp. 16-17) that the Australian's negative attitude toward "civilization" stems less from a dislike than from a fear that it is too alien to attain or too fragile to last. Stipulating that a love of gardening is quite different from, and indeed diametrically opposed to, a love of nature (it is significant, for instance, that aborigines do not garden; it is also significant that the purportedly nature-attuned Australian bushman is known to have disdained "bush tucker" just as much as the Australian suburbanite has historically disdained native flora), one might speculate that the obsession with landscaping testifies to the sheer intensity of the frustrated desire (like Richard Mahoney's yearning for the perfect house) that underlies the Australian's suspicion of "domestication." It would also, one suspects, exacerbate that suspicion. In a country as prey to climatic extremes as this one, the cultivated garden must be seen as providing an extremely frail bulwark against encroaching chaos.

One final comment before leaving Cairns: I have mentioned before, but have perhaps not emphasized enough, the prevalence of verandahs in Queensland architecture. At first I was inclined to dismiss this feature as simply another version of "front." I am now of the opinion, however, that the verandah represents a peculiarly Australian solution to the conflict between the necessity and the impossibility of conquering the landscape. Surficiality signals an antipathy to "insideness," along with a commensurate impulse to self-assert. Verandahs, however, can be read as the construction of a zone or space which is actually *between* inside and outside. This doesn't mean that verandahs *take the place of* "front" – many of them simply provide more scope for garish detail. It does, however, demonstrate that architecture, like literature, not only expresses in concrete terms a specific sense of being-in-the-world, but also operates to mediate, really and symbolically, the more ambiguous and troublesome aspects of that sense.

93

Man against the Land

"There are thousands of Australians today," wrote Rex Ingamells in 1941, "who, if they have not found eloquent tongue, feel nevertheless, with child-like devotion, the familiar beauty and utter loveliness of the outback environment in many of its moods" (in I. Turner, 1968: 299). Almost half a century later, the same refrain continues to be sounded by poets like Judith Wright and artists like John Olsen. Paeans notwithstanding, on the other hand, the fact is that the general public in Australia has historically evinced little respect and even less love for their landscape. "We have . . . submerged thousands of square miles of unique bushland in geometric sterility," says Ian Moffitt, "– and smeared the rest with debris. Our memorials are the rusted chassis, the burst mattress, the shining sheet of cement. We have polluted rivers and harbours, rubbed out rain-forests, filled marshes, eroded valleys, erased mountains, and cluttered once-handsome headlands with fibro weekenders. We have ravaged our beaches for rutile, chopped down our red cedar and ringbarked our mountain ash, gutted green landscapes for gravel, and obliterated ancient ecology beneath sheep runs and suburban backyards" (1972: 125-26). Such complaints are not unusual. Almost every contemporary social historian feels compelled to mention and to criticize Australia's deplorable record with respect to conservation policy. The rhetorical protestations only point up the real callousness of the average Australian toward the nature he/she professes to revere.

Neither the problem nor the duplicity are new in the history of man/land relations in Australia. If the fact is often obscured by rosy latterday retrospectives, an examination of nineteenth- and early twentieth-century letters makes abundantly clear the ambivalence, nay the outright negativity, felt by succeeding generations of Australian pioneers toward their environment (see, for instance, Gibson, 1984; L. Frost, 1984). So automatous was the alienation, in fact, that even those whose intention was to celebrate – like Banjo Paterson, most unequivocally optimistic of the *Bulletin* bush mythographers – were frequently unable to avoid ambiguous undertones. At the core of

Paterson's work, says Trevor James, "is an uncertainty which he seeks to resolve by imposing his own romanticism upon the landscape" (1984: 59). Paterson's reaction, and his reaction *to* that reaction, were in a sense exemplary. Simply by virtue of its *difference,* to the British-conditioned sensibility the Australian landscape was in-conceivable. Before it could be consumed, therefore, it had to be transformed – really or symbolically – into something more "normal." "As the colonists on the Cumberland Plain re-created the life they had either known or aspired to in England," says Alan Frost "– as they raised houses and towns, made roads, delineated holdings, raised stock and crops – so did they take progressively greater pleasure in their total environment" (1982: 77). Plausible as it sounds from a psychological point of view, this strategy unfortunately contained the seeds to its own undermining. The more strenuously the continent *resisted* such transformation – which, of course, it did – the more it confirmed its own unnaturalness. The more unnatural it seemed, on the other hand, the more it exacerbated the colonist's disquiet – *and* his need to cover up his weakness by denying that the landscape really was recalcitrant.

This disjunction perhaps explains why, quite apart from their values, Australians seem to have had so little *control* over their environmental transactions. Lacking empathy with the land, they had little intuitive understanding of its needs and rhythms. Much of the worst damage that has been done – ironically, given the accusatory tone of recent conservationists – has been inadvertent. Where most environmental deterioration in the United States is directly attributable to individual and corporate greed, in other words, the deterioration of the Australian landscape cannot for the most part be rationalized as a necessary adjunct of "progress" or even profits.

Part of the problem was the real fragility of what seemed to the invaders intimidatingly impervious to intervention. Even before the white man arrived, the Australian ecology had been substantially altered by its human occupants. Most importantly, in somewhat paradoxical contrast to their purported "harmony" with nature, the aborigines had for thousands of years used fire as a primary means of controlling the environment. The burning, says George Seddon, "was deliberate, regulated, seasonal, an immediate aid in hunting, and a future one by regenerating herbage for the grazing kangaroo" (1983: 13). If it had the advantage of favouring "useful" grass over "useless" scrub, however, the strategy also had the disadvantage of reducing soil fertility and increasing the rate of erosion. In consequence of this, what the white colonists found in Australia was an open, parklike environment only marginally productive in agricultural terms but spatially ideal for running cattle and, especially, sheep. Unfortunately, the latter in particular entailed some serious problems from a conservationist viewpoint. The animals' preferential grazing habits, and even more their cloven hooves, hastened the (in some places) already advanced degradation of the landscape. "When I arrived through the thick forest land from Portland to the edge of the Wannon country," wrote John Robertson in 1853, "I cannot express the joy I felt at seeing such a splendid country before me . . . the few sheep made little impression on the country for three or four years . . . [but then] many of our herbaceous plants began to disappear from the pasture land . . . the ground is now exposed to the sun . . . the clay hills are slipping in all directions . . . when rain falls it runs off the hard ground . . . into the larger creeks and is carrying earth, trees and all before it. Over Wannon country it is now as difficult to ride as if it were fenced. Ruts seven, eight, and ten feet deep are found for miles where two years ago it was covered with tussocky grass like a land marsh" (in Seddon, 1983: 17).

If the domestic animals deliberately introduced proved detrimental to the Australian ecology, more frivolous imports proved even more so. "The devastating effects of rabbits on the drier regions of Australia are well documented," says Seddon. "Foxes, cats, goats, pigs, donkeys and camels have also run wild . . . Feral cats are extraordinarily widespread, and very destructive of birds and small marsupials" (18). Introduced flora have been equally problematic. "Blackberries now infest some 663,00 ha of land in Victoria alone . . . The prickly pear in Queensland, the noogoora burr in the dry plains, and a host of other 'weed' plants have taken hold wherever conditions favour them. There are Mediterranean docks and sorrels on the Bogong High Plains; lantana chokes disturbed rainforest; Chinese privet . . . forms a dense understorey in the bushlands of North Sydney . . . veld grass . . . smothers the incomparably beautiful ground plants in Kings Park in Perth, while *Phytophthora cinnamomi*, a plant pathogen, infects the roots of jarrah, banksia, and much else" (18, 19; see also Rolls, 1984, for a full discussion of this issue). Economics and aesthetics aside, the psychological effects of these unforeseen and uncontrollable incursions must have been considerable. Insofar as the source of contagion was "outside," the phenomenon of the manmade plague would have operated to reinforce Australian xenophobia. Insofar as it flouted both human wisdom and human will, however, it would also have reinforced feelings of helplessness in the face of natural processes.

These feelings perhaps explain the relative ineffectuality of communal action throughout the history of the issue. It is not, as in the United States, a case of insufficient regulation. The Australian government has from the first kept a tight rein on land disbursement and management, using the grant and licence system as a means of exerting social control. As one might expect given popular antipathy to the native landscape, however, its priorities were just the opposite of preservation. "[W]e must recognize," says Alan Gilbert, "that the European colonizers of Australia were committed inescapably to ecological roles involving some sort of *rationalization* of nature" (1982: 10). Far from fostering efficiency, unfortunately, when disasters struck – when nature ran wild, as inevitably it seemed to do – the explicit progressivism of the official ideology, just like the romanticism of the bush mythographer, only served to emphasize the discrepancy between the heroic dreams and the comedy of errors. Loss of public confidence no doubt added to the problem. Even after widespread destruction made it necessary that some thought be given to conservation, government policy, as Gilbert points out, remained largely reactive – and thus inadequate. "In the Western Division *rectification* involved little more than a cutting of losses, followed by more sensible future management of the damaged environment. More often, however, the state as 'trouble-shooter' has been obliged to operate more directly as an agent in the ecological relationship between man and nature . . . [Such strategies] have been at best only partially successful, and . . . more often than not . . . have been both *ad hoc* and segmental . . . [dealing] with the natural environment without due appreciation of the integrated, holistic nature of ecological systems" (19).

The problems cannot, on the other hand, be laid entirely at the feet of the government. Despite conservationist images of "them" versus "us," official wrongheadedness in Australia has been much exacerbated by the duplicity of the popular imagination. Like their settler fathers, post-colonial urban Australians, while professing a fervent *spiritual* identification with the bushman, have shown little interest in protecting the "real" wilderness. The National Parks movement, which dates back as far as the 1870s, has thus been seriously undermined, at least from the conservationist's point of view, by the anthropocentric biases of the citizenry. "The concept of scenic value at least implied the notion that a natural environment might be worth preserving for its passive, aesthetic, unimproved qualities," says Gilbert. "Most of the early National Parks, however, were proclaimed purely in the interests of active public recreation." Far from guardians, "the managers of such Parks could be happily committed to the colonial usurper's role of subduing nature, of making a cultured, preferably exotic, landscape out of the wilderness" (20). Things changed little after the turn of the century. Bushwalkers' and naturalists' societies raised the public stock of the native landscape without much altering "real" public behaviour. At least until the sixties, Gilbert notes, "economic priorities pressed by mining, logging or grazing interests . . . [were frequently] less threatening to conservationist values than pressures from public bodies and service industries to develop National Parks for recreational purposes" (22).

Note that phrase "until the sixties." In the last two decades, under the influence of a strong, vociferous international conservation movement, ecology consciousness in Australia has finally come into its own. Given the persistence in art and literature of ambivalent images of nature itself, however (see, for instance, "SYDNEY," parts I and II, below), one can't help wondering if the "Greenies," like the urban bushmen of the nineties, are not simply trying to exert a symbolic control through the assumption of a proprietary stance. Gilbert himself, while giving full due to the enthusiasm of the new conservationists, casts some doubt on their effectuality. "Whether such changes amount to too little too late is partly a question of values, and partly a matter that only the future can determine," he says. "But (to conclude on a somewhat pessimistic note) if present indications are anything to go by, viable solutions to perhaps the gravest of Australia's existing environmental problems – the management of the Murray-Darling waters – do not seem likely to emerge in time to avert massive environmental and socio-economic dislocation in eastern Australia. The *ad hoc,* segmental approach of the past, the inherited indecisiveness of governments, which do not so much *act* as *react,* have been overcome in theory but not in practice by the holistic legislation and environmental rhetoric of the 1970s" (26). Particular issues aside, conservationist "practice" will in all likelihood continue to be undercut, I would add, as long as the Australian public refuses to recognize its own mixed feelings.

MOUNT ISA

But the bush, the grey charred bush. It scared him . . . it was so phantom-like, so ghostly, with its tall pale trees and many dead trees, like corpses, partly charred by bush fires: and then the foliage so dark, like grey-green iron. And then it was so deathly still. Even the few birds seemed to be swamped in silence. Waiting, waiting – the bush seemed to be hoarily waiting. And he could not penetrate into its secret. He couldn't get at it. What was it waiting for? And now, there was something among the trees, and his hair began to stir with terror, on his head. There was a presence. He looked at the weird, white, dead trees, and in the hollow distances of the bush. Nothing! Nothing at all. He turned to go home. And then immediately the hair on his scalp stirred and went icy with cold and terror. What of? He knew quite well it was nothing.

D.H. Lawrence, *Kangaroo*

Inland from Cairns, one climbs through some of the most spectacular scenery imaginable – classic rainforest. It doesn't last long, unfortunately, and the almost total absence of scenic lookouts along the steep, winding highway makes it difficult to get the full effect of the view. In many ways, though, the landscape on the other side of the mountains, while less spectacular, is even more interesting to anyone in quest of real Australiana. These are the Atherton Tablelands: high, rolling grasslands, well watered and wooded, and studded with snug, prosperous-looking farms and villages. It was the first area we'd been in that seemed really humanized. Again unfortunately, *this* didn't last long either. Descending from the plateau, we soon found ourselves back in the old, familiar drylands terrain.

The same – and yet not quite the same. One's sense of vulnerability increases as one penetrates further into the north. The distance from civilization seems mysteriously concomitant with a progressive, inexorable *natural* deterioration. The landscape here, especially in contrast with the tablelands, seems both wild and lifeless. The trees are smaller, scruffier, and more widely dispersed than they were out by the coast. Dry creek and river beds leave crumbling gullies across the parched red earth. The ground is thickly peppered with anthills up to three or four feet in height. There is little ground cover, and what there is seems more grey than green. Adding to the unease is the fact that the roads, too, degenerate along with the landscape. Much of the northernmost highway is what they call in the guidebooks "gravel." What this signifies in *fact* is sun-baked, bone-jarring, deeply rutted mud.

The most disturbing aspects of this scene, on the other hand, are not the roads per se, but the dead animals lined up along the shoulders. Cattle, kangaroos, the occasional horse – in one spot we even saw a pig. The road trains with their enormous reinforced grills and "roo bars" mow them down by the dozens. And there are, of course, no sanitary engineers to cart away the remains. The worst of it for me is not the fact but the *way* they rot. Scavengers usually take the kangaroos down to skeletons in fairly short order, but the cattle, perhaps because of the thickness of their hides, generally remain at least outwardly intact. After a few days in the sun, they blow up like grotesque balloons which then deflate gradually until there is nothing left but crumpled skins.

Equally grotesque are the enormous number of wrecked, stripped, rusted and/or burned-out automobiles that litter the bush. Alternate explanations for this phenomenon would have it either that the drivers of these cars swerve off the road to avoid animals, and go out of control, or that aborigines steal them from the city, torch and desert them. In either case, it certainly exacerbates one's feeling that one is penetrating a kind of no-man's land. The question is whether, in the long run, it means anything – with respect to *culture*, that is. For myself, I wouldn't rule it out. Economics can explain why the garbage, animate and inanimate, is allowed to accumulate this way, but one can't help wondering whether the practical motives are reinforced by an unconscious desire on the part of Australians to reiterate the exculpatory founding myth of the country's impenetrability.

"Civilization" makes a rather poor show of it in this area altogether. The only things that seem undaunted by the ferocity of the landscape are the pubs. To an even greater extent than its coastal cousins, the bush hotel – a sprawling, slovenly, often garish two-storey wooden building, surrounded by verandahs and clutter – tends to dominate, if not wholly comprise, the cultural text. The scruffy settlements which cling to their skirts seem almost an afterthought. No matter what the bush mythographers would have us believe, this is not a pretty scene. It's not even picturesque. Dust. Flies. Heat. I can't imagine living day after day against that unrelenting backdrop. Perhaps no one can, really. Next to our site in the Croyden Community Campground – a rather grand term for a graceless, grassless, treeless patch of undifferentiated sun-baked earth – was the half-wrecked shell of an old school bus tenanted by the half-wrecked shell of a young/old man. Watching this unkempt figure fumbling around the barbecue, muttering drunkenly to himself, I wondered whether he was crazy because he lived there or lived there because he was crazy.

Mount Isa, with its tidy yards and air-conditioned motels, is a modern Athens in comparison with these last few stops. Despite or perhaps because of its location, huddled in the midst of a broken, rolling rubble-scape criss-crossed by ragged ridges of weather-resistant dyke-rock, this medium-sized mining community is clean, compact, and thriving, with none of the slovenliness one associates with frontier living. Perhaps that's because this really *is* frontier living. If towns like Croydon are too small to resist or too apathetic to care, the determined normality of Mount Isa conveys the clear message that social forms are all the more important when one is cut off from "normal" society. Further to my comments in the "Oasis" section, for instance, it is interesting to note how these people cling to the psychological structure offered by a sense of season. This, though 25°C and sunny, is *winter,* and winter is when one drains the pool and gets out the flannel pyjamas. As one chance acquaintance put it, if we allowed our children to swim all year it wouldn't have any therapeutic value in the summer when we really need it. No wonder my companion was viewed askance when he ventured into the motel pool.

For myself, I have been dipping into the magazines that I picked up in Cairns. Of particular interest is *The Bulletin,* once renowned as the "bushman's bible," but now sadly degenerated to an American-style newsmagazine. What does this publication tell us about Australian society? The editorial bias seems to be at least slightly right wing; certainly it is anti-government. Despite this, there is something about its mode of presentation which at least hints at a kind of genuine ideological ambivalence that is palpably missing from the stage-managed contentiousness of its American counterparts. The readers' letters, for instance, are dominated by long and apparently unedited rebuttals from members of government and other public officials. This could mean either that the power elite is less aloof than tends to be the case in North America, or simply that it is more insecure. The dialogue strikes me as a healthy sign, in any case. The writing on the whole is slightly less "slick" than would be the American norm. Subjects of significance covered in this issue (May 27, 1986) are as follows:

(a) Trends in public opinion: The Morgan Gallup Poll's 1986 survey of professional virtue is reported to have recorded an upturn in the public assessment of professional ethics. More than the change per se, it seems notable to me that those most highly rated are individual professionals, with dentists at the top with a 63% affirmation and lawyers around the middle with 39%. After this there is a sharp drop to business executives at 23% and stockbrokers at 19%. Even lower is the class of public officials. State and federal members of parliament got 17 and 16% respectively. Union leaders – surprisingly in such a highly unionized country – got only 5%, a low surpassed only by used car salesmen. Journalists – and I'm not sure yet what to make of this – were fifth from the bottom with 12%.

(b) Phone tapping: The author of this piece sees the lack of public resistance to recent recommendations to increase police phone tapping powers as symptomatic of a kind of national naivete. "Behind the community's apparent acceptance of this state of affairs [law professor Robert] Hayes sees the lack of a deep national civil rights consciousness – unlike the United States tradition – and the ' "she'll be right" attitude of the average Australian. There's a complacent reliance in the belief that "I'm innocent so have nothing to fear" which ignores history'" (46-47).

(c) Profile of artist Kevin Pearsh: Pearsh is an expatriate painter based in London. In his earlier years he returned periodically to his homeland, and did a significant amount of work in the semi-arid regions of Western Australia. Then, as the article puts it, "in 1978, he visited India, fell in love with the place and decided to dedicate much of his time painting a country that is often said to be an assault on the senses." Why the preference? As Pearsh himself puts it: "'I don't see human involvement [in the Australian landscape]. It's not like the relationship with the landscape in India where people are working and moving through [it]. There are so many people you can't take them out'" (50).

(d) Women writers: "Australia's women writers are enjoying startling success both here and overseas," says the lead to this article. "But are they a conspiracy or merely a fashion?" My answer: although the fact that the United States is currently in a domestic phase (see G. McGregor, 1987b, Chapter 6) obviously has something to do with their international success, these women are far from a fluke. Despite the complaints of male writers like Gerard Windsor that the recent fad for feminism has produced an anti-male bias within the publishing industry, it is, in fact, no more than predictable that a country that associates art with the feminine should produce a disproportionate number of "good" women writers. The only question that occurs to me is why, out of the nearly thirty mentioned, I have heard of only eight and come across books by only six. Is this due to my own unfamiliarity or to a resistance among their countrymen? It will be interesting to see how difficult it is for me to acquire works by these women. It will also be interesting to read these works as a discrete sub-group to see whether the picture that emerges differs in any significant way from the more general pattern summarized in Chapter 2. Lumped with their male counterparts, as they were in that preliminary study, women writers were far from emerging as the distinctive force that this article invokes. Perhaps, though, with a larger and a more up-to-date sample the diagnosis will change.

(e) Australian theatrical exports: A review of international response to several recent Australian touring productions suggests that the success of the latter may be rooted in a kind of cultural imperialism. "Margaret Pepper sums it up as 'energy, rawness and edge.' But she also admits to a 'naive quality which lacks the tired old cultural influences of the northern hemisphere'" (98).

(f) Australian films at Cannes: Although it reports on the quantitative success and self-congratulatory mood of Australian filmmakers at Cannes, this article also hints that native assessments would rate this country's filmmaking skills considerably lower than North American opinion is wont to do. "Unfortunately the South Australian Commission won't be making many more feature films but will concentrate on television productions. One reason for this could have been voiced by Dr. Neustadt, boss of CEL, who pointed out that the 'B' movie industry had virtually disintegrated in the past few years and that the only cinema successes nowadays were arthouse films and blockbusters of the Spielberg mould. As the bulk of Australia's output falls, by design or not, into the 'B' movie category, this tends to cast something of a pall over Oz moviemaking." It is also interesting that the one "genuine 'arthouse' new Australian film" mentioned by the article was a production of outsider D.H. Lawrence's *Kangaroo*. Is this low self-esteem, or simply a reflection of reality?

(g) Technology: This comment is not directed at a particular article but, rather, concerns the implicit impression conveyed cumulatively by the advertising in the magazine. Out of a total of 109 pages or part-pages, 52 concerned some sort of high-tech product, and out of these, 30 were for computer technology. From what I have observed so far, Australia is *not* yet a widely computerized society. Outside of banks, in fact, I have seen virtually no evidence of computerization at all. When we booked train reservations in Townsville, for instance, the stationmaster still had to phone Brisbane for confirmation (the same station had train times chalked up by hand on a blackboard). The question is, then, does this barrage of computer ads signal a real burgeoning of interest here, or simply wishful thinking on the part of the merchandisers?

Actually, this raises the whole question of Australian attitudes to technology. Since the United States at the progressivist ("masculine") end of its cycle tends to be almost unequivocally pro-technology, I had more or less assumed that Australia would be likewise. So far, however, images of/reactions to technology have been conspicuous mainly by their absence. Even the automobile – which, given its almost universal phallic associations, one would expect to have replaced the horse as a symbol of masculine energy and assertiveness – has not, at least as yet, emerged in the course of this investigation as an important cultural symbol. One notable exception, now that I think about it, is in the Mad Max movies. Even here, however, the car symbolism is not quite what one would expect. If it is obvious that cars do epitomize masculinity throughout this series, it is equally obvious that the forces comprehended under the portmaneau label are by and large destructive ones. Even more interesting, technology *apart* from cars is associated in the series not with male dynamism but – implicitly in the second film, explicitly (in the person of citymaker Auntie Entity) in the third – with feminine centripetality. Which has some provocative implications for all this computer advertising. I will have to look into this matter further.

Ideology and the Press

There is a considerable difference of opinion among Australians about the power of the press. Donald Horne argues that "over the years, the media have been more significant than the politicians in setting the [public] agenda" (1985: 182). Keith Windshuttle, in contrast, attributes the downfall of *The Australian* to the disapproval among both public and professionals of its canon-violating involvement in the campaign against the Whitlam Labor government in 1975 (1985: 43-44). There is also considerable disagreement about who actually wields such power as exists. Though almost everyone concedes the existence of a conservative bias, while some commentators identify this as evidence of "establishment" control (Windshuttle: 264-65; Moffitt, 1972: 57ff.), others, like Margaret McColl, posit a more passive response to lowest-common-denominator market pressures. The general apoliticism of popular publications almost across the board suggests that McColl is right in downplaying the importance of the media moguls at least with respect to any "short term, immediate impact . . . on single elections or particular issues" (1980: 258). As she herself recognizes, however, the relative absence or ineffectuality of explicit propaganda says nothing about the influence of less tangible factors. Rowse and Moran (1984), among others, claim that the ostentatious neutrality of the Australian press carries more of an ideological burden than open sloganeering. Specific content aside, says McColl, "the pervasive, idealized message which is continually presented by the media is the notion that the Western world is being run in the best interests of the population at large" (257). Apart from this *general* message, we can perhaps see the most important ideological function of the press to lie with its construction of a reader.

What, from this point of view, are the critical features of the Australian press? First and foremost is its implicit anti-intellectualism. In terms of both size and presentation, the "news" part of the newspaper is definitely secondary to the features. Even within the news sections, moreover, both dailies and weeklies (with rare exceptions, to be discussed below) tend to play down hard news, with its appeal to the intellect, in favour of soft, and especially emotionally oriented, items. An impressionistic overview suggests that Peter Gerdes' content analysis of television news would apply equally to the print media. "Firstly," he says, "half of the time allocated to news broadcasts by the commercial stations was given to sporting items, weather reports, and commercial breaks ... Secondly: of the remaining time it can be said of all stations that almost half their news-time was devoted to stories on Law/Crime, Human Interest, and news from overseas [which itself stressed the exotic, the personal, and the sensational over political or hard news stories]. The rest of the time consisted of reports covering Industrial Disputes, the Federal Government, State Affairs, and Disasters and Accidents. Less than 5% of the news was concerned with Aboriginal Affairs, Unemployment, State Governments other than New South Wales, Education and Trade Unions" (1982: 83). It seems clear from this not only that the Australian news media are less concerned with information than with entertainment, but also that they tend to select the hard news items they do present from among those categories of issues/events which are least threatening to a rosy picture of the status quo. "Even the best of the dailies," says Henry Mayer, "have very strict limits. There are a hundred and one things discussed in the alternative press which the mass circulation press treats as non-existent to marginal. It won't feature news about socialist societies that over a period of time suggests that socialism might be a reasonable alternative to consider. It won't run material that over time suggests that land rights must be taken seriously to the extent of taking property ... away from whites and giving it to blacks. It won't run material on the ecological, or population, or nuclear, or resource crisis which, over time, ties these to the social system under which we live and suggests that solutions must overthrow the system" (1976: 132).

If the reader who emerges from the pages of the general mass-circulation press is passive, unintellectual, and almost wholly apolitical, the reader implied by the women's press is so conventional as, in this day and age, to be almost unbelievable. The oldest and most popular of the general women's magazines in the country is *The Australian Women's Weekly*. The *AWW*, reported Janet Jones in 1979, "is read by 3.7 million people over the age of 13. It is read by 46% of Australian women aged 18 and over, by 23% of the men, and it is trusted by its regular readers" (26). This entrenchment makes it all the more notable that since its founding the magazine has devoted itself, except for a brief interregnum during World War II, to affirming traditional female roles. In 1934, says Shirley Sampson, the *AWW* "centred around homemaking advertisements, and articles on personal appearance, child care, cooking, knitting, sewing, interior furnishing, decorating and other aspects of housekeeping. It catered for the woman who felt that she belonged at home. Children were regarded as a full time occupation, otherwise they grew into 'nervous, restless, irritable little beings . . .' [A neglectful] mother would one day be punished for her negligence: 'The time comes when the mother craves the love she has pushed aside, and who can say that which is the sadder – the almost motherless child, or the almost childless mother'" (1973: 10).

Recent studies indicate that little has changed in the last fifty years. If the image is somewhat less militantly domestic, it is still quite unequivocal in its affirmation of the values that underwrite patriarchy. At best it posits a combination of the new with the old ("[T]he *Weekly,*" says Jones, "presents the 'liberated' woman as slim, attractive, energetically enjoying stimulating and fulfilling paid employment while simultaneously maintaining a clean, attractive, efficiently run household" [30]). At worst, and – judging by the tacit role model one might infer from its advertising – somewhat more often, it reinforces the same old stereotype of passive, unintellectual, traditional femininity. "Success for the Australian woman is measured in terms of social acceptability rather than professional or economic achievement," says Tania Birrell. The ideal put forth by the media "tends to be a model beauty queen or loving mother. The approved areas of success are the arts, fashion or being an important someone's wife. Of course, women do other things. They work in factories, teach school, heal patients, write books, etc. The point is that these activities are seen as being of secondary importance to the idealized role . . . in which the uncomely female brain surgeon is less desirable than the pretty hat-check girl" (1985: 278).

Running in a sense at right angles to these general propensities is a recent trend toward greater fragmentation. In the area of newspapers, one of the most notable developments of the eighties, according to Windshuttle, has been the decline in the popularity or at least the profitability of afternoon tabloids like the Melbourne *Herald* and the Sydney *Sun* and *Daily Mirror,* and the concomitant rise of up-market morning papers like the Melbourne *Age* and the *Australian Financial Review.* While seeming at first to signal a change for the better, this phenomenon in fact indicates the splitting off of a new professional elite – young, educated, upwardly mobile, and (judging from the advertising) overwhelmingly male – from the reading public at large. Concomitantly, if the increasing turn to gimmickry on the part of television news programs is any indication (see Hall 1981), there has been a corresponding, even greater softening in the already soft-centred mass media. In the women's press, the fragmentation is even more striking. If the *Women's Weekly* is still going strong, for the past few years it has lost a substantial share of its market to glossy monthlies aimed at a younger audience: *Pol, Dolly, Belle, Cosmopolitan,* and *Cleo.* While superficially more "liberated" than their older sister, it seems clear on closer examination that these magazines, in de-emphasizing domesticity in favour of sex, have only substituted one patriarchal stereotype for another. What the narrower focus does do is to allow the advertisers to exploit group aims and anxieties more effectively. Whether the specific products one "must" have are cosmetics or home furnishings, in fact, the thing that is really being sold in these new publications, as in the old *AWW,* is an image of woman-as-consumer. Just as the "quality" press can be seen not to counter but to hasten the already significant marginalization of the average news-reader, *Cosmopolitan* and its ilk simply repackage old strategies in new guises. Far from signalling any sort of "improvement," one can only see the fragmentation of the mass media market as an effective means of rendering individuals more vulnerable to manipulation.

"HOMESTEAD"

Statistics of annual rainfall in Australia are not always revealing. When exactly the rain falls, how torrentially it falls, and how long are the lapses between each fall of rain, are as significant as the total rains of the whole year. The annual rainfall in many parts of Australia – and it might fall in two of the 365 days – is pitiful. An intensely hot area around Lake Eyre receives four to six inches of rain in the average year. Troudaninna, over a span of nearly half a century, knew only one year in which the rain exceeded nine inches; between 1895 and 1903, its annual rainfall was less than three inches a year . . . Those years embraced the first devastating drought in the British history of this land . . . The sheep population declined by fifty million, and cattle also perished by the million. It is a comment on how fragile is our understanding of this land, a land so new to us, that each major drought takes us by surprise.

Geoffrey Blainey, "Australia: A Bird's-Eye View"

Heading out from Mount Isa, the landscape continues to deteriorate. West of the Queensland-Northern Territory border we found ourselves driving through endless acres of raw, red rubble, utterly devoid of life. At about the same time, our waterpump started making noises and the temperature gauge began to creep upwards. We started fantasizing about breaking down out there, miles from everything. We speculated about heat prostration, sunstroke, dehydration. It was sheer paranoia, of course. The traffic on this highway isn't what one would call heavy, but there certainly wouldn't be any problem getting a lift. In such a landscape, though, it is difficult to avoid being defeatist. As luck would have it, we managed to limp into a roadhouse (gas station, variety store, restaurant and bar, campground and motel: these isolated service centres are communities complete in themselves) at the junction of the east-west Barkly with the north-south Stuart highway.

Did this mean our troubles were over? It seemed so. For a while anyway. They didn't have a replacement assemblage, but they were confident that they could rebuild the pump with what they had on hand. That was at three o'clock. At five o'clock they were starting to talk about having to order a new part from Townsville, two days distant. Since we have only four days to reach Port Augusta, almost 2000 kilometres to the south, we were less than thrilled by this news. They continued to work: by nine o'clock they were so fed up with our vehicle that the part-ordering option was no longer being bruited as a possibility. All they wanted was to get rid of us. Six hours earlier they had said that we'd be crazy to take a chance with a wonky cooling system. Now they assured us that with a little glop and a few minor adjustments we shouldn't have any trouble at all making it to Alice Springs, a mere 700 kilometres away.

I am beginning to realize that there is another side to outback friendliness. It's all on the surface. The rituals of mateyness are scrupulously observed – the cheerful g'day, the obligatory wave when you pass another car on a bad road – but it really doesn't go one bit beyond form. There is no interest in establishing real contact, not even very much curiosity. Salespeople, waitresses, gas station attendants frequently ask where we come from, but whereas in the U.S. such an inquiry would merely be the opening gambit in a game of ice-breaking ("Oh, you're from Canada, are you? Maybe you know my uncle in Montreal."), here the probing goes no further. Far from an invitation, this is obviously just a verbal version of the wave – nothing asked or offered, no strings attached.

I find it disconcerting. Although the American gush is equally foreign to our irritable Canadian reserve, it at least has the advantage of being readily readable. When one combines the desire to appear affable with a singular lack of empathy, the results can be extremely unpleasant. All too often in the last few days we have been cavalierly misled by the optimistic prognostications of the natives. *No one* wants to deliver bad news. "The roads to the west aren't bad at all," they assure us as we embark on 80 kilometres of teeth-rattling corduroy. Or: "I'm sure you won't have any trouble getting gas, mate." The first time I realized we'd been lied to I was terribly upset by it. These, of all people, must realize how dangerous this country is. Surely they must feel a sense of responsibility toward the unwary stranger. But that's obviously exactly what they don't feel. It puts me in mind of a story I heard in Mount Isa. An American geologist taking the mine tour was given such an ill-fitting pair of boots that he ended up with a sole-sized blister.

When he returned his gear at the end of the day, he replied to the stores-man's routine inquiry that they were the worst boots he'd ever had the misfortune to wear. Far from the apology he expected, what he got was a cocky grin and a cheerful "No worries, mate."

Actually, rereading this last paragraph, I realize that I haven't been entirely fair or accurate in these latest reflections on the Australian charac-ter. Because there *are* exceptions. If the inhabitants of the outback them-selves remain opaque, the other travellers we meet tend to be substantially more open. Why the contrast, I wonder? Is it simply that the locals, like locals everywhere, feel superior to the tourists? Or is it something more profound? Could it be that the Australian feels increasingly vulnerable the more he is pinned down or penned in? Where the traveller is protected from undue intimacy by the very fact of his transience, the permanent resi-dent feels himself to be very much on the spot. This would explain why the dichotomy between apparent friendliness and real callousness becomes more pronounced the further inland one gets. Out here, where the land-scape enforces a kind of unwonted huddling, the inhabitants put more emphasis on the outward signs of friendliness precisely because they feel doubly threatened by the real thing.

If Australians feel happier when they are travelling, this explains some of the peculiarities of their travel accommodations. In North America the typical hotel or motel room is a kind of facsimile home away from home. Besides the bed it contains a dresser where one can unpack one's belong-ings, a writing desk where one can work, and a pair of armchairs where one can read, relax, and socialize. The Australian one, in contrast, makes no bones about being a way station only. It contains the minimum of furniture and what it does have is geared to the transient's practical necessities: eat-ing, sleeping, cleaning oneself and one's clothes. In many ways it is more convenient for the traveller than its American counterpart – refrigerators and coffeemakers are virtually universal, free "makings" are provided, and most places outside of the cities also serve a pre-ordered breakfast to the room. It is, however, designed in such a way as to emphasize, rather than downplay, the fact that one is travelling. The standard 10:00 a.m. checking-out time – in comparison with the American norm of noon – only under-lines the implicit message carried by the room itself: it is the journey – per-haps even just the *idea* of the journey – rather than the real destination which is important in this culture.

Women Writers, Women Written

With some difficulty I was able to put together a sample of fifteen books – eleven novels and four collections of short stories – by the "new" women writers mentioned in James Hall's *Bulletin* article (1986: see pp. 75-76 above).[2] Comments on the recent burgeoning notwithstanding, considered collectively this oeuvre, it must be said, does not present a world picture substantially different from that yielded by the mainstream material surveyed in Chapter 2. Plotting is minimal, formal structuring naive or nonexistent. Far from an advance on earlier shapelessness, a majority of this sample[3] comprises linear or randomly accretive narratives full of aimless wandering, arrivals and departures, lonely and alienated individuals carried listlessly along the course of least resistance. Relationships, especially heterosexual relationships, are almost invariably problematic. Sex is mutually damaging. Marriages are unhappy or fractured. Inter-communication, even with same-sex friends, is at best partial, and often impossible. More critical, *self*-communication is also intimidatingly difficult. The women in these stories, exactly like the protagonists conceived by earlier (including male) writers, are restless, confused, unable to reconcile feelings with aspirations, self-image with self-knowledge. If there is one, at least vestigial, point of difference from the mainstream norm, it is in the implication carried by a few books that albeit the traditional "family" rarely survives

---

2. Helen Asher, Margaret Barbalet, Jean Bedford, Blanche d'Alpuget, Sara Dowse, Suzanne Falkiner, Helen Garner, Barbara Hanrahan, Shirley Hazzard, Georgia Savage, and Glen Tomasetti (novels); Jean Bedford and Rosemary Creswell, Beverly Farmer, Kate Grenville, and Olga Masters (short stories): see bibliography for details.

3. The one notable exception to the generalizations put forth here is Savage's *Slate and Me and Blanche McBride*. Even apart from its relatively sophisticated structuring, this book is strikingly unAustralian in its depiction of inner life, its implication that what we are confronting is not merely a set of social roles but an aggregate of discrete subjectivities. See "Tasmania as a Sub-Culture," pp. 159-64 for a possible explanation of this anomaly.

intact, a woman may still find hope and happiness through her children. Countering this, on the other hand, is the plethora of "bad" (remote, if not vicious) mothers who appear throughout the oeuvre. Negative imaging of mother figures, as Susan Gardner points out with respect to Miles Franklin (1986), is a clear sign of ambivalent if not negative feelings about maternity. Considering how often even the most cherished children in these books turn out to be an emotional liability, it seems clear that whatever they may consciously *think* they think, in their deeper selves these "new" women are still very uncertain about their roles *as* women. If we consider the evidence of the speaking as well as the spoken subject(s) in this sample, the mode as well as the content of writing, one would have to say, in fact, that the impression one takes from the group as a whole is of an ambivalent but persistent cross-sexual sense of identification.

Considering the results of the preliminary study outlined in Chapter 2, this finding suggests a quite striking continuity in the Australian literary sense of self, whether male- or female-generated. Nor have the Australians themselves overlooked the phenomenon. D.R. Burns, for one, has commented persistently on the preference evinced by both traditional and contemporary Australian heroines for taking the "man's part," as it were. Viewing such notably strong and self-reliant figures as Henry Lawson's drover's wife as normative rather than exceptional, he suggests that the Australian woman, at least as portrayed in literature, tends deliberately to model herself after a masculine ideal. "In feminist literature of the recent past, largely the sort originating in England, the need was expressed to ensure sexual equality by detaching the male from his macho model, by encouraging him to acknowledge and express feelings of a sort traditionally called feminine," he notes. "Our fiction and, increasingly, our social habit, may seem to indicate that for our society the reverse tack toward the ideal is the more desirable one" (1982: 50; see also 1975, 1986). The key phrase here, of course, is "our social habit." Literary imaging, like dream imaging, may function metaphorically rather than mimetically. If we look not only at women *in* Australian literature but also at the women who have *made* literature in Australia, however, there is much to suggest that the masculinized heroine bodies forth an authentic, if covert, image of felt reality.

The fact obviously has as many important implications for social as for literary psychology. Even more telling on this level than the qualities evinced are the qualities repudiated. Australian women writers have, as a group, been notably ambivalent about traditional women's roles. Even such eminently conventional colonial romancers as Catherine Spence, Ada Cambridge, and Rosa Praed, for instance, while accepting marriage as a necessary evil in a

society which viewed single women as objects of pity, were far from suggesting, either in or outside of their fiction, that the condition could be counted
on to produce any real happiness or fulfilment for the subordinate partner
(Thomson, 1983; Sheridan, 1982; Sharkey, 1983). Later writers rebelled more
completely. So much has been written about Miles Franklin's jaded views on
marriage – her conviction, strikingly expressed in *My Brilliant Career*, that
hetero-, and particularly sexual, relationships were not merely collaterally
but *of necessity* "brutalizing and degrading for the female" (McInherny,
1983:74; see also V. Kent, 1986) – that it sometimes seems as though her work
revolves entirely around the one theme. The life she wrote, moreover, was
also the life she lived. Like her fictional alter ego Sybylla, Franklin herself
chose to remain single. In this, Franklin was far from anomalous among
either her contemporaries or her literary descendants. Even more than the
masculine heroine, the misanthropic literary female has been one of Australia's hoariest literary clichés. There is, to be sure, ample pragmatic explanation for the phenomenon. Marriage *is* demonstrably constricting for
women in patriarchal societies like Australia. The question is, though, why
Australian women – or at least (since to generalize at this stage is perhaps pre-
cipitous) Australian women writers – should, from a surprisingly early
period, have *felt* this constriction so much more deeply than their similarly
constricted sisters in Britain and North America.

The answer, I would claim, lies in the fact that the Australian woman
writer's rejection of the woman's normal lot in life is *not* a political phenomenon – that is, a consciously conceived and wholly rational resistance
against personal oppression – but signals a far deeper dislocation. It is not
coincidental, for instance, that there is in Australian literature a strong element of sexual disgust directed not merely toward the "brutal" male but
equally, or even more, toward the ostensibly victimized female. It is not
coincidental that feminine fleshliness and bodily functions are treated just
as ambivalently by female writers as by male ones (see, for instance, B.
Walker, 1983: 218). It is not coincidental that the recent spate of lesbian
novels have all been chronicles of doom (M. Smith, 1986). Finally, it is also
not coincidental – as noted in Chapter 2 – that while childbirth is often
imaged as threatening to the mother, even more often mothers are imaged
as destroyers of their children (see, for instance, Modjeska, 1981: 137). Far
from simply a disadvantage, femaleness is depicted as literally ab-normal in
this oeuvre. From all this it would seem clear that the Australian woman
writer, just like the Australian woman-as-written, is rebelling not just
against artificially imposed patriarchal social constraints but against the
psycho-biological constraints of her own nature. Eve Langley's pea-pickers,

pursuing their peripatetic masquerade as men-on-the-move, can thus be seen not as eccentrics but as exemplars, acting out in concrete form the hidden desires that actuate the vast majority of their literary sisters. Writer or written, judging by her mode of being-in-the-world the Australian heroine wants to be, indeed, images herself *as*, a man.

This brings us back to the cross-sexual identification one may infer from the new women's writing. The question still remains, of course, as to the relevance of the phenomenon for the world of ordinary Australian men and women. Far from "masculine," the consensus of both popular and scholarly opinion is that Australian women are conditioned to perceive themselves as not merely disadvantaged but innately inferior (see A. Summers, 1975, especially Chapter 4; Healy and Ryan, 1975; M.J. Poole, 1986). Perhaps, then, masculinization is a specific byproduct of the literary avocation. Counter this, on the other hand, there is at least some indication in the sociological literature that cross-sexual self-imaging can be observed among groups as far removed from the intelligentsia as could be imagined. Linley Samuel's study of school resisters in New South Wales, for instance, reveals that delinquent working class schoolgirls tend to express their rebelliousness by deliberately adopting male modes of behaviour. Even more critical for the present discussion, however, is a corollary to this particular finding: that is, that despite their instinctive valuation of masculinity, even the toughest of these girls "could not see any real future for themselves outside the traditional feminine career (marriage and family) defined by the 'culture of femininity'" (1983: 371). Given this kind of conflict, it is no wonder that the Australian female is burdened with an inconsistent and untenable sense of self. Conditioned both to measure themselves against, and to disqualify themselves for, male social roles (Healy and Ryan, for instance, detail the extent to which female protagonists are absent from or devalued in Australian children's literature [1975]), yet withal subliminally encouraged by the covert deactivation of the male typos to continue to identify with such roles *despite* their formal disqualification, Australian girlchildren are caught between irreconcilable mythic and "real" role models.

This perhaps explains why women's autobiography is so rare in Australia (Walter, 1986). Perhaps, too, it explains why, as feminists have complained, one finds so few females among the country's historians and cultural critics (Dixson, 1984; Grove, 1984). It is not just the men, but the women themselves who find an explicitly feminine personae unsuitable for "expressing" – literally, "speaking for" – Australia. Much more critically, it may also explain why so many Australian women writers evince a radical confusion about their own as well as their protagonists' sexual identity. "She felt she could transcend sexual discrimination within the society," says Kay Iseman (Shaffer) of Susannah Prichard, "but she still unconsciously deferred to men. She could successfully compete with them professionally; but in the area of sexuality, she expected 'naturally' to be mastered. The desire both to dominate and be dominated led to an ambivalence towards sexuality for her, and for her heroines, which is seldom consciously explored in the fiction and certainly never resolved" (1982: 133). Prichard's problem was far more than academic. Propelled willy-nilly from a self-chosen but ever-chafing marital servitude (her husband committed suicide in imitation of the hero of her latest book, a mimesis for which she never forgave herself) into an even more crippling political servitude to the Communist party (see Modjeska, 1981, Chapter 6), Prichard can be seen as having sacrificed not only her peace of mind but much of her artistic freedom to what was at root an ingrained contempt for her own sex. It says much about Prichard's attitudes that though her books abound with strong women, the best of them always give birth to sons.

For other writers the price of sexual ambivalence was even higher. Eve Langley in mid-life became increasingly self-identified with cross-sexual role models. "She affected male clothing, developed a carefully constructed male persona, and grew closer and closer to her own autobiographical character, Steve," says Joy Thwaite. At one point "she changed her name by deed poll to Oscar Wilde . . . At other times, she believed she was the reincarnation of a Russian prince. [Eventually] the personae began to blur and dissolve, the writing to disintegrate. In trying to transcend the sexual stereotypes approved by her society, Langley created other roles" – roles that would eventually undermine not merely her work but her sanity. On August 14, 1942, Thwaite notes, "Langley was placed in Auckland Psychiatric Hospital, where she remained for seven years" (1986: 119-20, 118). This story gives one a whole new perspective on the penchant among Australian women writers for masculine pseudonyms. Franklin's "secret" assumption of the identity of Brent of Bin Bin, for instance, is usually explained as an attempt to escape derogatory stereotyping (see Kent, 1986). The lengths to which she went to protect the privacy and integrity of her alias, however, suggest – rather disturbingly, given Langley's experience – that on one level at least, this most overtly feminist of Australia's post-colonial writers was in fact acting out the fantasy of *being* a man. Taking the oeuvre as a whole, there is good reason to suspect that this is a fantasy which, albeit subliminally, the entire female population of Australia shares.

ALICE SPRINGS

The myths and legends of the aborigines have long populated this land with the shadowy forms of ancestral beings of the Dream Time, part human, part animal, whose pervading presence persists within their minds today.

Jock Marshall, *Journey Among Men*

Both Alice Springs and Tennant Creek have an apparent higher-than-average number of two income families, a relatively higher number of young families, children under 16 and single parent families. At the same time there is a relatively low number of residents over 50 – that is, of those likely to be grandparents. When coupled with factors like a high rate of transiency (and thus loss of friends), high alcohol consumption, and a situation in which a higher than usual percentage of husbands spend time away from home (and their average time away may be higher than is usual), the potential for stress on family life appears to be greater than in many other communities.

Gidley and March, "Community in Central Australia"

Well, we made it! The water pump complained but didn't collapse. It was a long day – 700 kilometres limping along at the "safe" speed of 80 kilometres an hour. It was also a tense one. The cost of towing out here is two dollars a kilometre. There were times during that trek when we were as much as 200 kilometres from anything, in any direction. We kept our fingers crossed. And we made it.

So now we're in Alice Springs. The mythical "centre." It isn't a bit what I expected.

For all that it is so often touted as the archetypal Australian town, Alice Springs has a different "feel" to it than anywhere else we have been on this trip. For one thing, it is genteel. Shop and restaurant windows are plastered with announcements for craft shows and theatrical productions. It is also far more "closed," far more reserved in its self-presentation than what we

have come to expect of Australia. Missing, for instance, is the usual sprawling clutter of motels and campgrounds and fast food outlets on the edge of
town. Motels in Alice Springs are tucked away out of sight. Missing also,
despite the omnipresence of "tourists," is the sense of a society geared to
the needs of the traveller. It was here that we encountered for the first time
on our trip a gas station in which the restrooms were locked. As a rule, gas
stations in bush country offer not only toilets but showers and camping
facilities. Here we were referred to the public toilets in the park down the
road.

The people seem more "closed" as well. Even the surficial displays of
mateyness are gone. Is this simply because a constant influx of tourists –
over 200,000 a year – is an irritant, or does it signal a real difference in communal psychology? One might, of course, simply put it down to paranoia –
a more extreme version of the kind of defensiveness that I talked about in
the last section. It seems significant, though, that Alice Springs, as revealed
in its tourist literature, is almost militantly self-conceived as being "at the
centre." It is, I think, at least possible that such an identification would ultimately result in a strained feminization of the symbolic ego.

One *could* perhaps see Alice Springs and Ayers Rock, the region's biggest tourist attraction, some 450 kilometres to the southwest, as representing the "good" and the "bad" anima, the civilizing versus the devouring
(m)other. The rock is phenomenal, mysterious, fascinating – but also
vaguely sinister. The controversy over the woman who claimed that the
dingo killed her baby is particularly interesting for this reason. Regardless of
whether the culprit was the natural predator *or* the human driven to madness, either way it testifies to the inimical effects of "the centre." Why, then,
the apparent widespread desire to exculpate the animal in this case? Judging by the way it is imaged in poetry and fiction, the outback is fearsome
above all because it is empty, impenetrable, a kind of dead zone. Under the
circumstances, I would have thought that the public would be *relieved* to be
offered a "real" monster on which to project their disquiet. I am obviously
going to have to give some further thought to this matter.

In the meantime, I have been reading what everyone tells me is the
seminal text in Australian cultural nationalism: Russell Ward's *The Australian
Legend*. Ward's main argument is that the classic Australian "type" epitomized in different ways by the bushranger, the urban larrikin, and the digger
is derived from the itinerant nineteenth-century pastoral worker who in

turn derived his defining characteristics – independence, egalitarianism, resilience, irreverence, pragmatism, and resourcefulness – from the convict. There are definitely some problems with this thesis. For one thing, although I am not in a position to pass judgment as yet on the historical accuracy of his description of convict society, there are a number of elements in it that simply don't seem plausible. In quite marked contradistinction to the Legend's romantic image of self-sacrifice and underdog co-operation, what modern concentration camp and hostage studies suggest – and this is certainly reinforced by my reading (as opposed to Ward's) of colonial novelists like Marcus Clarke and James Tucker – is that the physical and mental degradation endured by most Australian convicts would be far more likely to foster cravenness than confidence, debility than health, passivity than assertiveness, and opportunism than loyalty to a mate. Given Ward's emphasis on the "natural" roots of Australian democracy, this last is obviously the key point. If the bushman really was an exemplary democrat – and here I must point out that the union movement, which for Ward is simply synonymous with mateship, could easily be read quite differently, as a replacement for, rather than an expression of, a deep natural fellowship among pastoral workers – then it's unlikely he learned it from his convict forebears.

Rather than throwing out Ward's "history" holus-bolus, on the other hand, one might rather stipulate that he was right in his privileging of the convict inheritance; he merely erred in assessing exactly what that inheritance entailed. The approach offers a number of distinct advantages. If nothing else, it allows full due to Ward's obvious strengths. (That working class attitudes have exerted a disproportionate influence on the developing communal consciousness in Australia is, after all, indisputable – folk art canonized the "type" long before any scholars got hold of it – and Ward's reconstruction of colonial development, with the anglophilic upper classes increasingly self-excluded from the mainstream of Australian life, provides as good an explanation as any for the phenomenon.) It also, however, helps explain some of the ambiguities in the cultural text that Ward either ignores or rationalizes – the fact, for instance, that mateship is treated very ambiguously not just in contemporary literature but even by Henry Lawson, one of the two Bulletin writers whom he indicates as the primary purveyors of the myth. Reading The Australian Legend against the findings of my prelimininary study vis-à-vis Australian social psychology, I would suggest the following revisions or correctives:

(a) If only because of their obvious failure as both a class and a conglomerate of individuals to prosper under prevailing conditions, it seems reasonable to conclude that the lumpenproletarian offenders who formed the bulk of the transportees would tend to be repelled/bewildered by Victorian society. This does not mean, however, that they questioned its legitimacy. To transform a sense of personal failure into a self-conscious questioning of the status quo requires a degree of detachment and sophistication rare among the oppressed of the earth. It is important to keep in mind here that the American Revolution, though perhaps fought by the "common man," was both conceived and led by aristocrats. The aristocrats in Australia had other things on their minds. This may be why the bushman – again contra Ward – did not in fact respond to frontier conditions in the same way as Frederick Jackson Turner's American backwoodsman. Stripped of civilized constraints the backwoodsman became an entrepreneur – Davy Crockett or Jim Bowie. Similarly "stripped" the Australian simply became Penton's Cabell (see Appendix B). It is interesting in this regard to consider the different connotations of the word "squatter" in both countries. In the United States the squatter is (at least according to myth) a shiftless parasite encroaching upon the legitimate rights of the man who has won his land by the force of his will and the sweat of his brow. In Australia, by contrast, squatting is legitimized. The squatters *are* in fact the hereditary landholders. This usage suggests that the Australian pastoralist didn't really believe that the land *could* be conquered, and even less, "owned."

(b) Because the convicts were brought here against their will, the idea of "home" would be even more numinous for them than for the voluntarily transplanted; this in turn would make the Australian landscape seem all the more alien in contrast. Exacerbating the consequent sense of a good but unattainable "outside" versus a bad and equally unattainable "inside," moreover, would be the psychological implications of the prison experience itself. To be imprisoned is to be "shut up," metaphorically if not in fact. Even for those convicts working on the land, therefore, there would be a tendency to identify negatively with closure and positively with openness. At the same time, the fact that the "good outside" on this level is identical with the "bad inside" of the broader formulation would undercut their wishful escapism with very strong feelings of ambivalence. In the case of the Irish (who, as Ward points out, were both the most numerically important and, due to the strength of their group ethos, the most culturally prominent fraction of the convict population) these general effects would be further complicated by their racial matriphilia on the one hand and their hatred of Britannia on the other. "Masculine" rebellion against authority, especially – as in the bushranger's case – when codified as identification with the wild new land, would thus be construed as both an act of patriotism *and* an act of filial betrayal. At the same time, away from the civilizing influence of mother and church their religion would tend to degenerate into superstition, which itself would aggravate an inherent, almost nihilistic fatalism.

(c) The intensity of the ambivalence thus inculcated would go far to explain the vociferousness of the rationalizations historically offered by Australians as to why activity is preferable to contemplation, crudeness to polish, pragmatism to principles, and so on. They simply can't believe that anything else is possible. This says nothing, of course, about "real" capabilities. Convicts aside, it is probably true, as Ward claims, that the country did in fact "improve" the free immigrant at least with respect to usefulness and self-sufficiency. The decline-and-fall fable so common in literature must therefore be seen as reflecting a psychological rather than a physical reality. Might the negativity of this conceptualization simply reflect the relative discomfort of the self-ghettoized privileged minority? Since – at least until recently – a majority of Australia's better-known writers have tended to identify with, if not derive from, the working classes, it doesn't seem likely.

So much for Ward. As a final comment on the plausibility of his bushman typos, I might perhaps mention a series of paintings on display in the restaurant where we had lunch today. The name of the artist was Russell Morrison. Whether he is a local resident I don't know, but he certainly captures what I sense are the Australian's *real* feelings about the bush. Setting the tone for these pieces is a recurrent motif of bright, wingless birds plummeting head-first past ragged cliffs into a chasm. Whether one reads these creatures as "self" or "other," they project an incredible feeling of helplessness in the face of an alien and impervious nature.

Ned Kelly: The Ambivalent Hero

If someone asks a Canadian to name the country's most important national heroes, the commonest response is an argument about what the word *means*. If someone asks an Australian the same question, not only is there no hesitation in answering, but the candidates proffered are remarkably consistent across the board. Central to almost everyone's list are the three groups/individuals which/whom Veronica Brady identifies as underwriting the image of ideality one finds in Australian literature: Burke and Wills, Ned Kelly, and the Anzacs (1981: 14). It is notable that this slate ignores not merely the military leaders so beloved by the British but also the self-made successes, from Abe Lincoln to Horatio Alger, who crowd the American pantheon. The Australian heroes are *not*, typically, larger than life. Leaving aside for now the question of whether or not they are the out-and-out "losers" that some recent commentators have invoked (C. McGregor, 1981: 42), given the fabled misfortunes of these men it is at least obvious, as Donald Horne points out, that they have been memorialized "for their style rather than for their achievement" (1971: 31). The question that presents itself, then, is what qualities comprise this "style" – what qualities make a man such as to capture the public imagination in Australia? To answer this, I am going to put aside for now the less ostentatiously unconventional (though in context equally problematic) figures of the explorer and the soldier, and concentrate on Ned Kelly.

First: his antecedents. Even as a purely generic type, the bushranger has played a central role in Australian folklore since the early decades of the nineteenth century (see Ward, 1966: 146ff.). By the 1860s, when Ned Kelly was a boy, his attributes were well enough established to have become almost a cliché. He was strong, competent, physically courageous, a marksman, a woodsman, a ladies' man, a natural aristocrat, a lover of fine horses, a friend to the poor, a political rebel, and a notable rover. He was not – and this is an important point – violent. Nor was he essentially venal. Where the earlier crop had been for the most part runaway convicts, propelled into a life of crime by sheer desperation, the younger generation (so the myth claimed) were simply high-spirited "currency lads" who had been nudged along from such "innocent" – and, under the depressed conditions in which most natives lived (see Brown, 1986: 12, 21), economically necessary – activities as cattle-duffing and horse stealing to capital offences like robbery at gunpoint by the vindictive hounding of the law. It is easy enough to see the political appeal such a figure might wield. Few bushrangers prospered from their lives of crime, but for a short time at least they were able, collectively if not singly, to discomfit a smugly entrenched gentry. It didn't matter one whit that they were almost inevitably defeated by the superior resources and gunpower of the police: "the pastoral proletariat of the interior . . . [looked] upon the bushrangers as heroic figures of resistance to constituted authority" (Ward: 147). With prepackaging like this, it is hardly surprising that Ned Kelly would appeal. As the ultimate bushranger, he was also – again according to the "myth" – the ultimate "Australian."

The problem with this formulation – even aside from the question of the bushranger's own authenticity (in reality, says Humphrey McQueen, "bushrangers were no more, and often a good deal less, than louts of the contemporary bikie variety" [1976: 137]) – is that closer examination reveals just how poorly Ned Kelly actually fits the informing mould. Given that his primary business (apart from a youthful apprenticeship with gentleman-bushranger Harry Power) was not roadwork but bank and town robbery, there is some question, in fact, whether he can properly be considered a bushranger at all. And even if we stipulate a broad definition, there is the more troubling question whether he can be considered a "good" example of the species.

If success at outwitting the authorities is a criterion, then history might rather have focused on Frank Gardiner who, released by public petition after serving only eight years of his sentence, ended up a prosperous saloon owner in San Francisco (Clune, 1970: 487). If it is victimization *by* the authorities, alternately, then it should be Ben Hall. "Hall was widely balladised as the friend of the poor, driven to bushranging by official persecution," says Graham Seal. "[A] well-respected owner of a cattle station . . . [he] was arrested in 1862 for being present while Frank Gardiner, whom Hall knew well, bailed up a passing teamster. After a month in gaol, Hall was acquitted. He returned to find his wife had deserted him . . . Deeply upset by this, [he] fell in with Gardiner's gang. Twelve days after the Eugowra Rocks holdup Hall was arrested on suspicion of armed robbery. He was released two months later when an informer failed to implicate him as a member of the gang. While he was in gaol the police had burned his house and left his cattle to die, penned in the mustering yard. Six months later . . . [he was] found . . . in the company of a [wanted felon] . . . Knowing that in the eyes of the law [this made him] . . . an accomplice . . . Ben Hall galloped into the bush and into the beginning of his legend" (1980: 49). What kind of excuse did Ned Kelly have to set against this? Not much, in fact. While it is clear from the records that the police *did* persecute the Kelly clan, it is also clear that the clan, including Ned, were far from wronged innocents. Especially in comparison with Hall's case, Ned's retrospective aggrievement rings more than a little hollow. "I heard . . . that I was blamed, for stealing a mob of calves . . . which I never had anything to do with," he said in a written statement some years after the fact. "I began to think they wanted me to give them something to talk about. Therefore I started wholesale and retail horse and cattle dealing" (quoted in Clune, 1980: 40). While Ned may have been pushed over the edge by the arrest of his mother – and whatever the facts of the particular triggering incident (see, for instance, Molony, 1982, Chapter 7), Ellen Kelly was clearly not without her own share of guilt for the family's lawlessness – it is hard to see his claims of having initially been "driven" to crime by official harassment as anything but an exercise in self-justification.

Ned Kelly, then, did not quite fit the prescription for either victor or victim. And the "indomitable defiance" invoked by Ward (148)? Compared with Hall's glamorous demise in a gun battle with the police, no matter what subsequent romancers have made of it, Kelly's capture, trial, and hanging must be seen, at least from an aesthetic standpoint, as disappointingly anti-climactic. What about the personal charisma, the intelligence, the much-touted qualities of leadership? One of his victims wrote of him in after years that Kelly would have made "a magnificent general" (Brown: 84), and popular opinion has most often accepted that verdict. Science fiction writer A. Bertam Chandler went so far as to write an alternate-history fantasy called *Kelly Country* in which, as a *real* general, the bushranger successfully led a revolution against Britain that established Australia as a republic – with him at its helm. Historian Vance Palmer deflates this myth too. Kelly's letters reveal him, he says, as "a man with a vigorous, confused mind – an explosive fellow with a touch of the bully in his make-up, posing now as a defender of the poor cockie against the squatter, now as a rebel Irish leader whose family and race had been oppressed for centuries, but exposing himself in every line as a voluble peasant with a sense of guilt" (1963: 66-67). M.H. Ellis goes even further. "He was a compulsive, psychopathic murderer, [and] an equally compulsive boaster who subjected his audiences of prisoners . . . to harangues about his wrongs through which ran a whining note of self pity [overlaid by] . . . megalomania" (in Dunstan, 1973: 202). Even if we limit ourselves to the evidence of his *own* legend, it would seem clear that Ned Kelly falls considerably short of the "ultimate" exemplar cited above.

Again, then, we have to ask: what was it the popular imagination saw in Kelly that made him so irresistible? Because the fact is, unlike Jack Donahue, Frank Gardiner, Ben Hall, and the rest, whose popularity has never gone much beyond the pages of the ballad book, Ned Kelly over the years has become something of a national obsession. Since his death, says Seal, "a large industry has developed around Ned Kelly, or his image, and deluged a seemingly insatiable public with a flood of books, articles, songs, poems, a musical and a number of feature films, one of them Australia's earliest. By the 1940s Clive Turnbull found it necessary to grace the growing Kelly industry with a slim bibliography of forty-two published works, titled *Kellyana*. This only included the main publications in the field and did not cover newspaper articles, films, or works that dealt only in part with Kelly. A similar work today would run into hundreds of entries" (1980: 19). It would also delineate one of the country's liveliest feuds. Everyone, it seems, has an opinion about Kelly, and no two are the same.

During the sixties the burning question (*vide* the Palmer and Ellis comments above) was whether he was "worthy" of his canonization. More recently debate has shifted to the issue of whether Kelly worship reflects well or ill on the worshippers. "The Kelly legend," says John McQuilton, "has been seen as an illustration of a basic turpitude in the Australian character: or as a reflection of a national inferiority complex, a way of thumbing the national nose at a critical outside world. Others have argued that Australia is so desperate for a national hero we'll take anybody, and a bush criminal is good enough. There is also the view that Australians love a failure, and Ned was a spectacular failure . . . On the positive side, it is argued that the legend reflects basic Australian attitudes, particularly a deep-seated ambivalence when it comes to authority . . . [To those caught within] the dreary geographical reality of an urbanised society, Kelly . . . represents . . . the bushman, independent, self-reliant and game; a 'doer' rather than a 'talker'; a man capable of taking the local cop (and the boss for that matter) down a peg or two" (1981: 38). The most interesting thing about this list is not the diversity of opinion per se, but the extent to which that diversity – and the heat it has generated – documents a basic split in Australian values, perhaps even in the Australian sense of self. Graeme Turner notes that ambivalence is an essential, characterizing feature of Australian cultural production (1986, Chapter 2). Patrick Morgan goes even further, claiming that the national personality is typified by mood swings so extreme as to seem manic. At times, he says, the Australian is "solitary, withdrawn, quiescent to the point of indolence . . . But at other times . . . there is a heightened phase, characterised by outbreaks of feverish . . . energy and gregariousness" (1982: 131). If we stipulate that the split invoked here is not between the "sides" of a personality but between overt and covert, public and private, the official *actor* and the guiltily *acted-upon*, it would perhaps not be too far-fetched to speculate that Ned Kelly's appeal has less to do with his character, or even his specific mythic associations, than with the fact that, *qua* exemplar, he is duplicitous enough to "fit" the requirements of both the cultural text and its unacknowledged subtext.

This is not the place to embark on a full psychoanalytic reinterpretation of the Kelly legend – nor, considering the amount of verbiage that has already been expended on the subject, does it seem necessary. Let me merely mention a few of the elements in Ned's makeup – whether "real" or apocryphal does not matter – which I see as most pertinent to this kind of reading.

The first point to note is the extent to which Ned's familial experience may be seen as exemplifying the national pattern of absent, charismatic father and masculinely strong, inadvertently damaging mother (see Chapter 2). Ned's devotion to Ellen Kelly has in general been painted in approving terms, but it is clear from the extravagance of both his language and his actions (McIntyre, 1982: 42-44) that his feelings went far beyond normal filial respect. It is notable in this connection that throughout his life he showed no interest whatsoever in other women (Brown: 81; Seal: 157). It is also notable that *she* did not seem to reciprocate his devotion. Even apart from her well-documented sexual activity, Ellen Kelly was by all reports the complete opposite of the clinging, dependent female (Clune, 1980). This does not mean, on the other hand, that she was *indifferent* to her son. Quite the opposite, in fact. Reconstructions strongly suggest that she regarded him as an extension of her own will. The last sentence she spoke before his hanging, far from "motherly" comfort, was the stern admonition to "Mind you die like a Kelly" (Seal: 127).

Next, and of even greater importance are the intimations of "destiny" and "doom" that invariably undercolour the Kelly story. Much has been made of Ned's own fatalism – the title protagonist of Douglas Stewart's stage version, for instance, is quite clearly obsessed with death ("For all Ned's talk of outback freedom, what emerges most strongly from the play," says H.P. Heseltine, "is a sense of hatters baying at the moon" [1962: 48-49]); in Jean Bedford's *Sister Kate*, the madness, the suggestion of festering masculine irrationality, is even closer to the surface. Judging by those aspects emphasized in popular histories, on the other hand, it is evident that, even more than their admiration for his phlegmatic resignation, the tellers are fascinated with the extent to which Ned can be seen as the pawn of *outside* forces. All renditions make much of the impelling influence of police interference (see, for instance, Molony: 73ff.) – and not entirely as an alibi for the hero. Underlying the reiterated displacement of blame ("Gaol had made [Ned Kelly] into a criminal. From the moment of his release, [he] was at war with the community which had warped his life" [Clune, 1980: 37]) is the clear implication that it was society, history, fate – anything rather than the man himself – which was "responsible" for both actions and outcome. In Max Brown's book this element comes right out of the closet. By foregrounding Ned's own utterances, he makes us aware of the extent to which this supposedly notable individualist, in consciously modelling himself after his legendary precursors, was in a sense merely acting out a role already culturally inscribed. The only thing that set him apart, in fact, was the *reluctance* he evinced toward his ostensibly self-appointed destiny; a reluctance signalled by his slowness to act (Brown: 151), by his Hamlet-like volubility, and – pre-eminently – by the armour he donned for the final scene. In the ambivalence of his expressed attitudes, Australia's favourite "active" hero seems much more a dupe than a rebel – indeed, a dupe precisely because he was forced by "history" to *become* a rebel. In this he could be seen as modelling, covertly, the strain of passivity which critics like Graeme Turner (1986; see "A Quick History of Australian Film," pp. 209-15, below) attribute to ideological disablement.

The last element I would mention is the rather peculiar psychotypology intimated by that aforementioned suit of armour. Inasmuch as it hints at interiorization, Kelly's self-enclosure could be taken to suggest a covert sex role reversal. The idea, moreover, is at least provisionally supported by a number of adjacent facts. Just as it has long been conjectured that the over-valuation of mateship among Australian men is often a cover for latent homosexuality, there have been speculations about homosexuality among the Kelly gangsters (Dunstan, 1973: 204). As Miriam Dixson points out, on the other hand, far from signalling an identification *with* women, the kind of homosexuality associated (as is almost always the case in Australia) with rabid misogyny actually signals a fear/hatred *of* the feminine (1984: 24-25). Whether or not Ned Kelly was a homosexual, then, and whether or not this was behaviourally expressed, we probably should not take it as signifying femininization. So what are we to make of that armour? Certainly, it is hard to justify on purely pragmatic grounds. Accounts of the gang's last stand at the Glenrowan Hotel make it clear that their protective gear, far from an advantage, by impeding movement and vision was actually a major contributing factor to their defeat (McIntyre, 1982: 50-51). Nor, I think, can we dismiss it as simply an error in judgment brought on by an overactive imagination. Whatever it represented to Ned, to the Australian public the armour has come to be one of the most important ingredients in the myth. In Sidney Nolan's famous Ned Kelly paintings, for instance, the armour, especially the flat, black, slotted shape that represents the abstracted helmet, *is* the man (Hughes, 1970: 164ff.). What does it mean? Taking into consideration the above-mentioned inertia and fatalism, we might, I think, see the Kelly armour as expressing the Australian's inadmissible sense of immobilization by the intransigence of the world at large. Even more deeply buried, we might also take it as bodying forth an image of Australian man as empty shell; an opaque, impervious surface enclosing – the unknown. It is both interesting and disturbing that Nolan's iconic eyeslot sometimes reveals human features, sometimes opens on darkness, sometimes displays a fragment of inscape identical to the untenanted landscape in/on which the man-cypher is suspended.

Ned Kelly, then, models the Australian by presenting a plausible and poignant facsimile of both the actor *and* the man existentially deprived of the capacity to act. This is not, of course, to imply that his "meaning" is exhausted by these few isolated aspects. Indeed, as Seal points out, a large part of the appeal of the Ned Kelly legend is its ability to evolve, to mean different things at different times. Larrikin in the eighteen-eighties; bushman at the turn of the century; proto-Anzac during the war; battler during the depression; anti-hero in the forties; non-conformist and rebel in the sixties – Ned Kelly, it seems, is infinitely mutable. The constant that informs and energizes this amazing diversity – the thing that makes him *convincing* in all his guises – is, however, I would claim, the subversive understratum coded by his camouflaged disablement.

PORT AUGUSTA

In shape, Australia resembles a ragged square, but the real Australia where people live and work is a ribbon. Australia, economically, is more like Chile – a long coastal strip. The interior is largely deserted, and so too are most of the 12,200 miles of coast, but two strips of coast are settled more intensely. The most populous part of Australia is a curving strip, about two hundred miles at its widest and more than fourteen hundred miles long. It holds the country's biggest cities, Sydney and Melbourne, with a combined population of six million, out of Australia's fifteen million, people. This coastal strip holds most of the valuable farmlands, the best sheep pastures, most of the large tourist resorts, and almost eight out of every ten people. Occupying the southeast corner, it has sometimes been called the Boomerang Coast because of its shape. Another small strip occupies the southwest corner and includes Perth, the capital of Western Australia. Together these two strips of coast, occupying about one-tenth of Australian land, hold about nine-tenths of the people.

Geoffrey Blainey, "Australia: A Bird's-Eye View"

The trip out was even more daunting than the trip in. The worst of it was, having lost so much time over the van, we were now in a tearing hurry. It meant missing a lot of what one normally goes to the centre *for.* Despite what I have said about the bleakness of the landscape in general, there's some truly spectacular scenery in that part of the country: the gorges of the Macdonnell Ranges; the strange, cone-shaped domes of the Olgas; Stanley Chasm, which the sun at noon turns into a fiery cauldron of red and gold. We didn't see any of it. Not even Ayers Rock.

What we did see was spinifex, rubble plains, salt flats, and outright desert. Millions upon millions of unchanging acres of it. One can imagine the reactions of the explorers who first approached this land from the south. It is probably not accidental that the Port Augusta-Alice Springs stretch has been one of the last sections of the national highway system to be developed. Until very recently, it was wholly unpaved. Now, as part of a nation-wide pre-bicentennial program of civic spiffing up, the "horror highway," as it was known, has been reduced to a stretch of about 150 kilometres. Not that I knew this before we set out. In fact, I hadn't expected *any* of the bad roads we have been faced with. The map in the guidebook supplied by our travel agent didn't make any distinction between paved and unpaved surfaces, and as I mentioned above, it simply never occurred to me that a "major highway" could be a dirt road. I shudder to think what would have happened if we had been a year or two earlier. Given the slapdash way that we went about planning this trip — looking back on it, we really were remarkably naive — we probably wouldn't have found out about the road conditions until we were already out in the middle of the country. By then, of course, we would have been committed.

As it turned out, the 150 kilometres was quite enough for my taste. Most of it was the now-familiar sun-baked corduroy, but in one area a rare rainstorm had turned the surface to mud. Judging by the tracks, every vehicle had had to go a little further off centre to avoid the ruts left by its predecessors. By the time we came along, it was necessary to leave the road entirely and meander nervously through the bush. After our experience with the water pump, we no longer have total confidence in our vehicle. Where once we worried, if at all, about damage to the tires, now every time we have to negotiate a rough patch we expect a broken axle at the very least. The result, needless to say, was to make a long trip seem eternal.

Our feelings of vulnerability were exacerbated by the scarcity of gas stations throughout this whole region. One stretch south of Coober Pedy was more than 400 kilometres long. Before embarking on it we gave in to our paranoia and bought a second spare gascan. Bucking headwinds, our gas mileage had been so bad on the previous leg that we simply didn't think we could make it to the next stop. Again we were surprised by the cavalier attitude of the locals. At Pimba the roadhouse was out of gas; at neighbouring Woomera what was apparently the only other station within 150 kilometres closed up as usual at 6:00. Our options? Either stay the night and chance missing our train the next day, or set out to do the remaining distance with fingers crossed. We made it. But it wasn't much fun.

A *lot* of this trip has been rather less fun than we anticipated, now that I think about it. No time for sightseeing. No leisurely evenings taking in the local colour. Simply in order not to lose any *more* time, we have had to start early and drive late, nervously on the alert for the kangaroos which come out by the dozens to browse after dark. The moral, I suppose, is that anyone who wants to see the Australian outback should be prepared to leave North American ideas about itineraries and timetables at home.

There are other expectations one has to discard as well. The sense of everything shutting down at nightfall at first seemed very odd for a country renowned overseas for producing inveterate carousers. In fact, though, Australians at home would seem to be an entirely different species than Australians abroad: quiet, clean-living, domesticated – even when they're on holiday. The first night out of Alice Springs we stayed in a caravan park at a roadhouse at Kuljera. We arrived late, and by the time we got our dinner ready (around 9:00) ours was the only light on in the compound. No after-dinner drinkers. No cruising teenagers. No old codgers yarning around the campfire. Apparently not even a lone reader-in-bed. I couldn't help making a mental comparison with North America. From my experience, the chances of finding a campground in any popular tourist area in the United States or Canada on a Friday night – which this was – without at least one bunch of rowdies are very slim indeed.

Coober Pedy is an interesting place. Approaching from the north one enters a vast tract of what seem at first to be anthills but resolve themselves at closer view into giant heaps of sand, each marking the site of an excavation. These are in fact mines. Coober Pedy is in the centre of the richest opal district in the country. It is also in the centre of one of the country's most inimical climates. The town, consequently, has been built largely underground. When I first heard this I speculated that here, if anywhere, I would find an Australian version of Canada's garrison mentality. Far from feminized, however, this town seems one of the most "masculine" we have hit yet. It is seething with activity, slovenly in demeanour, crassly commercial. Perhaps this is because, definitively countering the psychological effects of a *literal* interiorization, opal mining – an individual rather than a corporate activity – epitomizes the masculine rape of the earth.

Port Augusta is a large-town-verging-on-small-city sited within a thin strip of fertile farmland between the Flinders Ranges and the upper reaches of the Spencer Gulf. Although it seems very cosmopolitan after our weeks in the wilderness, it's actually a relaxed and friendly place, neither chest-beatingly masculine nor overly culturally pretentious. The people – how can I put it? – are *ordinary*. They don't act as if one is invisible, but neither do they make a big display of mateyness. Though our exposure has necessarily been of short duration, the contrast with hinterland irritability seems pronounced. Casual to the point of complacency, Port Augusta actually does simulate the Oz of myth. It's also *much* cheaper. Although there are obvious economic reasons why costs have to be higher in a remote area, I can't help feeling retrospectively ripped off when I compare the comfort and spaciousness of our $35 motel room here – the very room, we are told proudly, where Linda Evans is going to be staying when she visits the city in connection with a film project next month – with the $63 closet we had in Alice Springs. It's not just the price difference, either. The difference in the attitudes of the proprietors is even more striking. In Alice the emphasis was clearly on profits, with skimpy towels and plastic glasses and a pay-as-you-go liquor vendor in every room. Here in Port Augusta the motel owners have not only volunteered to babysit our van free of charge while we are away out west, but are going to open their dining room half an hour early this evening so we can get a last decent meal before catching our train.

Actually, this will be the *first* decent meal since Cairns. Restaurants in small-town Australia are peculiar creatures. They only open at specific hours – 12:00 to 2:00 for lunch, 6:00 to 8:00 for dinner (waitresses obviously don't have much of a union). If one wants a meal outside those times – and it always seems that we do – then milk bars and junk food are the only option. In the outback proper things are a little less rigid vis-à-vis serving hours – roadhouse restaurants, faced with the necessity of being all things to all people, open early and stay open late. The menu, however, tends to be rather monotonous, leaning heavily to truckers' meals like hamburgers, steak 'n potatoes, and of course the inevitable mixed grill. The one thing one gets everywhere is good beer. Notwithstanding, it will be nice, especially since we are in the middle of Australia's biggest winegrowing area here, to treat ourselves to some wine that doesn't come in a cardboard cask.

Adventure Fiction

It is within the corpus of murder mysteries, spy thrillers, and detective stories, if anywhere, that one would expect to find a conventional hero type. The genre is not, unfortunately, an easy one to research. Like most popular culture productions, apart from the output of a few big names individual entries tend to have a very short market life. The situation is made more difficult in Australia, where neither publishers nor bookstores make a distinction between indigenous authors and the much bigger body of imported material. There is, further, no clear way to differentiate "popular" from higher forms of fiction. Much of what is accepted locally as "literature" is both qualitatively and thematically akin to what would elsewhere be considered as middle- or even lowbrow. Nor is there, as in North America, a critical consensus to aid categorization. Indeed, virtually nothing has been written on contemporary (as opposed to traditional) genre fiction in Australia. Students of literature tend to focus on what is more "literary"; students of popular culture on what is clearly less so. Despite this, taking packaging as my main criterion (if the publishers treated a book as a thriller, then I accepted it as such, even if its author was known to me as a "literary" writer) I was able to put together a small but representative sample (fifteen books by thirteen authors) of the Australian "adventure fiction" available in bookstores in mid-1986. Titles include (in alphabetical order): Peter Brennan, *Razorback*, Jon Cleary, *The Phoenix Tree*, Kenneth Cook, *Chain of Darkness*, Peter Corris, *The Big Drop* and *The Empty Beach*, Maxwell Grant, *Barrier Reef*, John Jost, *This Is Harry Flynn*, Leon Le Grand, *The Two-Ten Conspiracy*, William Marshall, *The Fire Circle*, Christopher Matthews, *Aljazzar*, Ian Moffitt, *The Retreat of Radiance*, Arthur Upfield, *Man of Two Tribes* and *The Sands of Windee*, Grahame Webb, *The Numunwari*, and Morris West, *The Naked Country*.

The first thing one notices about this body is the extent to which it images man, not as conquering, but as conquered by, natural forces. In three of the books, wild animals dominate centre stage. Particulars aside, what is notable about these is not the *choice* of theme (ecology novels were very big in the

United States during the seventies), but the ambivalence evinced by the authors toward their iconic creatures, *despite* their more or less overt sympathies with the conservation movement. In *Barrier Reef*, for instance, poached birds are offset by man-eating sharks. In *The Numunwari* a giant crocodile is itself both killer and victim of killers. In *Razorback*, even more extremely, a giant boar usurps the roles of both hero and villain, attacking indiscriminately a rapist and his victim, a tenderfoot and a conventionally competent bushman. The impression of personal impotence one draws from these novels is exacerbated by the fact that in two out of the three, the final denouement is brought about not by the protagonist himself but by agents of "otherness": in one case an aborigine, in another the police. This trend is not limited to the ecology thriller. Three other books in the sample (Cook, Jost, Marshall), by focusing on eruptions of almost inadvertent violence, as damaging to the perpetrator as to his prey, convey the clear message that the individual is as likely to be victimized by nature-within as by nature-without.

This is not to imply, on the other hand, that this corpus is totally lacking in conventional heroics. It is notable, though, that the heroic element – if we can call it that – increases systematically as the imagination ranges farther from home. Although no single book escapes entirely from pessimism (betrayal of/by a mate or kinsman, deliberate or accidental, is a recurrent theme), those set outside the country, such as *Aljazzar* or *The Phoenix Tree*, resemble more closely the American thriller in both the complexity of their plots and the dynamism of their personae. The difference tends to be most marked when the hero himself is not Australian, but judging at least by the present sample, the *key* element is not nationality but setting. Moffitt's protagonist, for instance, is not just Australian, but the classic Australian "type" – restless, empty, obsessed with an unattainable ideal of manliness. Even he, however, at the end of his story is able not merely to catch up with, but personally to defeat, the villain. LeGrand's young adventurer, in contrast, though technically an American exhibits all the stigmata of the Australian loser – deceived and manipulated by a woman, he has to be rescued in the end by an other-image, this time an American black. It is interesting but not, I think, coincidental that *The Retreat of Radiance* is set almost entirely in Indochina, while a substantial and significant portion of *The Two-Ten Conspiracy* takes place on the Australian continent. The clear implication carried by these novels is that the land itself is in some way to "blame" for the incompetence of its inhabitants. I am struck by the fact that when Morris West, a master of the conventional international bestseller, comes to write a novel set in his own birthland, *The Naked Country*, it has, in contrast to the rest of his oeuvre, a strikingly "Australian" flavour, not simply because it takes place in the outback, nor because of its (for him) anomalously simple narrative structure, but because of the way he treats his protagonist. Wounded by nature (in the person of the aborigine), an erstwhile dynamic and self-confident young rancher has to be rescued by a policeman. Reversing his fate, meanwhile, his wife, a conventionally helpless city girl, is herself not weakened but strengthened by her encounter with the wilderness.

The incompetence of the Australian on his home turf seems all the more striking when, as in the classic detective story, a "professional" hero is involved. According at least to local opinion, Australia's answer to Raymond Chandler is a Sydney journalist-cum-historian by the name of Peter Corris. Despite his surficial resemblance to the American hard-boiled detective, however, Corris's protagonist, private investigator Cliff Hardy, is a surprisingly unsuccessful aggressor. In *The Empty Beach*, for instance – characterized by Stephen Knight (1986) as the best Corris novel yet – he is ambushed, outgunned, kidnapped, beaten up repeatedly, rescued on one occasion by a colleague and on another by the police. In the end, moreover, it turns out that even his own client has lied to him. The pattern is not unique to this particular book. Hardy has intelligence, tenacity, and fortitude, but throughout his adventures he is constantly victimized and betrayed by friends and foes alike. He is also constantly victimized by "life." He can solve the puzzles, but he cannot control the consequences of his solutions. Four out of the ten stories in *The Big Drop* have "unhappy" endings at least indirectly attributable to the hero's own activity. He fails to prevent the revenge killing of a suspect he has tracked down; inadvertently triggers the murder of a gangster's adulterous wife; becomes implicated in a police plot to "allow" the death of an informer; faces the ordeal of informing a client that her husband is sexually involved with the beloved runaway daughter he has been hired to find. Even in the stories where the endings could be said to be "happy," Hardy's achievement tends to be undercut by a trivialization of the crimes involved. A death threat turns out to be an attempt to cover up a filmwriter's plagiarism. An accusation of embezzlement is merely part of a plot to induce an author to change agents. In the light of such qualifiers, Cliff Hardy is simply not a convincing effectuator. What he is, is the Australian "type" – exposed. "I wasn't very good [as a soldier]," he says in *The Empty Beach*. "I was very scared . . . But I was more scared of showing that I was scared. I did stupid things, risked other people's lives. Also I was erratic, unreliable" (1983: 61). Knight sees the erosion of Hardy's conventional macho position as a positive feature – and, of course, from a humanistic standpoint, it is. By in a sense deconstructing his hero, however, Corris also undermines (though without positively discrediting) the very conventions that his books explicitly invoke.

The pop-fictional professional hero, then, is for all his *formal* dynamism no more successful as an actor than his amateur brothers. Not, at least, when he appears in the guise of an alter ego. Given the role played by other-images in the action of some of the books mentioned earlier, it is obviously significant that the only wholly successful, conventionally dynamic hero-type to appear in the entire sample, including even those books set abroad, is Arthur Upfield's part aboriginal police detective, Napoleon Bonaparte.[4] It is even more significant that it is Bony's native half, not his white half, to which he owes his professional success. From his father, we are told in *The Sands of Windee,* he had inherited "the white man's calm and comprehensive reasoning" – a "passive" skill he shares with Cliff Hardy. From his black mother, however, he also inherited the "active" skills – "the spirit of nomadism, the eyesight of her race, the passion for hunting" – that Hardy and his ilk so notably lack.

---

4. The Upfield novels were originally published in the thirties through the fifties, and rereleased during the eighties.

KALGOORLIE

When the train stalls (which is much of the time), I can hear in my mind the steady dull scrape of metal on metal, the grinding and scraping of wheels. Wakened through the night by the haul and slam of linkages, ghostly sidings slide by. The thud of a mail bag. A solitary electric light bulb above a tiny platform. "See ya!" thinly in air. Flooded by loneliness, I wonder why I'm crossing this wasteland. I am nothing in the long dark night of this desert, part of a huge stolid silence. Small townships are swallowed up swiftly in the darkness. A fixed white pepper of stars. The earth is falling away. Endless Australia. Thrown out into unrolling vistas of outer space, I know no-one. All night shaking and bumping in berth 14 of car 6, I know that, for the moment, I am nowhere.

Fay Zwicky, "Living in Western Australia"

In 1892, some forty years after the Victorian goldrush gave Australia its first boom era, alluvial gold was discovered at Coolgardie in the dry interior of Western Australia by a pair of wandering prospectors. A year later an Irishman made a strike of such phenomenal richness that the news travelled around the world. The result, or one result, was the founding of the town of Kalgoorlie on what my guidebook tells me is the richest square mile of rock ever known. Living conditions in the early years must have been well-nigh unbearable. Everything in the way of food and hard goods had to be transported, usually by camel train, over 500 kilometres from the coast. Water had to be pumped through condensers from salt aquifers underground. It wasn't until 1903, when a pipeline was put through from the Darling Ranges, that the town began to take on any semblance of civilization.

Kalgoorlie today still carries reminders of its pioneer beginnings. Even aside from the more tangible relics – its pubs, especially the group that brackets the main intersection in the centre of town, are particularly spectacular — the predominating mood of the place is one of easy-going masculine camaraderie. Partly, no doubt, this is due to the continued emphasis on mining as the mainstay of the local economy. Partly too, though, the frontier atmosphere would seem to have been deliberately created by the local inhabitants. Although there is no sign that it is actually any less law-abiding than "normal" communities, the town not only allows but boasts about its "frontier morality." Much is made in tourist literature, for instance, of its quasi-institutionalized gambling (the only legal "bush two-up school" in the country) and prostitution. In this, despite its similarly beleaguered condition, it would seem almost the diametric opposite of Alice Springs.

Why *should* the difference be so acute? Kalgoorlie may not technically be in "the centre," but it is certainly a long way from the safety and civilization of the coast. Why, then, have Kalgoorlians been so much better able than Alicers to withstand the psychological rigours of exposure? The answer, perhaps, is that in fact they haven't. When one looks a little closer, it becomes clear that at least some of this free-and-easiness is an illusion. Take the matter of prostitution, for instance. Legitimized, it loses its aura of bounds-breaking — becomes, in fact, ideologically recoded as non-transgressive. It was notable in this regard that our first night here our hosts, a thoroughly middle class couple, insisted on driving us down to the red light district to show us the spectacle of the girls lined up in front of their cribs. In their eyes it's simply a tourist attraction. To co-opt antisocial behaviour to social ends like this is to redefine the line in such a way that there is no longer even the possibility of dis-order.

The physical aspects of the town also hint at a kind of subsurface rigidity. The layout of the streets is anomalously rational by Australian standards. Even more striking, the public architecture is so aggressively frontal that the effect is almost overwhelming. The buildings along the main shopping street, for instance, are so densely encrusted with surficial features — verandahs, arcades, parapets, awnings, columns, plaster castings, fancy brickwork, iron lace, ornate signboards, particoloured paintwork — that it is hard in some cases to make out their native shapes. This is *not* a free-and-easy architecture. It doesn't, on the other hand, suggest the Canadian fort in the wilderness either. The I-site here is clearly on the outside. It is on the outside, however, *uncertainly* — with the kind of trepidation that can only be balanced by a truly indubitable display of bravado.

After our train trip, I can understand why bravado would be called for. This is not easy country. The route from Port Augusta to Kalgoorlie lies largely within a region called the Nullarbor Plains. Apart from its mind-numbing flatness (the track runs as straight as a die for over 400 kilometres), the main feature of this terrain is amply evoked by its name. Not only are there not any trees, however – there is not much of anything else either. Red rubble, a patchy skiff of dirty grey dried grass, the occasional stunted bush – and kangaroos. Even in the most desolate sections it is common to see mobs of a dozen or more, hopping wildly in all directions as the train whistle splinters the dusty silence. How they survive out there is beyond my comprehension.

The trip took almost twenty-four hours. Not very scenic, but safer than a camel at any rate. How did those early explorers stand it? I seem to recall that the first white man who crossed this plain did it on foot with only a single aboriginal companion. In comparison with that, boredom seems an absolute luxury. I was disappointed that I didn't have more of an opportunity to meet people. Our fellow passengers were friendly, but reserved. Perhaps in the case of train travel the plus of moving is cancelled out by the minus of entrapment.

It may be a little different if one travels in coach class. Coach travellers are expected to be resourceful, and this in itself may be enough to offset the sense of enforced passivity. The seats are roomy and comfortable, and there are showers, but other than that, very little is provided. Passengers bring their own sleeping bags, pillows, towels, and (unless they want to subsist on the most minimal of fast food) their own comestibles. The only exception: they can "take out" alcoholic beverages from the lounge car – this is obviously considered a necessity of life. Sleeping class passengers, in contrast, are provided with hermetically-sealed two-person plastic wombs, complete with their own washbasins. Meals are included in the price of the ticket, and are totally regimented. One must appear promptly at the designated time, sit in the same place at every meal, choose from a very limited menu, and finish up quickly. Given Australian propensities, the felt difference between doing for oneself and being "done unto" could well make train travel an entirely different and less positive experience, psychologically speaking, for the "lucky" citizens who can afford something better than a coach seat.

The attitudes one may infer for those who *provide* this service are also a little peculiar. For one thing, the trip itself is obviously much longer than it needs to be. Both the speed and the long stops are in marked contrast to transcontinental routes in Canada. In some places the train lays by so long that the passengers can get off and have a guided tour of the town. Quite apart from its implications for the country's relationship with technology (the train in North America has traditionally been a symbol of progress and power), this could once again testify that for the Australians it is the journey that is important, not the destination. (Alternately, it could simply document the feeling that it is very difficult to "get anywhere.")

One of the ways that I amused myself on this trip was by dipping a little further into my growing collection of Australian pop fiction. During our brief stay at Port Augusta I went into a newsagents and picked out at random four Mills & Boon (the Australian equivalent to Harlequin) romances. This is obviously too small a sample to be "scientifically" respectable, but given the formulaic nature of the genre I felt that even so limited a dabble would give me a sense of culture-specific divergences from the Anglo-American norm, if any. And it did. Working within a palpably identical set of conventions (woman meets man, obstacles impede the course of true love, obstacles are overcome, man and woman marry), the Australian romance writer nevertheless manages to convey, subtextually as it were, a significantly different impression of and attitude toward both marital and familial relations. The salient features of this discourse are as follows:

(a) The main theme of all these books is emotional ineptness. In each case, one and often both/all of the major characters suffer(s) from problems of inadequate self-awareness. This is usually accompanied by serious difficulties in communicating.

(b) The emotional confusion is accentuated by the fact that nothing much seems to happen. The convoluted plots – the bizarre twists and dramatic discoveries – of the American neo-gothic are here conspicuous mainly for their absence. In fact, these books are dull. They make much ado about nothing. All the obstacles that have to be overcome are subjectively generated.

(c) The heroes, who tend to be both older than, and economically superior to, the heroines, are without exception portrayed as overtly aggressive but covertly childish.

(d) In all but one book (where the heroine is clearly flawed by her "masculine" independence and unselfconsciousness), the female protagonists, although conventionally "feminine" (i.e., they place more importance on love and marriage than on a career), are in fact more masterful than their male partners. Reciprocally, in one case the hero uses the traditional feminine ploy of a contrived pregnancy to win his mate.

(e) Sexual attraction strikes like lightning in these books. It is unexpected, often inconvenient, and always totally mysterious. Sex itself is treated like a kind of drug. It is shown to be both irresistible and dangerous.

(f) Children are set (overtly or covertly) in opposition to sexual fulfilment.

On the basis of this very preliminary sampling, it would seem that in Australia romance literature – the genre whose whole raison d'être is the celebration of love and marriage – in fact shares the same jaded views of heterosexual relations which we find in mainstream novels. Insofar as they *do* offer happy endings, these books may function collectively to reassure their readers that the emotional stigmata of the Australian psychotype need not debar happiness. To an outside eye, however, it is the stigmata that stand out, not the contrived solutions.

Making Connections

If Australia "is, indeed, a 'big country' as the television series sees it," there is also, as A.J. Rose points out, "the counterpoint of smallness." "[O]ur country towns are small," he continues, "and likely to remain that way . . . They are small for the reasons that the properties surrounding them are big and the cities are the centres of the growth that otherwise might have come their way. Within the cities, again, the smallness theme appears: people live, and most of them still prefer to live, in small buildings, single houses on separate blocks . . . It may be that these residents of small buildings also seek their social contacts in small and geographically restricted communities within their great metropolitan aggregations, communities focused on the local bowling green, the local church, the local club, paying only incidental and strictly 'economic' attention to the opportunities and demands arising from the existence of the surrounding urban mass, veritable country townships in the city" (1972: 64-65). The same phenomenon may be observed on the macro level. "Australia has never quite federated," says Keith Dunstan. In terms at least of self-consciousness, it is "six separate islands" (1973: 83). The question is, of course, how do we reconcile such marked and apparently deliberate fragmentation with the country's much-commented-upon propensity for "sprawl"? Judging by the felt relation between part and whole in the Australian world view, this is a people for whom, extraversion notwithstanding, the idea of interactivity is somewhat less than appealing.

The antipathy to connection shows up even more clearly in the nation's symbolic expressions than in its concrete ones. Unlike Canada, where systems of transportation and communication have played a central, perhaps key role in the productions of both poets and historians (see G. McGregor, 1985, chapters 3, esp. p. 61, and 11), Australia's attitude toward such themes ranges from negativity to neglect. Given the "real" importance of maritime history to the development of the country, it is notable, for instance, as Geoffrey Blainey points out, that "the sea and ships are . . . virtually banished from [Australia's] written history" (1983: 115). The most obvious explanation for so implausible an omission is anglophobia. The truth is, though, that communications *within* the country are treated even more ambivalently than communications with the outside world. The railway, in particular, turns up over and over again in Australian literature as a negative symbol. In Kenneth Cook's *Wake in Fright* it is the fragile lifeline that *fails* in its function of connecting the centre-haunted protagonist with the cool, civilized coast. In Xavier Herbert's *Capricornia*, even more extremely, it is associated repeatedly with images of death and disorder. Functioning "with deliberate irony to undermine the frontier symbolism of the development of a nation," says Russell McDougall, the railway symbol "deconstruct[s] narrative by conceptualising linear movement as meaningless" (1986: 337). Even such heroic episodes as the construction of the overland telegraph tend to be imaged ambiguously in popular history and fiction. In Hugh Atkinson's *The Longest Wire*, for instance, the emphasis is less on what is achieved than on the incredible difficulties encountered and on the price, in lives and suffering, that was paid. "In the period before the monsoon had made a sea and a quagmire of the northern section, poling down from Port Darwin had advanced a hundred miles. But the effort had strained both man and beast to the limit. The axemen, who had both to clear a track for the wagons and fell and strip poles, had wasted to sinew and gristle" (1986: 85). What one carries away from this narrative is not an impression of human might, but a sense of incredulity that the feat was accomplished at all.

This last sentence hints at an explanation for the fragmentation phenomenon. It seems likely that the antipathy to connection, at least originally, had less to do with a devaluation of its benefits than with the conviction that it was difficult and perhaps impossible to attain. There were, to be sure, good reasons why such a feeling should arise in Australia. Blainey, in his seminal text *The Tyranny of Distance*, talks about the absence of penetrating waterways, the difficulty of passing the Great Dividing Ranges, the inadequacy or at least unreliability of the rainfall in the interior regions. The physical conditions of Australia were such, in other words, as *inevitably* to foil attempts at trans-action. The "failure" of the railway to connect in a symbolic sense is thus in many ways no more than an accurate rendition of reality. On the one hand, says Brian Kiernan, the railway in *Capricornia* stands as a concrete representation of "'progress' and 'development.'" On the other, its very inefficiency exposes it as "a futile attempt to tame a wilful Nature" (1971: 84-85). It's the gap *between* wish and will, of course, that makes the whole subject such a painful one. As such, it's also the element that carries this phenomenon beyond the level of the purely pragmatic. Finding themselves most wholly blocked in those very endeavours most firmly enshrined in the ideology of conquest – penetration and expropriation of the land – as a psychological salve the Australians were forced to deny that they "really" wanted to reach out, to self-extend, in the first place. Hence the overvaluation of physical apartness, both personal and political, in the national mythos.

On one level, then, the deprecation of connection simply makes a virtue of necessity. It also, however, exacerbates the very problem that triggered it in the first place. Undervaluing the ability to communicate, the Australians created even greater obstacles for themselves than were posed by a recalcitrant nature. The "real" history of the railway, for instance, is as striking an example of counterproductivity as any novelist could possibly invent. In the year 1881, says Blainey, "Australia had nearly 4000 miles of railway . . . The most distant railway station in north Queensland was more than two thousand miles around the coast from the most distant railway station in South Australia or Tasmania. That did not mean, however, that a traveller could board a train at Townsville in the tropics and travel swiftly for 2500 miles around the coast . . . In that vast distance were at least fourteen distinct public railway systems, each running from a port to inland towns. Between each railway system was a gap that varied from half a mile to hundreds of miles" (1983: 243). The physical fragmentation was underlined by the discrepancies that existed on the level of planning and implementation. Because three different gauges were used throughout the country, even when the "pieces" began to be linked up, the network remained notably discontinuous. In the 1920s, says Blainey, "passengers with eight days to spare could . . . travel by train from Cairns to Perth, traversing nearly all the east and south coast of the continent. Their journey and often their sleep were interrupted, however, by the need to change trains at the break-of-gauge stations at the southern border of Queensland, the southern border of New South Wales, at the small towns of Terowie and Port Augusta in South Australia, and at Kalgoorlie in the hot interior of Western Australia" (303). It wasn't until the sixties that the country achieved a fully rationalized interstate rail system. Incompetence so striking can only be explained, it seems to me, if one adds to the purely practical difficulties a deep-seated psychological bias.

There is always, of course, the possibility that the malaise described here may be a specific rather than a general one. Some commentators attribute the historic and continuing problems not to conceptual difficulties but to the fact that the railways in Australia, in contrast with the United States, have been publicly rather than privately operated from the beginning. Gordon Jackson, for instance, compares the inefficient and uneconomical rail system with the "highly efficient" road haulage industry (1985: 243). Politics aside, on the other hand, I don't think that the relative economic "success" of the latter necessarily countervenes my suggestion that the Australians have a will to fail at communications. It is interesting, for instance, that the individual efficiency of the truckers, as measured by profits and productivity, is not matched by a commensurate *communal* efficiency, as measured by the extent and condition of the highways. That the road vehicle, unlike the train, stands not for connection but for anarchy is, moreover, supported by the *un*cooperative driving habits of the male population. "Australians drive their cars fast, aggressively, with considerable skill but even more danger," says Craig McGregor. "They approach the whole thing much as they approach so many other activities; the man with the most skill and 'push' wins. At intersections drivers try to hustle their way through with scant respect for the right-of-way of those less expert than themselves. Taxi drivers are the unchallenged masters of the road, and in some cities they drive with stout iron bars at front and rear instead of bumper bars . . . The result: Australia has one of the highest road death rates for its population in the world . . . In 1978 . . . The road accident has become the nation's fourth biggest killer; it causes half of all deaths by accident in Australia, and has already caused twice the number of casualties in all four wars in which Australians have fought" (1981: 43). Even apart from the rather disturbing adumbrations of Mad Max and the barbarian hordes, what these statistics suggest is that the social construction of "driving" in Australia, far from countervening, actually reinforces the symbolic implications of the train. By facilitating self-regulated motion the car allows the Australian to play the masculine (i.e., dynamic) role without violating the ban on "connecting." By demonstrating the dangerousness of extension, it also confirms the necessity, and hence the normality, of that ban.

PERTH

The gentry brought a grace and gaiety and a snobbery to life in the colony which still remains. There was something faintly absurd about them waltzing and quadrilling till after midnight, running musical soirées, giving dinner parties of roasted swan, wild duck, kangaroo and parrot pie, reproducing on their country estates, and in their public gardens, some rough facsimile of the ordered eighteenth century life of their English past.

It was all rather like dancing while Rome burned, for outside were the long miles of sea and scrub, the untameable jarrah and karri forests, the cattle rickety and poisoned by the samia palm, the shifting sand dunes, defeating land scheme after land scheme . . .

Dorothy Hewett, "Western Australia: No Ratbag's Eden"

In a way it's like coming back from the dead. Perth is a beautiful city of red tile roofs and lush green trees and black swans on a winding silver river. It shouldn't have been a shock – the countryside "improves" by slow but perceptible degrees all the way from Kalgoorlie – but it was. Realization comes suddenly somewhere around Northam that one is back in a humanized landscape again. Trees. Towns. Fields full of sheep. Only now do I begin to realize how visually starved I have been throughout this whole long trek through the outback. But perhaps that's an excuse. My sense of relief – of *release* – is triggered by something considerably more profound than aesthetics. I felt *threatened* out there.

We are staying with friends in a beautiful house in the hills above the city. Actually, when I say that their house is beautiful I misstate the case a little. The house is charming all right – a tidy little cottage full of plants and chintz and natural wood – but it pales in comparison with its surroundings. It's the gardens that truly make the place beautiful. I am amazed to discover how many widely differing varieties of eucalypts this country produces, barked and unbarked, from bright red to bone white, flowering shrubs to venerable giants beside which a maple tree would look insubstantial. My hostess tells me that there are over 200 species, a total constantly changing as the trees spontaneously mutate into new forms. She also tells me that they grow like weeds, achieving roof-topping stature in a mere handful of years. Such vigour and fecundity stand in odd contrast to the general aridity of this country. Perhaps a tree *has* to be unusually vigorous, unusually adaptable, just to survive. What I didn't realize, having formed my impressions from the drab and stunted outback gum, was how exotic, how utterly flamboyant these adaptations could be.

As much as the visual feast, I am delighted with the sheer hominess of this establishment. The indoor menage includes two children, a dog, a cat, and an axolotl in a tank. Dispersed around the grounds are a young horse, an old goat, several sheep, a flock of mixed poultry. The gander with his harem is especially picturesque. It's like Grandmother's Farm in the readers we used in grade one. The children are like escapees from an old-fashioned reader, too. They are bright, healthy, wholesome, the way American youngsters are supposed to be but aren't any more. Less sophisticated, they are also more independent, physically and socially. One little girl swings boisterously on a knotted rope across a rock-filled creek while her mother continues to talk placidly about the recent lambing. My North American friends would blanch at the sight of a child doing anything so *dangerous.* Her sister tells us how far afield they got on a recent all-day hike. Apparently it is quite normal for the children to take their lunches on a Saturday and simply disappear for five or six hours, off having who knows what adventures on their own. In North America that too would be considered dangerous, unfortunately often with good reason.

How much of this, I wonder, is simply culture lag – the big, bad modern world not having caught up with Australia yet – and how much relates to real differences in attitudes toward families? Certainly it casts some interesting reflections on the familial models we find in fiction. There, as I have noted, children tend to be problematic – a focus if not a cause of familial discord and often even disintegration. Maternity, especially, seems to be viewed with great ambivalence. The number of bad mothers suggests, aside from anything else, the *difficulty* of being a good one. Yet the reality would seem to be quite otherwise. Australia in many ways is a child-centred society. And the results are palpable. Far more rigorously disciplined than their North American counterparts, Australian children also seem more secure, more relaxed, *happier.* One feels it particularly in the streets.

Missing almost entirely is the undercurrent of rebellion, the obligatory self-conscious antagonism evinced by youth toward their collective elders. There doesn't seem to *be* any generation gap in Australia.

How, then, do we explain all those "bad" or damaged children in Australian novels? Perhaps it simply reflects a sense of insecurity; the subconscious conviction, despite all evidence to the contrary, that an association dependent upon anything as fragile and unreliable as human emotion could fall apart at any moment. If this is the case, then the ambiguous treatment of children in literature tells us much more about how Australians view their own chances and capabilities than about how they view their offspring.

Quite apart from our opportunity to get a closer look at Australian family life, our stay in Perth has been pleasantly touristy. We dined out, window-shopped, sampled the art gallery. We visited Fremantle, where we collected literary gossip and postcard views of the ocean. The local merchants are seething with excitement about the Americas Cup. The local artists' community is somewhat less enthusiastic. We also took the opportunity to check out the local academic scene. I was struck by the difference between the university and the institute of technology.[5] The former is old, staid, respectable, its architecture traditional, its campus disposed with equal components of grace and order amidst the trees of a lush but carefully manicured landscape. Unsurprisingly, its curriculum features the traditional disciplines taught by traditional methods. The latter, on the other hand, is brash and new. The campus seethes with parked cars and people. The quad is lined with fast food outlets and stores. There is a live band playing outside the pub. The intellectual dialogue is equally lively. Perhaps because they are less constrained by ivy-encrusted traditions, both students and teachers at this institution seem more outgoing in style, more innovative in their thinking, and far less oblivious to intellectual trends in the world at large. It is only, I gather, at these institutes and at the "new" universities like Deakin and Griffith that one finds any real interest in interdisciplinary studies. The academics themselves, on the other hand, are equally friendly and helpful on both sides of the fence. And like Griffith and James Cook, both kinds of campus are set definitively apart from the daily ruck.

---

5. Since my visit, the Western Australia Institute of Technology has been renamed the Curtin University of Technology. The differences, however, remain.

At the other extreme of the cultural scale, it was here in Perth that I finally had my first opportunity since arriving in the country to see a real Australian movie. The entry in question was a romantic comedy called *Crocodile Dundee*. Actually, I gather from the publicity that surrounds it that the Australians themselves consider this as an adventure story à la Stephen Spielberg. Considering the paucity of the plot and the inactivity of the hero, the designation seems somewhat absurd. Iconography notwithstanding, the title character of this movie is in fact less an embodiment than a parody of the classic bushman type. In quite marked contradistinction to Turner's legendary American frontiersman, for instance, Dundee is associated both overtly and covertly with the noble savage. His characterizing mode, therefore, is not a manly conquest of, but a feminine identification with, nature.

His masculinity is even more seriously compromised by the role he plays vis-à-vis the real female. Presented as pre-eminently masterful, Dundee nevertheless allows himself to be guided entirely throughout the film by the heroine, a New York reporter who is in Australia seeking local colour. Having heard of his encounter with a crocodile (significantly enough, a battle in which he suffered a less devastating defeat in reality than in his own hyperbolized retelling), *she* seeks *him* out. It is she who bullies him into taking her into the bush. It is she, too, who establishes the terms of their relationship. He kills a snake, frightens off some kangaroo hunters, saves her from a crocodile – but this is all simply reaction. He initiates nothing. It is she who invites him back to New York. And in the end, it is she who controls and eventually consummates their courtship. The penultimate scene shows her running down Fifth Avenue in hot pursuit of her obviously amenable but remarkably unselfassertive prey.

The question is, of course, how do we explain this? Not so much the fact that the hero has turned out this way – I have already noted the tendency of the literary protagonist to be somewhat less than impressively assertive – but the fact that *in spite of his quite obvious deficiencies* Crocodile Dundee has been received with incomparable enthusiasm by the Australian public. This film is already the biggest grossing homegrown production in the country's history. Yet the way he is depicted seems to violate every accepted canon of heterosexual relations in Australia. Is it simply that they don't see it? To me the role reversal seems too blatant to be missed, but perhaps for the insider expectations rule perception.

Supporting this is my strong sense that the Australians in the audience experienced that film in an entirely different way than I did. To me the caricature of the country hick in the big city was so crude and simplistic that I couldn't understand why they didn't find it insulting. But no – they obviously loved it. Clearly they didn't see that it *was* an insult. So maybe they didn't "see" the ineffectuality of the hero either.

Is that the whole answer, then – patriotic myopia? Perhaps. Another possibility, though, is that they *did*, at least subliminally, pick up on the subversive subtext to Dundee's character but were able to accept it, and indeed to recognize it as a portrait of self, because of the way it was mediated within the film. It is interesting in this regard that the female protagonist is an American. Where the Australian of both sexes experiences some disquiet when an *indigenous* female is portrayed as too independent (perhaps it is because they do not wish to accept the implications of communal complicity for the production of such an "unnatural" creature that the faithless wife is almost always construed in unsympathetic terms, as "other"), they may be both ready and relieved to allow the aggressor's role to an outsider, especially an American (symbolically, the wielder of irresistible power), since this would imply that the "unnaturalness" of the hero's subordination can be blamed on an outside agency. This in turn would reinforce the comforting implications of the main discourse. By denying the individual's self-responsibility, the public legitimization of passiveness works to decrease private anxiety.

Subtext aside, there's one further aspect of this movie that seems to call for some comment. The star, Paul Hogan, who also wrote and directed the film, is in some ways a more interesting character than his phony bushman. Hogan came late to the entertainment business. Until his thirties he was a typical Australian working bloke; I believe I heard somewhere that he worked as a welder on the Sydney bridge. Dared by his mates to enter a local television amateur show, he made such a hit with his irreverent wit and urchin charm that he quickly became adopted as something of a national folk hero. Well now Hogan is out to conquer North America. He makes no bones about the fact that this movie was designed to cash in on the international market. Will it make it? One wouldn't think so, given the "national" bias not just of its subject-matter but of its psycho-symbology. This is, though, to make the common mistake of assuming that popular culture products have the same "meaning" for out-group consumers as they do for their in-group producers. *Crocodile Dundee* will, I suspect, do very well in the United States, not merely because the Australians' implicit self-denigration will gratify its cultural chauvinism (which it will), but even more because, in a progressivistic (i.e., high-tech, jingoistic, pro-social) era like the eighties, individual Americans will themselves be gratified by the extent to which this film, while appearing to undercut (that is, make fun of), also in a sense covertly *ratifies* the now-disreputable, but for that reason all the more secretly appealing, sixties-style primitivistic fantasy.[6]

---

6. My prediction here has, of course, long since become history. *Crocodile Dundee* not only did "very well" in North America but was one of the biggest blockbusters of the year. The unexpected extravagance of this response takes on a certain additional resonance when one views it in the light of other, both concurrent and subsequent, developments in American pop culture. Numerous markers ranging from the revival of the consensually defunct TV western to the return of the "creature feature" to the drive-in movie screens indicate that the United States has now turned the corner on progressivism and is (in a sense) on its way back to the sixties. *Crocodile Dundee* appealed, then, not merely as a countertext, but as an early warning signal of trends to come. For more on the cyclic propensities of American culture, see "Television: Copping It," pp. 189-92, below; see also G. McGregor, 1993a.

War, Masculinity, and Violence

During the last couple of decades there has been much teeth-gnashing on the part of the Australians over the fact that, as mentioned above in connection with Ned Kelly, the country's most widely celebrated heroes are all "losers" (Souter, 1976: 228; C. McGregor, 1981: 42). On the face of it, the Anzac legend appears amply to confirm this pattern, not so much because of its subject as because of what has been "made" of it. Again, as in Kelly's case, it is a matter of the choices made from available material. Like the bushrangers, the Anzacs were not necessarily preconstructed as failures. From any broad perspective, in fact, Anzac participation in World War I has to be considered a rousing success. Especially in western Europe, the Australians appear to have comported themselves not just well but outstandingly. Historian Bill Gammage reports that "for a period in which 39 enemy divisions were opposed [by Australian troops] . . . of these 39, all were defeated, and 6 were disbanded. During this time[, although] the Australians represented less than 10 per cent of the British forces . . . they captured 23 per cent of the POWs, 23.5 per cent of the guns, and made 21.5 per cent of the British advances" (in Ross, 1985: 28-30). Yet it is not these triumphs that the "legend" celebrates. "Anzac Day, the only truly national day which all Australians share, whether at home or overseas, commemorates the bitter, bloody defeat suffered by Australians and New Zealanders at Gallipoli," says Craig McGregor – "a campaign which was doomed from the start, achieved nothing, wiped out 8500 young men and wounded another 20,000" (1981: 42; see also Ross: 36-37).

How do we explain such a choice? "It happened at the right time," says Gammage – a time of national insecurities, of adolescent doubts about whether the newly federated nation was capable of performing creditably on the world stage. "On 29 April 1915, news came. Australians were not told what had happened. They learnt only that their men were ashore in Turkey, and that the earliest cables from England were congratulating them. That was enough. Cheers, rejoicing, and editorials on nationhood swept aside the waiting months, anxiety gave way to exultation . . . [W]hat happened was irrelevant. The praise and the success were what mattered, for they made Australia a nation, and a partner to Empire" (1982: 57). According to this view, then, the country fixed upon Gallipoli simply out of relief that the Anzacs stood up under fire. Accepting the logic, one might go so far as to say that Gallipoli was probably all the more attractive *because* it was a disaster, inasmuch as it proved to the world that the Australians, as men and soldiers, could withstand the severest possible test of their fibre. This, of course, brings us back to our starting place, but with a difference. The Australians *do* have a penchant for public defeats (moving ahead a few decades, one might compare the relatively greater attention paid to the disastrous Battle of the Coral Sea during World War II than to the victory at Milne Bay [see Horne, 1985: 186]), but *only* because they give greater point to and occasion for private victories.

Leaving aside its logical flaws, the most interesting aspect of this formulation, it seems to me, is its displacement of emphasis from public to private. In this it is quite consistent with popular treatments of war among Australians. "The digger," if an anonymous figure, is still very much an individual one. The fact has some important ramifications. If nothing else, for all the overt connections made by commentators between war and nationalism (see, for instance, R. Poole, 1985), for all the harping on mateship (and here it is important to note that the much-touted male bonding of soldiers, in Ross's words, is "a relationship of convenience," based on "self-interest" rather than friendship, and involving "behaviour" rather than emotion [76]), it suggests that at least in terms of its psycho-symbolic function the Anzac legend has little to do with social existence per se. The Anzac is just as much an icon of man-alone as Ned Kelly. What, on this level, makes him so appealing? According to the myth it is simply his competence in those areas most central to masculine self-regard. Myths, on the other hand, rarely unravel themselves so neatly. While "manly" competence is certainly part of it, it is not necessarily, or at least not only, for the reasons officially given. I mentioned above (pp. 44-45) that sport was the single area in which the Australians seem able to envisage themselves succeeding (see C. McGregor: 145ff.). Similarly dependent on physical rather than intellectual prowess (the "brain is shown to be an unreliable and essentially un-Australian organ," says David Walker of Lawrence Glassop's classic war novel, *We Were the Rats* [1979: 130]), and on luck rather than will, soldiering could be expected to exert something of the same appeal. Unlike the intimidating worlds of business, or government, or art, or academia, the criteria of excellence in *this* arena are within the reach of everyman. This is, of course, to ignore the fact that soldiering, unlike sport, has to do with killing. The question is, does the difference invalidate the comparison, or merely render it more interesting?

Forming a persistent if largely covert subtext to Australian discussions of Australian attitudes toward war are intimations that it is the killing which, for Australians, itself comprises the greatest attraction. Going far beyond general precepts about "men's magic," womb envy, and the satisfactions of wielding life and death power (see, for instance, Farrar, 1985: 6off., on Brian Easlea), such contentions usually involve or imply the further assumption that Australians are more than usually aggressive by nature. "Violence of one sort or another is never far below the surface in the Australian community," says Craig McGregor (43). How is this accounted for? Xavier Herbert connects it with the convict inheritance ("There is a tradition of bastardy in Australia. We are a cruel people. It comes from bearing the chains" [in Dixson, 1984: 118]). Jon Cleary, making explicit a culturally entrenched image of war as "release," simply attributes it to a combination of temperament and opportunity. ("[T]he Germans and the Japs and our gallant allies, the Russians, haven't cornered the market on cruelty," says the soldier-protagonist of his novel, *The Climate of Courage*. "We Aussies have it too . . . We had it before the war, when Saturday afternoon pub crowds used to knock down a policeman and put the boot into him. You can see it in the crowds who go to fights and scream their heads off when they see blood. It's all cruelty . . . A man needs a streak of cruelty to be a good soldier" [98-99].) Whatever the explanation, however, the bottom line is simply that – as memorably phrased by the Anzac's most celebrated celebrator, World War I historian C.E.W. Bean – "the wild pastoral life of Australia, if it makes men wild, makes superb soldiers" (in Kent, 1985a: 158).

For all its surficial plausibility, on the other hand, the aggression theory falters in the face of the facts. Received opinion notwithstanding, there is evidence that outside of his driving habits (see C. McGregor, 1981: 43; Cunneen, 1985: 84ff.) the Australian male is in fact less, not more, given to violence than "normal." Certainly the rates of violent crime in the country are relatively low on a world scale. "In the United States," notes criminologist Paul Wilson, "the murder rate is more than ten per hundred thousand . . . In Australia . . . [it] is only four per hundred thousand" (1985: 18). Even when it comes to rape, the one crime that might be expected to run rampant in a nation of admitted misogynists, the rates – based on victims' reports, rather than the more suspect police statistics – are very similar in both countries (Braithwaite and Biles, 1980: 332). Despite the appetite for crime among "news" consumers (Harris and Raymond, 1985), in fact, the hard data paint a picture of an almost exemplarily obedient population. This not only goes against the myth of aggressiveness, of course, but contravenes the even more highly bruited myth of Australian anti-authoritarianism. Going all the way back to bushranging days, the Australians have been reputed, or at least have reputed themselves, as would-be lawbreakers, friends of the felon and sworn enemies of the police (Palmer, 1963: 61; Ward, 1966: 6). Closer examination, however, reveals that this antagonism, even in the early days, was more apocryphal than real. While there is little doubt that the shortcomings of the police inflamed already-smouldering anti-establishment feelings among the small selector class of 1880s Victoria (Seal, 1980: 58), the real problems would seem to have been political rather than temperamental. The same can be said about the notorious anti-police feelings on the Victorian goldfields. Sandra Wilson's study of "The Role of the Police in the Kalgoorlie Community, 1897-1898," inasmuch as, in a putatively similar environment, it *fails* to elucidate any evidence of normalized lawlessness ("The law as represented and interpreted by the police seemed to be accepted by most members of the public" [1982: 19]), suggests that the unrest which culminated in the Eureka uprising can be attributed not to the police presence per se, but to the specific regulations – and particularly the policing of mining licences – which they were charged with upholding. And so it goes across the board. In the absence of provocation, and to a large extent even in its presence (again contra popular images, it is remarkable how little real violence there was during the country's most notorious industrial action, the great shearer's strike of 1891 [Palmer: 147-48]), the Australian has usually proven himself a singularly peaceable fellow. So much for the theory that it is the unbridling of violence that makes war so attractive.

If we look at specific rather than general responses, the aggression theory seems even more implausible. For a nation which "loves" war, Australia has produced little military history (Kent, 1985a), and even less in the way of war literature. Quantity aside, moreover, outside of a recent spate of poetry that seems more concerned with lamenting the loss of innocence than with examining what that "loss" entailed (A. Taylor, 1985), such literature as does exist is ambivalent enough in its treatment not only of the moral but perhaps even more of the emotional issues ("while the soldier is generally portrayed as a tough, heterosexual male, there is a constant undertone of guilt and insecurity in the novels" [D. Walker, 1979: 126; see also Hoskings, 1979]) that it tends to ambiguate rather than clarify the basis for the popular conceptions. At least part of the reason for this is the fact that the actors in this drama were considerably less enthusiastic about their "performance" than the audience at home. Those who talked about it made no bones about its unpleasantness ("I would have stayed behind if I had known," says A.B. Facey, Australia's prototypical "ordinary bloke," in his autobiography, *A Fortunate Life* [285]); the majority refused to talk about it at all. "Returning veterans," says David Walker, "came to believe that the only people capable of understanding [what they had been through] . . . were other veterans" (124; see Stretton, 1985: 217ff.).

Where, then, did that image come from of the tough, irreverent, cheerful, fearless Anzac? Much can be attributed to the naive romanticism of C.E.W. Bean, the English public schoolboy turned historian who, according to Kent, selected the material for his influential anthology, *The Anzac Book*, along such lines as wholly to excise any suggestion that the battlefield was anything less than a grand adventure or the Australian soldier other than an insouciant adventurer. "The dirt, the flies, the cold, and the monumental discomforts of Gallipoli are all documented . . . with a grim humour," says Kent, "but the danger, the brutality, the suffering, the waste of life, and the dehumanising effects of warfare are conspicuously absent" (1985b: 381). How did he get away with it? Why didn't someone like Facey ("People often ask me what it is like to be in war, especially hand-to-hand-fighting. Well, I can tell you, I was scared stiff" [258]) stand up and contradict him? One could understand if it were only a matter of public ignorance, but there is ample evidence, if only in the phenomenal popularity of the anthology among the troops (Kent: 388), that the sufferers themselves were as eager to embrace Bean's inspiriting simplifications as the stay-at-homes. Obviously Bean's myth figure functioned as a positive referent even, or perhaps (assuming that no one was really naive enough to think that Bean's version of the war was the full truth of the war) *especially*, when one's mental image covertly conflated the tough and tender scapegrace of *The Anzac Book* with his silent but omnipresent dead companions.

The key to this whole thing might be found in an aspect that Bean *doesn't* talk about. The most frequent criticism of the Weir and Williamson film of *Gallipoli* concerns the extent to which it dramatizes the helplessness of the individual. "The film . . . present[s] us with a collection of more or less innocent babes," says Amanda Lohrey (1982: 146). Weir "places his characters within a natural or apparently natural cycle of events about which they can do nothing, except just register their vulnerability or bewilderment," adds Graeme Turner (1986: 101). For both of these commentators the strategy is a psychologically damaging and a politically suspect one. For others, like Sam Rohdie (1985), it is a major factor in the film's aesthetic excellence. For the public at large, judging by box office receipts, it clearly adds up to a plausible, moving, and meaningful reconstruction. The latter is, I think, the most important response, at least for present purposes. Ideological implications aside (for more on this, see "A Quick History of Australian Film," pp. 209-15 below), the appeal of this movie may well depend upon exactly the same factors that underwrite the appeal of the campaign it commemorates. If Gallipoli-the-film is perceived to demonstrate and, more important, to *justify* man's impotence in the face of fate (see my discussion of war novels in Chapter 2), Gallipoli-the-event is no less so. Gallipoli, says Gammage, "taught the Anzacs that guns were greater than men, and men must accept fatalistically what the guns might do" (66). What is so appealing about this? Only that *having* accepted their helplessness – a helplessness that both anticipates and redeems the condition of everyman – the soldier-heroes are henceforth free from the nerve-wracking task of trying to live up to (m)other-imposed social roles and obligations. "So they continued," says Gammage, "grim, mocking, defiant, brave and careless, free from common toils and woes, into a perpetual present, until they should meet the fate of so many who had marched before them down the great road of peace and sorrow into eternity" (55). Especially for the merely vicarious participant in the ritual, death seems a small price to pay for such a release.

BROKEN HILL

Intending visitors to the Outback should give considerable thought to plan-
ning their journey and equipping themselves and their vehicles for it . . .

The vehicle should be in first-class mechanical order . . . and some mem-
ber of the party should have a reasonable knowledge of running repairs . . .

In addition to the normal tool-kit which should include a good jack, tyre
pump, shovel, axe and tow rope, the following spares should be carried . . .

A well equipped first-aid kit and a fire extinguisher could be invaluable,
while a reserve drum of petrol, food and 4.55 litres (1 gallon) of drinking
water are necessities . . .

Drive according to the condition of the road and not to a rigid timetable.
Care should be taken when negotiating stock-grids . . . Dips and water-
courses are not always readily seen and, if travelling at excessive speeds,
could cause considerable damage or even overturn the vehicle. Keep a sharp
lookout for animals, particularly at night. As most roads are unfenced, there
is danger of collision with kangaroos, emus, cattle, wild pigs or sheep.

Broken Hill Tourist Information Guide

Green and friendly Perth has already begun to seem unreal. We arrived
back in Port Augusta at the crack of dawn, recovered our van, and immediately set out for the interior of New South Wales. I slept through most of
the Flinders Ranges, unfortunately; my guidebook describes them as
"majestic." By the time I was really registering again we were already well to
the east, having entered the Darling River pastoral district. This is sheep
country: rolling open ranges of close-cropped grass interspersed with the
inevitable shabby gums, acacias, and mulga shrubs. The visual gestalt is vintage Australia. For all that we are now in the most populous state in the
commonwealth, much of this region is well-nigh as desolate as the drylands
of the north. Especially as one approaches the vicinity of Broken Hill, the
impression increases that what we are seeing here is not nature tamed but

nature untamable. I find it hard to believe the reports of the jubilation felt by the early colonists when someone managed finally to find the elusive route through the Blue Mountains and penetrated this region. Far more appropriate is the sense of beleaguerment one gets when one reads that the area is protected by a 600-kilometre dingo-proof fence along the South Australian and Queensland borders.

Broken Hill is one of Australia's most famous mining towns. It sits on one of the richest lead-silver-zinc orebodies in the world. Discovered by a boundary rider who patrolled the Mt Gipps fences back in 1883, in 1885 the deposit came under the control of the Broken Hill Proprietary Company which remains to this day one of the most powerful corporations in Australia. Broken Hill is very much a company town. It is also, in reaction one supposes, a strong and militant union town. The Barrier Industrial Council, a federation of eight separate trade unions founded in 1923, has been notable – or notorious, depending on the side of the fence one comes from – for achieving on behalf of its members an exemplarily high standard of both wages and working conditions. Given our particular contacts, we tend to hear more about the negative than the positive side of this activity. Right now one gathers that BHP is resolved to take a firm stand in rolling back the "unrealistic" gains made by the unions during the boom seventies. Their latest move toward achieving this end is a lock-out.

As a physical presence this city lies somewhere between Alice Springs and Kalgoorlie. Like the latter, its streets are tightly gridded, its architecture strongly frontal. Though its older public buildings are somewhat less imposing on an absolute scale, it is interesting to note that its new civic centre sports a fancy openwork carapace. Unlike Kalgoorlie, on the other hand, it quite rejects the "frontier" label. "Many people are under the false impression that Broken Hill is a 'bush town' with few civilized amenities," notes a brochure produced by the Chamber of Commerce. "To the contrary, Broken Hill is a modern and progressive city with . . . everything required for comfortable living." Fodor goes even further in fostering an image of gentility. "Another unusual feature of Broken Hill," he says, "is its very low crime rate and its thriving cultural activities" (1986: 131).

Can we generalize at all from these variations in self-presentation? It is interesting that Broken Hill shares with Alice some of the mythic stigma associated with being "in the centre." In exploration literature, real and

fictional – John Hooker's book discussed previously is a striking example –
the area tends to be imaged as either a staging post, a last fragile bastion of
civilization, or, more critically, a first step beyond the fringe. It is perhaps
not, then, simple physical isolation which triggers the most extreme
response. The closer a community comes to the "dead heart" of the continent, either literally or figuratively, the more it is necessary to bolster the
merely physical panoply with a full gamut of cultural defences, even if this
means in one sense going over to the enemy – deploying the civilized
"mum" against the more dangerous natural (m)other.

The ambivalence implicit in such sleights as this might go far to explain
some of the peculiarities of the Australian folk consciousness. I mentioned
before my perplexity about some aspects of the Azaria Chamberlain case
(p. 91). I was especially puzzled by the reluctance of the public to believe
that a dingo could have been responsible for the atrocity. That this was a
wilful response, rather than merely a general misapprehension, seems clear
when one reads in John Bryson's recently published account, *Evil Angels,*
that the case against the mother was made – *and* won – not only on the
flimsiest imaginable positive evidence, but in the face as well of substantial
negative evidence from native trackers, dingo experts, and so on. Obviously the public *wanted* to find Lindy Chamberlain guilty of killing her child.
Why? I think the answer to this goes right back to the Australian's unique
sense of being-in-the-world, and particularly to his/her characterizing
apprehension of "centredness."

The first clue to the riddle is that the Chamberlain incident took place
not merely in "the centre" but specifically at Ayers Rock. Rocks have always
played a peculiar role in the Australian imagination. In literature, for
instance, they are commonly used to suggest not merely the mysteriousness of nature but, for no fathomable "real" reason, its dangerousness as
well. The sinister undertone can, I think, be explained if one examines the
landscape symbolism in Joan Lindsay's *Picnic at Hanging Rock.* In this novel –
which is based on a true story – two young girls who go rock climbing during a school outing disappear inexplicably and are never seen again. What is
most interesting about this book, aside from the mystery itself, is Lindsay's
rather idiosyncratic deployment of sexual imagery. Where normally one
might expect a rock to have phallic associations, here it is clearly feminine.
Images of caves and crevices convey to us vividly that the source of its

numen – and also its danger – is *inside*. Consonant with this, and even more intriguing, is Lindsay's quite unmistakable insinuation that the girls, far from simply victims, are, in some sense connected with their burgeoning sexuality, complicitous in their fate.

We find this same equation made everywhere throughout the oeuvre: rocks = femaleness = sex = death. What does it mean? The clue, I think, is contained in Damien Broderick's science fiction novel, *The Dreaming Dragons,* where, hidden in an ancient vault in the middle of the desert, the protagonist discovers the rainbow serpent which, paradoxically given its *conventional* sexual associations, here represents the chthonic anima: "nurturant, beguiling, exquisite," but at the same time an embodiment of the "archetypal Bad Mother which every child dreads in nightmare and fairytale" (219). The rock, then, the type image of nature in the dead centre, is none other than the phallic mother, who not only gives life (note that most of the water in "the centre" comes from underground aquifers) but also, and more critically, withholds it.

This would seem to take us a long way from Lindy Chamberlain. Remember, though, that I said the key was the location. Ayers Rock – its "natural" numen augmented by its strong aboriginal associations – is one of the most notable of Australia's great rocks. One might say, in fact, that Ayers Rock for many people *is* the outback – Nature. This, of course, means that it catalyzes a good many covert anxieties. It also – and here is where we get back to Lindy – catalyzes the full gamut of defence mechanisms that the Australian has generated in order to "manage" those anxieties. As with communities at large, the more the private person feels threatened by an alien environment, the more he/she will tend to put up a false front of blustering confidence as a means of deflecting, perhaps even (if it is convincing, and particularly self-convincing, enough) deconstructing that threat. What one might speculate happened in the Chamberlain case, therefore, was simply this: the more the public was forced to contemplate the possibility that nature really was as monstrous as – in the figurative shadow of the rock – they covertly feared, the more strenuously they had to deny it. They did so by borrowing from the ecology movement (which itself might be seen as simply another attempt to assert symbolic control by underlining communal guilt) a benign image of the dingo-as-victim, and substituting it for the disturbing image of the dingo-as-killer. The public, in other words, was far readier to attribute this incident to a kind of inexplicable malice on the part of the natural mother, who could be culturally controlled, than to give any conscious recognition to the fearful phallic potency of Mother Nature, who couldn't.

As a sign that the displacement was not entirely successful, on the other hand, it is interesting to note what happened to public perceptions of the alleged murderess as all this was going on. More and more, says Dianne Johnson in an essay entitled "From Fairy to Witch: Imagery in the Azaria Case" (1984), the Lindy Chamberlain portrayed by the popular press began taking on the attributes of the (m)other she had been elected to replace. Early speculations about post-partum depression started giving way to insinuations of supernatural evil. Her membership in the Seventh Day Adventist Church was parlayed into hints of bizarre rituals and blood sacrifice. Even more telling, during the trial itself the press gave an inordinate amount of play to her clothing, her makeup, her physical demeanour. The effect of this emphasis on physical details, aside from anything else, was to foreground the woman's sexuality. This could be seen at least partly as an attempt at deflation – the sex object image is one of the most time-honoured means by which the male in our society asserts his "natural" dominance over the female. Given that sexuality is one of the identifying characteristics of the neg-anima in both myth and literature, however, it seems clear that by this point Lindy Chamberlain, the quiet, unassuming, entirely unexceptional suburban housewife, had – for the Australian public – actually "turned into" the phallic mother.[7]

Only one last point remains to be made about this. The aborigines,

---

7. Subsequent to this writing, Lindy Chamberlain was cleared of all charges by a board of review whose convening was prompted at least partly by public reaction to Bryson's book. Despite this official vindication, however, and despite too the sympathetic treatment accorded the Chamberlain family in Schepisi's 1988 film, A Cry in the Dark, there is evidently a lingering reluctance within the community to give up on the original reading of events. On three different occasions during the last couple of years, chance-met Australians have proffered the opinion that the hearings, far from exposing earlier error, comprised a retroactive cover-up prompted by government sensitivity to international opinion. Though evasive when pressed for reasons, none of these individuals was willing to admit finally that Lindy Chamberlain had been proven innocent beyond doubt.

despite their explicit associations both with the real rock and the symbolic female, remain shadowy players in the whole story. The aboriginal angle seems to have been played down in the press, and doesn't really enter into the folk version at all. This isn't surprising. Like the dingo, the aborigines' connections with nature make them a dangerously unstable sememe. The result is to render them peculiarly invisible. This is perhaps why no aborigines have appeared in the pages of this journal. I have seen aborigines, of course – not many, but enough of them, especially in the outback – but I simply don't know how they "fit in." They seem so – apart. Slumped on the steps of country stores, crouched in the dust with a brown-paper-bagged bottle, or simply standing around in small, aimless, jittering groups in the interstices of white man's busyness, like clockwork toys in the last stage of unwinding. I can't pretend to have finished elucidating the myth of "the centre" until I look a little more closely at how the aborigine has been defined out of the picture.

The White Man's Aborigine

Australia is notable for its xenophobia, especially toward the oriental races. And I'm not merely talking of folk prejudices. Until recently, official immigration policies were such as to keep the country virtually 100% white. The historical factors usually cited in explanation for such policies are, in T.B. Millar's words, "remoteness from the sources of authority, power and protection, vulnerability to hostile forces deployed in the region, dependence . . . on . . . 'great and powerful friends,' and . . . fear that the hostile forces [would] descend and take away the settlers' hard-won physical or social gains" (1985: 259). Exacerbating the sense of military-cum-political threat, moreover, was the specifically working class "fear of an unarmed conquest . . . by cheap Asian labourers who would destroy the [white] labourers' prosperity and prospects" (McQueen, 1976: 43). Since both threats were at least potentially "real," Australian racism, if hardly laudable, at least had a rational basis. Or so the common explanation would have it. If, however, one takes note of the hysterical undertones to the rhetoric of the white supremacists – the social Darwinian harping on racial purity; the concerns about the debilitating effects of the climate on white vigour; the imaging of non-Caucasians and even the darker-skinned Mediterranean whites in terms of contamination and disease (White, 1981: 81, 141; for the popular view see Clune, 1970: 136ff.) – one begins to suspect that the phenomenon was not quite so simple as it may at first seem. If one examines the special case of the Australian aborigine, the suspicion becomes a certainty.

First, the facts. There is ample documentation of the extent to which the aboriginal peoples have been and continue to be victimized – literally, turned into victims – by white Australia. In a paper called "Racism Australian Style," Margaret Ann Franklin reports on the high levels of poverty to be found among the aborigines, on the chronic ill health, and on the consistently high school drop-out and unemployment rates. Such statistics show only the merest iceberg's tip of the social disadvantagement – the physical and psychological abuse – suffered by the black in Australian society. Bobbi Sykes

(1975) discusses how black women in particular are subjected to a demeaning mythology which makes it virtually impossible for them to function in any capacity except that of sexual receptor. Despite all this, and not to diminish its importance, it is also true, as Diane Austin points out, that while the "New World Negroes were incorporated into capitalist society," albeit through exploitation, the Australian aborigines have most often been "pushed to its periphery" (1984: 94).

This phenomenon may reflect as well on certain anomalies of representation in art, literature, and film. Just as they are in a sense ignored in social life, the aborigines have played a surprisingly small role in the collective cultural oeuvre (Pike, 1977: 592; Rowse and Moran, 1984: 264ff.). To the extent that they *have* entered the cultural record, moreover, the treatment has for the most part been relatively sympathetic. Even in colonial literature, for instance, where one might expect some self-exculpatory vilification, the aborigines were generally depicted in a positive, albeit unrealistic, light (see Webby, 1980). This could, of course, simply signal a patriotic desire to deny that the wild blacks offered any "real" threat to white civilization at all. If white barbarity has been downplayed by history (despite the widespread belief that it was only in Tasmania that the aborigines were massacred in any significant numbers, it has been estimated that over 20,000 of them were killed on the Australian frontier, of whom less than one thousand were Tasmanians [Watson, 1982: 141]), black retaliation has been even more so. Received opinion, says Don Watson, "tends to consolidate the view that the Aboriginals were passive victims. In fact, as a handful of Australian historians have been pointing out for some years now, the blacks resisted everywhere and displayed great ingenuity and resourcefulness in doing so" (141). The early and continuing tendency to treat the aborigines as hapless children, both in literature and in life (see May, 1983: 40), could thus be seen simply as an attempt at self-reassurance. This thesis is not, however, without its problems. Inasmuch as the passivity of the aborigine, as of the oriental, has tended itself to trigger some of the most extreme reactions (being "abnormal," says McQueen, docility on the part of adults, and especially adult men, is seen as "sinister and threatening" [1976: 49]), there is some indication that the image accorded the aborigine in Australian popular culture is *not* the most comfortable one that could have been selected. The question remains, then, why writers and artists have continued to emphasize those particular traits.

At least part of the white ambivalence can be explained by the fact, as pointed out in Chapter 2, that since colonial times the aborigines have been both conventionally and mythically associated with the land they inhabited.

"The use of Aboriginals as a metonym for the indigenous version of nature has been conventionalised," says Graeme Turner, and the ambiguity of "their representation in our narratives derives just as much from an uncertain response to the landscape as to the Aboriginal race itself" (1986: 26-28). Given other aspects of the Australian social psychology, however, it seems likely that an even larger part has to do with the fact – and this too emerged from the preliminary study – that, *like* the land, the aborigine is psycho-symbolically construed as feminine. This casts an entirely different light on that aforementioned infantilization. Insofar as they invited cross-sexual associations, the aborigines would naturally tend to take on such characteristics as passivity and interiority. The more passive they seemed, on the other hand, the more feminine this made them. And the more feminine, the more frightening. Like woman herself, therefore, the aborigines had to be symbolically distanced. One way of accomplishing this was to depict them as self-defeating. (It is interesting in this regard that one of the most powerful of the book/film treatments of the aborigine, Thomas Keneally's *The Chant of Jimmie Blacksmith*, can be seen both to act out the white's worst fears – the feminized/subjugated black reveals his/her deadliness – *and* to assuage them – "his" violence is directed not against the white male who is his true oppressor, but against the white female, his other self [see Kael, 1985: 204-210].) More often, however, relief has been sought by means of a kind of deconstructing mythology. Their reality well hidden behind such purportedly laudatory, extrinsically derived stereotypes as "noble savage" and "superwoodsman" (Kiernan, 1971, Chapter 4 [re Herbert]; Pike, 1977; Webby, 1980; White, 1981: 9ff.; B. Smith, 1985, Chapter 11; R. Dixon, 1986: esp. 7-12; J. Healy, 1987), the aborigines were brought symbolically if not "really" under white, masculine control.

One last point: though perhaps no more than predictable considering the aforementioned sexual associations, it is still interesting to note the extent to which conventional paeans to the aborigine have focused overtly on those same aspects of inner (that is, emotional-cum-spiritual) life more *covertly* associated with femininity in general. From the Jindyworobaks (a 1930s anti-European cultural movement under the leadership of poet Rex Ingamells which concerned itself "with locating and turning towards . . . the 'primaeval' traditions of . . . the land itself" [Goodwin, 1986: 134]) through to the more recent eco-artists (see Catalano, 1985), aboriginal culture, and especially aboriginal art and myths, have been seized upon as a source, perhaps the *only* indigenous source, of spiritual value. Quite apart from its confirmation of the trend to divest aboriginality of its alienness (the only forms of aboriginality "whites are prepared to accept," says Colin Tatz, are "those that are aesthetically pleasing and acceptable: One Pound Jimmy on our postage stamps, Albert Namatjira and his legacy of water colours, bark paintings on our dollar notes, goannas and turtles on an endless array of table linen, traditional corroboree performances for concert export" [1980: 356]), inasmuch as it seems to be on the increase, one might also question what this phenomenon implies for the evolution of the Australian psychotype. I will be discussing this further in my conclusion, below. For now, however, I would just like to point out that, assuming a correlation between anxiety and repression, the relatively higher or at least more open valuation of aboriginal than feminine "wisdom" provides strong evidence that ambivalence about the Australian natives *stems from* ambivalence about "femininity" rather than the other way around. Why is this of note? Because it suggests that the Australian's problematic sense of being-in-the world, being prior to and independent of the content of specific interactions with "nature," was structurally rather than historically inculcated. It also explains why Asians, despite the fact that they lack entirely the aborigines' problematic links with the landscape, tend to be imaged in much the same way. Because the oriental is almost perforce construed as other by Caucasian cultures (see Bird, 1983: 111), in any society where the most significant other is feminine the oriental will tend to be perceived as feminine too.

ADELAIDE

---

*For ten days early in 1837 [Colonel] Light walked about his [chosen site]
studying it deeply, visualizing, remembering, and pondering . . .*

*The final plan that [he] decided on consisted of two sections of building
blocks – one on the flat summit of the southern hill and the other on the broken rising slope of the northern hill. The gentle valley and the river banks
between the two were left as open parkland. The southern building area he
divided into a grid pattern with five widely spaced 132 feet wide streets running north and south, and eleven closer, narrower east-west streets. In the
centre of South Adelaide Light provided a large rectangular public space
which he intended should be formally landscaped and surrounded with
public buildings. Four lesser but still extremely generous squares were provided mid-way between the centre and the corner extremities of the town.
Each square was carefully centred on main streets with an eye to vistas.*

*Across the valley, Light divided North Adelaide into three different sized
rectangular sections, each disposed to take advantage of the rising site . . .
The smaller area, the breaking down into . . . sections and the natural,
stepped topography resulted in a more human, less formal and more domestic character than the southern town.*

*Finally, in a magnificent gesture of courage and enlightenment, Light
wrapped his towns in a leaf-green cocoon by declaring the entire surrounding area – a band about a mile wide – a natural parkland.*

J.M. Freeland, Architecture in Australia

Back to the coast again. I'm beginning to get dizzy from the perpetual
motion. At least we're finished with the outback for a while. The rest of the
trip, for me at least, will be spent in the big cities. The cities that Australians
profess to hate – and where they almost all live. Adelaide, the capital of
South Australia, 300 kilometres south of Port Augusta, was the first
on the list. Smaller, younger, and generally less colourful than the other

southeastern mainland capitols, this city is not as well known overseas as Sydney or Melbourne. Certain of its features, however, make it a good jumping-off point for the tour to come. Of these I will have more to say later. First, though, I want to talk a little about some recent insights I have had into Australian art.

Because of its ability to produce unmediated encodings of a sense of place, art is one of the most important diagnostic tools available to the semio-ethnographer. Ever since arriving in Australia, consequently, I have been looking at and thinking about Australian paintings. The high point of this investigation, so far at least, was my viewing of the Heidelberg show currently featured at the Art Gallery of South Australia. The Heidelberg painters – so-called because their work-site of preference was the outer Melbourne suburb of Heidelberg – were, according to myth, almost single-handedly responsible for teaching Australians to see and love their own landscape. "The popular view of the Heidelberg School," says Ann Galbally in her introduction to the exhibition catalogue, "is that Streeton, McCubbin, Roberts, Conder and Withers were the first artists to see and paint the 'real' Australian landscape while those who had gone before them . . . were lesser artists because they had only been able to paint . . . 'through European eyes'" (1985: 9). Gallery Director Patrick McCaughey is even more effusive. "They loved both the zenith landscape with the baking sun at high noon and a luminescent moment of moonrise . . . [Believing] that the task for the Australian artist was to paint Australian realities . . . they won for themselves, their contemporaries and for future generations a rich and stirring poetry from the spectacle of a landscape being transformed into a country which bore its own distinctive identity" (8). On the basis of such pronouncements, what I expected to find in that exhibition was something qualitatively different from the nature paranoia that permeates Australian literature. "Expected" is the key word here. Even leaving aside the question of their purported "Australianness" (early assessments have been qualified by recent investigations of the group's debts to European influences, particularly the Barbizon-type *plein air* painters and, to a lesser extent, French Impressionism), what I actually saw in these works was something rather different than what their countrymen claim for them.

It didn't emerge at first. What struck me immediately – exactly as per their reputation – was the incredible light that suffuses these canvases. In almost bizarre contrast to Marcus Clarke's much-quoted invocation of "Weird Melancholy" as a characterizing feature of the country's literary landscapes a decade earlier, the Heidelberg paintings are, if not quite quintessentially "Australian" (still missing are the pinks and puces, the brazen red-browns of the unreclaimed outback), at least strikingly non-European with their ostentatious outdoorsiness, their glowing palettes of dust- and heat-hazed golds and blues. Perspectival features add to the sense of expansiveness. If one postulates an ideal polarity of centripetal versus centrifugal, closed versus open, passive versus active, feminine versus masculine, the Heidelberg works clearly fall on the latter side of the fence. No wonder they were well received. Like nineteenth-century American landscape painting, this oeuvre, in asserting the dominance of viewer over vista, seems symbolically to confirm man's conquest over nature.

It's only when one begins to analyse the works more systematically that certain anomalies begin to emerge. For one thing, the vantage point is in fact considerably lower than that which typifies American works. While certainly far from the claustrophobic enclosedness of Canadian wood- and mountainscapes, the sense of distance one gets in Australian paintings is to a large extent dependent simply on the fact that there are so few real obstacles to vision in the Australian landscape. There is, further, a clear stratification in these pieces. Where American paintings are characteristically horizon-focused – and Canadian ones feature the near and the safe – the Heidelberg landscapes almost all emphasize the middleground. The middleground is where it all happens. A nexus not only of visual but of emotional tensions, it is an "active" zone sandwiched between an empty foreground and an idealized background. It is also where virtually all the human interest is located.

What does this mean? With respect to the subject in the paintings, there is at least a hint of entrapment. Especially in cases where isolated women or children are shown surrounded by bush (Tom Roberts' A Summer Morning Tiff [1886], Tom Humphrey's The Way to School [1888], or – most notably – Frederick McCubbin's Lost [1886]), we get a sense of the landscape as something that cuts one off from the safety and civility of human society. With respect to the subject-as-viewer, on the other hand, the implications are a little more complex. Because of the middleground focus, access would seem to be simultaneously offered and denied. And I'm not just talking about sightlines here. Granted, in many of the paintings the obstacles to penetration are purely visual ones. In Arthur Streeton's *Golden Summers, Eaglemont* (1889), for instance, the background is obscured by shadows. In Charles Conder's *Coogee Bay* (1888), Streeton's *Near Heidelberg* (1890), David Davies' *Warm Evening, Templestowe* (1890s), and Howard Ashton's *Through Sunny Meadows* (1898), similarly, we stand on or just back from a hilltop, the brow of which hides the path forward. In numerous other paintings, though, the barriers are more tangible: brush, bogs, gulleys. E. Phillips Fox's *Moonrise, Heidelberg* (1900), Davies' *Moonrise* (1894), Streeton's *Early Summer – Gorse in Bloom* (1885), and McCubbin's *Winter Evening, Hawthorne* (1886) are all alike in their careful invocation of fences in the middleground. If one sees a long way in these landscapes, it is clearly more difficult to actually get there. Added to this is the fact that in numerous paintings (Julian Ashton's *Evening – Merri Creek* [1882], Conder's *Stockyard near Jamberoo* [1886], Roberts' *A Quiet Day on Darebin* [1885], and Streeton's *Still Glides the Stream* [1890], among others) streams or rivers disappear in the middleground, giving us the clear impression of something sinister or sucking in the "centre," as if the landscape itself were determined to immobilize the human interloper.

What we have in the Heidelberg works, then, is a surficial optimism quietly undercut by a covert sense of menace. In order to figure out how such a vision arose, I did some delving into the art history books that I have been acquiring. The picture that emerges is a very interesting one. Allowing for some simplification, it would seem that there are six main phases within the colonial Australian oeuvre.

(1) Interesting primarily for their value as a negative example are those early nineteenth-century works that exemplify the Rousseauian noble savage theme, depicting Australia as an aboriginal acadia. Although not rare, the evidence – as Tim Bonyhady points out – seems to indicate that this type of painting tended to be either sent to, or painted in, Britain.

(2) In contrast with these is the corpus of topographical views taken in the vicinity of early settlements like Sydney and Paramatta. Far from celebrating noble savagery, their emphasis on the domestic face of the landscape is obviously intended to underline the triumphs of civilization. Where aborigines appear at all, it is as infinitesimal figures on the fringes of development. In the context of all these concrete testimonials to the

efficacy of white industry and order, their nakedness is now read as vulnerability rather than freedom. At the same time, because they are rendered
as childlike, their real dangerousness – like the dangerousness of the erstwhile untidy wild landscape – is put completely out of mind. No wonder
the colonists preferred the topographer's vision to the Rousseauist's.

(3) One of the most substantial and popular genres from the 1820s
through mid-century was the country house portrait. Often commis-
sioned by their owners, these paintings did for the private man what the
topographic townscapes did for the public at large. Although examples
range widely in both style and competence, several features are common
to the group as a whole. First, although it may seem an obvious point, the
vantage – and this is accentuated by the placement of staffage – is clearly
from the outside looking in.[8] Second, though their adjuncts may be more
or less scattered, the houses themselves typically occupy both the visual
and the physical middleground. There is the sense, consequently, that
although outside the house, one is not merely in, but surrounded by, the
natural landscape. Despite this, in most cases the sense of enclosure is
played down. Protective framing by means of fences is sometimes found in
paintings depicting the earliest stages of settlement (see Dixon, 1986:
72-75). The ideal, however, is the grand mansion set among broad, open
fields and gardens. There are no aborigines to be seen. White men and
women are invariably at leisure. There are no signs of the very real "work"
involved in winning a living from this landscape. Perhaps because nature is
more of a real threat to the settler than to the townsman, the more explicit
aspects of man's battle with the land and the elements are not properly
part of the subject-matter of these paintings.

(4) Concurrent with the fad for country house portraits, Australian
artists also produced a substantial body of wilderness views. Although
seeming at first sight to suggest a rationale diametrically opposed to the
topographic modes, the marked conventionality of this latter oeuvre

---

8. As a sidelight to this, it is interesting to note that the equivalent development in Canadian colonial art was the bourgeois portrait, a form which, in depicting its sitters in
opulently appointed parlours and libraries, surrounded by their most treasured posses-
sions, emphasized their self-identification with the inside, *not* the outside, of the
house.

suggests that the undomesticated landscape was only (quite literally) *conceivable* when, mimicking the physical process of settlement, it was transmuted into a facsimile of the European sublime. Even then there were tensions. Despite all the impassioned paeans to untrammelled nature, Bonyhady's discussion of the period clearly suggests that both the critics and the public felt easier with paintings in which the wilderness wasn't in fact overly wild or unruly. "The *Australasian* considered that because 'Buvelot's pencil . . . seldom strays many miles from Melbourne . . . [his work] is so comfortable compared with its sombre and magnificent rivals'" (1985: 111). It is evident from such unguarded comments that the conflict between European-influenced expectations and Australian experience was not to be resolved without a certain amount of anxiety. One strategy was to copy paintings rather than nature. Another was to introduce a few European personae to suggest that the landscape had already been appropriated. The latter, unfortunately, didn't always work out as planned. Far from suggesting some kind of proprietorship, most of these figures are palpably detached from their backgrounds. Slight, passive, and a little uncertain, they are clearly visitors to, rather than masters of, all they survey.

(5) By the 1870s, painting was becoming somewhat more realistic. Despite the common attribution of the "discovery" to the Heidelberg painters, it was actually the aforementioned Louis Buvelot who first rehabilitated the lowly native gum tree. At the same time as it was losing some of its exoticism, however, the Australian landscape was also becoming somewhat less benign. Denuded of its "artistic" trappings and conventionalized emotionality, it began to reveal its true colours. Or perhaps it was only that the artist, increasingly secure in an increasingly domesticated landscape, was able for the first time to show some of his own ambivalence. Typical of this vein was H.J. Johnstone's *After Sunset* (1876), the subject of which was described in a contemporary review as "a long lagoon [lying] . . . solemnly beneath a crystal sky" surrounded by sentinel-like swamp gums, "gnarled and twisted yet withal weirdly graceful, as our eucalypti to accustomed eyes always do seem" (in Bonyhady, 1985: 129). The emergence of the word "weird" into open parlance at this time – and it is notable that this was just one year before Clarke's aforementioned disquisition on the gloominess of the bush was to appear – suggests that in the boom climate following the gold rush at least some of the distancing mechanisms employed by earlier artists had been allowed to break down.

Re-viewed in light of this history, the practice of the Heidelberg school seems decidedly problematic. Far from signalling a final break from the bad old days of pessimism, the militant benignity of their landscapes would seem to suggest rather a regression to early colonial denial. Which is not really so surprising. In marked contrast to the earlier generation, these artists were working in the middle of a depression. Their celebration of the pastoral idyll, however patriotic it may have seemed in retrospect, was consequently in all likelihood nothing more nor less than a mass retreat from the encroachment of an increasingly unappetizing here and now.

If the Heidelberg painters "loved" the landscape, then, it was perhaps because it was too disturbing to do otherwise. This didn't mean that they never painted the dark side at all. It is interesting in this regard, though, that their "negative" subjects are almost all drawn from folklore. Far from affecting, such stock themes as the lost child, the swagman down on his luck, and the bush burial, as Astbury points out (1985), were already so conventionalized that they had long since lost their power to evoke unpleasant realities. The one notable exception to this rule is Arthur Streeton's *Fire's On,* depicting a mine cave-in that took place in 1891 in the Blue Mountains of New South Wales – and despite its subject this is hardly grim naturalism. In the absence of prepackaging, the artist this time distances through technique. In marked contrast to the heroic stockmen and larger-than-life shearers of other Heidelberg pieces, the figures in this painting are so small and the atmosphere so pellucid that the viewer doesn't realize at first that he/she is looking at a disaster.

It is ironical, of course – just as *Crocodile Dundee* is ironical – that the past in which these artists found their inspiration for the most part never really existed. Verisimilitude aside, however, it is clear that this displacement in time achieves exactly the same effect as the spatial displacements of the topographer. Once they are decontextualized, unruly elements can – with *almost* complete success (remember that ambiguous middleground!) – be ignored or perceived as innocuous.

This brings me back, as promised, to the city of Adelaide. Confronted with all this evidence of the Australian's ambivalence vis-à-vis "landscape," I suddenly had an insight into the semiology of Australian urban sprawl. Adelaide is supposed to be an exception among the capital cities. Where Sydney, for instance, "just grew," if not like Topsy then according to the exigencies of the landscape and the greed of the developers, Adelaide was *planned.* Despite this, Adelaide's layout merely makes explicit what is implicit elsewhere. Virtually all Australian cities have a more or less rigidly gridded commercial core. In Adelaide, however, where the area is segregated from its suburbs by an enveloping girdle of parklands within which are located all major government buildings, cultural and educational institutions, the real meaning of this arrangement becomes clear. Civilization is *inside.* And the people themselves? Where the outback forces an uneasy alliance with "mum," here it is the *cultural* (m)other who threatens. The result is predictable. Responding to their shared sense of fragmentation and dis-memberment by rejecting an identification with the feminized city (Australians live in Fitzroy or Paddington, not Melbourne or Sydney), "the people" have once again retreated to a space *between* inside and outside. In Adelaide as elsewhere, the suburb, sprawling and disorderly, is simply the verandah writ large.

Voss: The Ordeal in the Desert

As intimated in our discussion of Ned Kelly, along with bushrangers and foot-soldiers the Australians have been most fascinated by the figure of the explorer. Why? Perhaps it is simply his activity. Imaged iconically as a sharp line forging purposively across the map, the explorer can be seen as the incarnation of *movement*. And movement is *the* national mode. "Australians [are] . . . inveterate and capable travelers," says Nicholas Jose. They "go everywhere. Perhaps it is a compulsion that arises from their fear of geographical isolation and cultural poverty, or perhaps it is merely a necessity if they are to know what is going on in the world. At any rate, traveling provides an appropriate . . . metaphor for rootlessness, and a vantage point for looking . . . [at] Australia" (1985: 323). Counter to this, of course, is the fact, as pointed out in the section on "Connections," that the preferred *kind* of movement, far from purposive, is in a sense self-negating. "Even before we travel we're wandering in circles," says one of the protagonists in Murray Bail's *Homesickness*. Australians *don't see themselves as going anywhere.* This explains why, as Helen Daniel points out, Australian literati, though indubitably fixated on the journey, have proven far more apt in dealing with the picaro – "an incompetent . . . clown-buffoon moving restlessly through a protean world and himself reflecting . . . [its] disorder" – than with the goal-oriented questor (1978: 285). It also renders the postulated relationship with the explorer somewhat ambiguous. Insofar as the explorer is *by definition* purposive, it is difficult to see him as a convincing, or even – given that the antipathy to connection is based on real anxieties – a desirable, alter ego for the Australian.

This, on the other hand, is to underestimate the capacity of myth for swallowing its own contra-diction. If we examine which *particular* explorers show up most often in Australian fiction and folklore it becomes obvious, exactly as in the case of Ned Kelly, that the public is less interested in those who can be seen as successful in conventional terms, than in those whose enactment of the dynamic role is an ambivalent one. Sir Thomas Mitchell, the discoverer of the lush region known as "Australia Felix," has been virtually ignored. His contemporary, Charles Sturt, whose discoveries were of far less importance, has managed, on the other hand, to command a respectable amount of attention. Why? The difference between the two men may be summarized as a difference in *stance.* "The Sturt of *Two Expeditions into the Interior,*" says Ross Gibson, "is a patient, resolute man determined to survive in Purgatory until he has assimilated himself to the land, until he blends into it and attempts to understand it in its own terms. Mitchell, on the other hand, presents himself as an energetic conquerer, come to inherit the land in the interests of himself and the English nation" (1984: 120). Perhaps, then, we could see the public preference for Sturt simply as signalling a public preference for the Romantic myth of mergence over the Kiplingesque myth of conquest. If we look further, the folklore of exploration would seem to support this interpretation – up to a point. *Beyond* that point, it undercuts it completely. Ranked not just according to the amount of "official" recognition they have been given (for a review of the literary use of the exploration experience, see Gibson: x), but also according to their visibility in "popular" culture, the *most* preferentially cited explorers from Australian history are E.J. Eyre, Ludwig Leichhardt, and – especially – the team of Burke and Wills. All four of these individuals could be seen as exemplifying a movement *into* rather than a progress *over* the landscape. Unlike Sturt, who was "rewarded" at the end of his purgatorial journey with a glimpse of the fabled paradise, however, what these men experienced was near- or total annihilation. Eyre's journals, says Gibson, not only give us a sense of man's "minuteness against the backdrop of the environment," but awake us to "the horror which is latent in this elemental Australia" (133). The others on the list did not survive that horror. Leichhardt disappeared in the desert, never to be heard of again. Burke and Wills's fate was even more haunting. Having achieved the unachievable, made it *through* the dead centre, they died a miserable, lingering death from exposure and malnutrition because after five months they missed their relief crew by a matter of hours. Sturt notwithstanding, the message one takes from *these* lives is less a recommendation of neo-primitive self-abnegation than an admission that no other course is possible. The "purpose" is broken willy-nilly.

Patrick White's *Voss* provides the type literary treatment of the exploration motif. Considering the amount that has been written about this author in general and this book in particular, I will merely say by way of summary that the eponymous hero, having determined to test himself against the wilderness, like Eyre is forced to a progressive self-deconstruction by his sufferings, and like Leichhardt dies of it. Most interesting for present purposes, on the other hand, is not so much what White makes of his material (and he has obviously drawn on both Sturt's and Eyre's journals in order to capture an authentic sense of how the ordeal *feels* from the inside) as what the Australian critics have made of *him*. A significant faction – most notably Perth academic Veronica Brady – sees the defeat by nature, Voss's and others, as an ultimately affirmative experience. Far from defeatist, says Brady, *Voss* documents a "process of redemption. Initially so confident in his own powers that he 'has contempt for God because he is not in [his] own image' . . . Voss is humbled by his sufferings in the desert, learning that to be human is to be vulnerable and subject to necessity. Yet it is only when he accepts his humanity in this way that he comes to the vision of God" (1981: 74). Brian Kiernan disagrees. To privilege the Christian reading, he says, is to confuse the author's viewpoint with that of his protagonists. In withdrawing from the world, Voss and his vicarious fellow traveller, Laura, are in fact withdrawing from life. "Laura's and Voss's desires to transcend the flesh by mortifying it [can be] seen not only in terms of Christ's Passion but also in Freudian terms – as masochistic" (1971: 122). For Kiernan, the true exemplar in White's book is not the "explorer," with his fatal fixation on the supernal, but the ordinary, stay-at-home young matron, Belle, who, in accepting and enjoying her own thoughtless "animality," achieves "an emotional stasis *within* the flux of time" (116; italics added).

Who's right? If any version of the ordeal in the desert is a positive one, then White's, with its self-conscious metaphysicality, has to be it. But *is* it? The answer to this has to hinge, not on the interpretations of observers, inside *or* outside the book, but on the experience of the explorer himself. In the folk version there's no doubt: the death of the questor is a defeat. Burke and Wills aside, one of the most popular books of the century (see Bonnin, 1982: 237) was Ion Idriess's "true" story of Harry Lassiter's disaster-plagued attempt to re-find the gold reef he'd "discovered" while lost in the desert – and his literally fatal failure to do so. The literary version, though – and not merely White's – is considerably more ambiguous. "The sense of closure is strong in the final pages of [Randolph Stow's] *To the Islands*," says Anthony Hassall, "yet it is balanced by an open-endedness that eludes easy definition. The book ends but Heriot [is not yet quite dead]; he does and does not find God, or Wolaro; the islands may or may not exist; [he] is reconciled to Rex, but only by proxy. His last words, 'my soul is a strange country' . . . take us, and him, to the point where self-discovery begins rather than ends" (1986: 51; see also the Stow entry in Appendix B). To interpret this as positive *or* negative depends, it seems to me, entirely on the will of the reader. And so it is with *Voss*. Setting aside Laura's "special" knowledge as neither reliable nor disinterested (it is notable, I think, that this character ends up by choice a spinster – as sterile and aloof as the dead hero), what White actually shows us of Voss's *own* response is far from conclusive. Sustained by the luminosity of his hallucinations, he "felt that he was ready to meet the supreme emergency with strength and resignation" (393). But how did he feel when the moment actually arrived – when his aboriginal executioner entered the hut where he lay dying, knife in hand? Of this, we are told nothing. And afterwards? His severed head "knocked against a few stones, and lay like any melon. How much was left of the man it no longer represented? His dreams fled into the air, his blood ran out upon the dry earth, which drank it up immediately. Whether dreams breed, or the earth responds to a pint of blood, the instant of death does not tell" (394).

In considering the "meaning" of the explorer's story we must keep in mind the Australian's obsession with the image of a "dead heart." (For David Malouf, says Martin Leer, "Australia is a mere outline with darkness at its centre: a void" [1985: 3]). We must keep in mind the fear of "falling" that underlies this image. ("Refinement [is] maintained on the razor's edge on the edge of an abyss," says Shirley Hazzard of her propriety-obsessed protagonists in *The Transit of Venus*. "To appear without gloves, or in other ways suggest the flesh, to so much as show unguarded love, [is] to be pitchforked into brutish, bottomless Australia" [39].) Finally, we must keep in mind that what the centre-haunted Australian is afraid of falling *into* is not merely nature, but nature-as-The Feminine. Viewed from this perspective, it is not, I think, irrelevant to our subject that Voss's journey into the desert is also a journey into the mind of his absent lover. Nor is it irrelevant that the more perfect their communion becomes, the closer he approaches annihilation. David Tacey notes the significance of the Voss-Laura mind-meld in a damning critique of the book – or at least of the society that misreads it – subtitled "The Teller and the Tale" (1985). Far from the wholesome Jungian union invoked by critics like James McAuley and Judith Wright, and even further from Brady's Christian redemption, he says, what *Voss* really exemplifies is the soul-destroying search of the eternally infantile for self-dissolution within the womb of the dark, devouring phallic mother. Tacey's reading brings out the one essential ingredient our discussion has so far overlooked. Whether construed as centre or engulfment, the desert is not *merely* nature-as-The Feminine – which is bad enough – but an emblem of the human unconscious. By penetrating beyond its safe fringes, the explorer is thus confronting not merely otherness, but the particular otherness he carries within himself.

This, then, explains not just why the wilderness journey is so fascinating, but also why it is so fearful. It makes clear as well why so many critics should try so hard to *deny* that fearfulness by reconstructing the experience in positive terms. Insofar as it suggests a "heavily repressed but at the same time ever-present longing for extinction, oblivion, anonymity" (Tacey: 268), taken at face value the recurrent obsession with death in the desert could easily be taken to signal an unhealthily nihilistic strain in the Australian imagination. Hence the wishful fantasy of mystical translation. Hence, too, the implausibly optimistic reading of even the most cautionary of tales. The appeal of *Lassiter's Last Ride*, says Bonnin, "lay partly in the suggestion that Australia could find instant relief from the economic problems of the Depression in the untapped mineral resources of the outback . . . [and partly in] the idea that it was still possible for individuals to make their fortunes" (237). Considering that Lassiter not only failed on his quest but died in the process, this kind of response seems inappropriate if not incredible. Lassiter's bad luck notwithstanding, however, the Australian public, like Veronica Brady, and James McAuley, and Judith Wright, and the rest, seems unshakably determined to look on the bright side, no matter what. Idriess's book, which strikes the outsider as mounting the strongest possible argument for being *wary* of treasure hunts, "stimulate[d] a rash of expeditions and speculative investment . . . which ended repeatedly in tragedy" (Bonnin: 237). Must we, then, dismiss the myth of the dead but triumphant explorer as fraudulent? I don't think it's that simple. The Brady version of *Voss could* be seen as the whitewashing of a death wish, but insofar as the book itself does license such a reading – along with the more negative one offered by Tacey – we could perhaps see it as evidence of a genuine ambivalence within the communal imagination about the life of the spirit.

It is perhaps pertinent here to say something about religion in Australia. The most common view is that there "really" isn't any. According at least to received opinion, Australia is an almost wholly secularized society (see O'Farrell, 1982). According to Hans Mol, on the other hand, as recently as 1983, 79 per cent of respondents to a Gallup poll went on record as believing in God (1985: 130). This does not, of course, mean that they really do. Before we simply write it off as hypocrisy, however, it is interesting to note the widespread acceptance, among believers and non-believers both, that religious affiliation makes one, in moral terms, a "better" person (Mol, 137ff.). At the very least, then, Australians would seem to think that religion is not only a respectable thing to profess, but a "good" thing to have. Which makes it all the more problematic that very few of them do in fact "have" it. Public professions aside, the vagueness and incoherence of the belief system that emerges on close examination (see Mol: 132) make it amply clear that the *will* to affirm some sort of supernatural order is not matched by an *ability* to do so. O'Farrell attributes this to the fact that the beliefs proffered simply do not fit the Australians' conceptions of themselves and the world. "An uneasy tension exists between some sort of feeling of spiritual need, and the repulsion of the elements of foreignness or falsity in what is offered to satisfy it" (6). O'Farrell's use of the word "foreign" here is, I think, telling. If we assume that religion, like other non-corporeal aspects of experience, would tend to be associated by the Australian with the realm of the (m)other, then the mixed feelings to which Farrell refers can be taken both to parallel and to reflect upon the mixed feelings evinced by writers and readers alike about the ordeal in the desert. The desire for transcendent validation is both enhanced and undercut by the fear that any experience so alien to the masculine sense of self must perforce be deadly, *even, or especially, for those who succeed in penetrating to the heart of its meaning.* Like the other Australian folk heroes, then, if the doomed explorer holds a special place in the national pantheon it is *not* simply because he is a "loser," but because of what he is defeated *by.*

HOBART

The entire land-mass of Australia – most of it very dry – lies north of latitude forty. Tasmania, containing more lakes than any other region except Finland, lies south of latitude forty, directly in the path of the Roaring Forties. It genuinely belongs to a different region from the continent: in the upside-down frame of the Antipodes, it duplicates northwestern Europe, while the continent is Mediterranean and then African.

C.J. Koch, "Literature and Cultural Identity"

A weekend hardly seems enough to "do" an entire state. And not even a whole weekend: Saturday morning to Sunday noon. Unfortunately it's all I could muster. Tomorrow, Monday, my travelling companion is scheduled to head for the mining towns of the wild Tasmanian interior, and as for me, I have civilized appointments to keep in Melbourne. Despite the shortness of the time, however, this visit has been in many ways one of the most enlightening stops of the whole trip.

Tasmania is considered by Australian mainlanders to be a bit of a backwater. And I can see why. It may have been at least partly because it was an off-season weekend, but the impression I got right from the beginning was of a singular lack of "modern" bustle. Hobart itself has an old-fashioned air. I initially attributed this to the visual predominance, at least in its central core, of colonial, and particularly high Victorian, architecture. The fact is, though, that one could say the same of nearly every town of any age or size that we've encountered on this trip. The thing that made Hobart "feel" different was not, then, I decided, the *type* of architecture at all, but, rather, the particular features that have been emphasized. *Hobart shows less "front" than the average Australian city.* In part, of course, one may attribute this to the climate. The colder temperatures clearly obviate the need for verandahs. There is also, however, substantially less surficial display in downtown

Hobart. The quality I identified as "old-fashionedness" was in fact merely a kind of reserve.

Out in the countryside one continues to be struck by the same lack of flash. The scenery is spectacular: south of Hobart the mountains come right down to the serrated coast. Very little is made of this, however. In the back yard of the island's biggest city, there is virtually no visible tourist development – no scenic views, no roadside picnic areas, no concessions on the beaches. To the frustration of the camera buff, the highway doesn't even hug the shoreline that closely. Rather one gets the impression that this is merely a country road that happens to be near the ocean. And a *back* country road at that.

Inland the pastoral effect is even more pronounced. Here are snug little farms and orchards set in misty valleys among steep, rolling hills. The effect is very unAustralian. The grass is green. The sheep are fluffy and white. From a distance – ignoring the omnipresent gum trees – one could almost be in Europe. How much of this is natural, one wonders, and how much is due to a deliberate process of transmutation? *All* the early colonies tried to recreate Britain; perhaps the difference is only that on Tasmania the climate facilitated instead of frustrating the endeavour. Certainly there would seem to have been a considerable interest here in the institutionalized control of nature going right back to the earliest days. Hobart's botanical gardens, an exemplary fifty-acre array of (mostly) rare and foreign flora, were founded in 1826.

Apart from our quick sprint through the countryside, the two main highlights of my Tasmanian weekend could be considered to have spanned the entire range from low to high culture. Saturday night we spent in the Wrest Point casino. Having expected something like Las Vegas, I was struck by its low-key, low-pressure atmosphere. In the United States gambling is mythically linked with sex and power. In American casinos there is consequently a vast gulf between the in-group – the hard-faced dealers, the sleek, powerful pit bosses, the big money gamblers – and the ordinary tourists. In Tasmania the casino personnel are interchangeable with clerks or waitresses in any ordinary hotel anywhere in the country. The gambling is a good deal less frenetic too. In Reno or Las Vegas, an experienced blackjack player rarely spends more than half an hour at a single table. If his luck is bad, he cuts his losses. If it is good, he knows enough to quit while he is ahead. In Hobart the pattern is quite different. Most people seem simply to sit in one place until they have lost all their money or it's time to go home. Finally – and again in contrast to the American practice – no drinks are served at the tables here. This no doubt contributes to the relatively low level of emotional intensity. It also, however, suggests a rather different attitude on the part of the management. (The provision of free drinks is obviously calculated to reduce both a player's inhibitions and his skill.) Is this typical of Australian casinos, or is it a function of Tasmanian pokiness? I guess it's yet another thing I'll have to check out.

The morning after our big splurge we decided to do penance by playing the earnest tourist. Hobart is not a lively place on Sunday morning. Almost by accident we ended up at the state gallery. It would have been a shame had I missed it, because it was here I got the shock that put all the other local idiosyncrasies in context. Featured was a show of Tasmanian water-colour painting. As I walked through it, so soon after my confrontation with the Heidelbergers, I could hardly believe what I was seeing. I mentioned in the last journal entry the polarities of stance. In a centripetal culture – taking Canada as my type example – landscape painting tends to be characterized by a foreground focus, a low vantage point, an emphasis on the obtrusiveness of geographical features, and a vigorous denial of recession. The overall effect, in marked contrast to the (qualified) openness of the colonial Australian oeuvre, is one of almost claustrophobic enclosure. Why am I going into this? Because here on Tasmania, expecting vistas, what I found were all the stigmata of centripetality. The uphill vantage. The sense of being at the bottom of a bowl. The phallic mountain in the middle of the canvas.

The question is, of course, what does it mean? In my previous case studies, art has proven an almost infallible key to the way any given community constructs the self/other relation. Is Tasmania actually a distinct sub-culture, then, with a different social psychology than mainland Australia? And if so, why? I suppose the landscape itself may have something to do with it. Being surrounded by mountains does tend to make one feel a little crushed. However, one need only compare the paintings of nineteenth-century English artist John Glover, who didn't immigrate until very late in his career, with those of his younger contemporary, native-born W.C. Piguenit, to realize that there are different ways to "see" a mountainscape.

Where Glover paints supremely confident open vistas, Piguenit concentrates on deep, gloomy gorges, forbidding cloud-wreathed crags, and towering rock faces cutting off any glimpse of beyond. Whatever triggered the centripetalization process in the first place, it clearly had something to do with *being* Tasmanian, not just *seeing* Tasmania.

It wasn't just a historic phenomenon either. Contemporary artists manifest the same pattern. As in Canada, art here has now progressed from the passive *reflection* of centripetality to the active *management* of the anxieties that it entails. The claustrophobic landscape, in other words, is no longer so much depicted as deconstructed. It is interesting in this regard that photography has played such an important role in recent Tasmanian art. Insofar as a photograph literally freezes or "contains" its subject-matter, the use of photographs within a mixed media work or the juxtaposition of "real" and facsimile landscapes (see, for instance, Ray Arnold's *Florentine Valley: Displaced Landscape* [1984], or Marion Hardman's *Hill Series* [1978]; both are reproduced in Holmes, 1985: 504-505) underlines the artist/viewer's control over "nature." Self-announcing intervention can also achieve the same end. Arnold, for instance, uses mapping survey points in his works. Ann Harris tampers with her prints. David Stephenson makes photocollages by abutting series of contiguous but slightly mismatched shots. All these strategies are typical of the centripetal personality. Indeed, if it weren't for the specifics of content, the artists cited here could easily be mistaken for Canadians.

What about other forms of culture? I will have to take a second look at Australian literature now to see whether there is anything distinctive about the Tasmanians. I will also have to consider whether there was anything different about Tasmanian history, apart from the environment in which it took place, that might explain this unexpected divergence.

Tasmania as a Subculture

A key difference in the social psychological signatures of centripetal and centrifugal cultures has to do with attitudes toward time and space. Where the centrifugal personality seeks its meaning through extension, the centripetal one, turned perforce inward, does its questing vertically, in history (see G. McGregor, 1985, Chapter 11). A first point to determine, then, is whether Tasmania derives its sense of being-in-the-world from *elsewhere* or *elsewhen*. Like much else about the state, unfortunately, the question of orientation is not easy to decide. There is, for one thing, an overlay of "Australian" ideology which complicates if it doesn't actually obscure the local development. More important, there is also the problem of self-consciousness: the difference between what a community "thinks" and what it betrays.

For Tasmania the question of progenitors is particularly ticklish. Judging at least by public rhetoric, if this state is fascinated by its history, it is in a negative sense only, as something shameful to be hidden and denied. "While the rest of Australia came to accommodate itself to its past through a variety of mediating myths which sanitised history and made it ultimately irrelevant to the present," says Kay Daniels, "in Tasmania the idea persisted that the past had to be repressed and forgotten . . . In other states historic buildings languish for want of funds, decay or suffer neglect . . . But in Tasmania [there has been a] *wish to destroy* the physical remains of convict history as a deliberate, chosen way of wiping out the past itself" (1983: 3). *To wish* is, of course, quite different than *to will*. Even without dragging Freud into the picture, it seems obvious, if only as a matter of common sense, that the negative obsession is simply the reverse face of the positive one. Tasmania's desire to forget, far from signalling an extravert's *disinterest* in history, can be read as an admission that, as Daniels puts it, the past is "still important." This does not, on the other hand, solve our problem with classification, since the evinced perception of space is just as problematic as the relationship with time.

In Canada the inward turning is so clearly explicable as an aftereffect of the recoil from nature that the pattern seems not merely omnipresent but "natural." In Tasmania, however, the attitude toward the landscape is not nearly so straightforward. On the one side is the fact that this region has since colonial times been identified, and advertised, as a bastion of "natural beauty." "While nature in Tasmania is far from benign," says Daniels, "it has attributes which differentiate it from the mainland and which made it more easily able to be assimilated into the early nineteenth-century consciousness" (4). Counter this, on the other hand, are the efforts made by the early settlers to transform the purportedly sublime native environment into an exact facsimile of the lost homeland. "[T]he use of hawthorn trees for hedges, the suitability of the temperate conditions for fruit-growing and the construction of English gardens, and the presence of very substantial houses, were all used to evoke . . . another Merrie England," says Lloyd Robson. "The general picture painted by Tasmanian publicists was that of the sole colony in the Australias where the conditions were 'English'" (1985: 73). If the Tasmanians "loved" nature, therefore, it was perhaps only because it presented itself to them in a form that allowed them to deny the "natural." Even this, moreover, may fall somewhat short of the truth. A few of the less savoury aspects of the Tasmanian response suggest, albeit covertly, that the celebration of nature may in fact be as much of a red herring as the decrial of history. I am speaking, of course, of the genocidal extinction of the native population of the island. Since there is no reason to suppose that the Tasmanian aborigines were more dangerous, ultimately, than their mainland cousins, the extremity of the colonial response in this single case (the mainlanders were hardly innocent of atrocities [see p. 138 above], but nowhere else was the massacre so systematic) suggests that the reaction was more hysterical than pragmatic. It is perhaps possible that, for all their public enthusiasm, the Tasmanians privately experienced nature in exactly the same way the Canadians did – as an alien and ultimately life-threatening element.

Why? Inasmuch as it comprises the single most striking difference between the Tasmanian and the type Australian environment, on reconsideration I would still have to fall back on the claustrophic effect of the mountains. This doesn't mean that I am arguing for simple geographic determinism. It's a matter, rather, of the interplay *between* nature and culture. For all their differences (Van Diemen's Land was by far the most notorious of the penal colonies, both because of the kind of convicts sent there and because of the harshness of its regime) the earliest settlements in both places were self-identified with/against the "idea" of imprisonment. Where, on the mainland, the spaciousness of the landscape would tend, at least as a primary effect, to exacerbate the prisoner's negative identification with his enforced (whether real or symbolic) "enclosure," however, the sense of encompassment one feels in proximity to a literally over-whelming landscape would tend to reinforce and even, in a sense, to normalize the individual's interiorization. Some commentators have suggested that Tasmanian convicts were in fact more "submissive, unprotesting, [and] apolitical" than their mainland brothers (Daniels, 1983: 5), but even without hard evidence of *original* psychological differences there is considerable support for the argument in aspects of *contemporary* social psychology. Though Australia as a whole has been notably prone to xenophobia, where, as noted, the mainland attitude to prospective and particularly Asian invaders is tinged with an element of sexual disgust, the Tasmanian attitude toward the mainlander, in its combination of resentment *and* fascination (Robson, 1983), resembles quite strikingly the Canadians' love/hate relationship with their American neighbours (G. McGregor, 1985, Chapter 9).

As far as its social history is concerned, then, there are plausible if not irrefutable reasons for entertaining the notion that Tasmania, in contradistinction to the Australian mainland, could be a centripetal culture. Given the privileged relationship I have posited between literature and communal consciousness, on the other hand, I cannot claim to have made an airtight or even a prima facie case unless I can show the presence of at least a few diagnostic markers in Tasmanian writing. This is unfortunately much easier said than done. The Tasmanian oeuvre is not large to start with, and what there is, being neither packaged differently nor discussed separately from other Australian writing, is for the most part invisible. Even when there is some attempt to set out and to celebrate the local product, local chauvinism tends to obscure the question of "belonging." Of the fifty-eight identified contributors to an anthology of "Tasmanian" poetry entitled *Effects of Light* (V. Smith and Scott, 1985), for instance, only nineteen were born or spent any part of their childhood on the island; fifteen immigrated as adults, while twenty-four were short-timers, passers-through, or – even worse – outsiders for whom Tasmania was nothing but an idea.

Despite these difficulties, a little excavating turns up at least a few interesting indicators. It is significant in the first place that Tasmania produces more poets than novelists. The preference and especially the talent for poetic modes, as Russell McDougall points out (1987), is one of the key features differentiating the Canadian from the sprawl-oriented Australian. It is even more significant that the best known of these, A.D. Hope, is also the country's best-known apologist for classical formalism against "modernist" subjectivity (see Docker, 1974; also "Modernism in Australia," pp. 171-75 below). Although space prohibits a full review of the phenomenon at this time, one of the most notable findings of my Canadian study was that the centripetal personality, frightened yet fascinated by otherness, by both choice and propensity tends to mediate his/her relations with the at-large by emphasizing the public over the personal, the ritual over the casual, in all those social activities, from art through religion, which imply or entail self-transcendence; that is, to put it more literally, "going between" (see Appendix A; also G. McGregor, 1985, Chapter 12). That the Tasmanian can be seen to evince the same preference, no matter how vestigially, is a strong argument in favour of centripetality – especially given the much-touted casualness of Australian culture in general.

What about prose? Here we come up against the fact that the one "Tasmanian" novel included in the preliminary study, Christopher Koch's *The Boys in the Island*, did not seem to differ in any important fashion from Australian mainstream norms. This could be partly due to an original misreading. I interpreted the protagonist's obsession with the big city in that book as a variant on the typifying desire to escape. Given the imagery, however, it might equally well be taken to represent a kind of gravitation toward the human centre (see G. McGregor, 1985: 85). The same kind of ambiguity hampers elucidation of Koch's treatment of the mateship theme. If Australians are ambivalent about "connecting," Canadians are no less so. There are, on the other hand, differences in the way we people our relational myths – the way we conceptualize what we are relating *with*. This is particularly true where a masculine typos is concerned. While for the Australian the dynamic male represents an unattainable ideal self, for the Canadian, especially insofar as he resembles the American "hero," he is virtually always construed as other. The question is, then, what relationship does the dream-friend in Koch's book bear to the young protagonist? Depending as it does upon relative rather than absolute differences, this matter is almost impossible to resolve one way or the other. That he should so strikingly resemble the Australian "good mate" – a fact I previously took to confirm his derivation from the bush tradition – in truth says nothing, since we tend to construct our images of otherness from the projected images of those who comprise our most immanent "real" others. Does this mean, then, that there is ultimately *no* way to decide whether *The Boys in the Island* fits or violates the "Australian" model? Perhaps. Certainly it makes things no easier that centrifugal and centripetal are related as mirror images, not outright opposites. If we look elsewhere in Koch's oeuvre, however, we find some useful supporting evidence for the latter interpretation.

Apart from its emphasis on formal structuring, one of the characterizing features of the Canadian novel is a kind of ostentatious authorial reserve. *Like* the structuring, this feature is directly attributable to centripetality. In a culture where "going between" is not just problematic but in a sense taboo, the practice of art is perforce associated with risk to the self. In order to escape retribution for hubris, the writer hence tries to create the illusion that s/he is not really "creating" at all. S/he hides behind an "objective" observer like a journalist or historian. S/he presents the artifact as "found" or frivolous. Or s/he composes his/her text in such a way that any "meaning," far from intentional, appears to reside within a fortuitous concatenation of "facts" (see G. McGregor, 1985, Chapter 10; 1986). Given the psychological as well as the aesthetic implications of such strategies, it is obviously significant that Koch's best-known novel, *The Year of Living Dangerously*, should present an almost type case in narrative displacement. The author hides behind the speaking persona of Cookie, who in turn hides behind the experiencing consciousness of Guy Hamilton, who is himself absolved from responsibility for the "story" when it emerges, not least through the lurking presence of the Wayang shadow puppets throughout the book, that his experience has somehow been mediated through, if not created in, Billy's personnel files. Even before we get to its content, then, the form of this novel in itself is strongly suggestive of a centripetal orientation.

Its themes are equally suggestive. Recurrent throughout the Canadian oeuvre is a kind of identity fable wherein alternate life-modes are elucidated through an exploration of the relationship *to* or *between* passive (fool-saint, cripple, or freak) and active (gunslinger or magician) role models (see G. McGregor, 1985, chapters 8 and 9). This is exactly the fable that Koch gives us as well. Sukarno, the king-god with feet of clay, versus Billy Kwan, the half-Chinese (and therefore half "feminine") dwarf, with Guy, alter ego for the reader, caught uncomprehendingly between. If there *is* a difference from the Canadian model, it is such, moreover, as to suggest a more rather than a less extreme version of centripetality. Where the Canadian writer is generally careful to maintain the protagonist's distance from the fool-saint in a formal if not an emotional sense, in Koch's book the centre of consciousness slides almost irresistibly back and forth between the "normal" and the "abnormal" protagonists, such that Billy is not merely Guy's shadow but quite literally his other self.

The divergence seems even more significant when we note almost the identical pattern in another of Tasmania's very small stock of novels. In James McQueen's *Hook's Mountain* – a tightly structured, psychologically oriented, multi-vocal novel of a type exceedingly rare in the Australian corpus – the relationship between the passive and active exemplars is no longer merely exemplary (despite the token presence of a third, more "normal" voice), having itself emerged onto centre stage. It is interesting that McQueen's version of the fool-saint is again an abnormally small man. It is also interesting that his active typos is construed as the classic Australian bushman-cum-soldier. Most interesting of all, however, insofar as it reflects on the radical negativism of the Tasmanian fable of identity, is the fact that the erstwhile retiring Arthur in the end takes upon himself the mantle of his active idol, just like Koch's Billy Kwan – and with equally suicidal results. Unlike the Canadian, who has managed over the years to work out a kind of accommodation with his/her enforced passivity (see G. McGregor, 1985, Chapter 12), the Tasmanian, it would seem, feels it necessary to try to emulate his/her significant other, despite the deeply held knowledge that s/he is incapable of doing so. (The really poignant thing, of course, is that the "other" is not capable of it either.)

What are we to make of all this? At the very least it would seem incontrovertible that at least two Tasmanian novels express a "centripetal" world view. How far, though, can we generalize from a sample so small? And there aren't many more. Being "scientific," one would have to conclude that the case is not just unproven but unprovable. Speaking personally, on the other hand, I am inclined to feel that all the half-evidences add up to a rather convincing picture. I don't think it is coincidental, for instance, that the single anomaly among the women's novels reviewed above in the section on women's writing – Georgia Savage's *Slate and Me and Blanche McBride* (see fn 3, p. 85) – is by a Tasmanian, nor do I think it coincidental that the particular markers of its anomalousness – its multivocality, its psychological complexity, and its ambivalent playing on the theme of good/bad, passive/active "twins" – are strikingly reminiscent of McQueen's book. And besides, there's all that art. Received opinion notwithstanding, in the end I have to believe that those wall-like and phallic mountains speak louder than public protestations about the beauties of nature.

MELBOURNE

Gold may have made the fortunes of only a minority, but it had an enduring influence on the aspirations and ambitions of Melburnians. For a decade the city became the capital of El Dorado of the south, as colonists never tired of pointing out. They forgot, or did not know, the sinister implications of such a comparison. Not content with having ravished the Americas of their vast wealth, the Spanish vainly sought the fabled city. In Victoria, the golden city was a mirage in the vision of so many of the 1850s settlers and migrants, rushing from field to field in the hope of making a quick fortune: contemporaries estimated that a good half of the diggers barely recouped their costs, and that the rest (apart from the fortunate minority) actually paid in money, health or even with their lives, in the fruitless search for gold.

Paul de Serville, "Nineteenth-Century Melbourne"

Melbourne, physically, seems far more coherent than most of the urban centres in Australia. The inner city, a seven- or eight-kilometre square extending from Parkville in the northwest to St Kilda in the southeast, is (except, to some extent, the southerly section tucked in between the river, the parklands, and the bay) laid out almost entirely in a rectilinear grid pattern serviced by a complex and efficient tram and train system. Despite this, one still gets the impression in looking at a map or aerial photo of a subtly discoordinate patchwork of separate pieces. It is interesting, for instance, that the city centre, an almost obsessively rationalized latticework of streets eight blocks by four, is set at an angle to the predominantly north-south orientation of the surrounding areas. It is also interesting to note the extent to which it is buffered from its environs, on the south by the river, on the east by parks and gardens, and on the west by the railway yards. The main roads fan out at erratic angles from this central bottleneck. Again there is the sense of endless suburbs sprawling out over the countryside, becoming increasingly disorderly with their distance from the core.

Quirks of layout aside, the ambience of the city is both gracious and dignified. The streets are broad and often tree-lined. Front there is in abundance, but of a more substantial – more *serious* – type than much of what I have seen elsewhere. The public architecture is particularly imposing. Landmarks include the Neoclassical State Parliament Building, with its breastwork of Doric columns, the Italian Renaissance Old Treasury Building, the copper-domed French Renaissance Flinders Street Railway Station, the triple-spired Gothic Revival St Patrick's Roman Catholic Cathedral, and last but not least, the ornately facaded, fantastically embellished Princess Theatre. Domestic architecture is similarly frontal. I have been particularly taken with the iron-lace-encrusted working class terrace houses of the inner suburbs, and their more prosperous cousins, the multistoreyed, definitively verandahed and parapeted Victorian row houses near the University of Melbourne.

This element of surficiality I keep commenting upon is an aspect or close relation of what, I have recently discovered, Australian architect-cum-cultural critic Robin Boyd, calls "featurism." Though his definition emphasizes aesthetic rather than psychological aspects, and though he is more concerned with substance than with preferential disposition in space ("Featurism is not simply a decorative technique," he says in an acerbic little book called *The Australian Ugliness*, "it starts in concepts and extends upwards through the parts to the numerous trimmings. It may be defined as the subordination of the essential whole and the accentuation of selected separate features" [1963: 23]), it is clear from his descriptions that the phenomenon under consideration – at least as it appears in Australia – is largely concerned with, or constituted by, external elements. "The terrace buildings" of 1880s Melbourne, he says, "were plain and solid: stucco on brick or bluestone, and the ornament was confined to a perforated skin of iron standing in front of the front verandahs . . . The balustrades . . . offered the broadest scope, but from there the ornamental iron crept up the thin, fluted columns and edged along the upper bressumers, hanging in festoons like pressed wisteria . . . For [the richer mansions] Italianate was the only accepted costume, and it sometimes inflated even single-storey cottages with extraordinary pretensions until they dripped with plaster encrustations round every marble feature" (60). How does he explain this "love of display, so inconsistent with the character and situation of settlers in a new country" (61)? The first great building boom in Melbourne took place in the aftermath of the gold rush, and much of the excessiveness, as Boyd indicates, can be attributed to the natural desires of the newly rich to make as much splash as possible. The bravado is so striking, however, as to suggest that it documents an underlying uneasiness – also natural among a people whose fortunes were built largely on luck – about the unpredictability of nature and the vagaries of fate. Whatever the reasons, colonial Victorians were obviously obsessed with putting on a good face. "Motives came and went," says Boyd, "styles came and went . . . [but] Featurism remained unchanged" (61).

Partly, I suppose, because of its civility (among other things, this is the first place I've hit where off-campus bookstores rise one whit above the militantly middling level of how-to manuals, American best-sellers, fad philosophy, and popular history) but also because of the climate, I feel more at home in Melbourne than in most of the other places we have been. This is not an entirely positive feature, unfortunately. While certainly no cooler than autumn in southern Ontario, winter weather in coastal Victoria is damp and even raw. And central heating seems to be a rarity. The flat where I have been staying is equipped with one feeble electric heater that has to be dragged from room to room. I don't think I've been warm once for the whole week I've been here. The lowest blow was the fact that the unit came equipped with a bathtub, the first I'd seen since arriving in the country. (Australians prefer showers.) On checking in I immediately began to fantasize about long, therapeutic soaks. The reality has fallen somewhat short of my expectations. The bathroom is so frigid, even with my token heater turned up as high as it will go, that bathing is a teeth-chattering ordeal.

The human elements have been much warmer. Working my way through my list of contacts at the various universities in the area, I was gratified to find them free with both information and hospitality. I have been pleasantly surprised throughout the whole trip by the almost universally ungrudging helpfulness of Australian academics. I had expected to encounter a certain amount of reserve, especially since I am in a sense trespassing on their turf. What I have found instead is a rather peculiar eagerness to know what *I* think about *their* culture. This could be, I suppose, because many of them aren't sure what *they* think about their culture – or indeed whether they should think of their culture at all. Australian Studies is in its infancy. Not only is it the new boy on the block but, cutting as it does across a number of fields, it "looks" different than the traditional disciplines. This is enough in itself to trigger a certain amount of defensiveness. And to make matters worse, many of its own adherents seem to be struggling against the unvoiced concern that self-examination might simply be parochialism. The status of the field is rendered even more equivocal by the fact that it has been relegated almost entirely to "soft" faculties like English, History, and Humanities. Apart from a few Sydney sociologists, virtually no Australian social scientists seem to be working on their own culture. Much has been written lately on the migrant phenomenon, and even more on the aborigines, but social scientific studies of the life modes of modern white Australians are few and far between. This isn't to denigrate the work that is being done on the other side of the fence. It does, however, tend to produce a somewhat biased picture, if only because of its privileging of certain types of subjects and certain classes of data. It also suggests a feeling on the part of the Australians themselves that introspection is as difficult and ambiguous an undertaking for the community at large as it is for the private individual. As such it is more akin to the unrational arts than to the objective sciences.

While in Melbourne I have taken the opportunity to push a step or two further my investigation into Australian painting. Noting that the state gallery was featuring an exhibition of Australian modernism, I made this one of the first stops on my agenda. My initial reaction to the show was disappointment. It seemed to me lacking in both quality and focus. The non-representational pieces – which in North America would be considered to carry the burden of the modernist aesthetic – were a particularly poor lot, in many cases barely surpassing the level of art school exercises. They ranged from highly cerebral and rather laboured early experiments in cubism to a motley selection of scruffy, self-conscious, calligraphic and gestural paintings that were undoubtedly intended as abstract expressionism. Lacking entirely the buoyant self-confidence of their American models, these latter were unpleasant without actually being disturbing. Too frenetic to even seem healthily self-indulgent, they struck me as providing a peculiarly nihilistic version of Australian sprawl.

One facet of the show that *did* strike me as at least interesting, on the other hand, was a fairly large body of figurative works. Again supplementing on-the-spot observations with a bit of dabbling in secondary sources, I have determined that figurative expressionism was, at least until the sixties, the only modernist mode in which the Australians achieved any real competence or originality. The corpus seems to be divided into two phases. The first, stimulated – so critical opinion would have it – by the terror and turmoil of the war, comprises a sizable number of pieces (done mostly by Melburnians, interestingly enough) depicting the terror and turmoil of life in the modern city. The second is, at least on the surface, somewhat more benign, the artists having moved out into the countryside again. In both cases, however, the sense of environmental threat is expressed less through its direct representation than through its effect on its inhabitants. In town and out (and it is interesting that the suburb, the "safe" zone, has been almost entirely excluded from the oeuvre) this is a world which *makes people monstrous.* Albert Tucker's concupiscent homunculi, Russell Drysdale's stickmen, John Perceval's frog-children, Arthur Boyd's leering wraiths and wild-eyed dwarves: there is hardly a "normal" figure to be seen anywhere. The personae of these paintings are caricatures – diminished, distorted, perverted.

Reinforcing the impression of a humanity damaged by its transactions are a number of recurrent themes having to do with the relations *between* individuals. This is a world, as well, in which, ultimately, everyone is alone. Even in the cityscapes, as Virginia Spate points out in her introduction to the 1984 Sydney Biennale catalogue, the sense of a social life, of collective experience or co-operative action, is not merely devalued but missing almost entirely. "Figures tend to be shown alone, or in a hostile or indifferent environment; if they are depicted together their relationship is characterised by menace, separateness, or less often, violence. They are rarely shown looking at one another, let alone interacting" (Spate, 1984: 7).

The *dérangement* of complicity also disturbs the relation between work and world. One doesn't know how to "take" these paintings. Partly it has to do with a destabilization of the iconography. There is an obvious fascination, for instance, with the passive and/or subordinate figures of aborigines, women, and children. One is also, however, struck by the ambivalence of both the subject *in* the painting (the children are evil and innocent; the women both sexual monsters and sexual prey) and the painting subject, whose feelings seem to run the gamut from guilt to open hostility. What this suggests is not identification but (in Derrida's sense) *différance.* Which shouldn't surprise us, I suppose. The victim figure may in fact invite a displacement of the artist's own apprehensions, but inasmuch as she also denotes otherness *righteously* reviled, she is pre-construed as a scapegoat, not a potential image of self.

This doesn't mean, of course, that the self doesn't appear in these paintings. Indeed, it's the sense of self which, present or absent, localizes most of the tensions in this oeuvre, the *same* tensions – and indeed the same sense of self – that one finds everywhere in film, in folklore, and in fiction. What is this creature? It's masculine, there's no question about that, but it's also, and equally important, a self beleaguered. Carrying implications quite different from those of the "natural" victim, its shadow and antithesis, it is bodied forth at its most typical as the dynamic hero – again: the explorer, the bushranger, the digger – who, like Crocodile Dundee, has been rendered passive and helpless by the "plot."

Next question: what does it all mean? Quite apart from their reworking of the Australian legend, the figurative expressionists add an interesting coda to the ongoing debate with the land. The city in these paintings is clearly inimical. The countryside, in contrast, though certainly bleak enough, has in a sense been demythicized, turned into geometry. As a result it registers more as an absence than as a threatening presence. Why the difference in treatment? Received opinion would simply put it down to the Australian's love of nature. But if this is the case, how do we explain the strikingly detrimental effects which are obvious even in those works most inclined to sentimentalize rural life? Drysdale's bush families, for instance, have been praised for their monumental dignity, their heroic resistance in the face of adversity, but they are also quite clearly the losers in a battle to wrest more than the barest and meanest living from the land. "In the emphasis he placed on the heart-breaking aspects of country life," says Gary Catalano, "Drysdale was surely the custodian of Henry Lawson's melancholy vision" (1985: 26). So why make the land itself so benign? Perhaps it has something to do with the reluctance to cognize the enemy that I noted in connection with Lindy Chamberlain. The city harlot is safely offset with the socially constructed figure of "mum," but (m)other Nature is so potent that the only thing to be done with her is to wishfully insist upon her benevolence. The concomitant insistence that humans *in* nature are at best disabled and at worst outright monsters seems to suggest that the ploy is not altogether successful.

Modernism in Australia

Modernism had a hard time of it in Australia. Modern poetry, in particular, was attacked on both moral and aesthetic grounds from the twenties right through the forties. Part of the problem, especially in the earlier years, was simply an ignorance exacerbated by distance and culture lag. Lacking the theoretical background to grasp the intentions behind the technique, even the most open-minded were inclined to find it "unintelligible." Part, however, was an entrenched reactionism to which the popular misunderstanding merely added fuel. Capitalizing on public fears of "foreign" decadence in the period following federation (see White, 1981: 143), mainstream literati found it easy to dismiss the new poetics as, at best, a "camouflage for laziness and incompetence" (McQueen, 1979a: 8). This does not, of course, explain *why*, in such a (purportedly) politically "advanced" country (see Chapter 4, *"National Fictions,"* pp. 254-64 below), the response to what was in essence merely a natural outgrowth of High Romantic individualism should be so unequivocally negative – why, indeed, the most "radical" of Australian literary movements during this century have been conservative and backward-looking rather than, as has generally been the case even in North America, liberal and progressive.

This shared conservatism has made strange bedfellows in the history of the anti-modernist movement in Australia. The first and perhaps most strident attack was launched by the *Vision* group gathered around Norman and Jack Lindsay in the early twenties. Describing themselves as Vitalists, much given to bohemian behaviour and "uninihibited" subject-matter (Norman Lindsay himself favoured fleshy nudes and cavorting satyrs), this clique was most potent as a defender of the faith precisely because its anti-establishment stance on matters social and sexual made it difficult for would-be modernist apologists to accuse them of stodginess. "While [*Vision*] rejected Modernism, it was up-to-date in a way that almost no other local publication had managed," says McQueen. "Its contributors scoured the cultural presses of the world in search of decadence to attack. The cadavers of literature, music, art and science were dissected with amused horror . . . [*Vision* shared with] Modernism . . . a 'violent rejection of the society that had begotten the 1914-18 war.' [But] where the Dadaists and early Surrealists accepted irrationality as their inspiration, *Vision* ached for Classical certainties. Civilisation had to be defended by reasserting its hard won lessons of ordered, yet vital creativity" (1979a: 19).

This combination of classicism and cerebralized neo-primitivism can be seen in a sense literally to set the agenda for most of the later resisters. When the Jindyworobaks turn to the aborigines rather than the European masters for their inspiration (see p. 139, above), when A.D. Hope combines formalism with an emphasis on platonic-cum-Jungian sexuality (Docker, 1974, Chapter 3), like the *Vision* group they are rejecting naturalness while seeming to worship nature. Quite apart from its sexist implications (Modjeska, 1981: 16ff.), the psychosymbolic bias of this strategy has some important implications for the "meaning" of Australian anti-modernism. The key question here is what was actually being reacted *against*? Where those involved have tended to rationalize their distaste in social and even political terms (the social realist movement of the thirties merely updated twenties claims that "free verse spelled social anarchy" [McQueen, 1979a: 11]), H.P. Heseltine's assessment hints that there was a somewhat less measured side to the response. "It is my contention," he says, "that Australian literature is signalized by its . . . recognition of the nature of the social contract and by its long-standing awareness of the primal energies of mankind, an awareness which has known little of the sweetening and freshness of early Romantic optimism. Australia's literary heritage is based on a unique combination of glances into the pit and the erection of safety fences to prevent any toppling in" (1962: 39-40).

The message emerges even more clearly if we compare the attack on poetry to the – initially, at least – somewhat more temperate reaction to modernist art. For the first few decades of its existence, modernist painting in Australia was safe, timid, derivative, and almost wholly intellectual. It was also simply not a bone of contention. If it failed to win much in the way of either critical or popular support, it also failed – even in its more radically non-traditional forms – to stir up much furor. "They met with little fuss," says Robert Hughes of the Sydney cubist-constructivist group that congealed around Grace Cowley and Rah Fitzelle in the early thirties. "[Y]ears later the public found the work of Dobell and Tucker actively offensive, but it shrugged at the constructivists" (1970: 252). Why the anomalous tolerance on the part of an establishment that found free verse literally demoralizing? Partly, one supposes, it was because, in Hughes' words, their abstraction was so "mild." More important, however, it seems clear – if one compares both the concurrent case of literature and the later case of figurative expressionism – that the non-reaction related specifically to the fact that it was *not* subjective. "During the 1920s and 1930s," says Bernard Smith, "the modern movement in Australia[n art] tended to be classical and impersonal in its manifestations, preoccupied with the achievement of significant form" (1971: 221).

The implications of all this are confirmed by subsequent developments. In the late thirties, after decades of disinterest, the resistance suddenly hit the fan. In 1937, in his opening address to the annual exhibition of the Victorian Artists' Society, Prime Minister Robert Menzies called for the establishment of an Academy to stem the increasingly evident deterioration in public taste. In 1939, J.S. MacDonald, director of the Victorian state gallery, responded to the Melbourne *Herald* exhibition of European post-impressionist painting with the statement that "most modern art was produced by 'degenerates and perverts'" (Serle, 1973: 164). And in 1942, the aging Lionel Lindsay published a diatribe entitled *Addled Art* in which, in Geoffrey Serle's words, "he set out to prove that Picasso, Matisse and the surrealists were part of a vast Jewish conspiracy" (164). Why the *volte face*? We find a clue to the reaction in one of the country's most celebrated art scandals. In 1943, a European-trained academist by the name of William Dobell was awarded the annual Archibald Prize for portraiture. In January 1944, two of his unsuccessful competitors instituted legal action against the Gallery Trustees on the grounds that the winning entry was "'not a portrait but . . . a caricature'" (in McQueen, 1979a: 43). The case failed, but in its course managed to stimulate a level of vituperation rarely equalled since the war on modern poetry waged by the *Vision* group almost a quarter century earlier. "One of the plaintiffs' witnesses," says McQueen, "a prominent Sydney doctor, testified that the picture represent[ed] 'the body of a man who had died in that position and had remained in that position for a period of some months and had dried up'" (43). The real irony was that Dobell (described by Hughes as "an occasionally interesting but always minor eclectic" [1970: 183]) neither was, nor claimed to be, a modernist. The portrait in question was mildly distorted, but far from non-representational. The only way to explain the extent and the heat of the controversy it triggered, therefore, is to suppose that the Australian public, while quite ready to accept the geometrical fantasies of the abstractionists, were roused to fury when an artist took such liberties as to suggest that the human form was not immutable – or even worse, that one's being was somehow a function of "psychology."

The propensity could equally well explain the *general* reaction to modernist painting throughout this period. During the war years, Smith notes, the "temper of the contemporary movement in art changed from one of classical impersonality to one of romantic involvement" (1971: 221). It is evident, reviewing responses to the figurative expressionists ("The public refused to buy or see their work; this indifference was occasionally relieved by a bout of vandalism, as when a visitor threw green paint at some of Nolan's pictures" [Hughes, 1970: 137]), that this was a change the public didn't like one bit. Why? Because it licensed subjectivity. And subjectivity was something the average Australian preferred to pretend did not exist. The "wholesome" view of life was the view that kept to the sunny surface of things (see White, 1981: 143; see also Eagle, 1982, re the preference for exteriorization in Australian art) – the view that celebrated the sane, the solid, and the normal. Hence the resistance to anything that hinted, be it ever so subtly, that a gap might exist between appearance and "reality." Long before the forties, the one aspect of modernism that unfailingly attracted the rancour of both its foes *and* its friends was surrealism. Lionel Lindsay summarized the opinion of his whole generation when he described the mode – "emanating from Freud's 'dirty mind'" – as "decadence without equal since it aimed 'To see life foully'" (McQueen, 1979a: 42). It is clear from the shrillness of such epithets that for all the pretense of protecting the at-large from profanation (*pro*-modernist Adrian Lawlor, for instance, complained that surrealism "'falsif[ied] the world as *object*'" [McQueen: 28]), the real concern of the protestant is the protection of, or perhaps from, his own inner integrity. To the extent that the landscape is not only *equivalent* to the inscape, but also as threatening to the (masculine) sense of self, the Australian cannot bear the suggestion carried by any form of distortion that it(they) is(are) perverse, irrational, or – especially – beyond conscious control.

It is in the light of this anxiety about interiority that one has to read the notorious "Ern Malley" affair of 1944. "What happened," says McQueen, "was that two young anti-Modernist poets, Harold Stewart and James McAuley, made up some verses which they attributed to the recently deceased 'Ern Malley' whose sister 'Ethel' sent the poem 'Durer: Innsbruck, 1495' to Max Harris, the Adelaide-based editor of the ultra-Modernist journal, *Angry Penguins*. Harris, who adored Durer, took the bait and brought out an 'Ern Malley' special, complete with a Surrealist cover painting by Sidney.Nolan, and an editorial announcing the discovery of 'one of the most outstanding poets that we have produced'" (88). What is interesting about this hoax is less the fact that it was successful – a circumstance greatly celebrated not only by the anti-modernists themselves but by a much-amused public – than the light it casts on the subtext to Australian cultural history. McAuley in particular is an interesting figure, not because he represents the forces of entrenched and militantly know-nothing reaction, but precisely because he doesn't. Having himself dabbled in modernist modes at an earlier period, he can perhaps be seen more in the light of an apostate than a "natural" enemy (see Dutton, 1985, chapter 9). This makes somewhat more plausible his opponents' claim that the poems "worked" only because "their authors had allowed their unconscious to dictate the lines" (McQueen: 91; see Dunstan, 1973: 246ff for a summary of responses). In suggesting a more personal motive for the masquerade, however, it also connects the Ern Malley affair with much broader issues of social psychology. This takes us, in fact, right back to Heseltine's invocation of "the pit." It is not too fantastic to see McAuley's attack on modernism as a displacement of the anxiety he experienced in practicing it. One could, indeed, say of McAuley exactly what Geoffrey Dutton says of A.D. Hope. His "enmity towards modernism was based on style. It symbolized his own internal conflicts, in which a turbulent Romantic sensibility is caged by a formal syntax and verse technique. David Brooks has percipiently expressed this in a review ... 'Bars of iambic pentameter ... shield us from (or is it allow us to glimpse?) a panther of unresolved emotion prowling behind them'" (1985: 161). Once the bars were removed – which was, of course, what modernism threatened to do – who knew what would emerge.

A final footnote to this discussion: in the last intertext I suggested that Australians in general do better with novels than with poems. Following on the above, however, one might speculate that the relative preference is due as much to the fact that poetry is the most personal of literary genres – and therefore the most in *need* of formal constraints – as it is to any purely technical inaptitude. It is intriguing to note in this connection that since 1961 James McAuley has been living in Tasmania.

CANBERRA

The Griffins' drawings showed a city and a suburbs composed of interlocking circles and hexagons. At the center lay two axes at right angles, a land axis running northeast from Capitol Hill to Mount Ainslie, and a water axis running southeast from Black Mountain along the river. The Molonglo would be transformed into a chain of lakes and basins accessible to the people. From Capitol Hill would run two principal avenues, one to the north of the land axis and one to its east, intersecting with the water axis to form a triangle occupied by national institutions. The northern avenue would continue to a hill where municipal activities would cluster, and from there to suburbs of radial layout; the eastern avenue would lead to a commercial center and railway station. The avenues and waters, the placing of national and municipal and commercial activities, all bore an orderly relationship to Griffin's two axes; the axes, he declared, delighted at the harmony of geometry with nature, were "determined by the most important natural features of the site." It was his tender reading of the landscape that appealed to most of the assessors.

K.S. Inglis, "Ceremonies in a Capital Landscape"

Perhaps his concept was too swaggering and ambitious from the start, as many asserted. In any case it never had the opportunity to prove itself. The suburban areas were not strong elements of Griffin's plan, but these, characteristically of Australia, grew most rapidly. By the time of the Second World War they were Spanishy, shaded, and cosy. Then wooden war-time cottages occupied acres of treeless grounds on the less favoured side of town, and afterwards new suburbs grew almost as undisciplined as any other Australian city . . . [In 1954] The centre was still dry and empty, Parliament House was still the "provisional" 1927 building next door to the permanent site, and as ill-assorted a group of offices, banks and commercial buildings as ever were built – blue tiles, bacon-striped stone, yellow porcelain, concrete grilles, aluminium – began to disgrace the once-sleepy, arcaded Civic

Centre. There were no effective building regulations. The airport reception building was a wooden shed.

Robin Boyd, *The Australian Ugliness*

Canberra is a totally artificial city. At Federation the rivalry between Sydney and Melbourne was so intense that neither could countenance the idea that the other should house the new national parliament. A Capital Territory was consequently designated at a compromise location in the highlands of central New South Wales. The story of its development from sheep pasture to metropolis is so absurd and yet so typical that despite its historical *a*typicality, Canberra could almost be seen as a paradigmatic exemplification of Australian urban planning.

In 1911 an international competition was announced to find a design for the city. The winner was Chicago architect Walter Burley Griffin, a former associate of Frank Lloyd Wright. A government committee subsequently decided that Griffin's plan was impractical and put forth an alternative of its own. Outraged at such presumption on the part of amateurs, the Australian architectural community, which had hitherto been distinctly lukewarm, swung its weight behind Griffin. Public outcry ensued. Finally, after a change in government in 1913, the American was invited to Australia and appointed Federal Capital Director of design and construction. His problems were far from over, however. For seven years he was hindered at every turn by the bureaucrats whose plan had been rejected. By 1920 all he had been able to accomplish was the laying down of some of the main roads. At the end of that year Griffin's enemies finally had their way: the position of Director was abolished and the task of building the capital fell to an uneasy alliance of civil servants and private entrepreneurs.

In the years that followed, the original conception receded further and further from view as piecemeal development replaced the holistic vision of its creator. The basic layout was retained – looking at the map we can still see the spider-webbed triaxial core that here replaces Colonel Light's rectilinear grid – but abandoned entirely was the vision of a rational and integrated architecture. The public buildings, not one of which was designed by Griffin himself, represent such a motley collection of styles that no matter what their value as individual entities – and some of them, like the High Court with its soaring glass walls, truly are admirable – together they create a visual cacophony. The result, even though Griffin's lake was finally filled in the mid-fifties, is a cityscape like all Australian cityscapes, where a vestigial remnant of "foreign" order sits precariously at the centre of a dis-orderly sprawl.

At right angles to the implications of its mega-text, Canberra's architecture also yields some rather interesting readings on a local level. Considering the rather odd pairing of the High Court with the National Gallery – what link is there, one wonders, between art and law? – it suddenly occurred to me that a significant fraction of the recent architecture I have seen, both here and elsewhere, seems not merely not to demonstrate, but in a sense actually to deconstruct "front." By opening up entranceways, merging halls with arcades, using more glass, and, perhaps most radically, integrating landscape elements into the basic design, many of the newer public buildings seem, rather than reasserting, to obscure or even erase the line between inside and outside. One could read this phenomenon two ways. The first possibility is that it represents a "feminine" substrain within the ultra-masculine mainstream tradition. This is reinforced by the fact that the style seems particularly prevalent in academic and cultural buildings. An alternate possibility, however, is that it's not really feminine at all; that the hitherto buffer zone of domesticated outsideness has now been appropriated as part of the masculine "front." In this regard I would instance in particular the Victorian Arts Centre, where the entranceway is flanked by a wall of water harnessed between two sheets of glass.

The question is, of course, how do we arbitrate between these seemingly irreconcilable readings? My answer: perhaps we don't need to. Perhaps the whole point of this style is that it can and must be read both ways. Take the (in mid-1986) soon to be finished Parliament Building, for example. Inasmuch as it sits on a height of land, dominating its environs, this complex can be seen as epitomizing masculine assertion. The giant flagpole on top thus merely reconfirms what is already structurally determined. Inasmuch as the building itself is designed in such a way as to hug closely and even burrow into the contours of the hill, however, it also has a womb-like aspect that more than offsets its formal bravado.

Such semiological duplicity is, of course, highly appropriate for a site which is not only affectively ambiguous (Australians profess to hate and despise politicians, but at the same time they accede almost eagerly to government regulation) but critical to national self-imaging. That they should have achieved it bodes well for the public psyche – and perhaps for the private individual as well. The new suburban style, in which the structured zoning of yard and verandah has been replaced by the French door and patio, also suggests, albeit in vestigial form, a desegregation of symbolic spaces. That Australians continue to relate more to the outsides of their houses than the insides attests that the characterizing I-site has not changed its basic location. That they are less obsessive about compartmentalizing, however, suggests that they have, at least to some extent, been able to come to terms with the anxiety generated by marginalization.

Leaders

Its egalitarian mythos and disdain for "tall poppies" notwithstanding, Australia's strongest or at least most resilient political leaders have traditionally been those who were most self-announcingly "other." Sir Robert Menzies, for instance, the country's longest-ruling prime minister, was not only strongly identified, in terms of both attitude and policies, with the mother-land-across-the-sea ("Menzies was more British than the British," says Donald Horne [1971: 98]), but on a personal level comported himself in a manner in which there was not the slightest trace of, nor deference to, that purported national icon, the "ordinary bloke." "Bulky, white-haired, patriarchal, a man equally impatient of fools and those who had the temerity to oppose him," says Craig McGregor, "Menzies held absolute sway over the Liberal Party from the moment he created it in 1944, and the Liberal government from the moment he took the oath of office in 1949. Ruthless in his treatment of those within the party who might have challenged his authority and in promoting those whose loyalty he could rely upon, he built up a quite unrivalled edifice of power. In parliament his imposing, heavyweight form ... was always treated with great respect, even by the Opposition, whose members rarely dared interject when Sir Robert was speaking. At his rare press conferences he was arrogant and abrupt ... Like another prime minister before him, Lord Bruce, he enjoyed the pomp of London and other overseas capitals, visited them regularly and liked nothing better than to be seen at the Queen's right hand" (1981: 206). Menzies was far from anomalous. Until recently, in fact, Australians have shown an almost overwhelming preference for leaders as different as possible from the much-touted national "type." How do we account for this oddity? One might give some thought to the aforementioned ambiguities of Australian science fiction. In a culture where individuals are "taught" to fear power – or more accurately, to believe that they are incapable of wielding it effectively – the choice of (symbolically) out-group leaders is in one sense no more than predictable. It is also no more than predictable that the image of an "appropriate" power-wielder should be borrowed from those who have historically been viewed as wielding it.

It will be noticed, on the other hand, that I said "until recently." During the sixties Britain was definitively eclipsed by the United States as Australia's primary external referent. This meant that the Britannic typos lost much of his symbolic ascendancy in the power game. The Australian response to the change was not, however, quite what one might have expected. Whether it is a transition phenomenon or whether the new "most appropriate" model is simply too difficult to emulate (see Chapter 4, "*The Lucky Country*," pp. 264-73 below), the last two decades have seen an at least vestigial shift in the pattern of leader-preferences that may just possibly presage a shift in self-, or at least self/other-, imaging. This isn't to imply a total reversal, of course. The revised version is still a long way from the bushman writ large. He does have something of the bushman's charisma, though – and even more important, some of his key failings. Most critical for the topic at hand, he evinces a good deal of the bushman's mythic duplicity. It is not merely interesting but telling how often, in discussions of recent leaders, the picture that emerges is an *explicitly* ambivalent one. Gough Whitlam, for instance, is described in terms of an almost schizoid two-sidedness. "One side of him appealed to the Australian love of the respectable," notes Horne. "He dressed well. He spoke well. He had neat hair. He was a credit to us all . . . But the honest, blunt, witty, and sometimes child-like side could offend respectability . . . One side of him was civilized, rational, enlightened, humane . . . Yet on his other side there was the style of the crashthrough, the mad itch to throw away reason and give it a go" (1976: 92).

What does it mean? Perhaps nothing. Many politicians in many different cultures have been accused of hypocrisy. Whitlam's two faces, however, don't seem quite so simple – *or* so functional – that one can write them off as political opportunism. It is intriguing, for one thing, that his "sides," as Horne describes them, should mimic so closely the larriken/good citizen polarity that Patrick Morgan sees as constituting the "dual Australian personality" (1982). It is even more intriguing that we find the *same* kind of duality in the leader who – after the country's short-lived late-seventies regression to other-direction under anachronistically conservative millionaire landowner, Malcolm Fraser – emerged as the eighties' most powerful figure, Bob Hawke. Hawke not only *sounds* schizoid (he has "two voices," says Ian Moffitt: "a grating pleb one on TV . . . and a mild, cultured one off camera" [1972: 212]); he *is* schizoid, in his essential self. A "tamed larrikin . . . with few obvious airs and graces," he is also, as Richard Walsh points out, "the last in a generation that completed their education at Oxford and Cambridge" (1985: 434).

Beyond its intrinsic significance, like the architectural trends delineated in the last journal segment this phenomenon is interesting primarily for what it reflects on the mechanics of the Australian mythopoesis. As the last quotation makes clear, Hawke, like Whitlam, is seen not merely as a new type of leader, but in a more important sense as reconciling the old *with* the new, the international with the indigenous. Going one step beyond this, however, there are intimations between the lines of Blanche d'Alpuget's biography that the reconciliation Hawke effects – "on behalf" of his auditors, as it were – is actually the more profound reconciliation of male and female modes achieved by such folk heroes as Ned Kelly. For all his macho demeanour – the overt womanizing and covert misogyny (d'Alpuget, 1984: 197-98; all further quotes in the section are from the same source) – there is some indication that Hawke suffers from a latent sex role ambivalence going all the way back to his childhood.

This is obviously not the place to embark on a full-scale psychoanalysis, but a few provocative points might be mentioned. First, Hawke was apparently "meant" to be a girl – a fact of which he was made well aware during his childhood (6). Second, his relationship with his mother, a notoriously independent woman who explicitly rejected conventional domestic servitude, was a complex and problematic one characterized by the kind of "test of wills" more normally associated with same-sex parent-child, and particularly father-son, relations (12, 6). Alternately, his relationship with his father was so intense as to suggest, far from Oedipal rivalry, a kind of Electra complex. "When Clem was not around," says d'Alpuget, the child, being denied his sole contact with the world, "retreated into nervous, almost hysterical demanding and isolation." Once when he was away in Melbourne for a few days "Hawke announced, 'I can't live without him. Send a telegram for him to come home. I'm going to die'" (17). Given such a start, it is perhaps not far-fetched to see Hawke as fighting, and even more important being *perceived* to fight, an exemplary battle not just against the feminine world-at-large but against his own inner nature. D'Alpuget herself makes the phenomenon *almost* explicit. "It took him half a century," she says, "to make a sort of peace between the warring states within him, a confrontation that arose from his biological maleness on one side, and on the other, the phantom Elizabeth against whom he, Bob, had to fight from the beginnings of life" (6). The corollary possibility that d'Alpuget *doesn't* note is that it was perhaps the lingering shadow of that feminine "other" self – passive, emotional, intuitive – which, in the absence of more explicit coding, made Bob Hawke seem an appropriate power-wielder in the first place.

ARMIDALE

The typical [Australian] town is a service town supplying the needs of the agricultural district around it. There are three or four banks, solid two-storey brick buildings with a rusticated stucco facade, all on the main street; two or three pubs, usually with an Irish licensee . . . The pubs and banks generally occupy the corner sites. There will be a War Memorial in the strip of parkland running down the middle of the main street, with a statue of a digger of the First World War, slouch hat to puttees; and an improbably long list of names for so small a town. A much shorter list is added on for World War II. There will also be three or four churches . . . a primary school, and a high school if the town is big enough; a District Hospital and an Olympic Pool, built largely with locally raised money; a recreation oval and showground, and a golf course, tennis courts and a park; usually a railway station; petrol stations and motel; fish and chip shops and "cafes" that rarely sell coffee, and are often run by Greeks. A few shops . . . and a simple geometry of rectangular streets and of suburban bungalows. The doctor has the best house, the schoolteachers and railway workers have the worst, and the retired farmers have the best tended gardens, generally. The structure of the town will also reflect the clear social distinctions of rural Australia. There is a "good" end of town, on a hill if there is one, with the houses of those who send their children away to private schools; and then there is the rest of the town which provides the raw material for the local high school.

George Seddon, "The Man-Modified Environment"

Back on the treadmill again, thankfully for a short time only. Our van has been increasingly crotchety of late. Since the camping portion of our trip is finished in any case, we decided to make a detour back to Brisbane – a mere 2000 kilometres – in order to trade it in on a car. Figuring we might as well see as much as possible in the process, we made a long loop up the western flanks of the Great Dividing Range and down the east. It was far

too much to digest in three days. Or perhaps, like the Australians themselves, as an aftereffect of the outback I have begun to detach myself from a
backdrop I can no longer hope to assimilate. Whatever the explanation,
the only thing that remains with me from that trip is a vague, kaleidoscopic
impression of a patchwork landscape punctuated with sheep, cows, and
country towns: some rustic and Victorian, some "western" in feeling, some
exhibiting the unmistakable symptomology of the tourist trap. The scenery
itself is as variable as the economic activities it supports: from rugged
mountains to banana plantations to high, rolling tablelands. The roads, too,
are variable: paved but primitive for the most part – winding two-laners
that never go around a town they can meander through. It was a long haul.

Now we are in Armidale, a bustling small city (population 19,000) in the
heart of the New England Region of northeastern New South Wales. This
was once bushranger country. Today it is noted for its educational institutions (one university, one teachers' college, one technical institute, and a
handful of secondary schools) and its spectacular cathedrals. According to
my guidebook, it also boasts an excellent collection of Australian paintings
which are housed in the Hinton Benefaction Art Gallery. Unfortunately I
am too played out to participate. For me Armidale is a motel room and the
rare opportunity to spend a day loafing.

Despite the discontinuous nature of our journey, I have now been in the
country long enough to have gotten a feel for Australian television. Several
points in particular strike me as significant. First, the system as a whole is at
least in one sense somewhat less monolithic than it is in the United States.
Almost as if it represented a literal outering of the communal sense of self, a
comparison of programming across the country reveals a familiar combination of homogeneity and disco-ordination. Everyone everywhere seems
to get the same basic mix, but in marked contrast to North America,
where network schedules are virtually identical from one side of the continent to the other, the schedules here vary considerably from place to
place. This isn't simply a matter of which day a program appears. Country
stations, in particular, can diverge significantly in their choices re frequency,
segment length, and even order of episodes. A given series hence proceeds at different rates in different locales, with the result that no two
regions are in the same "place," metaphorically speaking, at the same time.

The bias of content is equally interesting. The public network, as one

might expect, broadcasts a much higher proportion of cultural, educational, and current affairs programming. Its imports, especially in the category of prime time entertainment series, tend to be British. The private
networks have much more of an American flavour. Although I don't have
any figures on this, it is obvious that imports comprise a very significant
percentage of their prime time programming. One's impression is that
almost every important and/or popular American series is available here
on a near-current basis. The only exceptions I am aware of are the daytime
soap operas, some of which, disconcertingly enough, are running a year or
more behind.

I have been disappointed in the sparsity of indigenous production. Judging at least from current schedules, Australians make very few action/
drama series, and virtually no comedy.[9] For the former they typically go to

---

9. This seems like a good place to address some potential criticisms. It is more than likely
that indigenous observers, with their special knowledge, will object to both the broad-
ness and the baldness of the kinds of generalizations I have been making throughout
this narrative, particularly when it comes to a complex techno-aesthetic phenomenon
like television. "References to the sparsity of local production strike me as not support-
able unless one makes it clear what kind of production we are talking about," wrote
Graeme Turner in a personal communication in 1988. "For instance, there is one production house which alone produces something like forty hours of television a week . . .
this is a mixture of soap and game shows. It is still television. Also it seems a little naive
to expect a population of sixteen million to have a strong and active television production sector. There is less local production in Australia than in Italy. So I am leery of
[your readiness to] . . . jump to conclusions about 'Australian TV' from what is available
[in a single] year . . . For instance . . . [despite the historical] shortage of comedy, there
[has been] a plethora of satiric shows – Mavis Bramston was the first ratings success for
homegrown shows and it was a satire [– though] none may have been screening during
the time [you were] watching. With a small industry . . . it is necessary to have experience or knowledge of their products over a number of years. There simply is not enough
produced to claim that one year's output is . . . typical." Turner is right about this, of
course. Though it is clearly telling what a country chooses to *do* with a limited production capacity (one might note, for instance, that Canada, with similar economic and
technical handicaps, has preferentially produced drama and documentaries, neither a
popular form in Australia), it is equally clear that a single cross-section is unlikely to
be perfectly representative. I also can't disagree with his further complaint that the

North America; for the latter to Britain. Perhaps the problem is that both these genres are highly structured and formulaic. Just as Australian writers have historically evinced a preference for the loosely knit, naturalistic linear narrative, the two categories of programs that the country does produce for itself are the mini-series and what is locally known as the "soapie." Although the former provides some interesting sidelights on the Australian attitude to history (I will return to this later), it is the latter which, for me, offers the most trenchant commentary on communal psychology.

Despite the name, and despite, too, what the Australians themselves seem to think of them, the soapies are not really much like American soap operas. Nor are they a homogeneous body. All of them have continuing casts of characters and background "situations" that carry over from week to week. In many the primary narrative also carries over. There is a substantial subgroup, however, which preferentially utilizes discontinuous plot segments complete in two or three episodes. Lacking the continuity of the true soap, the latter might be better characterized as continuing series than as serials.

Series or serials, on the other hand, there are a number of features that almost all Australian soapies seem to have in common. In no case I came across were the storylines either as complicated or as drawn out as American ones. Other differences from the American model include: differences in structure (where the American soap tends to distort chronology – weeks can be spent on one focal incident, while a child grows up literally overnight – the Australian soapie, though certainly it compresses time, is

_____

intertext which follows and complements this section, being focused narrowly on program types of special interest, does little to offset the arbitrariness of the synchronic optic of the journal narrative. What I would not agree with is that the failure to achieve inclusiveness – here as elsewhere – necessarily vitiates the goals of the project as formulated. My concern in this study, as I have said before, is not an exhaustive documentation of social facts but a demonstration of how a consensual version of "reality" is cumulatively conveyed through key redundancies across the full range of cultural production. That my scattergun sampling misses some features and misrepresents others is less important than the fact that, despite its randomness, it does turn up regularities. This is not to deny either the existence or the significance of non-regular features, whether due to economic or subjective factors, but only to emphasize that they are not the business of this book. My goal here is to elucidate the common themes that *underwrite* the multiplicity of culture.

relatively naturalistic in the pace of its unravelling); differences in "subject" matter (where the American soap personae are always exceptional in personal appearance, in social status, and/or in life experience, the Australian ones – with some exceptions – tend to be "ordinary" people in "ordinary" circumstances coping with "ordinary" problems like broken romances and family misunderstandings); and differences in emphasis (where the American soap is interminably talky and endlessly introspective, the Australian soapie coasts along the surface of events, privileging action over dialogue and invoking rather than anatomizing emotions). In terms of its general mood, the average Australian soapie, in comparison with the American soap, is less intense, less subjective, and certainly a good deal less angst-ridden.

What, one wonders, are we to make of all this? The surficial bias is certainly no more than predictable. The preference for shorter and more self-contained plot segments seems, on the other hand, to run counter to the general propensity for sprawl. If one looks more closely at the *distribution* of open versus closed structuring, however, an interesting pattern begins to emerge. At least in the series I have been following, storylines become systematically looser and more expansive as one moves from nature to culture. Episodes on *The Flying Doctors* are often virtually complete in themselves. *A Country Practice,* set in a small town in the Wannan Valley, seems to favour two-part sequences. *Neighbours,* set in a working-class suburb, though technically continuous, tends to close out given subplots within a few weeks. Only *Sons and Daughters,* with its substantially more up-scale urbanity, is leisurely enough in its pace that it could really be considered open-ended.

Other features vary concomitantly along the same axis. As we move from the country into the city we also move, in relative terms, from naturalism to melodrama, from extraversion to interiority, from simplicity to complexity, from static to dynamic, from passiveness to wilful self-assertion. One way of reading this is simply as reflecting a higher degree of "Americanness" in the more sophisticated settings. Against this possibility is the fact that the one program which most strikingly epitomizes the urban end of the spectrum, in terms of both its pacing and its symbology, is the very *un*American *Prisoner,* a series set in a women's prison.

The implications one may draw from this alignment are obviously very provocative. For one thing, it clearly confirms my previous identification of "the city" as feminine. More interesting, however, is the fact that the marker traits one may impute to the polarity are not exactly what convention would lead one to expect. If femininity is traditionally associated with inwardness, it is definitely *not* normally linked with either activity or aggression. We may read this divergence in two ways. The first possibility is that both the narrative constriction and the reactivity of the personae in the masculine realm of "country" may simply reflect the anxiety of the individual in the proximity of nature. As in the bush paintings I talked about in the Melbourne section, this would also explain the (defensive) overinsistence on the pleasantness and wholesomeness of the rural lifestyle. The second possibility, running in a sense at right angles to the first (though by no means incompatible with it), is that women – perhaps because of their symbolic associations with *both* landscapes – really are construed as the active agents in the Australian arena.

If the latter is true, it raises some interesting possibilities vis-à-vis the ideological function particularly of the last in the above list of programs. Inasmuch as its focal protagonists are deviant women, *Prisoner* seems to invite the viewer to identify with both women and deviance. Inasmuch as these women are depicted as "unnatural," however, in much the same way as the victim figures in those expressionist paintings discussed earlier, they are simultaneously devalued as self-symbols. What is really going on, therefore, is that the viewer, far from identifying *with* deviant women, is being invited to identify women *as* deviant. At the same time, he (for we have to assume that the audience here is being coded as masculine no matter what its "real" gender) is also being provided with a symbolic means of distancing and defusing the threat that they carry. The fact that these women are being punished is reassuring in itself. The fact that their punishment is "explained" in terms of simple rule-breaking is even more so, inasmuch as it allows us to avoid giving cognizance to their real crimes; that is, their unnatural activity and wilfulness. Finally, the fact that the prison cell may be seen as actually *standing for* femaleness means that their degraded condition can be construed as "normal." It seems obvious from the richness of this subtext that the soapie, far from the trivial and derivative form it is usually considered, plays a central and critical role in the Australian communal mythos.

Television: Copping It

During my stay in Australia, I was surprised not merely by the number but even more by the kind of imports one found on TV. Of particular note, it seemed to me, was the fact that the focal protagonists of approximately half the dozen-plus American action/adventure shows scheduled for prime time viewing in mid-1986 were neither loners nor rebels (as per the great Australian myth of national anti-authoritarianism), but the duly accredited personnel of law enforcement or state security/intelligence agencies. Of the three British entries, similarly, two were out and out police shows. I have demonstrated elsewhere the real ambivalence of the purportedly uncompromising Australian attitude toward authority figures (see, for instance, "War, Masculinity, and Violence," pp. 125-30 above). The combination of cop-dominated imports with a total absence of home-grown action drama struck me, however, as peculiar enough to require some explanation. When I reviewed the history of Australian television production, the picture that emerged seemed at first to muddy the issue even further – it quickly eliminated the thesis that only "foreign" cops were acceptable, for instance – but when the situation was reread against the international and particularly the American context, an interesting pattern began to emerge.

The first Australian television program, aired live on Channel 2, Sydney, on November 5, 1956, was a play, *The Twelve Pound Look*. My sources do not comment on its quality. Good or bad, however, the fact that it was a dramatic production is itself enough to set it apart from the bulk of programming that followed. The early years of Australian TV were, as Sandra Hall notes, dominated by low-budget, almost militantly amateurish variety-and-chat shows. "Possibly no country in the world has given so many people the opportunity to sit in front of a television camera and talk about the inconsequential," she says. "The only qualification has been that they be mildly extrovert" (1976: 85). How, apart from the obvious financial considerations, does she explain the apparent not merely acceptance of, but preference for, mediocrity? Pretensions being anathema to the national mythos, she says, "a strain of television . . . developed in Australia predicated on the assumption that people like to watch other people like themselves." Hence the almost-institutionalization of talk shows populated by second-rate "personalities," talent shows in which amateurs were both exposed and insulted, and quiz shows "based on the notion that [the viewer] can do just as well as the person [he/she is] watching" (Hall: 85).

Early imports seemed to express the same preference. "The two most popular programmes in Australia during the first two years," says Christopher Day, "were *I Love Lucy* and the archetypal wholesome family situation comedy-drama *Father Knows Best*" (1981: 140). Within two years, however, there were clear signs of the radical split between home-grown and imported programming that I comment upon in my journal. "Richard Boone in *Have Gun Will Travel* and Hugh O'Brien as *Wyatt Earp* were the first to clatter into the Top Ten in 1958," Day notes. "A year later westerns and crime shows had captured nearly everybody . . . At one stage there were more than 30 westerns running in prime time TV in the US and Australia saw most of them" (140). As the years passed, the trend to depending on imports to fill the national appetite for excitement only became all the more entrenched. "The nation stayed indoors on the nights Raymond Burr's monumental *Perry Mason* filled the screen," says Day. And "in 1962 – just as things were beginning to happen in local production houses – . . . a new programme, *Ben Casey*, leapfrogged the established *Bonanza* and *The Untouchables* to take first place in the ratings" (141).

Apart from a few sporadic one-shot historical dramas (ABC, the national network, according to Day screened one historical play per year between 1960 and 1963, while the Seven network aired its first in 1962), the situation remained generally unchanged for almost a decade. After the mid-sixties, however, there were increasingly widespread complaints about the endemic Americanization (see O'Regan, 1986: 9ff.). For the first time, it seemed, there was a *will* within the community to produce its own heroic fictions. When it did, intriguingly enough, it was the police drama which became *the* national genre. "On the night of 20 October 1964," reports Brian Davies, "HSV-7 screened . . . the first episode of a new Australian drama series the station was trying out called *Homicide*. The first Anderson rating survey gave Episode One a rating of thirty-three. McNair estimated a twenty-eight. The next episodes surveyed, Four and Five, were measured at thirty-one and thirty-three respectively" (1981: 96). Early indicators were not misleading. *Homicide* ran for eleven years, for a total of 509 episodes (O'Regan: 14). For nine of those years it placed in the national Top Ten; for five it was number one (Beilby,

1981: 58ff.). Scoring as high as thirty-six in 1965, says Davies, it "really took off in 1966, hitting ratings of forty regularly and a peak of forty-two. In the following year, 1967, it ran for forty-eight weeks and its ratings in Melbourne rarely fell below forty" (98). Was *Homicide* a fluke? Apparently not. Other networks quickly got on the police show bandwagon, and while none quite equalled the popularity of the prototype, it was obvious from the ratings that the Australian audience was just as happy – indeed, happier – with homegrown "cops" as it had been with American ones. In the fifteen years between 1965 and 1980, *Division 4* made the Top Ten six times, *Cop Shop* twice, *Hunter* and *Matlock Police* once each.

Even apart from its reflections vis-à-vis the nation's purported identification with the law-flouting larrikin, the *Homicide* phenomenon raises a number of intriguing questions. For one thing, and most obviously, we have to ask why the trend did not continue? In 1972 the Ten network initiated a soap opera about the excitements of life in an inner Sydney suburbs, and from that moment, though it would take a decade to become fully apparent, Australia's own action drama was a doomed species. By 1986, as I noted in my Armidale entry, it was apparently extinct. The question is why. If Australians hate the police, or even if they only think they do, why did they virtually canonize the cop show? And if they *don't*, why, in the eighties, did they turn their backs on what was such a popular form? Because they were tired of it? Perhaps. No fashion lasts forever. But in that case, why resume importing exactly the genre that they had ceased to produce for themselves?

The answers to these questions are, I think, to be found not in Australia itself, but in the United States. I have elsewhere (1987b, 1993a & b) shown how American culture, far from monolithic, tends to oscillate on an irregular but systematic basis between two "positions" or mind-sets one might epitomize as *primitivism* and *progressivism*. Particularly pertinent to the subject at hand is the fact that the country's preferential hero also changes systematically with the shift in public mood. During primitivistic periods, he tends to be introspective, socially isolated, and aligned with "nature." During progressivistic phases, on the other hand, he is just the opposite, deriving both his legitimacy and his power from outside sources like technology, The Law, and/or formalized (whether domestic or institutional) social alignments. On the basis of the Australian's much-touted traditional self-image, it is obviously the former, more independent, typos who *should* appeal. Counter to this, however, is the fact that it was during the primitivistic sixties that the American hero fell out of favour, and during the progressivistic eighties that he was rehabilitated again. If this isn't enough to hammer home the point, it

is clear from the character of those briefly regnant homegrown cop shows –
and particularly from their emphasis on the institutional/communal background rather than the lone protagonist (Moran, 1985, Chapter 8) – that during the hiatus, unable to purchase a satisfactorily domesticated hero from
their usual sources, the Australians set out to produce one for themselves.

What are we to conclude from this? One possibility is that the Australian
sense of self is really quite different than advertised. Another and (viewed
contextually) more likely explanation is that, their native pessimism exacerbated in the case of television by an equally ingrained technophobia, the Australians were unable to imagine a version of self sufficiently competent to
satisfy the perceived norms of the electronic fantasyland. Just as in life they
have so often looked to the U.S. for both policy and hardware (see pp. 271ff.),
they were hence almost bound to construct their version of "television hero"
in the image of the, or at least *an*, American. But why fixate on the policeman
in particular? Given that they are even more ambivalent about nature than
about technology, and especially given the disquieting omnipresence of
strong women in adjacent genres (see, for instance, Moran's discussion of the
phallic mother in the soap opera, *Sons and Daughters*, 1985: 200ff.; also
Stern, 1977), the primitive hero, with his "feminine" dependence on natural
instrumentalities, is obviously not suitable for local consumption. American
pioneer myths notwithstanding, the only one capable of holding his own
against Australian "nature" is a formally designated agent of the *cultural*
(m)other.

SYDNEY I

Sydney is a huge, sprawling, turbulent city, full of bustle and a zestful mate-
rialism . . . It arouses violently conflicting emotions among those who know
it; perhaps this is because it is a moody city, sometimes dominated by the
beaches and brilliant sunshine which persuade men that life is for enjoying
and sometimes by the grey skyscrapers and ugly, narrow streets which per-
suade men that life is for making money. It is centred on a superb yacht-
studded harbour overlooked by genteel homes, but the bulk of Sydney is a
mass of redbrick bungalows with pocket-handkerchief lawns . . . Brash, pos-
sessive, vulgar, it is an uneasy compromise between the nouveaux *riches*
with their powder-blue power launches and tax-evasion companies at one
extreme, and the burly dark-singleted road workers grown fat on beer and
sunshine at the other . . . Yet those who call it "unfeeling" are simply not cor-
rect; its people are warmer, friendlier and quicker to shake your hand than
the inhabitants of many a cold provincial city.

Craig McGregor, *The Australian People*

I'm having a hard time getting into this section. Perhaps it's because I can't
help flashing back to the hard time I had getting into Sydney itself. Sydney is
the most confusing city I have ever been in. *And* the most alien. For all its
surficial friendliness, ever since I arrived here I've had the sense of being
rebuffed. Part of this, no doubt, is a result of my feelings of isolation since
my travelling companion returned to North America. A larger part,
though, is Sydney itself. This is not a city for strangers. Even by Australian
standards its layout is both erratic and irrational. Such through routes as
exist are convoluted and badly marked. Even maps don't help much. As if
only the initiate "counted," the main roads are often without signs. The
downtown core is particularly daunting. Time after time I have found
myself driving in frustrated circles through a maze of one-way streets, lane
shunts, and required or interdicted turns. Once deflected from one's
objective, it is a major undertaking to get back on track.

We had a bad beginning, Sydney and I. This is a city renowned for its beautiful harbour. *Our* approach, unfortunately, was not from the water, but from the land – a much less inspiring proposition. Because of its low density, the outskirts of the megalopolis seem to drag on forever. Because each suburb is labelled like a separate town, on the other hand, it's difficult to discern where the "city" actually begins. Not that I should have been surprised to be confronted once again with the stigmata of disconnectivity. At least by reputation, Sydney *is* Australia. And if the past few months have taught me one thing, it's that the Aussies, despite their hypothetical love of travel, are in fact quite hopeless at trans-action.

Suburbs apart, to even get *near* this city is difficult. Eager to see more of Australia's famous coastline, we deliberately took a roundabout route from Armidale. It was a mistake. As it turned out, there were very few places on the "coastal" highway where one could even see the ocean. South of the fruit belt, the road winds interminably through wooded parklands along the edge of the escarpment, following the course of least resistance. Too close – too *closed* – for the long view, apart from the occasional too-brief moment on the brink of some sudden valley, it seldom rises even to the level of picturesque. On the practicality scale it rates even lower. The narrowness and steepness of the way, the density of the traffic, and the preponderance of heavy trucks and recreation vehicles ensure a virtual snail's pace through the entire region. And this is the main route from the north! Below Newcastle, there are, it is true, several stretches of multi-lane freeway. Because these are discontinuous, however – and how typical *that* is! – they tend to exacerbate rather than relieve the bottleneck effect. As usual, we were in a hurry. And as usual the Australian reality fought us at every turn. We finally crawled into Sydney around nightfall in the midst of a mob of Sunday drivers. And spent what seemed like a lifetime trying to unravel the labyrinth in time for my partner to catch his plane.

I dwell on the issue of impenetrability not in order to show what a "bad" city Sydney is – in fact, as cities go, Sydney has a lot to recommend it – but, rather, to underline the difference between conceptualizing and assimilating a culture. By the time I got to Sydney I had begun to feel that I had Australia "taped." What I didn't give enough thought to is the fact that a mental map is *at best* only homologous, not identical, with the territory it purports to elucidate. No matter how accurate the survey marks, a gap still exists – a gap that can only be filled by experience. Take the matter of pedestrian rhythms, for instance. Once I had been around Australian cities for a while, I became aware that I was subtly out of step. It wasn't just imagination. I actually kept bumping into people. I thought at first it might be an unconscious left-hand, right-hand thing related to the left-hand driving. On closer observation I realized that Australians don't always walk on the left, any more than North Americans always walk on the right. So it's something more complex than that. Something that operates on the level of instinct. Something a casual observer will never pick up. There are, I've come to realize, a lot of little things like that. I never did figure out the semiotics of drinking – what difference there is between the various public rooms in a hotel, and which ones it's "all right" for a woman to drink in. Nor the etiquette of public transport – how one manages eye contact, body language, etc. Perhaps because Sydney is at once the most American and the most unAmerican of Australian cities, during my stay here I have been made constantly aware of the gap between subject and object.

This hasn't stopped me from playing tourist. Nor from adding some very provocative new tidbits to my store of information. Once I got myself settled in a shabby bed-and-breakfast in a posh east end suburb, I spent a lot of time just walking around the city. Even apart from the irrationality of its traffic pattern, from a semiotic standpoint I found it a tough nut to crack. Sydney at first seems all sprawl, with little beyond the most vestigial remnants of an ordered grid. There is no distinct core as there is in Adelaide and Melbourne. Only Hyde Park, with its gardens, pool, and fountain, its memorial to the vanquished hero, remains as a token of the feminine centre. And even this is overshadowed by the stark, phallic presence of Sydney Tower looming nearby, above a shopping complex called Centrepoint. Nothing in my stock of precedents had prepared me to account for this ostentatious masculinization of what I had come to read as an *essentially* feminine location.

It seemed even more anomalous when I considered the other aspects of Sydney's iconography. In its own public imaging Sydney has historically emphasized two major landmarks, the Harbour Bridge and the Opera House. Both of these are clearly feminine, the first through its function as a mediator, the second through its association with "art" and its explicitly womb-like structure. Equally important, both were difficult to achieve.

From the date the bridge bill passed through the state parliament in 1922, for instance, a full ten years were to elapse before the structure was completed. Reading the history of those years – the accidents, the labour troubles, and the political controversy – it seems a miracle it was completed at all. Perhaps this is why Sydneyites were so proud of it; why for decades afterward it was touted at home and abroad as a pinnacle of cultural achievement, *despite* the fact that there was nothing particularly exceptional about either its aesthetics or its engineering.

The opera house was even more of a *cause célèbre*. Designed by a Dane (it's interesting how much of Australia's most notable architecture can be attributed to foreigners or immigrants!), its construction was marked by engineering problems, soaring costs, and bitter feuding between the architect and his clients. On completion it revealed many practical flaws. Its two main halls are undeniably impressive, and the outside visual gestalt is nothing short of breathtaking. Other aspects, however – especially of its interior – have been severely criticized. "The other four public areas," says David Saunders, ". . . offer [little] architectural pleasure. They also have some severe . . . backstage problems. Their foyers, and the Exhibition Hall itself, are inadequate, architecturally negative, shabbily finished and ineptly furnished. In the case of Drama and of Music . . . the auditoria themselves are acceptable but mediocre. Many municipal halls or suburban cinemas offer as much" (1974: 45). Despite all this, like its forerunner, the bridge, the Sydney Opera House is regarded by its proud patrons to represent a landmark not merely within the local scene but within the annals of modern architecture.

The message seems clear, then. From the prominence accorded these two items in the cultural text, we can infer that Sydneyites, like other Australians, have been predisposed to identify their city with the feminine. From their chequered histories we can also infer a psychological incapacity to deal competently with such an alien reality. Sydney Tower notwithstanding, in other words, on the evidence of icons one can only conclude that Sydneyites have historically imaged their sense of "place" in exactly the same way as the rest of their countrymen. So how do we explain that phallicized centre? I must admit I was at a loss here, until someone showed me an article on the tower in *Island Magazine*. The fact is, within its *own* ambience, Sydney Tower is construed not as masculine but as feminine. This structure, says Meaghan Morris, "is not . . . an anachronistic symbol of growth as expansion, but rather the reverse – a focus for a mini-spectacle of implosion . . . There's no doubt . . . [it] could be described as a phallus . . . But as the phrase 'Ned Kelly in skirts' suggests, the Tower's shape permits it to be seen as the feminine object of an assumed masculine gaze" (Morris, 1982: 55, 57). What does this mean? There's only one thing it *can* mean as far as I am concerned. *In the heart of Sydney the phallic mother has been allowed out of the closet.*

Once I solved this riddle, the rest of the city quickly fell into place. The sprawling, self-consciously differentiated suburbs, the braggadocio of the architecture, the segregation of major government and cultural buildings within a large tract of parklands adjacent to the central core – it all fitted. At least on an intellectual level, the pattern was beginning to assume the lineaments of an old friend. As was the broader pattern of psycho-symbology of which it was a part. Or so I thought. I decided to put it to the test. The Sixth Sydney Biennale was currently in progress at the state gallery. I made a mental bet with myself that I could pick out the Australian paintings simply by their "look." And I won. I didn't get them all – I'm not familiar enough with the corpus of mixed media, construction, and performance art in Australia to adequately cognize works of this type – but I did catch most of the paintings. Even more interesting, I didn't identify one single piece as Australian which wasn't. The following excerpts from my notes provide an interesting illustration of the degree to which a base pattern may vary without losing its recognizability.

(a) Immants Tiller – In *Lost, Lost, Lost* (1985) a bloodstained forest dissolves into swastikas at one end and violently graffitied urban alleys on the other. The Melburnians' nightmare city is here clearly and disturbingly conflated with its "natural" counterpart. In *The Nine Shots* (1985) a human figure is itself grotesquely merged with a deconstructed and largely symbolic landscape. In both cases, the encounter-trauma is "managed" by means of strategies strikingly reminiscent of those used by the Tasmanian artists for managing nature. These pieces are collages, scavaged together from the cut-up, worked-over fragments of magazines and catalogues. With respect to the element of sprawl, it is interesting to note that the artist views his collective oeuvre as comprising "*one painting,* vast and ever expanding, into which every new work is absorbed" (Sixth Biennale of Sydney, 1986: 270).

(b) Tim Johnson – Combining the graphic strategies of the aborigine with the stance of the cartographer, this artist builds up his images through a rhythmic layering of crude dots and striations. Surface tensions are minimal, and visual density is almost uniform throughout the canvas. The subject is landscape. *Western Desert* (1985) presents an aerial view of a subtly differentiated plain in pale pinks and browns. *Illusory City* (1985) is a fragmented townscape. In *Blue Fire* (1985), tiny aimless figures crawl across an amorphous ground. Johnson's deconstruction is more radical than Tiller's. Even when the subject is man-in-nature, it is so distanced as to be entirely drained of threat.

(c) Dick Watkins – "With not much premeditation," says this painter, "I move in with a few big brushes and splash a bit of paint around" (Sixth Biennale, 1986: 284). The artlessness of this comment anticipates nicely the artlessness of the works. *Echoes of the Jungle* (1982), for instance, is chaotic, sprawly, crude – a child's version of the tropics, in bright primary colours of blue, orange, yellow, and green. While lacking the boundary-challenging aggressiveness of American abstract expressionism, Watkin's paintings are notably decentred. Almost devoid of focus or structure, his shapes spread lushly across the canvas, coming obediently to a stop at its edges.

(d) Vivienne Shark Lewitt – This artist paints very small, rather disturbingly cut-up (dis-membered?) family scenes on pieced-together sections of wood. *Now and at the Hour of Our Death* (1986), for instance, comprises two entirely separate sex-coded "spaces." On the left, a crowned woman dressed in red holds out a child whose legs (though the fit is inexact between panels) seem to disappear into the mouth of a naked man whose right arm and side are cut off by the intervening fracture. While the iconography of this piece is obviously intended to remain ambiguous, one reading might suggest that it alludes to the destructiveness of family life. Alternately it may be construed as an image of the vulnerable self, caught between feminine culture and (a common defensive miscoding) masculine nature. Whether the infant is emerging from, or being devoured by, the latter is entirely a matter of conjecture.

(e) Tony Clark – The central focus of the central panel in a three-piece composite entitled "Designs for a mural painting with sections from CLARKE'S MYRIORAMA 1985-86" is a tiny brick building surrounded and overshadowed by a black-on-black ground full of looming, half-sensed, animate presences. This might be seen as an ironic version of the country house portrait. Echoing the Australian attitude toward the feminine interior, the hut here, as viewed from the outside, seems both precarious and impenetrable.

(f) Colin Lanceley – This artist paints bright, childishly colourful, quasi-surrealistic and highly stylized landscapes. Identified in the catalogue with both "catastrophe art" and "kitsch" (Sixth Biennale, 1986: 168), these pieces are not just discontinuous but disorderly: unfocused, unstructured, fortuitous. The sense they convey of diffusion or disintegration is exacerbated by the superaddition of unidentifiable or inappropriate carved wooden "things" to their surfaces. In *Midwinter Spring, James's Garden* (1986), for instance, the dissonance between elements is so extreme that the picture seems almost to be decomposing before one's eyes.

(g) William Robinson – These were my favourites: primitive landscapes full of affectionately rendered dogs, cats, cows, birds, farm folk, and squat, lumpy trees. What makes them "Australian"? Even more than by its content, Robinson's world can be identified by its "middleness." Denying both extent and centre, the land in these paintings curves up to canopy or contain a sky dotted with stylized clouds or stars. "I make works in the same way that we make a home," says Robinson – "a secret world full of personal meanings that often I do not understand" (Sixth Biennale, 1986: 240). For all its idiosyncrasy, Robinson's sense of "home" is strikingly consonant with that of his countrymen. The sky may perhaps be taken to represent the mystery which is both inside *and* outside.

The Question of Regionalism

"Strangely enough," says Craig McGregor, "there are virtually no regional accents in Australia, despite the vast distances between the main centres of population" (1980: 35). Speech is not the only thing that unites the country. Architecture and town layout are remarkably consistent across the board (Freeland, 1972). There is a "broad homogeneity of popular leisure and recreations" (Alomes, 1986: 240). And though there have been several attempts to promote "regional" writing during the last decade, there is, according to Susan McKernan, little evidence of "natural" differences in literary production from different areas (1986). Despite all this, Australians conceive *themselves* in regional terms. From the days of the earliest settlement, says Richard White, inter-colonial rivalries were "surprisingly strong" (1981: 63). Though Federation was achieved with little trouble in 1900, far from an expression of national unity, it was regarded, in Vance Palmer's words, "as an alliance between countries foreign to one another and having rival economies" (1963: 142). The attitude persists today. "There are few national matters in Australia," says Donald Horne. "[T]he way Australians see Australia is largely the way they see their own States. State differences and State conflicts run through almost every national institution – the political parties (even the Communist Party), the trade unions, the big pressure groups, the Churches, and private firms" (1971: 156). This discrepancy between what is thought and what is revealed calls for some explanation.

The case of Sydney and Melbourne can be viewed as paradigmatic for the country as a whole. So strong is the traditional rivalry between these cities that they are imaged most often in terms of polarities. The (not entirely self-consistent) picture that emerges from an anthology entitled *The Sydney-Melbourne Book* (Davidson, 1986) sets – among other things – beach against dinner party, philosophy against history, flamboyance against decorum, egalitarianism against elitism, scepticism against optimism, romanticism against neo-classicism, abstraction against social realism, sensuality against intellectualism, tolerance against righteousness, conservatism against liberalism, business against academy, ocker against wowser, internationalism against nationalism, individualism against social responsibility. At the same time, the very writers who elucidate these contrasts seem largely convinced that the differences are trivial ones, differences not of substance but of style. "The two cities may play different codes of football," says James Jupp; they "may have different climates and lifestyles, may present different images to the rest of Australia. But in measurable essentials, using social statistics normally believed to give guidance to political characteristics, they are not very different" (79). Is Jupp right? And if so, how do we explain the divergence in temperament? These questions are important ones, especially in the present context. At least some of the characteristics imputed to Melbourne – its reserve, its subordination of private whims to public interest, and its pro-social bent for collectivity – could be interpreted to delineate a vestigial feminization, thus undercutting the claims made earlier that Tasmania should be viewed as singularly distinct from its neighbours.

We perhaps find our "answer" to Melbourne if we look at the case of Queensland. Reputed to be the most primitive of Australian states (see McQueen, 1979b), from at least one perspective Queensland can actually be seen as intermediate in position between Sydney and Melbourne. On the one hand, says Glen Lewis (1974), is its historically notable propensity for anti-social behaviour and masculine aggression. This, of course, is the tie-in with Sydney. On the other, echoing Melbourne, is the rigorous – both tacit (the rituals of mateship) and institutionalized (punitive legal sanctions against deviance) – social regulation that has been brought to bear as a means of *controlling* this excessive individualism. What, we must ask, does lawless, macho Queensland have in common with the most "civilized" state in the union that would explain their shared, albeit differently "expressed," repressiveness? Lewis, as intimated in his epigraph to the "CAIRNS" section above, identifies both the initial dis-order *and* the reactive authoritarianism as reflecting the effects of a brutal, unpredictable environment. Taking this clue, we might also see the difference between Sydney and Melbourne as environmentally determined.

How does this work? We have elsewhere described the Australian as impaled between the equally alien realms of nature and culture. As can be amply inferred from the structural differences between outback towns and coastal cities, however, the two (m)others are not always experienced as equally *immanent*. One might hypothesize that when culture is felt as the greatest threat to individual integrity, as would certainly be the case in a penal colony, then nature tends to be relatively idealized. When nature is most threatening, however, as is the case in the north, then the beleaguered individual is forced to work out an accommodation with "mum." Where

does Melbourne fit into this schema? Unlike Botany Bay, the Victorian colony was founded despite, rather than by, the long arm of the Crown. "The
pursuit of fortune and the worship of success have been numbered among the
attributes of Melbourne from its foundation," says Paul de Serville. "The settlement [was] . . . established by groups of capitalists and entrepreneurs from
Van Diemen's Land, joined by equally restless men from New South Wales . . .
[It] was a triumph of private enterprise and individualism" (1986: 56). Cultural triumphs notwithstanding, on the other hand, these same successful
Melburnians were somewhat *less* successful when it came to dealing with
nature. Far from protecting them, indeed, the early triumph over the cultural
(m)other, by inflating their self-confidence, left them ill prepared to deal with
setbacks when they came along. And they *did* come along! Especially in the
aftermath of the gold rush, Melbourne's history is an almost exemplary demonstration of boom and bust. For every man who profited from the grand
schemes of the mid-century, de Serville notes, "there were twenty failures,
destroyed by bad luck or misfortune, by the economy, or the climate. Melbourne has never learned to control nature, and drought, flood, fire and disease remain the four horsemen who have stalked every generation in town
and country since 1834. Against the ravages of these, the proud battlement of
Melbourne's buildings has been as impotent as the Maginot Line" (57).

Quite as much as Queenslanders, then, the Melburnians had strong incen-
tives to adopt the tools of the cultural (m)other as a means of buffering their
confrontation with an inimical environment. This doesn't mean, on the
other hand, that either of these communities is *essentially* different from
bush-loving (Kiernan, 1980) Sydney. Re-viewed from the perspective of
betweenness, in fact – and this, I think, is the bottom line to the question of
regionalism in Australia – both Sydney *and* Melbourne can be seen as
expressing in their different ways a similar sense of radical (though
ambivalent) disablement. Where they diverge, as the following table demonstrates, is *only* in the routes they took to get there.

The Tale of Two Cities Retold:
A capsule comparative psychohistory
of Sydney and Melbourne

Sydney		Melbourne
authoritarianism	*early*	aggressive individualism
feelings of personal impotence*		feelings of self-confidence
	fin-de-siècle	
cynicism/ sentimentalism		guilt/retrenchment triggered by boom and bust cycle**
greater individual freedom, less public morality	*post-world war II*	more public regulation of private experience; more radicals too – but they have to move to Sydney to escape the repression

* leads to fear of culture   **leads to fear of nature

SYDNEY II

Who today is unaware of those things called Australian films or the Australian music industry . . . [or] the new Australian art? While particularly the Australian music that is celebrated in America is far from the best produced in the country, the image of a nation having come of age assaults us every time we open a fashion or music magazine, survey exhibition catalogue and film journal. Australian culture hasn't necessarily "come of age"; rather, it is the beneficiary of a worldwide loss of confidence and nostalgic yearning for lost utopias. How else can the endless cranking out of Australian landscape myths and tales of our youthful energy – that is, a perpetually cute young adulthood – be explained?

Paul Taylor, "A Culture of Temporary Culture"

Myths make a good introduction to a society because the further they are from reality, the more they may tell us about a society's tensions. One can ask: if humans can delude themselves to this extent, what has gone wrong? What is (in effect; whatever the intentions) being covered up?

Donald Horne, "Who Rules Australia"

More about the mini-series. I've seen quite a few of these now. Good and bad, the one thing that has struck me is their lack of topicality. Though often depicting "true" events, they tend to be set either in the past or in the bush (a mythological space which by definition carries an aura of "pastness" no matter what the date). This retrospectivity is, I gather, typical. If one were to judge only by their film and television production, in fact, one would have to conclude that these people are not merely interested in, but downright obsessed with, history. On the face of it, the finding is more than a little surprising. The concern with lineage, a centripetal trait, is clearly inconsistent with other aspects of the Australian psychological profile. One might, on the other hand, suggest several reasons for an apparent historicism, *apart* from, and in some ways counter to, the centripetalist desire to

204

establish continuity. First, the use of historically derived storylines obviates the necessity of artfulness. Second, the use of either "real" or premythicized personae obviates the necessity of character development. Third, and most important, the fact that the events have already happened, at least figuratively, makes possible the happy ending which is so difficult for the natural pessimist to conceive – or defuses the tragic one that he/she suspects to be inevitable.

History, then, is the writer's best friend. Utility aside, on the other hand, this last item also points up the reason that "historical" themes are so popular with the Australian public. The kind of past depicted in TV films and mini-series is inevitably a rosy one. Whatever hardships the protagonists may suffer, whatever social disasters fill the background, they are offset or framed through the invocation of a sustaining matrix community. Even – perhaps especially – in tales of catastrophe, therefore, the audience is offered a reassuring picture of a time, or a place, when life was simpler, moral choices more clearcut, and interpersonal relations more wholesome.

Sentimentalizing the past is nothing new, of course. This is exactly the tack taken by the Heidelberg painters, back in the depression of the nineties. Nor, *qua* strategy, is it particularly "Australian." The United States recycles its history almost as fast as it happens. A comparison between the western and the bush tale, however, points up a peculiarity in the Australian *handling* of history that virtually always betrays nativity. Where Americans revise the past in order to make it more accessible, more consonant with the present, the Australians tend to emphasize its *differentness* from "now." One might speculate that when a community lacks faith in futurity it becomes important to prove that the ideal society – radical utopia, workingman's paradise, or what have you – really did exist at one time, *even if doing so means a further devaluation of the present.*

History aside, another interesting feature at least of the current crop of TV films and serials is their preoccupation with, and indeed apparent rehabilitation of, the "bad" woman. *The Lancaster Miller Affair,* a three-part series recently shown on the Nine network, is particularly intriguing in that it not only renders sympathetically a type who is normally anathema in Australian fiction – the promiscuous cosmopolite – but actually allows her to take over the hero's role. In the most immediate sense, what this series is "about" is the chequered relationship between Australian aviatrix,

Chubby Miller, and British ace, Bill Lancaster. Symbolically, what it represents is a female who proves successful in the very realm – ad-venturing – that means so much to (it is fitting that the review in *Cinema Papers* is entitled "Fear of Staying on the Ground"), yet proves so difficult for, the would-be dynamic Australian male. That Lancaster dies alone in a plane crash in the desert – and what an "Australian" fate that is! – only underlines the ironic implications of the story as a whole.

Chubby Miller is not an anomaly. Female potency is a major theme in recent feature films as well. The strong woman has never been a stranger in the annals of Australian fiction; what is different about this recent version is that, like Chubby, she is neither compartmentalized as "mum" (the strong mother of *Coonardoo,* the dutiful helpmeet of *Richard Mahoney*) nor dismissed as "evil" (the bad wife of *The Passage,* the sexual predator of *The Tilted Cross*). This does not mean, on the other hand, that the fable of the new woman (or the new woman's fable? – the genealogy of this recent burgeoning is as yet unknown) is without its own somewhat sinister subtext. As usual, this subtext is connected both causally and conceptually with the realm of (m)otherness, nature. *Unusually,* the female in the case is now construed (at least on the surface) not as a scapegoat, but as an exemplar.

Take, for instance, two recent releases: *Fortress* (a small town schoolteacher and her pupils are kidnapped by terrorists) and *Fair Game* (a lone woman living in the outback is harassed by sadistic hunters). In both of these films it is made clear that the wilderness uniformly releases the natural violence of those who enter it. The *effects* of this process, though, as shown here are notably *not* uniform. Whereas for a man to become violent is to become a brute, for the female protagonist it is shown to be a morally positive transformation. Pushed too far, the prey becomes the predator. The victims emerge from the shattered shells of their social personae (in both films, the house has to be destroyed/denied as a first step to realization) to avenge themselves on their oppressors. *"Mum" becomes phallic mother.* The key symbol here, made explicit in the former film, is the cave. At first, as the ad says on TV, it is a prison; later it becomes a fortress. Before and beyond its "social" functions, however, it seems clear that we have to read this structure as a womb. This, of course, gives us a new whole slant on the myth of the rock. Or does it? Released from her social subordination by the wilderness, the woman is born into her "masculine" (i.e., active) self. At the same time, however, it is not possible to avoid the uneasy feeling – even if one accepts the *overt* destruction as justifiable – that in doing so, she has subverted the finer (because more "feminine"?) aspects of her inner being.

The ambivalence of these films could be interpreted several ways. By using a rebirth motif to validate the phallic mother (and it is notable that both films, and particularly *Fortress,* make much play with sharpened stakes, spears, etc.), the writers have in a sense normalized the sex role inversion that has always provided an energizing undertone to the national mythos. By attributing her potency to nature, on the other hand, they also underline the psychic danger she represents. It is telling, for instance, that the protagonist of *Fortress* is shown explicitly as having sacrificed the innocence of "her" children in order to win her victory. It is even more telling that the single act by which that sacrifice is confirmed is the castration of the defeated male antagonist. Rhetorical approval aside, it is unclear, then, whether the new woman is in fact being reconstructed as "good" in these recent films, or covertly re-presented in her same old guise – as something unnatural, a threat against social order.

It is interesting in this regard that the hero of the latest television outback drama, *From Alice to Nowhere* (a two-part series aired on the Ten network), while clearly unmanned by his ordeal in the desert, relinquishes the role-defining task of defeating the villain, not to the heroine this time (this transplanted city girl is the classic passive female), but to her covert alter ego, the natural (m)other, here imaged as the river. It is possible, then, that Chubby Miller and her ilk can be accepted only when they are distanced by time. The closer a subject comes to "reality," the more likelihood there seems to be of a filmmaker falling, albeit unconsciously, into the old strategies of either denigrating the strong woman or displacing her power onto nature. In the latter case, since feminine passivity is only a wishfully displaced image of nature in the first place, it is no wonder that the hero himself, unnerved by an ineradicable sense of existential precariousness, is content to ride like flotsam on a sea of circumstances.

The new filmmaker thus clearly evinces the same old ambivalence as his/her predecessors. It is true, on the other hand, that at least some of these films have devised more successful or at least more interesting means of expressing and managing this ambivalence. The same might be said of recent art. It is no accident, I think, that those recent artists who have turned back to the landscape with the greatest enthusiasm are also those whose deconstruction of that landscape is most vigorous. "The thing which I always endeavour to express," says John Olsen, "is an animistic quality – a certain throbbing throughout nature" (in Hughes, 1970: 260). Animism there is in abundance in his writhing vegetation and fleshy terraforms, but it is an animism from which, *despite* its anthropomorphic undertones, the observer has been carefully removed. Viewed from a distance these landscapes resolve themselves into dreamscapes, lively and fecund: the dead heart brought to life by the will of the artist – and, like woman herself, long since conventionalized into passivity or irrelevance, by that same will kept well at bay.

The same message is conveyed even more baldly by Fred Williams. In his desertscapes the land is reduced to its most basic qualities: "a few tiny marks on an empty ground," unfocused, inconsequential, and utterly structureless (Mackie, 1979: 248). Eschewing the usual strategies of familiarization, unlike Olsen's mega-amoeboids this is nature at its most unhuman. "We can never get close to this land," says Alwynne Mackie, "never become part of it – coulisses, large trees framing the picture plane, all the devices of intimacy are avoided. It is as if there is always an unseen barrier preventing us from approaching the scene any closer" (250). Far from daunting, however, it is this very reserve that makes Williams's landscapes – like Olsen's *apparently* quite different ones – assimilable. By removing the subject from the expressionist landscape, by obviating the necessity of interacting, these artists also remove the point of strain. By backing off for an aerial view, converting horizontal to vertical recession, they create the illusion of a wholly appropriable space – still other, perhaps, but powerless now beneath the arrogant masculine gaze.

Where, we might ask, does this leave the Sydney Tower? Given that the most typical response to anxiety is denial – and certainly Olsen and Williams fit this bill – its literal outering of a communal bogey *could* be taken to mean that today's Sydneyite is somewhat psychologically stronger than his forebears. Given the mixed messages we draw from other aspects of the current communal oeuvre, however, it is possible that Sydney's hermaphroditic Centrepoint simply signals the feeling that in an increasingly alien urban environment, the bogeys are immanent.

A Quick History of Australian Film

"The past, in terms of Australian feature film production," says Andrew Pike, "is a distant one. After a short burst of activity between 1910 and 1912, the production of feature films declined sharply and continued at a level of rarely more than 10 features a year until World War 2. Efforts to revive production after the disruptions caused by the war failed, and during the 1950s and 1960s only a few locally-made features were completed . . . This period of inactivity ended abruptly . . . in 1970" (1980: 11). The reason, or at least the immediate impetus, for the recent revival is well enough known – a sudden infusion of government money into the industry – but what caused the long hiatus it ended? "The most common cry of producers, from the 1920s to the 1960s," says Pike, "was that the grip of powerful foreign production companies over the Australian distribution and exhibition trade was stifling the local industry by making Australian screens inaccessible to Australian film-makers." When one looks a little closer at the situation, however, it becomes obvious that the supposed freeze-out, while undeniably *contributing* to the problem, does not provide an ample explanation for it. "[T]he Americans, who had begun to arrive in force towards the end of World War 1," notes Pike, "merely perpetuated a trading environment that was already established." The Australians themselves, it would seem, simply lacked the necessary interest or faith to support their own industry. The question remains, then: why?

The picture becomes clearer if we consider the problematic that confronted the Australian filmmaker right from the beginning. Probably because of its emphasis on the *given*, film, more than any other medium until the advent of television, has an affinity for the con-textual. Reflecting almost perforce not merely what a community would like to think about itself but how its self thinks, it expresses, structurally as it were, an authentic if largely covert sense of being-in-the-world. If this sense is an ambivalent one, and especially if it conflicts with aspects of conscious or "official" self-imaging, it will also inadvertently express a kind of *sub voce* or subversive uneasiness.

Only if a given feature offers an adequate means of containing or managing this unexaminable tension will it "work" on an emotional level. Partly because they were breaking ground in a new field and partly because Australian culture at large had not yet normalized its displacing strategies, early filmmakers had difficulty in achieving such a balance. *Especially* since the most disquieting aspects of their psycho-social ambience were also the most (literally) fixating.

What aspects? Australians, says Graeme Turner, have generally imaged themselves in terms of a bracketing polarity. Discussion of this polarity, he continues, "has been dominated by three connected arguments, of which only the third is specifically generated by the Australian context. First, there is the proposition that [the] . . . basic opposition [is] between the city and the country; second, it is stipulated that this is essentially a Romantic opposition between Society and Nature, an opposition which is resolved in favour of the search for some harmony with Nature; and third, it is proposed that the search so initiated is usually fruitless because of the hostility, vastness, indifference or cruelty of the Australian version of Nature" (1986: 25). Impelled by their patriotism to *deal* with this subject (visual appropriation not only models but in a sense affirms the act of physical appropriation), yet denied the shifts employed by artists for re-making the recalcitrant environment, filmmakers were even more than most caught on the horns of this dilemma. Confronted with not merely one but *two* irresolvable oppositions – between the self and the landscape, between the landscape and its own image in culture (see G. Turner, 1981: 52) – they were forced to devise a means of sidestepping the whole issue. They did so, interestingly enough, by exactly the same means that artists, architects, and town planners have always used in Australia: by using "tamed" or token elements of the "preferred" but unassimilable otherness to create and then validate a space "between." What was this space? "The central thematic structure which generates the narratives . . . of Australian silent cinema," says John Tulloch, may be resolved, despite surficial diversity, into the simple triplet: "under-cultured (nature)/country culture/over-cultured (city)" (1981: 355). The film's version of the verandah, in other words, was simply a humanized version of "the bush."

Already, of course, it is easy to see how this strategy might contain the seeds to its own demise. For one thing, the main means available for achieving the requisite domestication of "country" entailed the foregrounding of an element which in itself replicated the tensions generated by the original polarity. Because nature was experienced, at least covertly, as feminine in Australia, the only way "she" could be convincingly tamed was through personification as a convincingly "tame" female (Tulloch: 376). Since women were as dangerous as the landscape they imaged, however, the only way to ensure that the creature would remain manageable was to denude her of her femaleness. The women in early Australian films are hence split into two groups: the strong but sexless "bush girl," and her evil alter, the sexy, wilful, weak-charactered city vamp. Even apart from its purely iconic functions, the geographical segregation had the dual advantage, first, of minimizing any suggestion of contamination or – worse – identity between types, and second, of supporting the pretence that what is being offered as I-site in these films is, in fact, nature. As neat as this schema sounds, unfortunately, in practice it was simply not believable enough to contain the psychological threat carried by its own subtext. Insofar as a not-quite-deactivated sisterliness (both types are, after all, equally alien under the skin) threatens at any moment to effect a symbolic reconflation of cultural power with natural sexuality (see, for instance, Tulloch's discussion of female virility in Franklyn Barrett's films, 396ff.; also Lawson, 1982, 28-29), the bush girl in the end carries too much psycho-symbolic baggage to be wholly amenable to masculine reconstruction.

The fragility of the bush-girl vehicle was unfortunately underwritten by the evasiveness of the cultural shifts for which it fronted. What was involved, in a sense, was an attempt to have one's cake and deny it too. The Romantic world view was important to the Australian not merely because it was European but because it confirmed, if only by assuming, a positive and, more important, dynamic relation with nature. In order to avoid implicitly unmanning himself, therefore, the filmmaker was debarred from openly admitting that *his* bush – the-bush-as-neutral-zone – was not wholly coincident with the-bush-at-large. This presented a number of problems. For one thing, there was the difficulty of maintaining its integrity. No matter what displacing mechanisms were invoked, as long as the terminology was indiscriminate, the decidedly ambiguous associations of the "wild" bush (see *"The Legend of the Nineties,"* pp. 237-44 below) were almost bound to carry over, albeit covertly, to the ostensibly tamed one. Second, and connected with this, given the *un*naturalness of the landscape which had been normalized in art (see section 12, above), there was the difficulty of presenting through the passive medium of film an adequately de-cultured setting which was not at least subtly alienating. Third, there was the problem of emotional alignments. Even leaving aside the liability of lurking adumbrations, if the "country" were to be accepted as good, even in conventional terms, it had to be signally endorsed with respect to the city. The only way this could be achieved was to make the moral threat of the latter loom larger than the physical dangers of the former. The difficulty, of course, was that even so early in Australia's history, far more viewers lived in than out of town. In order to downplay the *un*winnable battle with nature in favour of a positional triumph over culture, therefore, early filmmakers were forced to emphasize their protagonists' differentness from – indeed, their agonistic relationship to – the very people whose identification and sympathy they were courting. The fourth problem went somewhat deeper. Offsetting its benefits to a considerable extent, the tripartite schema, simply by virtue of its existence, had the concomitant effect of confirming the very opposition it was mounted to defuse. By tacitly criticizing its own stance, it also raised some disquieting questions about intention versus reaction. Tulloch himself sees the construction of a mediating category as (if somewhat politically problematic) fulfilling a positive function in the process of national self-definition. Considering the reluctance of its "creators" to cognize it *as* mediate, however, it could equally well be seen as an after-the-fact rationalization of the marginal status they had had thrust upon them. As such – and this was the really ticklish point – it was always in danger of self-deconstruction.

Lumbered with this kind of ambiguity, it is easy to see why the bush film – which might, as Tulloch notes, be taken as a paradigm for the entire early output – would present problems for both *auteur* and audience. The coming of sound was the final straw. Technical problems aside, by demanding or at least suggesting a conscious articulation of what was essentially inarticulable (it is notable, as Susan Dermody points out, that sound remakes of silent classics like *On Our Selection* and *The Sentimental Bloke* were far more "artfully" structured than the originals – and that this comprised their greatest flaw [1982: 43ff.]), they made a difficult proposition impossible. So – for the lack of a myth, an industry died. The question now, of course, is what made possible its revivification? What did filmmakers have in the seventies – and money alone is not enough of an answer – that their predecessors lacked in the twenties, the forties, even the sixties?

If we turn to the oeuvre itself, one of the first things that strikes us is that the "problems" so strenuously denied by the bush film have now apparently come out of the closet. The early seventies ocker comedies, as Jack Clancy points out (1979), not only document misogyny but expose the male fears of impotence that *underlay* the national antipathy to the feminine. Women themselves, as noted above, have become aggressors. Sex is linked openly with violence, while romance is either devalued or "impossible" (Morris, 1980). Even on a physical level, success is elusive. Indeed, the most active of heroes are often not just passive but defeatist (J. Clancy, 1982; Turner, 1986, especially chapter 3). The environment, despite the persistence of rhetorical nature worship, is at best problematic and at worst downright deadly. *Picnic at Hanging Rock* is not the only film where nature "devours" the protagonists. Colin Eggleston's ecological thriller, *Long Weekend*, as Dermody puts it, takes the "theme of the guilty alien despoiler . . . one step further, from judgment to sentencing" (1980: 84). As the word "guilty" implies here, nature itself is still usually construed as "good" in this genre. The fact, though, that we are allowed to see "her" naked menace is a considerable advance on earlier attempts at whitewashing. What does it mean? The most attractive possibility is that the Australians have simply stopped "pretending." The new filmmaker makes better films than the old one because he/she is no longer burdened with an unviable ideology. Closer attention to the *mood* of these films, however, suggests that, for all their *appearance* of normalizing the unpalatable, recent filmmakers have in fact been as assiduous in distancing unpleasant realities as their forebears. The only difference is that they have devised more effective means for doing so.

How? Brian McFarlane comments on the way that Peter Weir, in films like *Picnic* and *The Last Wave*, diffuses the ostensibly foregrounded threat of nature through an emphasis on atmospheric effects (1980, 62-63). Other critics note the propensity for temporal displacement I mentioned in my last journal segment. More important, they also note the extent to which the historical film virtually always subordinates the individual to event. "Perhaps the most significant recurring narrative pattern is that which locates the characters in a position of powerlessness in relation to the movement of the historical periods in which they are placed," says Tom Ryan. "In contrast, say, to American narratives which are 'typically stories of strength and energy expended in the pursuit and acquisition of or extension of control over geographic areas or political enterprises,' these Australian narratives decline the option of . . . tracing [their] characters' rises to power . . . Films as different as *Between the Wars, Mad Dog Morgan, Caddie, Break of Day, The Irishman, Newsfront, Dawn!, The Odd Angry Shot* and *My Brilliant Career* . . . [are] peopled by characters who are governed by forces beyond their control, and who are shown in a position of defeat at the close of the film" (1980: 120). Left-leaning commentators like Graeme Turner interpret this feature as both negative and ideological. By naturalizing "a grim and static view of the powerlessness of the individual," he says, it short-circuits potential revolt on the part of the disadvantaged proletariate (1986: 125). Whatever its incidental political *effects*, however, I think we have to see the strategy first and foremost as an attempt to rationalize or "excuse" what is felt to be an environmentally determined and therefore *unavoidable* impotence. The ultimate implication of this narrative pattern, notes Ryan, is "that the individual, and those with whom he/she is likely to come into contact, can play no part in the construction of history. Its course is in the hands of the powerful institutions which . . . exist outside the framework" of the film (125). Debarred a priori from efficacy – swept "against intentions, against all will . . . to actions and courses [he] cannot understand, nor control, nor alter" (Rohdie, 1985: 195) – the ordinary bloke need feel no guilt for his failure to "make it" as a hero.

The thing the new film does, then, that the old film does not, is to emphasize what is normally taken for granted, the *givenness* of the story. It does this, moreover, not only through its content, but even more through its "shape." It is interesting, for instance, to note the collective implications of what Tim Burstall lists as the "formal characteristics" of the new oeuvre: (1) "A preference for the structureless and episodic. Follow a life in the manner of a saga or a television series"; (2) "The pace, whether documentary or lyrical, is . . . slow"; (3) "A marked antagonism to style except for the purely aesthetic and visual"; (4) "Resistance to confrontation, drama, intensity of feeling"; (5) "Recessive heroes but not heroines"; and (6) "Even when [the pictures] are contemporary they betray very little sense of the present" (1985: 220-21). What all this adds up to – besides a striking facsimile of sprawl – is a narrative which literally announces itself as "not contrived." Why is this important? In the first place, it naturalizes the "inactivity" of the filmmaker just as the content does that of its inner personae. (It is notable, in this regard, that so many Australian films have been based on extant literary texts; see McFarlane, 1983: 206ff.) In the second place, and more important, it implies that since the events shown are purely fortuitous, it is absolutely unnecessary that they "make sense" or "add up" to anything beyond themselves. Where the early filmmaker was stuck with supporting an incoherent moral schema, therefore, the new one can set aside "values" as irrelevant, yet without actually having to *deny* any of his country's sacred cows.

While accounting for their success, this still doesn't explain, of course, why – apart from the financial shot in the arm – Australian films took off at the particular time that they did. Part of it no doubt was the fact that, with the distancing of the "real" bush, the erstwhile problematic mediating category of bush-as-idea (for the schema still imprints the subtext if not so often now the surface of the Australian film) had lost virtually all its ambiguity (see Rowse, 1978b, and Moorehouse, 1982, for different perspectives on suburban bushophilia). Part was the extent to which the conventions of the "new realism" of the sixties seemed to license that all-important shapeless-ness. Part, too, might relate to some critical point in the growth of the liter-ary reserves from which filmmakers could draw their material. It is not overly farfetched, though, to speculate that the political climate also helped. Insofar as the rhetoric of the anti-Vietnam and pro-ecology movements invoked the image of a world out of control, "reality" itself may well have been perceived as legitimizing the passive stance that these films collec-tively recommend.

SURFER'S PARADISE

[D]espite the bush mystique, there has also developed in Australia an urban attitude that disdains country life as vulgar and uncultivated . . . On the other hand, it is not easy to find this attitude issuing in much positive enthusiasm for Australian towns and cities . . . In both rhetoric and action, defenders of cities have [traditionally] been drowned out by their critics . . .

. . . Since the early 1970s, however, a new kind of large urban area has emerged. The first example was the Gold Coast, which comprises a string of coastal settlements stretching from Tweed Heads on the north side of the [Queensland-New South Wales] border to Southport, which have little industry and are not commercial centres for any large region. Holidays, retirement, recreation and some long-distance commuting to Brisbane seem to be its primary functions. It became a major urban area in 1976, and between then and 1981 it grew faster than any other major urban area (38%) to reach a population of 155,000 . . .

By comparison with other Australian cities, these new combined urban areas seem to have "no visible means of support." More than anything else, they are a product of affluence . . . [They] cater for pleasure as distinct from work: hedonism rather than fundamentalism is their religion.

Max Neutze, "City, Country, Town: Australian Peculiarities"

The last leg of my journey. Having fled New South Wales on the eve of a petrol strike, I am now heading back to my starting point. En route I decided to break my trip with a few days in Australia's most popular vacation spot: Surfer's Paradise. Now that I'm here, I am hard-pressed to explain the appeal. It's not surprising that Australians should prefer to holiday at the beach rather than the outback – the beach is, after all, the ultimate buffer between inside and outside, the dead heart and the green homeland, the natural and the cultivated (m)others. Surfer's Paradise, however, is the ultimate in urbanism. For miles along the coast the ocean is lined with rank upon rank of towering multi-unit hotels and apartment buildings. For a race of self-professed city-haters, this seems an odd spot to come to relax. Yet they do – in droves. Even though it is off season right now, and the weather is marginal, the main highway is lined with NO VACANCY signs.

It could, I suppose, simply reflect the desire to escape as far as possible from the humdrum and the usual. Despite the blanket implications of the word "urban," this isn't, in fact, an Australian's home away from home. Surfer's Paradise is the "other" city, the North American city, a high-rise ghetto seething with humanity and *action*. It's also, of course, not real. Perhaps this is the key. Just as the Australians have always looked to their painters and writers and filmmakers to provide them with a safe – that is, contained – version of the bush, what Surfer's Paradise may represent in the national iconography is a habitable facsimile of the archetypal city, domain of the phallic mother, *which has been made safe through its containment within the buffer zone of "the beach."* Carrying a subtext like that, the place could hardly help but be popular.

Just to check out one of my own loose ends, I have spent several evenings in the casino since I arrived. Although the general atmosphere here is glitzier than Tasmania, I really can't detect any significant differences in ambience. Again there is little sign of the kind of power games that go on in American gambling establishments. Missing also is the palpable greed, the almost desperate edge of excitement. For the Australian, gambling is obviously less liminal than it is for the American. Why this difference? Part of it must obviously reflect the extent to which the activity is normalized in mainstream culture here. Australians, I am told, are the biggest per capita gamblers in the world. Much of their betting, moreover, is done in the relatively domestic surroundings of the neighbourhood T.A.B. shop or the suburban club with its shiny ranks of poker machines. The experience offered by a full-scale casino, like the one in Hobart or the one here, is thus only quantitatively and not qualitatively different from everyday experience. To my eye, though, there is something about the Australians' *attitudes* toward their gambling that suggests the contrast is based in something a little more profound than increased familiarity. In American casinos everyone images him or herself as a winner. Here I get the impression that most casual gamblers don't, at least in the long haul, expect to come out on top. Nor do they seem to care overmuch one way or the other. Indeed, they are almost absurdly cheerful losers. I was struck by a domestic interchange that I overheard at one of the blackjack tables the other night. The wife was ready to go home. "Just hang on until I lose the rest of these chips," her husband replied. Surely this is fatalism in its most amiable guise.

Just one further point before I close for the day. Much has been said about the Australian accent, mostly by the Australians themselves, and all of it bad. Personally, perhaps because my standard of comparison is American rather than British, I do not find the dreaded drawl all that dreadful. Indeed, in comparison with, say, the brassy, nasal streetspeak of New York, it is rather pleasant. Which isn't to imply that it doesn't have some distinct peculiarities. To my ear, Australian speech sounds weak, tentative, somehow feminine, even when spoken by a male. The rising inflection at the end of the sentence makes every statement sound like a question. This may be pretty flimsy evidence on which to construct an entire theory of existential uncertainty, but it is interesting to note the extent to which the aural pattern is reflected on a semantic level. Others have noted the Australian tendency to infantilize their language by shortening common multisyllabic nouns to their diminutive forms (journalist is journo; barbecue, barbie; football, footie; afternoon, arvo; portable radio, trannie; and so on). I don't know whether anyone has gone the one step beyond observation to offer the obvious speculation that the habit reflects an attempt to make more manageable an essentially *un*manageable reality.

Decoding the Beach

The Australians themselves have not failed to recognize the importance of the beach as both a real and a symbolic locus. One of the most interesting of Australian popular culture studies of the past decade was John Fiske's "Surfalism and Sandiotics: The Beach in Oz Popular Culture" (1983), reissued in modified form as part of a 1987 book entitled *Myths of Oz*, written jointly by Fiske, Bob Hodge, and Graeme Turner. Because Fiske's conception of "mediation" in one sense complements but in another conflicts with the notion of a buffer zone put forth in early sections of this book it is worth taking a closer look at this paper.

Borrowing Don Grant's summary, Fiske's thesis can be seen as a variation on the Lévi-Straussian biaxial schema. "[H]e argues," says Grant, "that the text constituted by the set of Perth beaches reveals a . . . set of signifying categories or zones, operating vertically as well as horizontally . . . The beach [itself] is 'a physically anomalous category between land and sea . . . The land becomes culture, the city, civilization; the sea becomes nature, untamed, uncivilized, raw. The beach mediates this terrifying boundary.' This is the horizontal operation . . . The vertical operation . . . shows 'the same physical and conceptual movement from culture to nature, only this time in a south to north direction.' Commencing at Cottesloe beach with its prohibition notice, lawn and esplanade, all of which, Fiske argues, are attempts to naturalize culture, [he] takes us on a journey north . . . [towards] raw nature, [throughout which] the vestments of culture are [progressively] loosened. We move through zones of 'scandalous behaviour' represented by surfboards, dogs and topless women, finally divesting ourselves at Nude Beach" (1984: 132-33). What's wrong with this conceptualization? Grant himself suggests, first, that Fiske's reconstruction of the vertical development is oversimplistic, and second, that differences on this axis, as signalled by the presence or absence of regulatory notices, are less attributable to spontaneous communal codings than to the specific political leanings of the eight different local authorities that control the shoreline between Fremantle and City Beach.

Being inadequately acquainted with either the terrain or the local politics, I am unable to comment on this proposition beyond suggesting that since the regulation of the beach, vis-à-vis both posting and zoning, would appear to be more explicit and more rigorous in proximity to the most "urban" areas, the variability Grant comments upon could be seen not as an effect of the attempt to humanize a threatening nature, as Fiske would have it, but as a reaction to the omnipresence of an equally threatening culture. It is here, of course, that my own reading would depart most markedly from Fiske's. Though he doesn't explicitly say so, it is obvious from his emphasis that Fiske assumes that the human occupants relate normatively to the cultural side of the fence. The mediating function of the beach is therefore simply a means of naturalizing relations with the alien zone of nature. In stressing – indeed, taking into consideration Grant's critique, misrepresenting – the systematic aspect of the gradation, moreover, he also seems to assume that the desired accommodation *is*, in the end, achieved. The question, leaving aside quibbles: is he right about this?

Even apart from its intrinsic interest, the issue has some important ramifications for broader aspects of Australian social psychology. For all that he foregrounds the geographical schema in his original paper, the most critical aspect of Fiske's thesis lies in its historical dimension. Leaving the beach aside for now, it is interesting to note the thematic parallels in some of the other topics covered in *Myths of Oz*. Whatever the authors intended, the picture that emerges at least from the first half of this book is of a culture which has recently gone through a number of very major changes. If one were looking for a pat phrase, in fact, its subject might well be described as "the evolution of mediate spaces in Australia." In the first chapter, for instance, we are told how the pub, formerly a no-woman's land (except for the co-opted barmaid, as much a token of male dominance as the foreign flowers in the front yard) located between the public world of work and the private world of home, has recently been feminized, made more domestic in both ambience and function. In the second chapter, supporting my own observations in the "CANBERRA" segment above, we are told how the "outdoor living area" has replaced the verandah in the new suburban home. Both of these developments, though in a sense semiologically opposed (one breaks down barriers between the [male] self and "inside," while the other, in "affirming nature over culture," actually *counters* the domesticating ideology of suburbia [43]), can be seen as signalling not merely the relatively more successful "adjustment" that I suggested in my discussion of new trends in public architecture (pp. 178-79), but a real, albeit vestigial, *reconciliation* with the feminine. If true, this would obviously have tremendous implications for the future of Australia. *This* is why John Fiske's semiology of the beach is so important.

If we return to Fiske's schema we will note that the progressive naturalization suggested by the geographic gradation from regulated to unregulated beach is parallelled in the historic evolution of its proprietary typos. Between the wars, the Bondi lifesaver was not only a local hero but in a sense came to represent a national ideal of manhood. Since the fifties, however, says Fiske, the lifesaver has lost much of both his real and his symbolic ascendancy. "If he is still an heroic figure rowing out to scare sharks from the urban beaches, his heroism is counterpointed and qualified by the . . . surfers suicidally straddling their boards further out to sea, affecting a nonchalant disinterest in the proceedings" (1987: 65). The surfer himself, concomitantly, has assumed an increasingly central role in both folk and mass culture. What does this mean? One way of interpreting the development is as a shift from a culturally oriented self-image, set in opposition to nature, to one in which nature has been, if not conquered, at least assimilated. Richard White's more specifically grounded description of the lifesaver would seem to support this latter reading, and at the same time to suggest what it was that triggered the change. "Although most aspects of the lifesaver conformed to the traditional Australian 'type' – the 'sun-bronzed' physique, the masculinity, the cult of mateship, the military associations, the hedonism and wholesomeness of the beach – there were," he says, "important differences. Unlike the bushman and [C.E.W.] Bean's version of the digger, the lifesaver was identified with the city rather than the bush" (1981: 155-57). What White implies here – as, on a different level, does Fiske – is that the lifesaver was an unsatisfactory alter ego, ultimately, because he was too clearly an opponent, rather than an agent, of nature.

While agreeing that the lifesaver's associations with the regulatory function of the city would tend to undermine his symbolic authority, I have to question the collateral assumption White makes here. Inasmuch as the bush is itself culturally constructed as a mediate zone (see "A Quick History of Australian Film," pp. 209-15 above), the bushman is no more truly aligned with nature than the lifesaver is. The reason, I would claim, that the lifesaver has been replaced in the popular imagination by the surfer, therefore, is not the latter's nature-association but the fact that, *like* the bushman, he is semiologically located exactly on or in the interface. Construed almost invariably in Australian fiction and folklore as feminine – and this is what Fiske overlooks – the ocean is not just "nature," but the unconscious. Because he skates on its surface, then, rather than penetrating it as either opponent *or* victim, the surfer is able, far more than the swimmer, to exemplify for his auditors a reassuring immunity to both animal (and here it is interesting to note the iconic significance that the shark attack, real or metaphorical, has accrued in the Australian communal text; see Sanders, 1983) and *anima* danger. At the same time, his notoriously antisocial behaviour dissociates him definitively from the lifesaver's pro-social policing role. Given the literal ambi-valence of this imaging, one would have to say that the "development" implied by Fiske et al. is at least somewhat less clear-cut than it surficially seems.

BRISBANE

Yet here is the irony. If Australianness is elusive as a center, an essence, a destiny, it is everywhere to be found as a refracting perspective, a melange, a quirk. The baffling circumstances that defeat the search for the center may well prove to be the thing itself.

Nicholas Jose, "Cultural Identity"

My last stop is my longest one, but also probably my least eventful. I spend most of my days in the library, browsing through bibliographies, rifling the stacks, and endlessly photocopying. I am amazed at how much good journal literature there is on Australian culture. Perhaps because so many of the book-length cultural studies tend to be written from a generalist rather than a scholarly standpoint, one doesn't get the sense of this dense body of commentary floating beneath the surface. If it is somewhat inadequately synthesized by North American standards, on the other hand, by the same standards this material is refreshingly animated. Having somehow resisted or perhaps simply misunderstood the rigidly objectivist creed of the New Critics, Australian historians and literary and art scholars virtually always write from a specific and often highly politicized point of view. There is a lively tradition of scholarly debate going all the way back to the eighteen-nineties. Literary-cum-cultural affairs journals like Sydney's *Southerly* and Melbourne's *Meanjin Papers* have been around since the forties. Despite, or perhaps because of this, there is an element of amateurism in the way that intellectual resources on a national scale are, or rather are not, mobilized. The impression one gets on the whole is of a thriving intelligentsia lacking badly in both self-awareness and confidence.

I continue to be impressed by the helpfulness of my academic colleagues. My first day out at Griffith I dropped by the School of Asian Studies to speak to the co-ordinator of a conference at which I am scheduled to give a paper. Before I knew it, I was fixed up with an office, a library card, and photocopying privileges. While the assistance is generally of a somewhat less concrete nature, the attitude implicit in this response has proven much more the rule than the exception. Australian Studies specialists at all three of the local post-secondary institutions have – if somewhat bemused by my (to them) rather idiosyncratic approach to cultural history – been particularly generous with their time and advice. Where their generosity stops, on the other hand, is at the gate of the college. I am invited for lunch, or tea, or a late afternoon drink, but never for dinner. Not one of these people has asked me into his or her home. Given their apparently quite genuine friendliness, I can't help wondering why. It may be me, of course, or it may be that they simply don't know what to "do" with an unattached, middle-aged female. It may, on the other hand, reflect a kind of social ineptness or even outright asociability.

It is my impression that Australians – or perhaps, to give fair due to the limited nature of my face-to-face contacts here, Australian academics – do not, in fact, do much socializing. Certainly I see no sign of the kind of on-campus pub-centred cross-strata fraternization that is common in North America. Part of this may be attributed to a more rigid hierarchization of the academic community. Part, too, may relate to the fact that these people seem to work harder, or at least more *regularly*, than their American counterparts. They put in their eight hours, and then go home to their families. This, of course, is the final ingredient: domestication. I have already commented on the rather surprising reclusiveness of the Australian. It is notable that the only individuals apart from old friends or business contacts to have offered us a more personal brand of hospitality on this trip have been a childless couple and two single (divorced) women.

If I have been kept officially outside the Australian home, I have, however, been afforded a few more covert glimpses into the private lives of Australians. The balcony of the flat in which I am currently installed overlooks the back yards to a block of old-style working-class suburban housing. After all my comments on gardens, I am fascinated to note that apart from a sparse skiff of grass these anterior spaces are virtually bare. There are sheds, toys, tools, clotheslines, barbecues, bicycles, old furniture, and a few vegetable plots, but absolutely nothing ornamental: none of the flowers and fancy shrubs that embellish their faces. Contra my remarks about the recent incorporation of nature into the buffer zone, it seems from this that there was *always* an element of "front" in the Australian garden. It also becomes apparent to what extent these marginal spaces, while seeming to "open up" the I-site, are actually coded as restricted. Not only are the yards here *physically* fenced, but virtually nothing goes on in the way of *social* interaction that might violate the tacit barrier between households. Neighbours go around to the front if they want to visit. I have seen two boys who fraternize on the street playing side by side separately in their respective yards without, apparently, either taking the least notice of the other.

I, too, feel a bit as though I'm living in a hermetically sealed space these days. In some ways it's rather liberating. Perhaps it's because I'm a short-timer now, or I have found other ways to valorize my detachment – perhaps it's even because I am becoming more "Australian" myself – but I no longer feel rebuffed the way I did those first few days in Sydney. More accurately, I am no longer disturbed by it. I am still trapped on the surface of things, but now, rather than feeling that there is something I'm missing, I have the sense that I am only one among a multitude of essentially segregate lives. As I walk around downtown with my camera, knowing that observers will construe me, simply and anonymously, as "tourist," I begin to see the appeal rather than the limitations of surficiality. Denied intimacy, I am also free of all expectations but my own. I go to movies in the afternoon. I get my dinner from one of the several take-away restaurants in the base of my building. I spend my evenings watching television and packing books for mailing.

I find myself increasingly fascinated by the now familiar repertoire of programs. Early evening is devoted to the soapies. Later come the American or, less frequently, British drama series. There's virtually nothing between. For me it is all equally foreign. For the Australians themselves, however, there must be an element of schizophrenia in this unmediated juxtaposition of the familiar and the strange. What do the imports "mean" to them? It's a sticky question, but an important one. Given their popularity, these action/adventure shows, with their feisty, wilful guys and dolls, must – notwithstanding discrepant subliminal effects – play a role in constructing a public understanding of social "reality." Given the gap between what is consumed and what is "made," however, it clearly can't be the same role that they play for their own creators. Canadians are fascinated by the Great American Hero because he represents our significant other. Perhaps Australians are fascinated because he represents a wishful but unattainable ego-image, while they themselves are construed as shadow. This may explain why the internationalist strain in Australian culture seems in some ways a more important characterizing feature than the nationalist one. If, rather than being assimilated, the imported myth is viewed as normative, then it is inevitably going to foster a doubleness of vision, an irreconcilable tension between felt self and willed self. By subverting the criterion of source (internally generated artifacts are relevant, out-group ones are not), it must also complicate immeasurably the task of differentiating between significant and non-significant aspects of culture.

The problem of discrimination becomes particularly acute in the area of youth culture. Given the nature of the music industry, for instance – given that Australian musicians are not only economically dependent on the big international labels for their marketing, but *culturally* dependent on the British and American trendsetters vis-à-vis both visual and musical style – it would seem not only difficult but pointless to look for indigenous patterns in rock music and videos. The key word in this sentence is "seem." No matter how other-directed the host, I do not believe that there is any such thing as truly international culture. Assuming (1) that individual musicians must have *some* influence on the packaging of their product, and (2) that social psychology will bias them in the choices they make among available models, one should still find at least relative differences in the way that any given nationality *adapts* the international idiom. In order to prove this point I have spent my last few Saturday mornings in Brisbane watching rock videos on TV. Although the resultant sample is far too small (analysis was carried out on one or more videos each by eighty-three different groups and/or artists, of whom twenty-five were identified as Australian) and the methodology too crude to allow for any definitive conclusions, in the context of this broader study some of the general patterns that have emerged are at least provocative.

First, the music itself. Here I have found little that is distinctive. The Australian sound seems a little "softer" than the international norm, but this may have something to do with the speech patterns I talked about in the last section. Lyrically, too, the Australian songs seem largely to recycle the same themes, the same feelings, even the same phrases that fixate their British and American counterparts. If there is a distinct substrain of nihilism and despair (AC/DC's "Who Made Who," for instance, with its images of schoolboys caught in a science fiction nightmare, or Flotsam/Jetsam's "Distraction"), there is plenty of precedent especially among the British and

European examples. It does seem to me that there is less, or at least less convincing, heroic posturing on the part of the Australians than among the Americans; it also seems that the former have less control over their irony. Since the desire to promote local talent tends to establish lower standards for Australian entries than for the imports, however, this may simply be a case of unsuccessful imitation.

The visual level yields far more interesting evidence. Again there is, of course, a high level of what we might call "background" homogeneity. Despite this, the Australian sample as a whole reveals a number of rather interesting culture-specific propensities. First among these is a general art-lessness. Antipodean videos are not only less technically innovative (which could be put down to economic causes), but also strikingly unstructured. The most common form is an open-ended, slackly additive, anthology-type sequence of anecdotal segments intermontaged with performance shots. Narrativity is offset, ambiguated, or simply overwhelmed by a barrage of inappropriate or irrelevant visual imagery. Particularly popular are fire and water images, damaged or threatened children, (sub)urban rot, and inexplicit violence. Transitions tend to be abrupt, and pacing erratic. The effect of discontinuity is in many cases further exacerbated by the use of strobing, flickering, fuzzing, label babble, torn, decaying or fragmented images, and manual tampering with the film.

Differences in form carry over to homologous differences in content. A few of the Australian examples employ crudely nationalistic themes featuring the beach or the outback (Boom Crash Opera's "Hands Up in the Air," Midnight Oil's "The Dead Heart"). More interesting, however, are those cases where they *attempt* to adapt an international-type storyline – and fail. Paradoxically, the area of greatest failure is in the area of their greatest conventionality. Where the American videos in particular are self-consciously recursive, parodic, and interactive, Australian attempts at allusiveness generally undermine themselves by decontextualizing or otherwise disorienting the stereotypic patterns. My running notes on Dragon's "Speak No Evil," for instance, clearly imply a failure on the part of the writer to control the intertextuality of his construct.

Hand-held camera (signalling "presence"?) moves through bush to backwoods-type farm – dramatized confrontation with old woman – shots of farmer-daddy, children, baby doll-type girl, alternating with fire images, band shots, dramatized pursuit (brute chasing blond), nostalgic swimming hole scenes – strong hints of southern gothic – but is the brute the villain or the protagonist? Has the "brother" figure done something to him? There is no closure to this narrative – we are left hanging, with vague hints of Deliverance.

Dragon is untypical in attempting to present, or even suggest, a coherent narrative at all. It *is* typical, however, in its handling of that narrative. When the conventions of film or fiction are invoked in these videos, instead of helping to stabilize the reading, they themselves tend to become ambiguous. The only notable exception is INXS's "Listen Like Thieves," where a band concert is staged in a grotesque post-atomsmash world strikingly reminiscent of *Mad Max*. In their attempts to "use" the conventions of non-indigenous and particularly American popular culture, the Australians generally prove unable to appreciate which elements are optional and which (like the marking of the hero/villain) essential to the underlying myth.

Failures aside, if the Australian oeuvre has one positive characteristic of its own, it is its emphasis on motion. Just as the Australian writer follows the course of least resistance with his loosely linear plotline, the Australian videomaker seems to be most comfortable when s/he is simply scanning across the landscape. In many cases, the *sense* of movement is tied to explicit *images* of movement: cars, boats, planes (but not trains). Sometimes, as in The Ups and Downs' "The Living Kind," with its sinisterly discordant flash-past views of working class suburbia, the observer bespoken by the camera is actually *in* the vehicle, speeding through cities or careening across the countryside. This strategy of mobilization is not, to be sure, unique to Australia. I think it notable, however, that a "travelling" persona is employed in a quarter – six out of twenty-five – of the Australian videos in my sample, but only around 10 per cent of the non-Australian ones.

What does it mean? To my mind it means that for all his/her surficial Americanization, the young Australian has exactly the same sense of the world, and of him or herself *in* the world, as his/her elders. Baulked in the task of rationalizing reality-as-given by an inability to see or to "make" connections, he/she relieves anxiety by (at least wishfully) keeping on the move. More important, it also means that the communal consciousness imprints not only those products which are overtly nationalistic, but *all* a culture's artifacts, without awareness or intent, *and whether the ostensible creators will it or not.*

4

ALTERNATIVE READINGS

I have made mention throughout my perambulations of the extent to which both expressive and instrumental productions seem, in Australia, to reflect the same underlying structures – structures that can be related directly and systematically with aspects of Australian social psychology. The term "sprawl," for instance, may be applied with equal aptness to literature, to painting, to urban development, and to habits of mind (McDougall, 1987). The same can be said of the antithetical/complementary trait of disconnectedness. Vance Palmer notes how the editorial practice of the early *Bulletin* encouraged fragmented and discontinuous prose (1963); Susan Dermody comments on the episodic nature of early films (1982) – literary and cinema critics are making exactly the same kinds of comments about the work that is being produced today (see, for instance, Burstall, 1985). Tim Rowse, in a discussion of short story writer Frank Moorehouse, makes explicit what is only implicit in most of these critiques: the fragmentation of the artifact echoes the fragmentation of culture-at-large. Imputing a specifically mimetic intention to his subject ("Moorehouse sees his preferred narrative form, the discontinuous narrative, as 'a map of how the world – Australia – appears to me'"), Rowse proceeds to demonstrate how Moorehouse's "map" fits the current political scene. "The CPA [Communist Party of Australia] reflects the fractionated condition of contemporary Australian radicalism," he says. "The differences [between factions] are not . . . [indicative] of mutual hostility, but of discontinuity – a dispersion of efforts which is both healthy and problematic . . . No activity of intellectual comprehension and unifying programmatic assertion pulls this together" (1982: 251, 259; see also Jose, 1985). Though Rowse himself implies that the phenomenon is somehow related to the country's new cultural pluralism (see Chapter 5, below), such "discontinuity" is, in fact, just as consistent and predictable an aspect of Australian cultural production as McDougall's sprawl. More important for present purposes, it is also a consistent, predictable aspect of the discursive modes that Australians use for "talking about" their culture. The primary characterizing features of Australian "fiction" are, as we shall see, the primary characterizing features of Australian scholarship. Using a few key texts as jumping-off points, this chapter will offer a number of rereadings of the Australians' own readings of Australian cultural history. Before I address this task, however, inasmuch as they can be considered as propaedeutic to the entire corpus, it is useful to examine a few of the more important of these shared formal predispositions.

First and perhaps most highly visible is an element I have elsewhere called ambi-valence or duplicity. This is not simply a matter of the bifurcate "literary" patterns that Graeme Turner talks about in his exemplary study of *National Fictions* (1987, especially Chapter 2). Australians, as, indeed, Turner himself recognizes, seem actually to experience their world in dualistic terms. It is hence hardly surprising that they are inclined also to *formulate* their world in dualistic terms. John Colmer comments, for instance, on the tendency of Australian autobiographers and memoirists to construct their "lives" around antitheses. "Even in . . . works that make no specific claim to describe and analyse cultural conflict, there is an uneasy preoccupation with conflicting life-styles and values," he says. "The characteristic oppositions are those between Bush and City; Ocker and embryonic artist; Wowser and Bohemian sophisticate; nationalist and cosmopolite; the older generations and the younger" (1984: 138). Quite apart from its relevance to the theme of "middleness," this apparently persistent binocularity perhaps explains why so much Australian cultural critique focuses on questions of either/or. And I'm not just talking about quibbles. The dialogue mentioned in the last Brisbane section (p. 223) is not, commonly, limited to academic side issues, but concerns the kind of all-embracing socio-political dichotomies embodied concretely, as the myth would have it, in the two great cities of Sydney and Melbourne (Davidson, 1986). We will be looking more closely at some of the constituent feuds in the sections that follow (for an overview, see D. Walker, 1976: 194-211). For now, however, I would just note that an obsessively agonistic intellectual position may well signal an inability to "think" culture except in terms of black and white.

The second feature was also presaged in my comments in that concluding journal segment. I have noted on numerous occasions – as, indeed, have numerous indigenous critics – the "shapelessness" or "artlessness" of Australian literary productions (Kiernan, 1971: 82ff.; Daniel, 1978). I also noted, in connection with McDougall (1987; see "Sprawl, Urban and Otherwise," pp. 50-52 above), that at least some of the latter are inclined to view the propensity as a positive one. The reason most commonly offered in justification is that an unpretentious matter-of-factness achieves a "truer" image of reality. Geoffrey Serle, for instance, talks with approval of the "documentary" bias of thirties novelists. "[I]n a period when there were still few Australian historians and almost no political scientists or sociologists," he says, writers such as Leonard Mann, Eleanor Dark, Vance Palmer, Christina Stead, M. Barnard Eldershaw, and Kylie Tennant "were almost alone in attempting to define, analyse and comment on the nature of Australian society" (1973: 123). Political rationale notwithstanding, on the other hand, the Depression era social realists were far from unique in their practice. Drusilla Modjeska suggests that the "indigenous tradition" may have exerted as great an influence as Russia on Australian Marxists. T. Inglis Moore would agree. "The general temper of the society," he says, "has been strongly utilitarian, extrovert, with little feeling for the life of the mind and spirit . . . [A]ll these characteristics . . . are . . . reflected in the outward-looking realism of [Australian] literature – a realism in literary form, opposed to romanticism, and a philosophical realism, opposed to idealism, with stress on things as [opposed] . . . to the invisible realm of ideas" (1971: 123).

The question is, of course – since my task here is not literary criticism but ethnography – what does this preference "mean" to/for the actual practitioners? While disagreeing neither with Moore's contentions about the entrenchment of utilitarianism in the Australian mindset, *nor* with claims widely made about the causal relationship between this mindset and the feature of artlessness, I would have to query, for one thing, whether the strategy is so much a matter of rational choice, based on social and personal priorities, as it is a fallback position, based on the felt impossibility of alternatives. For all the attempts to make it seem a virtue (some of the best of recent Australian writers, says Nicholas Jose, work "for a coherent, comprehensive understanding, scrupulously eschewing the simplicities of myth and, instead, reckoning with the resistance to coherence exerted by the stubborn, broken, actual world" [1985: 332]), the refusal to give "form" to experience – the preference of filmmakers for historical subjects, as well as the penchant among novelists for pseudo- or quasi-autobiography ("'Unreliable Memoirs' . . . or 'The Education of Young Somebody Else who used perhaps to be me'" [Grove, 1984: 161]) – could well be diagnostic of much more profound problems of comprehension.

This suspicion becomes more acute when we turn from literature, where one can at least *debate* the issue on the basis of opposing aesthetics, to scholarly discourse, where the aim of the writer must be assumed, at the very least, to involve some sort of elucidation of his/her object. In this realm, unfortunately, the feature of artlessness combines with the feature of discontinuity to militate against synthesis. "The received overview of our Australian literary tradition is oddly superficial," says Turner, "noting details without attempting to relate those details to their source in our tradition" (1981: 51). One could say exactly the same thing of the country's non-literary critique. When Stephen Alomes complains about the "simple-minded empiricism" of media research (1981b: 13), or John Uhr criticizes a notable local political scientist for the ostensibly *opposite* error of "rest[ing] his case on abstract truths which do not illuminate the specific situation" (1981: 107), or Diane Austin complains about the mutual exclusiveness of conservative and Left factions within Australian sociology (1984: 87), they are all, essentially, talking about the failure of the country's scholars to make meaningful connections among texts or between text and context. Leonie Kramer claims it is the lack of "a rigorous, constructive critical tradition" that makes Australians so naively prone to embrace imported theories, usually belatedly and with "very little understanding as to whether or how they might be adapted to Australian conditions" (1985: 295). Viewing it from a slightly different perspective, one might simply say that they are handicapped by the lack of any natural talent for intellectual as for other forms of systematic trans-action.

The third key feature of Australian scholarship is also one that has been noted in a number of connections in the foregoing chapters. Again taking a start from literature, a common theme of contemporary criticism has been the shallowness, the opaqueness, and particularly the lack of self-awareness of the characters in Australian novels. At best, as in Patrick White's novels, it is a peculiarity of content rather than of presentation (White's *Tree of Man*, as Kiernan points out, "succeeds in dramatically objectifying the characters' inner consciousness, even when it may remain puzzling to themselves" [1971: 107-8]). At worst, and more often, however, the authors seem no more sure of what Moore calls "the inner life of the emotions and the imagination" (123) than their creatures. "In [Martin Boyd's] *Lucinda Brayford*," says Brian McFarlane, "the third-person narrative skirmishes around [the heroine's] most painful moments, not quite offering a sharp enough insight into Lucinda and not offering a compensating dramatic interest in the narrative voice" (1983: 183). The complaint is a common one. It is also more than a little relevant to the practice of those self-same literati who make it. Why? Because what we are talking about here is not merely a technical flaw but a peculiarity of stance that goes far beyond the creators of fiction. Australian critics, says Graeme Turner, have traditionally evinced a "reluctance to enquire too closely into the structures, the experience, of life itself." Far from "immanent in the self," meaning is preferentially seen by these people as "a system of customs and practices which have a determined secularity and practicality, priding itself on its ability to deal with the world as it is" (1986: 83). Note those terms: *secularity* and *practicality*. What we have here, of course, is an exact discursive equivalent to the exteriority of Australian painting.

When we look at cultural studies, the deformative effects of the bent become more palpable. Paralleling the writer's disinterest in the inner lives of his characters is the Australian scholar's apparent disinterest in the inner lives of his/her subjects. Australian social science in particular has been fixated on the level of effects, preferring not even to speculate about the ineffable causes of behaviour. As late as 1965, a critical anthology entitled *Australian Society* contained not one single psychology text in its 204-item bibliography (Encel, 1984: 5). Why the bias? Judith Brett blames history. "The slight impact of psychoanalytic thinking on our culture must . . . be understood partly in terms of Australia's relative inhospitality to immigrants at a crucial time: partly too, I think, in terms of the preoccupations of many Australian intellectuals, particularly of the left, with forming an identity from the Australian past. Psychoanalysis with its central European origins was of no help to such an enterprise" (1982: 340). This last sentence is the important one. That the Australians should think of psychoanalysis as something "foreign," and therefore irrelevant, is much more telling than Brett apparently realizes. From an outside perspective it seems clear that less weight should be placed on the purely historical factors than on the issues of national temperament she mentions almost by way of afterthought. "Judith Wright talks of the way we are constantly turned away from emotions," she notes. "Australia's indifference to psychoanalysis may then be part of a wider indifference. Psychoanalysis, like poetry, is [a] way of attending to . . . inner life . . . of understanding emotions . . . of approaching the self" (341). The comparison is a provocative one. We have already noted the Australian's ambivalence about poetry.

Whatever the combination of reasons, the fact is that there is virtually *no* psychological dimension to Australian cultural studies. One finds the odd psychoanalytic piece in the literary field, like David Tacey's aforementioned paper on *Voss* (1985; see pp. 149-54, above), or Annette Hamilton's fascinating study of children's literature (1975), but apart from these the pickings are slim indeed. Australian historians, even biographers, as John Rickard points out in a *Journal of Australian Studies* symposium on psychohistory, have almost always stopped short at "hard" facts like works and dates and events (1981). Judging by the tone of the respondents in this debate, moreover, the oversight is far from coincidental. Within the academic establishment, psychohistory is clearly viewed as somewhat less than respectable. "Only when a change in the subject, or sometimes a lack of change, cannot be narratively explained," says Richard Ely, "will the conventional historian resort to . . . theories" (1981: 123). With such attitudes among those who actually purport to be dealing with personalities, it is not surprising that social studies in Australia tend to be overwhelmingly phenomenal and circumstantial. It is also not surprising that such psychologically oriented studies of culture as do exist should be relatively naive in their grasp of theory. Ronald Conway's *The Great Australian Stupor* is particularly interesting in this regard. Although the author explicitly cites Freud and Jung as his primary authorities, a scan of the notes reveals that he allots them only one quote apiece in the entire 250-page book. Pop psycho-philosopher Erich Fromm gets four references. None of Freud's "hard" descendants, from Rank and Adler through to the recent post-structuralists, are even mentioned. And this despite the fact that Conway – "a practising clinical psychologist and therapist for over 25 years . . . and . . . Senior Lecturer in Applied Psychology at the Royal

Melbourne Institute of Technology from 1975 to 1981" (1985, back cover) – would seem as close to an expert on the subject as the country can muster.

Does it matter? This, of course, is the bottom line. And the answer? I think so. It seems clear from an overview of the scholarly oeuvre that these peculiarities of stance not only bias but maim the Australians' attempts at self-analysis. *As* we shall see in the following sections.

The Legend of the Nineties

There has been ample opportunity throughout this study to note the mixed feelings held by Australians about their land. From one viewpoint ambivalence was inherent simply in the landscape itself. "Not only was the continent less attractive the further inland one went," says R.L. Heathcote, "but the condition of the environment ... changed significantly ... from season to season, [and] year to year ... The exploring accounts as a result are full of conflicting reports of country seen at different times, 'plains of promise' were 'barren deserts' depending upon whom you read and when (or whether) they had been there" (1972: 78-79). From a broader perspective, however, it seems clear that the "real" paradox was only the least of the problems. As hinted in Heathcote's parenthetical "or whether," a much more critical factor was the expectations projected *on* the country before the fact. If the antipodes were often viewed by Europeans as literally "freakish" (White, 1981: 6ff.), there was also a strong and extremely emotional paradisial strain in early conceptualizations. More important at least with respect to its psycho-symbolic ramifications, this strain almost always expressed itself in fantasies of the "middle." Ross Gibson, for instance, in a fascinating study of Australian exploration literature entitled *The Diminishing Paradise*, notes the persistence in the folk consciousness of an image of an as-yet undiscovered lush green heartland – sometimes even a great inland sea – beyond or, more accurately, *within* the purgatorial desert. He also notes the extent to which public prehension of this image was influenced by wishes, rather than by facts. "[T]he spirit of the goldrushes," he says, "obscured . . . the contradictory and experientially validated image of an Australian Purgatory . . . The explorers' vision of the country was not [accepted] . . . because the more alluring notion of the Australian golden age" seemed to be validated by "the prospect of favourable material conditions" (1984: 137). This did not, to be sure, mean that the negative image of "bizarre dead lands" (136) was expunged from the communal memory. One might speculate, indeed, that it was the concomitant thought of purgatory – especially given the archetypal associations with (m)otherness – that made the paradise fantasy so numinous. It seems clear, in any case, that it was the tacit juxtaposition of irreconcilable good/bad visions of the interior that laid the ground for the aforementioned sense of existential dichotomization.

Having been established as a given, this dichotomization took on a life of its own. Not only did it predispose the Australians' sense of being-in-the-world; it also predisposed the way they conceived – literally, gave birth to – their past. One of the most rancorous, voluminous, and long-lived debates of the last half-century has been the controversy over whether the colonial experience itself was "good" or "bad." Russell Ward's *The Australian Legend* (1958; rpt. 1966) served as a catalyst in this matter (for a range of representative responses/rebuttals, see Roe, 1962; Barrett, 1972; Wilkes, 1977; Carroll, 1982; Bolton, 1983; see also my own discussion on pp. 91-94 above), but the terms of the argument were clearly entrenched in the communal text long before. Vance Palmer's 1954 re-examination of fin-de-siècle Australia in *The Legend of the Nineties*, for instance, while lacking Ward's enthusiasm for the convict (Palmer was more inclined to associate the impulse toward democratization with the hordes of foreign-born adventurers who poured into the country during the gold rushes; see 1963, Chapter 1), certainly anticipates him in its ratification of bush-begotten egalitarianism, and its admiration for the Furphy-Lawson school of writing associated with *The Bulletin* which (according to him) most saliently expressed it.

Wherever it began, on the other hand, a scan of journal literature and book bibliographies makes it clear that the debate is far from over. What, exactly, is at issue? This is not the place to get too deeply embroiled in the details of the controversy – nor, in view of the sheer volume of paper already expended to that end, should it be necessary. For present purposes I will merely note that the pro-legendists believe with Ward that the best and most authentic elements of the Australian tradition can be traced to the mores and values of the nineteenth-century pastoral working class, while their opponents claim that the "history" on which this hypothesis is based is at best revisionist (Ward is found "guilty of legend-mongering, romanticism, false sociology, wilful disregard of multicultural precedents, and promulgation of an ethic . . . of unAustralian origins" [Bolton: 48]), and at worst an outright lie. The task for this section is not so much to arbitrate these opposing claims in any full or systematic manner, as to determine how they "fit in" with some of the less explicit aspects of communal self-imaging examined in earlier sections of this book.

Let's start with the putative "facts" of the matter. Many of the debunkers over the years have been preoccupied with proving that this or the other aspect of the Lawson-Furphy portrait of bush life – the portrait around which Palmer and Ward built their theories – was inaccurate. Some of the most damning documents in this vein have been those that take on Ward's rather naive contentions (based at least in part on the stories of *Bulletin* writer Price Warung; for a critique of this usage see Hergenhan, 1980) about the positive after-effects of convictism. If Robert Hughes's *The Fatal Shore* is the most impressively panoramic of these, M.B. and C.B. Schedvin's study of "The Nomadic Tribes of Urban Britain" – one of the slate that John Carroll puts together in an early eighties anthology entitled *Intruders in the Bush* – is perhaps the most delving. Even apart from its scarcity value, the Schedvins' psycho-socially oriented analysis of the population from which the majority of the convicts were drawn is both interesting and (perhaps unintentionally) provocative, providing as it does not only a definitive rebuttal of Ward's optimistic inferences about the roots and meaning of mateship, but *also* – insofar as their elucidation of convict behaviour patterns reveals an almost startling consistency with the behaviour patterns presented as normative in Australian popular culture – an equally definitive confirmation of his claims that the convict inheritance was a critical factor in the development of the national psychology.

Their . . . characteristics included restlessness and unwillingness to accept the personal investment and self-discipline implied by continuity of work and purposeful action; uncertain restraint of libidinal impulses illustrated by periodic bouts of excessive drinking; the evocation of fantasies of independence which masked an underlying reluctance to assume responsibility for oneself or one's actions, demonstrated by reliance on chance and addiction to gambling on the one hand and a tendency to rely on externally provided support on the other; the juxtaposition of this dependency need with a habitual quest for scapegoats to bear the blame for failures; hostility to outgroups and authority figures; release of aggression in acts of cruelty and savage humour, abuse, swearing, and vilification; wariness of personal intimacy, and an underlying mistrust between men and women which reflected an inability to relate to the opposite sex on a basis of mutuality; ambivalent and reticent relationships between mates; and a marked preference for egalitarian modes of social behaviour which would minimize anxiety occasioned by manifestations of difference. These characteristics . . . represented a style of personal adaptation which . . . served to confirm and defend a fragile identity. [1982: 108]

Given this inheritance it is no wonder, as Graeme Turner notes, that the convict should be preferentially used in Australian films and fictions as an emblem, not – as Ward's thesis would lead one to expect – of egalitarianism, but of powerlessness (1987: 6ff.).

An even more popular target for the anti-legendists than convict brotherliness has been the myth of pastoral felicity. Where Ward saw bush society as exemplifying both political and social enlightenment, numerous critics have pointed out that its much touted egalitarianism was largely illusory. John Rickard, for instance, notes the respectful treatment accorded the squatter not just by the romancers but by Furphy himself (1979). G.A. Wilkes, even more intriguingly, notes the proletarian disdain for the underdog figure of the "cockie," or small selector. "As the cockatoos come from the lower classes, as seekers of independence, it is natural for the squatters to resent them," he comments. "But they are also resented by the lower classes themselves. Although they seek the freedom that is part of the Australian ethos, show a willingness to contend with hardship, to wrest a living from a recalcitrant soil, none of this has recommended them to the democratic and egalitarian legend. Their place in the legend is that any misfortune they may have incurred, they have deserved" (1977: 324). How do we reconcile this attitude with explicit professions of working-class solidarity? Taking a clue from the Schedvins' elucidation of the seminal convict mentality, we might speculate that the plight of the cockies aroused less than comfortable feelings among the bushworkers. On the one hand, their hardships underlined the individual's very real vulnerability in the face of Australian nature. On the other, their attempts actually to grapple with it were a constant reproach to the passiveness of those who chose not to participate. In either case, the reaction is hardly an exemplary one.

Humphrey McQueen goes even further than Wilkes, claiming that the entire "myth" was a product of capitalist ideology. Far from evidencing enlightenment, he says, early political reforms, in combination with the illusion of social equality, actually retarded the development of working-class consciousness. "There was no revolution, virtually no violence and not even a mass movement comparable to the Chartists," he says. "Impetus for reform came from the colonial middle classes and from the Colonial Office. The broad mass of people were enfranchised free of charge. Consequently, they did not come into conflict with the bourgeoisie . . . to the extent that they were forced into even defensive ideological or organizational positions or structures" (1976: 180-81). Aside from its immediate political effects, this retardation perhaps explains why, as McQueen details (Chapter 1), the union movement in Australia has been conservative, apolitical, and non-militant. More indirectly, inasmuch as the covert undercutting of solidarity would tend to exacerbate tendencies already present, it also helps explain the ambiguities that undercut the purportedly interknitting institution of mateship. Like Australian class consciousness, Australian mateship is in fact a hollow facsimile rather than the real thing. As intimated in earlier sections, it *replaces* rather than fostering "relation." "[O]ur endorsement of the convention of mateship," says Graeme Turner, "allows us to ignore the complicating moral and personal contingencies . . . [W]hat makes mateship possible is not the authenticity of the particular relationship. Its primary attribute is rather the *negation* of individuality or even specificity of character." Given the Australian's weak sense of identity, and even more given his dependence on external structures for self-definition, it is easy to see why the "naturalness of the institution of mateship is never questioned, but is continually reinforced" (1987: 95). It is also, on the other hand, easy to see why it wouldn't be allowed to go more than skin deep. "Deep in our brains," says Ian Moffitt, "is a vast wasteland of bush marked 'No Trespassers'; approach too close and we throw down a brusque triviality like a barricade. 'There you are, my friend!' grates the publican . . . as he slaps down a glass. The 'my friend,' however, is no invitation to intimacy, but a hand pushing the [intruder] back" (1972: 228).

The "myth," then, would seem not to be supported by the "facts." The question that begs to be asked now is why, in that case, the *Bulletin* crowd were so eager to validate it. Michael Roe proposes a political motivation. "My argument," he says, "is that these writers felt, with varying degrees of deliberation, the need to create an Australian type. They put him in a rural setting. This was not only orthodox Romanticism, but orthodox Nationalism too. The premise that living in a particular corner of the world shapes character has the corollary that the closer a man is to the soil, the more he must feel that effect. So even the Old World nationalisms stress the rural theme, while the emphasis becomes overwhelming in New World nationalisms" (1962: 365). Graeme Davison goes one step further than this, suggesting that patriotism was in this case energized by a negative response – partly conventional, partly genuine – to the increasingly constricted and unsalubrious urban environment. His interpretation is given weight when we consider that the country was in the throes of a depression during the period that saw the development of the *Bulletin*'s characteristic themes. Considering the real impoverishment that confronted them, it is hardly surprising that urban writers like Henry Lawson, Banjo Paterson, Edward Dyson, Price Warung, and Bernard O'Dowd should, like their contemporaries, the Heidelberg painters, escape into nostalgic neo-primitivistic fantasies of easier and earlier times. "The 1890s," says Davison, "have been rightly interpreted, by Russell Ward, Vance Palmer, and others, as a watershed in the creation of an 'Australian Legend.' But that 'apotheosis,' as Ward calls it, was not the transmission to the city of values nurtured on the bush frontier, so much as the projection onto the outback of values revered by an alienated urban intelligentsia" (1982: 129; see also Kiernan, 1980).

While not disagreeing in essence with Davison's analysis, I would suggest that the situation was not quite as simple as he implies. For one thing – and this is something that has been obscured by the tendency of critics to concentrate on the question of whether the *Bulletin* version of history was "true" or not – the *Bulletin* writers themselves were hardly unequivocal in their much-touted nature worship. As Veronica Brady points out, the feelings expressed by Marcus Clarke in his notorious 1877 preface to A.L. Gordon's poetry ("The

Australian mountain forests are funereal, secret, stern, their solitude is desolation, they seem to stifle, in their black gorges, a story of sullen despair" [in I. Turner, 1968: 101]), far from anomalous, were in fact common coinage at the end of the century. "A similar sense of melancholy is to be found in the work of Baynton, Lawson, Furphy, and their followers," she says (1981: 5). How, given their now-conventional associations with the rural idyll, do we account for this? Brady attributes it to the pragmatic bent mentioned in the last section. "What A.G. Stephens has called the 'spirit of Australia . . . a sceptical and utilitarian spirit that values the present hour and refuses to sacrifice [it] . . . for any visionary future lacking a rational guarantee,' may be its obverse side: disappointment . . . make[s] for scepticism." When one considers Lawson's ambivalent emotionality (see A. Taylor, 1982); when one notes the undertone almost of terror carried by Baynton's bush stories, it becomes clear, however, that the reaction is a little more profound than mere scepticism. Running through this entire oeuvre, in fact, albeit covertly, is a "sense of spiritual darkness emanating from the land itself" (A. Phillips, 1980: 81). This takes us right back to the *base* dichotomy mentioned at the beginning of the section. The intimations of disquiet one derives from at least the more sensitive among the *Bulletin* writers (it is interesting but hardly surprising that it is the urbane middle-class Paterson, rather than the working-class, bush-reared Lawson, who gives the "myth" its most unequivocally positive expression [see, for instance, Nesbitt, 1971]) are clearly correlative to the purgatorial adumbrations that offset those early fantasies of an interior paradise. Like their forebears, the nationalists of the nineties preferred to concentrate on the "good" face of nature. Also like them, unfortunately, they were rarely able to repress entirely their awareness of the "bad" one. Hence their overly loud assertions of confidence. Hence, too, the development of all the displacing mechanisms observed throughout the foregoing chapters.

If the bush mythographers did *not* paint the wholly or, indeed, predominantly sunny picture that has been attributed to them, how, we must ask, did their vision come to be so oversimplified by their latter-day proponents? The answer is obvious: Ward and his cohorts saw what they wanted to see. But why *this* particular fantasy? The reasons most frequently given – again – are political ones. Whether their motives are *general*, like Vance Palmer's ("Palmer maintained that Australian writers should cling to the traditions of the 1890s . . . so they might more effectively resist the corrupting influences of the post-war world" [D. Walker, 1976: 197]), or *specific*, like those of McQueen's ruling-class ideologues, the pro-legendists are held to proffer a politically useful (to them) version of the past. Given the evidence, the argument is eminently plausible. Whether it was retroactively co-opted by the forces of conservatism, as Amanda Lohrey claims in her examination of post-World War I shifts of emphasis in the offshoot digger legend (1982), or whether, as McQueen asserts, it was conservative from the beginning, the fact is that the bush myth, by defusing inter-class tensions, has, as noted in "A Quick History of Australian Film" (pp. 209-15 above), served obvious ideological functions during the last century. "In Marxist theory," says Graeme Turner, "the elision of culture into nature is the classic bourgeois use of ideology, [inasmuch as] it converts the contingent and interested actions of men and history into the inevitable and disinterested processes of the natural order of things. Its most important effect is that it pre-empts calls for change by removing it from the agenda – one cannot change nature" (1987: 35). Without challenging the accuracy of Turner's analysis as it relates to effects, on the other hand, I would have to question whether it quite gets at the *causes* of this phenomenon. It is at least interesting that neither the process nor the problems of revising the past are limited to any particular period or political interest group. Just as there was a will among the colonial public to fantasize an idyll else*where*, there seems to be a desire on the part of modern Australians to confirm better days else*when*. Whatever their secondary political uses, then, both the recurrent wishful myopia *and* the polarization of response can be seen as knee-jerk reiterations of what, for Australians, constitutes the "primal experience" (see G. McGregor, 1987a).

Lion and Kangaroo

Australia's relationship with Britain was problematic almost by definition. Even more troublesome than the relatively short-lived tensions inherent in the penal function was the fact that right from the beginning the country was treated less as a potential entity in its own right than as the means to someone else's ends. "The mystery of why

England decided to send many of its convicts to the opposite side of the world was brilliantly probed by Mr. K.M. Dallas ... in 1952," says Geoffrey Blainey. "He suggested that England needed a new sea base and refitting port in order to strengthen her commercial empire in the East. Botany Bay ... was to be that maritime base" (1983: 23). Implicit in this intention was a serious difference in interests which – or so the indigenous legend would have it – in the long run would succeed in driving an indissoluble wedge between the two countries. In the short run, however – and on this point the indigenous legend remains largely silent – the result was quite the opposite. Far from stimulating the focused discontent that led the Americans to rebellion, in Australia the subordination of local interests to imperial ones – exacerbated, no doubt, by the failure to conquer the land in the definitive fashion managed by the Americans (see White, 1981, Chapter 3, for a discussion, or rather a debunking, of the nineteenth-century "land of opportunity" myth) – seems rather to have *weakened* the colonial sense of self-worth. "Preconstructed" as overridingly important in the colonial hierarchy, England provided the daughter-country with its aesthetic standards (see, for instance, pp. 68 and 160 above), its social standards, and above all – underwriting the apparently endemic fears of contamination or degeneration (see "The White Man's Aborigine," pp. 137-40) – its sense of racial identity. "How *can* [we] be like people born in the green Motherland?" asks Rolf Boldrewood in the mid-1880s. "My answer is – that 'race is everything.' A little heat more or less, a little extra wayfaring, the prevalence of ... abundant food – these things do not suffice to relax the fibre and lower the stamina of the bold sea-roving breed" (in I. Turner, 1968: 140).

Such statements as this provide a necessary corrective to the popular view, a corollary to the "myth" discussed in the last section, that separatist feelings were increasingly rampant in Australia toward the end of the nineteenth century. "Looking back through the pages of the *Bulletin* during the 1890s," says Gavin Souter in *Lion and Kangaroo,* "one could easily gain the impression that Australia, seething with radical and optimistic impulses, was about to strike out on its own. It should be remembered, however, that the twine of Australian identity had another strand to it: 'the crimson thread of kinship' ... During the 1880s many nationalists were uncertain whether Australia ought to remain part of the British Empire much longer; *but*" – and this is the important point – "'schizoid love-hate' for Britain was an important part of Australian reality" (1976: 21-22, italics added).

Without disagreeing with Souter's primary point here, taking collateral as well as direct evidence into account one might go so far as to say that "schizoid love-hate for Britain" was not just a part, no matter how important, but in a sense comprised the horizon to Australian reality. It is difficult otherwise to explain why, in an era renowned for nationalist rhetoric, there was (as noted in "The Question of Regionalism," pp. 200-203 above) so little real enthusiasm for union; why there was "no 'peak' in Australian literature to correspond with the achievement of Federation in 1901" (Wilkes, 1981: 1); why, most of all, it took over a decade to name a capital and another half-century to transform it into a city. The *Bulletin* notwithstanding, it is clear from such indicators that the Australians had great difficulty with self-reference.

This is not to say, on the other hand, that other-reference didn't offer problems as well. While they failed signally to effect the emotional break promoted so vociferously by the nationalists, events in the period leading up to Federation did contribute to a marked erosion of Australia's ability to believe in Britain's maternal benevolence. Despite the enthusiasm with which the country initially sprang to the aid of its Queen, the Boer War, for instance, was an almost unmitigated disaster from the viewpoint of imperial accord. Exacerbated equally by the not entirely unmerited British disdain for the slovenliness of the Australian volunteers and the, again not unmerited, Australian distaste for Kitchener's ruthlessness, before the fighting was over the relations between the colonial forces and the British high command had degenerated to such a point that it became a matter of international scandal (see Souter, Chapter 3, for details). Australia's sense of fair play was outraged by the summary nature of British military justice. (The trial and execution of Breaker Morant was only the best known of several incidents.) Far worse, Australia's pride was offended by public accusations of incompetence and cowardice.

If the South African experience was a deflating one, it at least had the advantage of being soon over. Much more damaging in the long run was Britain's apparent prioritization of trade interests over Australia's national security. Humphrey McQueen summarizes:

[D]uring the struggle for [a "White Australia" policy] . . . the distinction between the "British Empire" and "Britain's Empire" became of practical importance. [The problem] commenced with the difficulty of excluding from the gold fields Chinese who came from Hong Kong since they were British subjects . . . [and] intensified as Britain established treaties with the Chinese Government which expected its nationals to be accepted as equals in Britain's colonies . . . Australians looked upon this as an unwarranted interference in their affairs – an interference which could only occur because Britain placed commercial considerations above those of blood and race.

At the 1897 Colonial Conference, Joseph Chamberlain attempted to gain equal immigration rights for Indians with the argument that "the traditions of the Empire . . . make no distinction in favour of or against race or colour . . ." Although Chamberlain did not press the point he increased colonial suspicions regarding the sincerity of British race patriotism. Indians, however, were not the real substance of the dispute. That honour was reserved for the Japanese with whom Britain had signed a Commercial Treaty in 1894 . . .

. . . [N]ot content with negative prescriptions [like non-ratification, Australia quickly] set about producing legislation which would positively exclude Japanese immigrants. Some of these Bills were so blatantly offensive . . . that the Colonial office refused them Royal Assent and eventually hammered out a formula which was acceptable to the Japanese but resented in Australia . . .

Even crusty old conservatives like Sir William McMillan [reacted negatively to this last straw] . . . [R]ather than allow Asians to land in Australia he felt it was better to cut loose from Britain. [1976: 25-27]

Cut loose from Britain. Pretty strong words! Easier said than countenanced, of course. But if anything could sever that emotional umbilical, it was a challenge to Australia's xenophobia. It didn't, in point of fact – but it certainly strained it. Once the country began to suspect that a mercenary and unmotherly Britain could not be depended upon for military support (a common theme in early twentieth-century pop-cultural invasion fantasies, as McQueen points out, is the withdrawal of British warships from the Pacific [59]), what was at first merely filial resentment deepened into real fear.

This fear would continue to backdrop relations between the two countries when the slights of the Boer War were long forgotten. A decade after the events that McQueen describes, in the wake of an obviously cautionary visit-by-invitation on the part of the American fleet, Franklin Matthews, a correspondent for the New York *Sun*, summed up the Australian feelings. "It was Australia's way of telling Great Britain something extremely important," he said, "something

... that she has had difficulty in telling the mother country about up to this time. It was that if England expects, as she has the right to expect, that [Australia] shall come to the assistance of the mother country when that country may be enfeebled ... the mother country must take heed at this very moment of Australia's dread ... [of] the yellow peril" (in Souter: 143). Matthews was undoubtedly right in his interpretation of the Australian intentions. *Qua* gesture, however, the flirtation with the United States should not be given undue weight. Why? Because the context makes clear that it did not, at least at that time, signal any real pulling away from the neglectful parent. Despite – or perhaps because of (I'll come back to this later) – the country's undoubtedly real sense of betrayal, the period which marked the high point of xenophobic anxieties also saw a tremendous burgeoning of imperialistic sentiment among both public and private Australians. After an initial half-hearted attack on "Vampire Day" when the holiday was first inaugurated, even the *Bulletin* gave in to the general mood (Souter: 116-17; see also Serle, 1973: 89ff.; Firth and Hoorn, 1979).

How do we explain this volte face? Part of it no doubt can be related to a reactionary sense of vulnerability. The *way* this reaction expressed itself, however, and particularly the insistent dissociation of Britannia from her minions ("There is more evidence of loyalty in Australia than I have ever met with in any other part of the King's dominions – not even excepting home," said Sir John Foster Fraser in 1910. "But it is loyalty to the Empire, not to Great Britain" [in Souter: 155]), suggests that the Australians were in fact practising a rather interesting sleight-of-mind. Being "independent," they could tell themselves they were no longer at the mercy of Britain's whims (see McQueen: 37). Being linked with the Empire, on the other hand, they were also still part of a greater (and the greater, the better) whole. If the comfort provided by this mental reorientation were largely illusory – for all the patriotic fantasies being bruited about (within the "protective shield" of the Commonwealth, Australia "could aspire to be an equal partner with Great Britain, and in some respects ... might even be able to teach [its] northern archetype a thing or two" [Souter: 112]), Britain was still after all the member with all the clout – Federation-plus-imperialism allowed the Australians at least symbolically to have their cake and eat it too.

The trend climaxed with World War I. I have already noted how important it was to Australia that its soldiers make a good showing. The almost mass-hysterical enthusiasm that greeted the outbreak of hostilities (see Adam-Smith, 1981: 17ff.) perhaps makes more sense when we realize the critical emotional function played by that perceived "tie" with Empire. The profundity of the consequent disillusionment – documented most poignantly by such *negative* features as the veterans' reluctance to talk about their experience and the historians' propensity to play down the danger – is also more understandable. Because it *was* (whatever C.E.W. Bean might say afterwards) a traumatic confrontation! The shock of discovering the *un*heroic reality of trench fighting, added to the even greater shock of discovering the unheroic reality of their glorious allies ("Everyone here is 'fed up' of the war," wrote Major Garnet Adcock in a letter home in 1917 – "but not with the Hun. The British staff, British methods and British bungling have sickened us" [in Souter: 240]), were more than enough to sour at least the participants themselves on jingoistic slogans.

Though a better front was maintained at home, there too the flaws that emerged when rhetoric became reality succeeded in seriously fraying the erstwhile almost seamless dream of Empire. Souter summarizes:

The nation was divided – not neatly into two camps, but into several overlapping ones which all drew their acrimony from the war against Germany. To start with, the families of men who had gone to the war, and perhaps even lost their lives, looked askance at those who had not volunteered. The working class was less enthusiastic about the war than the middle class, for it was the more severely affected by wartime wage freezes and rising prices. Many Labor politicians resented the extent to which the war effort had taken precedence over social reform, and in this they were at odds not only with the Liberal Opposition but with their own parliamentary leaders. Religious sectarianism could also be relied upon to set neighbour against neighbour. Despite their professed early intention of sinking Irish grievances in imperial loyalty, many Australian Catholics found it increasingly difficult to reconcile Britain's solicitude for the independence of small European nations with its denial of Home Rule to one small island in particular. Protestants, on the other hand, regarded agitation for "Rome Rule" as almost treasonable. [244]

These strains emerged into high profile during the fight over conscription in 1916. Something else that emerged into high profile at the same time, however, was the reluctance, perhaps even inability, of the Australians to give up on their erstwhile external referent. For all that the conscription referenda *were* defeated, and definitively so, the seemingly paradoxical re-election of their author, arch-hawk Billy Hughes, seems clearly to indicate that the problem at least for the general populace was less an antipathy to the war per se than a fear that the coercion of participation would undercut the illusion of a strong *natural* commitment between Australia and Britain.

This is not to imply that the relationship was not *in fact* eroded by the wartime experience. It was. And after the war things only got worse. As if the sacrifice in lives and suffering had been nothing (Australia's casualty rate, as Ross points out, was more than 10 per cent higher than Britain's, and almost twice that of the other Dominion participants [1985: 28]), it became amply apparent during the peace talks that the "mother" country was once again less concerned about antipodean security than determined to protect and promote her own mercantile interests. Needless to say, this hit a nerve. The Australians' "deep-seated fear of Japan," says Souter, "had been reinforced during the war, despite the latter's status as an ally, by [its] rapid industrial growth and undisguised imperial ambition." They hence "saw nothing but danger in [the] proposal that the German Pacific territories should be administered by mandatory powers acting as trustees for the League of Nations, which would soon come into being. How could Australia be certain of receiving and retaining the mandate for New Guinea? If it did receive the mandate, would it be able to restrict Asian immigration into that territory . . .? And would it have to accord Japan equality of commercial opportunity in the mandated territory?" (276). The fact that Britain seemed all too ready to dismiss such concerns as trivial served to confirm earlier suspicions about her unreliability. By exacerbating the country's sense of vulnerability, on the other hand, it also made it all the more critical that the illusion of "ties" be maintained. The result? Although, as Firth and Hoorn point out (1979), the *rhetoric* of Empire would remain "intact" at least through the next war (when shifting power relations would render the whole problem academic), the feelings evinced toward Britain herself became increasingly problematic and anxiety-ridden.

One major source of evidence for this ambivalence is the long-lasting and still ongoing debate on Australian literature. From the nationalist camp examined in the last section emerged not only a specific literary canon enshrining (in Tim Rowse's words) "'the common man' . . . egalitarianism and . . . spontaneous fraternal 'socialism'" as "basic" Australian values, but also an image of the artist as a "reflector of a communal experience, an active interpreter . . . of a common culture" (1978: 231). For all the vociferousness of its adherents, however, at least until the last couple of decades this view made little impression on the concomitant and seemingly paradoxical tendency of a bush-bemused public to think of England as "home." "Our education system, not the Japanese, betrayed us," says Ian Moffit, recalling his childhood. Deluded into misidentification by "our inherited race memory . . . we yearned for starfish and buckets and breakwaters and Pop and Grub on pebbly beaches 12,000 miles from our golden sand. English meadows drenched with English history, English swords buried beneath English acorns, English battleships and fighter planes and Billy Bunters – they all sat up there on a shining ledge beside our Lean Bronzed Australian Anzac" (1972: 35-36). It was this conditioning, even more than "real" cultural stultification, one suspects, that led generation after generation of Australian writers – not just Anglophiles like Martin Boyd, but also a good many of the country's most notable "nationalists," up to and including Vance Palmer himself – to take ship as soon as they could get together the money (see Serle, 1973: 124ff.; Modjeska, 1984, Chapter 2). And it was the same conditioning, more deeply submerged perhaps, but still powerful, that made nationalism continue to seem suspect long after Britain itself had been demoted from its symbolic position as "the" other. A.A. Phillips' phrase, "the cultural cringe," though ostensibly coined to denote the "twin attitudes of boastfulness and provincial special pleading" (Rowse, 1978: 230-31), inasmuch as it came to be applied to almost any cultural phenomenon which underlined its own "Australianness," could equally well be taken to signify the assumption on the part of the new internationalists that to be identifiably Australian is inevitably to be inferior.

This last sentence points up one aspect of the "cultural nationalism" debate that a purely historical review of movements and players might tend to obscure. *Qua* controversy, it has been just as (and perhaps even more) rancorous as the related but more general argument over the "legend." Why? Part of the reason is the tendency of the participants to let *non*-literary, and especially political, considerations enter into their pronouncements (Kiernan, 1979: 152ff.). An even greater part is the fact that the *particular* non-literary elements invoked invariably involve issues – *polarities* – of personal as well as public self-conception.

I am not just talking about ideological wrangles here – like Phillips' claim that the Marxist McQueen distorts his evidence (1971), or McQueen's criticism of Robert Dixon's (to him) politically naive reading of colonial history (1986). Nor am I merely talking about the social divisions that underwrite the aesthetic ones. All these things contribute, of course. But they are secondary rather than primary factors. Besides, the alignments don't work out that neatly in any case. "The Left has historically seen itself as leading the nationalist opposition to the exploitation of Australia by overseas powers while conservative parties have looked gratefully towards our 'great and powerful' friends," says Stephen Alomes (1981: 5). How, then, do we explain the post-war right-wing co-optation of the nationalistic digger myth mentioned above? Or the nostalgic neo-primitivism of arch-conservative James McAuley? And where does someone like Patrick White fit in? White posed "a difficult challenge for the upholders of a left-Australianism to meet," says Rowse, "since [he] appeared to adhere to a subject matter of which they approved (there is no man more 'common' than Stan Parker, in *The Tree of Man*), and in fact treated 'his' nature and destiny as a Grand Theme. Yet [he] placed its concerns on a universal and metaphysical level . . . [that was anathema] to the average Australian" (1978: 234). This is not the place to review all the quirks and anomalies of Australian literary politics of the last quarter century – for this the reader is referred to Rowse's chapter on "The New Critics" (191-245) or, more contentiously, to John Docker's *In a Critical Condition*. The important point, anyway, is that the proponents on both, or all, sides of this fence see the issue not simply as one of aesthetic preferences but of national – and hence, of course, personal – survival. When Brunton Stephens in 1897 calls for a literature which is "'positive' as well as 'independent'" (Nesbitt, 1971: 14), as when Peter Coleman in 1962 demands that his countrymen be prepared "to criticise Australian life frankly and firmly, to see it clearly and wholly with all its limitations" (11), the suggestion is being made that the national health and well-being are going to be affected, perhaps critically, by the strategies that the country's literati decide to adopt. Framed in such life-and-death terms, it is hardly surprising that the issue should catalyze a lot of ambivalent emotion!

This would seem to take us a long way from the relationship with Britain. Actually, though, the subjects are not as divergent as they may at first seem. Insofar as this relationship represents Australia's type relationship with otherness, its "construction" must be seen as exemplary for all later reactions to outside influence. The most critical aspect of this construction is already implicit in the foregoing review. When it came to imaging their history, Australians for over a century have evinced a preference not merely for a biological, but for a specifically familial metaphor. "This is largely a story of progress," says David Walker, "pervaded by the view that nations like individuals inherit stages of development which take them from childhood dependence on their parents, through a spotty, awkward and rebellious adolescence to mature adulthood" (207-208; see also Souter, 1976, Chapter 2; White, Chapter 9). Formulated thus, the problems immediately become palpable. Inasmuch as such metaphors tend not merely to reflect but to constrain the reality they purport to describe (see McGregor, 1986, 1987a), the corporate entity that was Australia began to manifest all the developmental stigmata of its private counterpart. Particularly important for the present subject is the tendency to see the mother as alien but dangerous (an identification made all the more frighteningly plausible by Britain's "unmotherly" behaviour) and the father as charismatic but inaccessible or dispossessed. Debarred thus from both its potential role models, the child is literally *unable to grow up.* The continued debate over Australia's maturity ("the image of a nation having come of age assaults us every time we open a fashion or music magazine," said Paul Taylor in 1984, retro-invoking the parade of similar pronouncements which have greeted every significant political or cultural event since Federation) suggests that the same thing may be true of the country as a whole.

I shall be looking at some of the political consequences of this phenomenon in the next section. In the meantime, hearkening back briefly to the nationalism debate, I will merely note the problems it presents for self-imagers. "Austrophobes . . . [are those who] look to some place, some centre outside of and quite other than Australia to provide the standard of what is ideal," says D.R. Burns disapprovingly (1982: 46). What Burns doesn't recognize is that when one *by nature* locates authority "outside" the self, it is almost impossible to do otherwise. "The Australian habit of looking back to England – which has lasted for generations – is not only a looking back to the society from which our forefathers were exiled," says Graeme Turner, "but to a social norm *unavailable in delinquent Australia"* (1986: 76, italics added). This sense of an absence at the centre of social reality perhaps explains why, in constructing "Australianness," Australian writers and filmmakers have tended to fall back on "hard" or "given" items related to *mise-en-scène.* It also explains why, even more provocatively, Australians seem ready to affirm even the most bizarre and unflattering stereotypes projected on them from outside. "The British . . . think of Australia as an uninteresting country inhabited by beer-swilling louts who talk in a comic accent," says Michael Davie. "Their misconceptions are fed by some of the best-known, and highly talented, Australian expatriates . . . Australian businesses go along with the tide. Qantas airline advertisements feature sheep, koalas, and men with corks suspended from their hats on strings to ward off the flies . . . Australian winemakers have tried to ingratiate themselves with British drinkers by labelling one of their red wines 'Kanga Rouge,' which suggests that even the producers do not expect their product to be taken seriously" (1985: 385-86). Going Davie one step better, it also suggests that any identity is felt to be better than none at all.

National Fictions

Nationalism is not the only issue that ambiguates the Australian political spectrum. Viewed from abroad, the "sides" seem strangely skewed. Part of it is the lack of congruency with North American norms. In the United States it is the right-wing (that is, anti-communist) faction which connotes cultural conservatism, religious fundamentalism, and xenophobia. In Australia, in contrast, it is the Left which (though not characteristically religious) has tended toward racism and reaction. The problem goes far beyond imported expectations, however. Within the country, alignments and associations are even harder to sort out. The rural populists, for instance, have historically been divided into what Brugger and Jaensch call left and right-wing "tendencies." "The former sought common cause with the itinerant rural worker, whilst the latter" – finding the common

denominator between the small farmers and the large landholders –
"began to see the interests of labour as identical with the interest of
the cities" (1985: 9). Labour, too, has been plagued by bedfellows who
evince as much antipathy to each other as to their common enemies.
Popular wisdom claims that the main reason the Australian Labor[1]
Party (ALP) was debarred from power for most of this century was its
tendency to split, irretrievably, between right and left-wing factions,
Catholics and Communists (see Horne, 1964: 161-70). Given these
kinds of complications, it is hard to talk about anything as systematic
as a "spectrum" at all.

It is not, on the other hand, merely the elusiveness of the players
that makes it difficult to unravel Australian politics. It's the inherent
peculiarities of the game itself. Take the lead text selected for this section, for instance. Far from a political tract, Graeme Turner's
National Fictions is, as its subtitle explains, an examination of "literature, film and the construction of Australian narrative." Why
choose such a work for a section on public affairs? One possibility: I
could be trying to underline the fact that political ideologies are just
as "expressive" as literary fictions, and therefore susceptible to
exactly the same kinds of informing pressures. Or it could be an
oblique way of referencing Australia's much-touted apoliticism (see,
for instance, Rowse, 1978; Emy, 1980 a & b; Alomes, 1981a). Both
these factors are relevant. My real reason for singling out Turner,
though, is that he elucidates a number of psycho-social preconditions
which, I believe, are more important to the understanding of Australian politics than any agglomeration of "mere" facts. "If Australia is a
'delinquent' society," he says, "if the myth of exile proposes that life
does not go on here as it does elsewhere, and if there is an intuition of
a society beyond these shores in which the 'norm' resides, then 'universal' philosophical solutions to the problems of existence within
the society may not be convincing" (1986: 80).

If it is difficult to elucidate a spectrum for the country, can we at
least talk about political "climate"? According to the nationalist
myth, the "real" – that is, the bushman's – Australia is left-leaning if

---

1. Reflecting provocatively on my claims about Australian reliance on extrinsic
   role models, given that the nation as a whole adheres rigidly to British spel-
   ling patterns it is clearly noteworthy that the ALP's founders opted deliberately for the Americanized form of "Labor."

not socialist. "We are all Socialists now and the only qualification you hear from anybody is that he is 'not an extreme socialist,'" said soon-to-be-prime minister Andrew Fisher in 1908 (in McQueen, 1976: 194). Rhetoric notwithstanding, however, numerous commentators – none more acerbically than Humphrey McQueen – have pointed out the speciousness of the purported socialist bias. From its earliest days, says McQueen, the movement was atheoretical and non-revolutionary. Its leaders were malcontents who threw around a few disembodied Marxist tags. Workers' hero William Lane was "an authoritarian racist who conceived of himself as a latter-day Messiah" (191-2). The Labor party was corrupt and conciliatory. ("Socialism for the [ALP] . . . has very often meant nothing other than state intervention to aid capitalism" [202].) Even the unions, so-called protectors of workers' rights, in giving up political militancy for social panacaeas, have covertly confirmed the dictum "that the interests of society as a whole are identical with the interests of the rulers of that society" (235). How do we explain this? Some commentators invoke the fragmentation of the labour force, or the relative prosperity of the country, or the (purportedly) high mobility rates. None of these factors in itself is enough, however – as Brugger and Jaensch point out (11-12) – to explain the gaping discrepancy between words and action.

Sydney sociologist Tim Rowse, some of whose views on literary nationalism were touched upon in the last section, claims that the dominant discourse in Australian political history, contra "popular" opinion, has not been socialism but liberalism. If correct – and there is much evidence to support it – Rowse's thesis could explain a number of the more puzzling features of the so-called climate of the country, including even its ostensive inconsistency. One of the main reasons, traditionally, that liberalism has been so successful in post-industrialist societies is an almost incomparable strategic flexibility that allows it to diffuse dissent. "Our state has developed vast apparatuses for negotiating and absorbing into itself class and intra-class tension," says Rowse. How? By means specifically of its liberal ideology. This is not, he underlines, "a monolithic nor simply apologetic doctrine. Its different emphases can sanction a variety of ruling-class strategies of government – from the harshly conservative to the subtly conciliatory and reformist" (1978: 10). Stipulating the appeal of such elasticity to the heuristic strain in the Australian character, however (see Uhr, 1981: 100), there are other aspects of liberalism which create more problems than it solves.

First and most obvious is the problem of plausibility. The optimistic and progressive bias of liberalism assorts ill with the Australians' native pessimism. This is only the least of it, though. Less obvious but far more important is the problem of what we might call *assimilation* – the tendency for socio-political metaphors to become generative, to create the world in their own image (G. McGregor, 1985: 76ff.). One of the most basic features of liberalism is its personalization of the social realm. "Society is conceived of as an ensemble of atomistic individuals," says Rowse, "and the state's actions are taken to be a pursuit of the 'collective interest' of that social ensemble" (15). What's wrong with this? First of all, it's dysfunctional. While the projection of a fragmented society both confirms and is confirmed by the institutionalized discontinuity noted in pp. 115-18 and elsewhere above – indeed, it is probably this congruence that makes liberalism attractive to the Australian in the first place – it also has the effect of discouraging or discounting or undercutting cooperative action even more than natural propensities would. For the United States, with its myth of heroic enablement (G. McGregor, 1988, Chapter 6), such a prejudice poses no problems. In a nation fixated on images of entrapment and powerlessness (G. Turner, especially Chapter 3), it is wellnigh disastrous. Despite the plaints of left-wing critics about the ideological undermining of solidarity (see, for instance, Connell, 1977; Dwyer et al., 1984), it is *not* just the working class that suffers from the endemic incoherence of Australian society. Australians "do well wherever individual performance suffices," says Hugh Stretton. "They do less well where, as in big business and government, the individual performances need complicated organization and direction" (1985: 197). I shall be discussing this further in the next section. For now I will merely point out that in an age which has come to be synonymous with big business and big government, a built-in antipathy to co-ordination must be viewed as a very serious liability. This brings us to the second drawback to the liberal model. Inasmuch as the individual in Australia is – covertly, if not consciously – well aware of his/her own impotence (we need only look at the self-images carried in film and literature for confirmation of this), the imputation of self-responsibility is covertly, if not consciously, a locus for anxiety.

The individual is not, of course, the only element in the liberal equation. Standing against the "atomistic individual" is the "social ensemble" mentioned above. But what exactly does that mean –

ensemble? The dissociation of the actor from intermediary group-
ings, like classes or strata or occupations, says Rowse, means that
"social structures are understood as systems of intersubjectivity"
(1978: 15). Semantics aside, however, in the popular *imagination*
what stands against the individual is simply the State. This, needless
to say, inserts its own ambiguities into the melange. Why? Part of it
simply boils down to unfamiliarity. The system so-called is a mystery
to the average Australian – indeed, judging by the literature, even to
the not-so-average Australian. "[N]one of our best novels, and very
few of lesser rank," says Dorothy Green, "have power structures as
their principal concern . . . We are never taken inside the board-rooms
of great companies . . . we are never introduced to the great merchant
bankers; never taken inside the exclusive clubs frequented by the rich
and influential; never confronted with the leaders of powerful
bureaucracies, or the leaders of pressure groups . . . we are never
present in a Parliament when crucial issues are being discussed"
(1982: 17). Ignorance, on the other hand, is less likely to be a cause
than a symptom. The real problem – the underlying problem – is, I
think, the fact that for most of Australia's history "the State" has
simply been synonymous with "the Crown" – and we have seen what
feelings of ambivalence *that* has the power to raise. Or *did*, at least.
That's all in the past now.

Or is it?

On 11 November 1975 – the anniversary of Ned Kelly's execution!
(see Turner and Sturgess, 1979, for a discussion of this "coinci-
dence") – the Australian Governor-General took it upon himself to
dismiss Labor Prime Minister Gough Whitlam on the grounds that
his loss of control over the purse strings-holding upper house
endangered the country's well-being. More significant, despite the
fact that this office has for years been a figurehead office only, filled on
the recommendation not of the Home Office in London, but of the
Australian government itself, so great, apparently, is its residual mystique that neither Whitlam or anyone else resisted Kerr's high-
handed action. "When Whitlam was sacked," says Donald Horne,

he went back to the Lodge and drafted a motion to put before Parliament. He
didn't act like a figure from British history using modern methods to defend
freedom against a tyrant. He didn't ring up Bob Hawke and ask for a general
strike. He didn't ring up the Australian Union of Students and ask them to get

10,000 students to picket Government House. He didn't make a speech from the steps of Parliament House saying that the Governor-General had acted against the Constitution and that he would get the House to pass a resolution telling Queen Elizabeth to fire him. Whitlam didn't force a crisis which might have ended in Kerr's resignation, with the appointment of a new Governor-General and the government's survival.

A good reason for not doing so is that it may not have worked. I can't think of any other good reason. [1976: 89]

The *reason* it wouldn't have worked – and in this regard one might note that inasmuch as Whitlam was defeated handily in the subsequent election, it would seem that the public was inclined to accept Kerr's judgment, *whatever* the proprieties of the matter – is, of course, in all likelihood the *same* reason that deterred Whitlam from attempting it: the Australian's habit of deferring to "outside" authority. To defer is not, on the other hand, to trust. To the extent that a faceless State tends to take on the semblance of outsideness simply by virtue of its power, whatever its *defined* responsibilities under liberal doctrine it is *in fact* read as inimical to the interests of the individual. To shift the emphasis from citizen to state, self to other, in the liberal equation is therefore no solution at all.

The primary effect of this disquieting subtext is to destabilize the political scene. This is not a case, as in the United States, of oscillation between two equally appealing but incompatible political philosophies (see G. McGregor, 1988): the "preferred" ideology in Australia is in practice self-deconstructive. We're talking about *recoil* here, in other words, not simply rebound. How does it work? Besides liberalism, Brugger and Jaensch single out populism and utilitarianism as the key strands in Australian ideology (1985: 49). Refining the model slightly, one might, rather, see these adjunct "strands" as representing fall-back positions on either side of the unattainable, or at least un-*maintainable, liberal ideal. When "the State" or "the System" or simply "the World at Large" seems too overwhelming – as in the 1890s and again in the early 1930s (Brugger and Jaensch: 51) – the Australian retreats into populism, with its emphasis on the virtues of ordinariness, its vision of corruption in high places, its vague, non-militant, and backward-looking millennialism. In the later stages of crisis, when communal faith in either self-sufficiency or utopian fantasies is at its lowest ebb – like the mid-thirties or the latter war years

(Brugger and Jaensch: 35ff.) – there is a commensurate swing back to various utilitarian or managerial strategies in which "responsibility" – for ill *or* good – is displaced from the individual to the system. This node, unfortunately, isn't stable either. When the "machine" is perceived to be getting out of hand there is a quick retreat to individualism again. "Opposition from the right was to lead in 1944 to the defeat of the Powers Referendum which the Labor Government felt was necessary to achieve the new social liberal and managerialist vision . . . It led later to the defeat of Chifley's attempt to nationalise the banks" (Brugger and Jaensch: 39) – *and*, one might add, to Whitlam's more recent defeat. No wonder one gets a feeling of *déja vu* in reading Australian political history. "Australia . . . apparently [came] of age" during World War I, Brugger and Jaensch point out, falling back on the country's favourite metaphor. "Or [did] it? As [our] next Chapter will note, people were to remark at several times in the following decades that Australia was coming of age and the debates outlined . . . [here] were reiterated time and again" (23).

From a practical viewpoint, the destabilization is less detrimental than its secondary effects. *U*ncertainty – the lack of a consistent enabling world view – prompts a lowering of expectations (McLaren, 1981: 28); certainty of disappointment, more critically, catalyzes a withdrawal of affect. Among the public, this produces attitudes ranging from "apathy" (Rowse, 1978: 4), through scepticism ("the community at large appears to have lost faith in the government's ability" [Jackson, 1985: 254]), to outright anti-politicism ("The Australians appear to a man to regard their politicians as time-serving crooks or simple-minded hirelings" [James Cameron of the London *Sunday Times*, in Dunstan, 1973: 138]). Among the politicians it produces cynicism, timidity, inconstancy, and a tendency to attribute both failure *and* success to "chance" (Higley et al., 1979: 171; see also Walsh, 1985: 435). Neither the electors nor the elected, in other words, will admit to placing any faith in the process at all.

What sort of government, in practice, results from such an unpromising meld? One of its most frequently noted features is its pragmatism. "Unlike that paradigm of the liberal polity – the United States," says John Uhr, quoting Dennis Altman, "Australia is not founded on any 'vision of creating a society that can be a model for the rest of the world' . . . [O]ur tradition is 'relentlessly opposed to speculation that goes beyond the confines of the immediately practicable.'

Our political culture is . . . rooted in the 'bourgeois values' of 'economic development and material wealth as the central good in society'" (1981: 100). While not disputing the finding per se, I would question whether the praxis is in fact as efficiently mercenary as such
statements imply. Indeed, given current economic realities, and especially the complexities of international capitalism, the anti-intellectual bent invariably linked with the feature of pragmatism (Horne,
1964: 213ff.; Rowse, 1978: 112ff.) must be seen not as a sacrificing of
"frills" to profits (as the businessmen would have it), but as an
extremely *im*practical indulgence which has cost the country dearly
in terms of both profits and opportunities (Stretton, 1985, especially
209-10). Nowhere is this manifested more strikingly than in the area
of long-term planning – or in the vacuum where the plans would be if
there were any. In fact, as Stretton points out, Australians are not
planners at all, but reactors. They are well aware of this, of course.
Many of them, indeed, would see it as one of the country's most
endearing qualities. "The saving Australian characteristic," says
Horne, "is the ability to change course quickly, even at the last
moment" (1971: 221-22). Stretton documents some of the consequences for business of that kind of thinking. These are bad enough.
But when the "game" is politics, the entrenched shortsightedness
that Higley finds in his "elites" can take on downright sinister implications.

During 1975 Australian elites saw few really ominous clouds on the horizon.
Most were confident that the specific problems on which they were working
would be effectively dealt with and that the principal economic and political
problems of 1975 would not persist. Consequently, when [asked] about . . .
future problems, they tended to settle for broad, relatively unspecified foreign and defense problems, to continue thinking in terms of 1975 issues,
often in order to make partisan criticisms, or to produce standard, somewhat
platitudinous, forecasts of social psychological, political and environmental
adjustments which the future will require.

The significance of these assessments lies mainly in what they did *not*
include. One principal omission was any widespread suspicion that further
economic expansion would be more difficult to achieve than it has been during the post-war period. A second was any substantial scepticism about the
ready availability of lucrative export markets for Australia's natural
resources. A third was any widespread apprehension about the ability to

provide the population with sufficient and satisfactory employment. In addition, no notice whatsoever was made of ... the growing reluctance of middle-class taxpayers to support public sector social insurance programmes, particularly those aimed at the poor and the occupationally excluded. [279-80]

Naivete within government is less dangerous to the extent that the electorate is untrusting, of course. And if there's one thing Australians know, it's that they *don't* trust politicians (remember the poll noted on p. 75 above). Unfortunately – and here's where the popular wisdom falls down – trusting or no, history reveals them as almost absurdly eager to defer to such figures. I mentioned above the penchant for strong, "otherly" leaders (see also Rowse, 1978: 165ff.); I noted in the last section the preferential location of symbolic authority apart from the self: put these together, and what we have are the grounds for a kind and degree of dependency which totally explodes the nationalist myth of self-reliance. From the so-called "rural conservative," with his expectations of "government intervention to provide a variety of schemes that minimize his risks, soften his hardships, and protect the market price of his produce" (Walsh, 1985: 430), right through to the modernday suburbanite ("There were arguments, from 1900 onwards, for parks and playgrounds, nurseries and kindergartens, then for housing for the poor, and finally for jobs for everyone ... And as each of these arguments was in turn accepted, the role of the state was extended to being that of a much more *active* provider or instigator or, at the very least, supervisor of the quality of life ... in the cities" [Sandercock, 1983: 71]), the Australian has not merely accepted but demanded state intervention.

Is this merely, as Albinski would have it (1985: 410), a result of the "stern conditions" that faced the original colonist? If one compares the reaction to reactions elsewhere, it would seem clear that more is involved than simple necessity. "[E]ven in rural areas, where the traditions of self-help and individualism are strong," says S. Encel, citing A.F. Davies, "the habit of leaning on the bureaucracy is too deeply embedded to be resisted... During the depression years of the 1930's, this led to a proliferation of bureaucratic agencies to help the farmers, whereas a similar situation in the Canadian prairie provinces led to the creation of a network of self-help agencies" (1980b: 314). We are reminded again of the aforementioned inaptitude for co-operation. We are also, however, reminded of the nagging respect that underlies the equally nagging fear of the (m)otherland. In Australia there is *always* a tendency to displace responsibility onto something larger: the "state" (it is perhaps no more than predictable that local government – the realm, literally, of "self" expression – is weak to the point of non-existence [see Neutze, 1985]), the transnationals, Uncle Sam, the World Bank – *fate.* "Australia leads the way in a process whereby every country and every provincial area is becoming, through the internationalization of culture and commerce, a dependent province of the major world metropolitan centres," says Stephen Alomes (1981a: 19; see also Austin, 1984: 91-92; Wells, 1986: 76).

Deference is not, of course, an entirely negative feature. Just as their self-protective cynicism makes Australian politicians more ideologically flexible, conditioned deference makes individual Australians more governable citizens. It also makes the *process* of governing a more "reasonable" one. Because the politicians, though publically construed otherwise, are as deeply conditioned to self-deprecate as their constituents, they too manifest the national propensity for displacement. The result is that many, perhaps most areas of deep-cutting public disagreement tend to be resolved in Australia not through spontaneous confrontation but through *structured* compromise. "Nowhere," as Jackson remarks, "is this more evident than in the labour market":

[A]s early as 1892, legislation was enacted to provide for the compulsory arbitration of wages. Industrial courts were set up in New South Wales and Western Australia; the other states, taking a less judicial approach, established wages boards. In 1904 the federal arbitration court was established. While this system has been modified repeatedly over the years, the broad framework has been little changed.

The institutional framework and highly centralized nature of the wage-fixing arrangements disguise the complex and cumbersome workings of this Australian arbitration system. As Justice Ludeke noted, "In the name of public interest, the Conciliation and Arbitration Act of 1904 has become a multi-armed miscellany which reaches into nearly every nook and cranny of industrial relations." In addition to wage rates, separate state and federal tribunals regulate such disparate matters as hours of work, annual leave, sick leave, long service leave, penalty rates for overtime and shift work, recognition of union rights, and resignation and dismissal. [1985: 250-51]

I would not like to imply that such a system is necessarily either efficient (note Jackson's use of the term "cumbersome") or fair. In fact, as numerous critics have pointed out, the pro-management and pro-masculine bias of both the architects and the adjudicators have produced gross injustices for working men, and even more for working women (see, for instance, McQueen: 1976, 219ff.; A. Summers, 1975: 396ff). Considering the country's temperamental antipathy toward trans-action, however, it seems likely that conflicts would exact an even higher social cost if they had to be dealt with individually, and without predetermined guidelines.

The Lucky Country

Though their reasons for doing so run the gamut from social stability through political freedom to material largess, Australians, according to popular mythos, have traditionally viewed themselves as more fortunate than most mere mortals. Donald Horne's book, *The Lucky Country* (1964; third edition 1971), both celebrates and condemns that particular habit of mind. Why? The celebration part is easy – the critic himself cannot resist the wishful fantasy of the workingman's paradise. The condemnation is a little more complicated. On the surface Horne would seem primarily concerned with the dangers of clinging complacently to an outmoded set of prejudices and expectations. And in this at least, the events of the last two decades have amply proven his perspicacity. Especially in the material realm, there seems no doubt that the designation "lucky" is no longer, if it ever was, appropriate. Though the crisis was allayed, at least temporarily, by yet another mineral boom, the Australian economy, already beginning to slip by the mid-sixties ("It may be worth noting," said Horne in 1971, "that since I wrote . . . the first edition of this book, according to one set of estimates, Australia dropped from fifth to tenth in the list of the world's prosperous countries – in one year" [223]), has slid steadily downhill throughout the seventies and eighties, with no bottom-out in sight (see Dunkley, 1983). "Real" problems notwithstanding, on the other hand, my own reading of this situation would place more weight on the intangible factors. The "lucky country" syndrome can be seen as not merely a symptom of, but a complication to, many of the problematic psycho-social propensities we have seen in the foregoing sections.

For the private individual, the real danger was perhaps not the failure of the dream but the extent to which it succeeded. In the first
intertext section above I noted the apparent *embourgeoisement* of
Australian society. Whether the implied de-classification was real or
illusory (see C. McGregor, 1981, Chapter 3, versus Dwyer et al., 1984:
32ff.), the fact is, as even the Marxists admit, the post-war years of
"full employment and rising real incomes" (Connell and Goot, 1979:
5) gave ample substance to the myth. The most immediate effect of
the relative affluence – unsurprisingly, given traditional lifestyle
preferences (Rose, 1972: 69ff.) – was to facilitate a tremendous boom
in domestic construction. Between 1947 and 1976 home ownership
in the capital cities jumped by between 17 and 34 per cent (Berry,
1984: 40). At the end of this period, owner-occupancy rates – the
highest in the world – ranged from 69 per cent in Sydney to 74 per cent
in Melbourne. The secondary effect, since there was nowhere to put
all these houses but "further out," was, unfortunately, to maximize
not merely the physical but the "mental" suburbanization of Australian society.

Why "unfortunately"? "Distance from the centre and the very
existence of the separate plot of land on which the cottage, of necessity, stood, combined to foster an overweening interest . . . on purely
local and domestic activities," says Rose (1972: 71). This enforced
parochialism on the one hand exacerbated the already entrenched
anti-intellectual bent ("local activities . . . concentrate heavily on
sporting and social activities . . . as opposed to cultural ones" [71]);
more critically it also exacerbated the equally entrenched social fragmentation. Women, at least on the face of it, were the greatest sufferers from the enforced isolation. Their social identities tied almost
exclusively to their familial and particularly their maternal functions, they were, as feminist critics have amply elucidated, trapped as
surely by conditioned intellectual and emotional limitations as by
their physical circumstances (see, for instance, Summers, 1975;
Brophy, 1975). For all the myths of male camaraderie, however, there
is ample indication that men, too, are not just affected but delimited
by the artificial "separateness" of suburban living.

It is important to note that I am not simply talking about separateness from the "city" here. If that were the whole of it, the problem
would be a far less serious one. There is ample indication, though,
that there is just as much fragmentation within as between the

suburbs. As I noted earlier, structures operative on one level tend to replicate themselves on other (emotionally or metaphorically) contiguous levels. The relationship between the bungalow and the subdivision hence tends to reflect – almost perforce, as it were – the relationship between the subdivision and the metropolis. "Privacy is a valued commodity in [the suburb]," we read in a *National Times* article called "Living the Australian Dream." As horrifying for its dispassionate tone as for its "facts," this essay is worth quoting at some length.

Kathy Pippet is 35, originally from England and a Davidson resident for just over two years. When her baby was born her neighbour, also a young mother, brought in a pot plant as a gift. The two women had lived next door for three months but until that day had hardly exchanged a word. Since, they haven't said much to each other either.

Around the corner Sue Webbe, 32, a Davidson resident for seven years, told a similar story. She had given a bouncinette to her neighbour but since the birth of the neighbour's baby the two women had hardly spoken. As she said: "You say hello, but you don't mix socially. There is nothing worse than having people living on top of you, popping in" . . .

Life revolves around the nuclear family, rather than community or friends. Davidson is bereft of community places: no pubs, no clubs, no corner shop, no hall to break the landscape of houses. No accessible walls offer themselves for posters or graffiti. There are no signs except street signs. The Glenrose shopping centre, in the adjoining suburb of Belrose, must be reached by car. Public events are poorly attended, except for the end-of-year ballet school concert with its cast of 500. [Horin et al., 1985: 7]

These journalists' observations are amply borne out by more scientific studies. For many Australian suburbanites, kin interaction comprises a large proportion of *all* off-the-job interaction (Stivens, 1985), and home-oriented activities like reading or gardening are preferred by a significant margin over outings to restaurants, theatres, or clubs (McNair, 1975: 69).

Commentators like J.M. Freeland (1972) and Leonie Sandercock (1983) have made clear the social costs of the endemic suburbanization. Without denying the importance of such factors as socio-economic ghettoization, transportation problems, and youth unemployment, of more importance for present purposes – indeed, since they undoubtedly exacerbate the more purely structural problems, for social purposes as well – are the psychological ones. Middleness may, as we have seen, suggest safety to the beleaguered Australian; it also produces, as a byproduct, apathy, pessimism, secret self-loathing, and a fear of otherness so acute as almost to qualify as paranoia. Again without denying the substance of feminist complaints, from my particular viewpoint it is the male who suffers most, or at least most profoundly, from what is essentially a deactivation. Why? If, as Stivens points out, "being a good 'family man' and a good provider is" – at least theoretically – "an important source of self esteem" for the suburbanized male, the lack of any active function *within* the home (increasingly inappropriate norms for a sex-based division of labour – all the more rigorously enforced as the traditional tokens of male "superiority" erode – make it almost inevitable that participation in domestic and child-rearing chores will be viewed as effeminizing) means that this same male is in fact reduced to the position of a passive consumer of "care." The result? Not just despite but *because of* his careful role maintenance, "suburban man is . . . emasculated" (Stivens: 17, 18).

The worst thing about this situation, at least as far as the participants are concerned, is that it brings uncomfortably close to the surface a secret truth too terrible to contemplate. Ronald Conway, building on the work of American psychologist, Dr. Dan Adler, claims that the dominant pattern in present-day Australian family life, if not matriarchy, where the mother is formally superordinate, is matri-*duxy*, where she is functionally so. "Matriduxy or mother-leadership," he says, "implies a greater assertion of influence by the mother because of the domestic indifference or nurturing impotence of the father" (1985: 72). Conway also makes clear the intensity of the Australians' resistance to such an idea. "The reaction of most ordinary adult Australians when told of Adler's conclusions," he notes, "was one of incredulity, astonishment or downright ill-temper." Insofar as it is the most strenuous repression that localizes the most negative affect, we could take this response in itself as strong evidence of a shot too close to home. Even without the reverse psychology, though, there is ample support in culture to support Conway's conclusion. "Mothers," as we have seen, are virtually always construed as strong in Australian literature and popular productions. That they are also almost always construed as negative (in terms of "sympathy,"

Conway's matriducal household, with its nurturing mother and indifferent father, is in some ways quite opposite to the fictional model) simply indicates the desire to deny or repudiate the disapproved gender constructions that underlie real behaviour. Where does the suburb come into it? Though these constructions go a lot further back than Conway seems to realize, the suburban erosion of macho illusions, for good or ill, makes them loom more ominously in the folk consciousness. Given that humour usually expresses communal anxieties, it is interesting to note the *almost* explicit linkage of mother-dominance with the eclipse of the father in Australia's longest running comic strip, *Ginger Meggs*. "The decline after 1922 in the number of Ginger's confrontations with authority," says Barry Andrews, "corresponded to an increase in John Meggs' troubles coping with the world . . . [and with] the evolution of Sarah as an important character in her own right, less a one-dimensional oppressor of Ginger than his worthy adversary and verbal foil" (1983: 216). One doesn't have to look very deeply between these lines to understand why, if the long-term effects might be less than unequivocally negative (see the next chapter), at least in the short run the suburbanization of Australia would be detrimental to the masculine sense of self.

One of the most interesting indicators of anxiety is the change undergone by the critique of suburbia during the last two decades, and particularly by the erstwhile symbol of that critique, the ocker. What is an ocker? At his worst, as Oxley describes it, he is "a self-satisfied vulgarian, a beer-sodden slob uncouth in behaviour and thought, an ignorant bigot opposed to anybody unlike himself, of narrow outlook never rising above hedonism and prone to sneer at anything or anybody rising higher, a loudmouth obsessed by his own plastic masculinity, a conceited braggart, 'one of the boys' spending his time and money in the pubs and giving no thought to the morrow, a grunting pig and a male chauvinist one at that" (1979: 193). At best he is Paul Hogan. What this dichotomization obscures, on the other hand, is that the "good" ocker and the "bad" ocker do not signal divergent conceptions, but merely divergent evaluations of the *same* qualities. "[T]he ocker-knockers do not talk about improvising ability while Ward and his like are silent on male chauvinism," says Oxley. "But on most points these two accounts are of the same fellow, described respectively by those who do not like him and by those who do" (195).

The question is, of course, how do we explain this apparently quite radical split within what has heretofore revealed itself as an essentially homogeneous community? Craig McGregor posits a temporal dimension. *Initially* a negative construction, he says, as the "good old days" of the "working class bloke" receded further into the past – as the "real" ocker, that is, became less of an immediate threat to middle class sensibilities – the suburban larrikin paradoxically began to take on the temperamental semblance of the legendary bushman (1981, Chapter 5). McGregor is not alone in this interpretation. Though the ocker typos "originated as a satire on Australian boorishness," says Richard White, it "became an affectionate tribute to the national identity and ended up as the most effective way of selling cigarettes to children" (1981: 170; see also Horne, 1975).

Given the Australian penchant for rosy revisions of history – the pastoral age as seen by *The Bulletin*, the nineties remade by Ward and Palmer, Bean's expurgated World War I, the forties à la long-running "period" TV soapie, *The Sullivans* (McLaren, 1983: 4) – it would not be surprising if, by the seventies, the cultural wasteland of fifties suburbia should start to be repainted in more appealing colours. This doesn't, however, explain why the ocker, even in his most overtly affectionate renditions, remains an explicitly obnoxious character. The key to this, I think, lies in his ambivalent expression of masculinity. If, as I suggested above, the most disturbing aspect of increasing suburbanization is its covert undercutting of the myth of male dominance, then the one thing the modernday auditor would wish to establish by means of his nostalgic reconstruction would be that that dominance *did* once exist. But why emphasize negative rather than positive traits? Like all versions of the Australian "type," beneath his bluster the ocker is profoundly passive (Oxley: 206). To depict him as otherwise would violate the Australian's ineradicable, if unacknowledged, sense of impotence. Hence the obnoxiousness. Like Ginger Meggs' "controlled" floutings of authority, anti-social behaviour of the type exhibited by "ockers" is in essence simply an adolescent form of rebellion against an all-too-immanent "mum" – the *only* form the adolescent can muster.

Taking both of its sides into account, the ocker myth can thus be seen as a means of simultaneously expressing *and* denying castration fantasies. The fact that the negative aspect is rarely recognized only testifies to the wilful myopia of the deniers. This comes through with particular force in discussions of seventies "ocker films" like *The*

Adventures of Barry McKenzie or *Alvin Purple*. In the closing frames of the latter, says John Hinde, the eponymous hero is shown "fleeing naked through the streets of Melbourne closely pursued by a procession of screaming, rapacious girls. What fun for early adolescents! Otherwise how harmless, how trite, and – surely – how culturally inexact and pointless" (1985: 185). Given the omnipresent subtext of gynophobia elucidated throughout this book, it is impossible to believe that an Australian male could view that scene without at least subconsciously reading into it a meaning that is neither "fun" nor "harmless." By keeping attention focused on his excess of masculine "display," however, the ocker provides a means of managing the resultant anxiety.

The public response during the last few decades has been just as ambiguous as the private one. I have already noted how the entrenchment of passiveness and self-deprecation tends to militate against the development of effective governing strategies. The same factors, as hinted above, are even more dysfunctional when it comes to business. Like Australia's politicians, Australia's businessmen are above all *timid*. The impression one gains from Higley's sample, says Hugh Stretton, is of "an elderly, under-educated or narrowly educated business elite of a predominantly cautious, bureaucratic kind." The 1983 *Business Review Weekly* list of the country's wealthiest individuals reveals a similar pattern: "[L]uck, inheritance, and predatory activities figure largely, wholesome productivity rather less in the making of [Australian] multimillionaires," Stretton notes. "Very few have invented anything or done much technical research and development; scarcely any have made any significant use of Australian science. The brainiest one who showed the greatest technical ingenuity got rich by inventing a computerized betting system" (1981: 201; see also Jackson, 1981). The lack of imagination, the lack, even more, of entrepreneurial drive, has tended to stifle initiative and hamper efficiency even within the country's biggest and most powerful corporations. It is telling, for instance, that Tom Sheridan, discussing BHP's handling of the 1945 steel stoppage, should observe, exactly as I have observed of individuals, that the company can be "seen as much reacting to events as initiating them" (in Stretton, 1985: 203). While some, perhaps much, of the recent economic downturn can be blamed on world climate – as the old saying goes, a paranoid's problems are not necessarily all imaginary – one cannot therefore simply dismiss the systemic flaws as irrelevant. If only for its effect on national self-image, it is *not* irrelevant, as Stretton points out, that for "seventy years past, Australian business and political leadership has been generally mediocre and uninventive, missing many good opportunities" (225).

Profits and even productiveness aside, from a long-term perspective the most harmful consequence of recent poor business performance is the way it has reinforced the habit of dependency. This is not *quite* a case of more of the same. If the first half of the twentieth century was dominated by dreams of empire, over the last forty years, as numerous commentators have observed, the role of primary referent has been taken over from Britain by the United States. By now, says Henry Albinski,

American intellectual as well as popular cultural trends are the dominant overseas influence in Australia. About seventy thousand Americans are domiciled in Australia on a permanent or long-term basis, and over a hundred thousand American tourists visit annually. There are extensive scientific and technical cooperation programs between the two nations. By the early 1980s, the U.S. had become Australia's principal source of imports and its second most important export outlet. The United States had also become the foremost overseas investor in Australia across a broad range of industrial, resource, agricultural, and service industries. Since 1952, Australia's security has been linked to the U.S. through the ANZUS alliance. Bilateral military exercises and intelligence exchanges are widespread. [1985: 395]

The question is, of course, does the change of content affect the *form* of the response? One factor that obviously has to be borne in mind is that, judging at least by its effects on indigenous popular culture (see especially "Adventure Fiction" and "Television: Copping It," pp. 106-9 and 189-92 above), the United States, unlike Britain, is symbolically construed by the Australian as masculine. This *could* mean that Australia now has at its disposal a less inherently alienating model of culture. Despite laments about loss of national identity, however (see, for instance, Alomes, 1981a), the aforementioned discrepancies between home-grown and imported television programs reveal that – fortunately or unfortunately – the felt gap between self and other remains intact despite the shift to a same-sex referent. And so does the absence of effective "imitation" in Australia's conduct of its public affairs.

One area where this "gap" reveals itself most strikingly is in the Australian response to world high-technification. Where the United States carries on a constant love-hate relationship with technology (see G. McGregor, 1988), in Australia, corporate timidity notwithstanding, what we find most commonly is neither love *nor* hate, but something at right angles to both. To Australian children, as Shelley Phillips notes, "'Science is like magic.'" "The power aspect of the pipe dream theme [is] encapsulated in the scientist's ability to perform miracles which over[come] adversaries and adversities" (1979: 175). To adults, judging by both rhetoric and practical applications, it is scarcely less mystifying. Thomas Mandeville and Stuart Macdonald comment on the ignorance displayed by both sides in the recent "technological change" debate. Behind both Labour resistance *and* employer enthusiasm, they note, is an alarmingly "uncritical and unanimous" belief in the potency – the job-displacing efficiency – of high technology (1980: 216). Stephen Alomes, identifying this naivete as the latest version of "cultural cringe," opines – quite rightly, I think – that its "hard" disadvantages are equalled, perhaps even outweighed, by the less tangible ones. Conditioned dependency, he says, "distorts the perceptions of one's own society, which is usually seen as inferior to the metropolis" (1981a: 11). This is far from the whole of it, though. The more disabled Australians feel with respect to technology, the more they are forced to dissociate themselves from the recently[2] almost wholly technophilic American role model. And the more disabled they become in fact.

Like the ocker phenomenon, on the other hand, this development may not be quite the unequivocal disaster it surficially seems. Counter the Ward thesis, both history and popular culture suggest that there is something in Australians that hungers for a safe, suitable, and, especially, non-feminine authority to subordinate themselves to. Although it may seem a far-fetched analogy to make, one

---

2. Since this book was written, the climate in the U.S. has – as mentioned earlier (see note 6, p. 124) – changed rather drastically, with the eighties infatuation with technology giving way to a new wave of primitivism. This change, which is entirely predictable in light of my cyclic model of American history (for different aspects of this, see G. McGregor, 1987b, 1993a & b), may, for reasons given above (pp. 191-92), be expected eventually to usher in a new round of Australian cultural nationalism.

might instance attitudes toward officers during World War II. Received opinion would have it that the Australian private soldier was purely and simply insubordinate. Jane Ross disputes this. Though leery of institutionalized authority, she says, the Australian diggers were quite willing to accept the leadership of those who proved themselves intrinsically worthy (1985, Chapter 12). The way she *explains* their response, on the other hand, merely invokes a slightly revised version of the traditional view. Exactly like the outright anti-authoritarianism posited by Bean and his cronies, the insistence on passing judgment before awarding allegiance is viewed simply as a symptom of the much-touted Australian independence of mind. There is no doubt an element of this in the reaction. Considered in light of our observations on attitudes to war, however, I don't think the motives involved were quite that simple. The reason the Australians set such high standards for their officers, I would claim, was that they needed to be able to maintain a positive image of authority in order to justify their covert (unmanly) deference to it. What does this have to do with the American? Simply this. The only culturally validated image in the digger's conceptual repertoire capable of fulfilling this function was the image of the remote but charismatic "good father." The operative word here is "remote." The only way the officer – or anyone else, for that matter – could be accepted as a permissible object of reverence was for him to be definitively dissociated, by real or symbolic means, from the self. This, of course, is where the tie-in comes. Though one can do little more than speculate at this point, it is at least possible that the distancing of the American role model, as evidenced in the dissociation from both technology and techno-heroes, while in practical terms clearly counterproductive, as a means of rationalizing the *fait accompli* of dependency is an emotional necessity.

5

AFTER WORDS

This brings us to the bottom line. The question, of course, is what, beyond another "view," a study like this adds. The answer, I would claim: another view-*point*. And not just *an* other viewpoint, but a viewpoint capable of compensating for the blind spots in Australia's own. To the extent that they probe causes at all, Australian interpretations of Australian history tend to emphasize material factors. For Geoffrey Blainey (1983), for instance, the shape and rhythms of colonial development can be explained entirely in terms of distance, both *from* and *within* the country. Blainey and his ilk are at best half right. If it is true that the geo-historical facts determined the way that Australia was experienced and expressed by its inhabitants, it is equally true that the expressed experience itself determined which and how "facts" would be perceived. Both supporting and extending my initial predictions about intrasystemic homology, the foregoing survey demonstrates that the Australian "world" is not just structurally *self*-consistent, but consistent as well with the structures of consciousness by means of which it was both created and comprehended.

Quite apart from its almost literal pre-packaging of art and literature, this fact has some important consequences for indigenous cultural studies, especially in light of the *particular* predispositions that emerged from the mind/matter collision in this particular case. If it is revealing that Australian scholars, like Australians in general, have excised not only "woman" but "the feminine" from their conceptual/descriptive repertoires ("the now familiar signification of the sign 'woman' as the 'other,' the 'unconscious,' the 'instinctual' and so forth," says Delys Bird, "extends in Australia to include all those things classified as [non-masculine]" [1983: 111]), it is even more revealing that so few of them have noticed the absence. "In fact," says Kay Schaffer – an American now teaching at the South Australian College for Advanced Education – "no commentators on the Australian Tradition, to my knowledge, have registered or analysed the

significance of the enunciation of the land-as-woman. Yet, if one
re-reads the texts on Australia which constitute an historical tradition, from Dampier's *A New Voyage Around the World* (1697) to
Manning Clark's recent five volume history, what becomes apparent
is that although references to actual women as historical agents are
rare, references to the idea of woman, embedded in linguistic constructions of landscape, are everywhere" (unpub.: 3-4). This is not
just a special case of the general antipathy to "psychoanalytic" interpretations. Relations with and perceptions of feminineness are critical elements in the Australian construction of self. As such (and now
I am going one step further than the passive mapping of culture I
promised in my introduction), they provide a useful tool for elucidating and – more important in Australia's case – discriminating
between real and apparent cultural change.

Why more important? Given the obsession with "coming of age"
metaphors, change is almost guaranteed to be a major theme in Australian cultural histories. The recent period is no exception. Judging
by both scholarly and popular publications, there seems to be almost
unanimous agreement that Australia has recently undergone or is
currently undergoing some kind of critical shift. More surprisingly,
considering the pessimism of concurrent economic and political
prognostications ("It seems likely that the manufacturing crisis and
the environmental and fiscal crises of our major cities will remain . . .
The industrial labour movement . . . will continue to provide leadership, but will be reminded constantly of its powerlessness to transform the international economy" [Wells, 1986: 76]), most commentators read this development as a change for the better. "The old rigorous, uniform, single-ethic society has lost its clarity," says Craig
McGregor, "and in the process it has become more cosmopolitan,
looser, more worldly." "[I]n this fragmentation, this exploding-out, of
the old stale consensus, lies Australia's best hope for the future"
(1981: 313). Is McGregor right? Here is where those "markers" come
in. If the change remarked upon really is more than simply a shift of
emphasis – the replacement of the verandah with the "outdoor living
area" (Fiske et al., 1987, Chapter 2), or the integration of the garden
into architectural "front" – then we should expect to find a change in
the way self-other relations are conceptualized and expressed.

At first sight there would seem to be some reason for believing that
this could indeed be the case. Insofar as the recent "maturing" event

is most commonly attributed to the social and psychological incorporation of such erstwhile dispossessed elements as "Women, Aboriginals, and Post-War Immigrants" (D. Burns, 1982: 44) – insofar, moreover, as the country's significant other is now construed as masculine – one might postulate an at least relative femininization of the symbolic ego. In real life, unfortunately, the problematic doesn't resolve itself nearly so tidily. Far from the catalyst hypothesized by indigenous observers, closer examination of the invoked phenomena reveals that much even of the supposedly substantial surface change to Australian society is illusory.

Take the matter of women. The mid-seventies saw a spate of impressively researched and overtly impassioned feminist publications intended, so their authors and editors said, as a corrective to the blatantly sexist histories and sociologies that had hitherto been accepted as normative in the Australian popular imagination (Mercer, 1975; Summers, 1975; Dixson, 1976, revised 1984). Once out of the closet, the subject of women quickly became one of the hottest academic properties of the decade. By 1980, no collection of essays on social or historical topics could appear without its requisite Chapter on "gender" or "families" or "women in the workforce" (see, for instance, McLaren, 1983; Encel et al., 1984; Graubard, 1985). Despite all this consciousness-raising, however – and despite the fact, too, that concomitant economic developments ensured that it would be accompanied by a good many "real" changes (where once it was simply assumed that a woman's place was at home, says Leonie Sandercock, a "second income has [now] become essential for ordinary families wishing to participate in the great Australian dream" [1983: 75]) – there is considerable evidence that any consequent attitude modification was temporary or surficial. "Sinister symptoms, such as the growing numbers of highly qualified women underemployed or unemployed, the massive unemployment figures for young women, political tokenism, and the concerted attack on working women by governments and newspapers, are cause for disquiet and anxiety," says Belinda Vaughan. "Break the vigilante mood, and the gains could disappear almost overnight" (1983: 131; see also Richards, 1985, xvff.; Burns, 1986).

Part of the problem (as usual) has to be attributed to the political climate in the world at large. The American women's movement, too, lost more ground than it gained during the Reagan years. A

greater part, though, is due to those same psycho-social predispositions that created the sexism against which the seventies Australian
feminists were rebelling. Presaging ill for the hopes pinned on
"enlightenment," recent researchers, as Vaughan points out, have
come up against the fact that they are not really breaking new ground
at all. "[F]ar from a dearth of women's history," she notes, once
broached the archives were found to overflow with "positive and radical material from women in late nineteenth and early twentieth century Australia" (128). How, she asks, could such a degree of "activity
and furore" be so totally "smothered and extinguished" as to produce
at mid-century the *Australian Woman's Weekly*'s suburban mum?

Someone more optimistic than Vaughan would undoubtedly attribute the regression to the inherent weaknesses of fin-de-siècle feminism. The suffragettes and even more the Temperance Unionists,
says Summers (1975, Chapter 11), had so completely internalized the
delimiting stereotypes projected upon them by a monolithically
patriarchal world-at-large that they were literally disabled as political
actors. By working politely within the system, by shunning direct
political action, and by focusing their energies on moral reform, they
were in effect merely transporting the maternal role to a wider stage.
Today's feminists are no longer constrained by such foolish misappre-
hensions. Or so it is claimed. If it is obvious that the "new" Australian woman no longer identifies herself solely as a homemaker, however, it is *not* clear that she is any more immune to "patriarchal"
indoctrination. Quite the opposite, in fact. Though patently less
decorous than their great-grandmothers, for instance, post-seventies
feminists have shown little advance in the way of either political
astuteness ("Consciousness-raising groups, agitation for the right to
abortion and for equal pay, and radical lesbian organizations advocat-
ing women's rights all developed in urban centers in the 1970s," notes
Jill Conway. "What did not accompany these developments was the
parallel concern for access to higher education, the professions, and
the management levels of business . . . [More women entered] the
helping professions – nursing, librarianship, social work – but the
rates of the entry of educated women into non-traditional fields, and
their rates of persistence in higher education do not indicate major
social change" [1983: 357]), *or* – of somewhat greater import – self-
awareness.

Two points in particular bear mention here. First, virtually every writer in this field reiterates the common view of Australian women as psychologically as well as socially disadvantaged by their conditioning. What strikes the outsider most forcefully, however, is that nearly all the "handicaps" they lay claim to – passiveness, apoliticism, technophobia, a poor sense of self-worth, and so forth – are, albeit covertly, attributable to the population at large. Second, as if they had even more invested in the "official" image than their male counterparts, virtually every writer in the field also buys the national myth of masculine strength and aggression. And not merely buys, but *reinforces*. Where, accepting their plaints at face value, one might expect them to search out evidence or instances of "distaff" superiority, most of them in fact reject indignantly any suggestion that the Australian female is *not* totally subordinate. Especially interesting are responses to the Adler study. Lois Bryson's essay in Jan Mercer's 1975 anthology, *The Other Half*, is typical. If one may judge by the logical absurdities in which the attempt to rebut involves her (she claims, for instance, that the "rationalizations" of parents are a more trustworthy guide to power structures within a family than the artless observations of children), this purportedly objective social scientist would seem to feel more threatened by the matriduxy thesis than the males whom it ostensibly discredits (compare Horne, 1971: 82).

How do we explain this? The most obvious interpretation is the political one: by augmenting their Antagonist, the Australian feminists are using the old ploy of a straw man to strengthen their own position. And undoubtedly there is an element of this in the equation. The implications of the women's fiction that came out of the seventies, however, would suggest that something rather more insidious is at work than simply political trickery. No matter how fervent their rhetorical disclaimers, there is every indication, as noted in "Women Writers, Women Written" (pp. 85-89 above), that Australian women actually identify *with*, rather than against, the masculine ideal. The only difference between them and their menfolks, therefore, is that they are conditioned to recognize rather than denying/hiding the extent to which they not merely fall short of, *but actively betray*, the exemplary picture. No wonder the Australian women's movement lacks conviction. The guilt these women feel simply for being feminine continually erodes their sense of purpose. Not to mention their praxis. Whether one sees it as penis envy or vicarious castration anxiety, the harder they attack the male mystique, the more it seems they feel impelled to shore it up, albeit negatively. Apart from anything else, this clearly rules out the "influence" theory. If Australian women are simply wishful-males, it is foolish to suggest that their increased visibility in Australian public life is likely to alter attitudes in any real way.

Given equal scrutiny, the other factors cited above seem equally unpromising. Much has been written about Australia's new cultural pluralism, for instance, but apart from a few determined optimists like Craig McGregor ("Australia, which was once the most homogeneous of countries, has become surprisingly multi-cultural, multi-ethnic, even multi-racial, and in doing so has drawn closer to the American pattern of strong, self-defining and self-generative minorities" [1984: 94-95; see also Horne, 1971: 84-89]), most, at least among the specialist commentators, agree not only that immigrant groups, proportionate to their degree of obvious "differentness" (Lippman, 1983: 125), suffer substantial real disadvantagement when it comes to education, employment, housing, and so on, but that xenophobic feelings remain firmly entrenched in the public at large (see Poole, et al., 1985, especially de Lacey, Smolicz, and Barlow). As in the case of women, then, the greater visibility of minorities, though speedily incorporated into the political rhetoric (and here one might keep in mind the probable abstract appeal of catch phrases implying social fragmentation), cannot be said to have modified community *attitudes* in any significant way.

The same can be said about the recent fad for aborigines. Despite the specialized attentions of artists and social scientists (Benterrek, Muecke, and Roe's *Reading the Country* [1984] combines a bit of both), and notwithstanding the recent glut of pop-scholarly publications on aboriginal myths and customs, it is important to remember, as noted above (pp. 139-40), that the commodification of aboriginal culture is a way of distancing, not of redeeming, its "subjects." "[I]t is not the aborigines at issue, but ourselves as so-called 'free' individuals," says George Alexander (1985: 37; see also Tatz, 1980). Here, of course, is the hidden truth which (again) underwrites the gap between word and action. If the "official" policy toward aborigines has become – at least in theory, and where no corporate interest is at stake (it is notable but not surprising that the greatest resistance to aboriginal land claims has been mounted by the major mineral-producing states of Western Australia and Queensland [Franklin, 1979]) – somewhat more enlightened than it used to be, there is absolutely no evidence either in popular culture or in the manifest behaviour of the public at large that attitudes toward the real flesh-and-blood aborigine have changed in any essential way at all (see Rowse and Moran, 1984: 264ff.).

Does this mean that the "transition" so hopefully touted has been entirely apocryphal – one more in the endless series of comings-of-age? Perhaps. In fact, almost certainly. If, however, we make the effort to dissociate ourselves from the insider's wishful vision of metamorphosis – if, even more important, we turn from official pronouncements to more spontaneous kinds of indicator – what I think we can see in recent Australian cultural history, if not a *change* per se, is at least a re-cognition of old motifs. If it is true that the psycho-social distortions remain essentially unaltered, it is also true that Australian popular culture would seem recently to have discovered an incomparably more effective way of psycho-symbolically "managing" the endemic ambivalence.

The exemplary case in point here is the *Mad Max* series. If on the surface these films seem to express the ultimate in post-modern nihilism (*The Road Warrior*, says Paul Taylor, "describes an anarchic race to the end, a world where all participants are racers, greedy, deceitful and self-interested" [1984: 98]), from a slightly different perspective they can be seen to resemble a uniquely Australian version of what Ross Gibson calls a "*primary* myth, a myth of origins" (1985: 26). Max himself is the type Australian protagonist: destructive, disinherited, deteriorating; a pawn of incomprehensible forces; above all, alone. He is also, however – and here is where the "myth" comes in – significantly *different* from his both real and fictional forebears. How? Gibson puts his finger on the key point. "Max is still a failure . . . in the tradition of Leichhardt *et al.*," he says. "[H]e still cannot return from his self-transcendent wanderings with any prize, or grace, or answers. He is still defining himself through negation: finally, yet again, he abjure's society's pleasures and responsibilities. In these respects Kennedy-Miller are riding with the energy still contained in the old myths. *But most significantly, Max is still alive*" (32; italics added).

The question, to be sure, is: accepting that the Max character really is as significant an indicator as Gibson implies, what exactly does the departure from convention *mean*? That Australians are less defeatist than they used to be? Again, perhaps. But the social and economic indicators certainly show no sign of it. That they are becoming more Americanized? For the same reasons, it doesn't seem likely. So how *do* we account for the fact that Max, without either straining our credulity or diminishing his stature – more important, without undercutting in any way the essential "Australianness" of his character – unlike Ned Kelly, Burke and Wills, the Anzacs, can be allowed to survive his ordeal in the desert? It's simple. There is one thing, apart from his fate, that sets Max apart from Gibson's "transcendent failures." *Max is not wilful.* All Max's deeds, all his decisions, all his inter-actions, are thrust upon him by chance. Max, therefore, is both the epitome *and* the antithesis of the Kiplingesque "hero." The duplicity is critical to the power – and, even more important, the reassuringness – of the myth. Insofar as he is *formally dynamic* (as a reactor, Max is so impressive that one quite overlooks the amply reiterated reluctance), the new protagonist avoids the stigma of effeminacy. Because he is at the same time *functionally passive*, however, he does not have to pay the usual price for self-assertion against (m)otherness. From here it is only a short step to the open legitimization of what, with great difficulty, had formerly to be disguised or denied. "The logical project for *Mad Max 4*, should it ever eventuate," says Gibson, "would be to show Max learning to *love* again" (33). As Gibson himself will undoubtedly have realized by now, that task has been achieved by a surrogate. Mad Max *sans* angst is simply – Crocodile Dundee.

APPENDICES, BIBLIOGRAPHY, AND INDEX

APPENDIX A

"Voice in the Wilderness":
A Note on Grounds and Precedents

When this book went to press it was suggested to me that it might be useful for the reader to have a better sense of the preceding volumes on Canada and the United States. I agreed. It seemed an easy enough chore, to provide synopses of work already safely between covers. It wasn't until I sat down to my computer that the enormity of the task began to strike me. Even in their original condition, the books in question were too long, too dense, and too convoluted to yield easily to capsulization. Exacerbating the problem was the fact, as I discovered, that in my head neither of them actually exists in that condition any more. Subsequent work in both areas has extended, augmented, and in some cases significantly transmuted the initial picture. To unravel hindsight from first thought at this point would be difficult if not impossible. Complicating the task of producing a "series outline," moreover, was the fact that the material was inhomogeneous to begin with. Due partly to changes in my own development over the last decade (including both a shift of affiliation from the Humanities to the Social Sciences and an expansion of my area of research to encompass a far wider range of artifacts and practices) and partly to variances in the "styles" of the communities in question, the three entries in this series diverge widely not just in their findings, but in the "kind" of discourse they represent. All three do, it is true, take as their primary task the attempt to capture the historical development of a site-specific sense of "place." The way they approach this task, however, is significantly different in each case. First written but second published, The Noble Savage in the New World Garden: Notes Toward a Syntactics of Place *(1988), despite its theoretical framework and concluding attempt to schematize its findings, is for the most part a relatively conventional literary history focussing on a small number of thematizations connected with the American "errand into the wilderness." The* Wacousta

Syndrome: Explorations in the Canadian Langscape *(1985), in contrast, is specifically "postmodern" in conception. Intended initially as a chapter in the American study (before irreducible differences made this lumping impossible), and building on its findings regarding the problematization of identity under frontier conditions, it focuses far more than the earlier book on the formal features (rather than the content) of culture, using the tools of post-structural analysis to elucidate connections between modes of expression and their social and psychological grounds. Considering only the variance of aims, therefore, to synopsize these books as a set would clearly entail either a reductive homogenization or a distracting attention to the incommensurability of ways and means. I tried the first, and hated it. I tried the second, and the result was a tome-unto-itself. On the verge of giving it up, it suddenly occurred to me that what was needed here was not a synopsis but a* representation. *What I am offering, consequently, to "stand in for" the rest of the "Voice" series is the text of the paper I presented at the Canadian Studies Conference I talked about in my introductory chapter on Brisbane. Allowing for a rather too-obvious element of traveller's chauvinism, this piece not only summarizes some of the more salient findings of my work to that point, but also provides a good sense of where I was "at" in my thinking when I began the journey that produced the present book. Its title on that occasion was "Transforms: A Metamorphology of the Canadian Mind."*[1]

Like the United States, Canada began with a group of civilized Europeans set down in the middle of an untamed wilderness. Unlike their southerly neighbours, however, Canadians did not find anything the least bit garden-like about this setting. "Official" rhetoric notwithstanding, the Canadian was in fact utterly repelled by the "rude grandeur" of the northern landscape. How do we know? Not, admittedly, from what we are told explicitly by early writers and historians. Because the reaction was not only an unconscious but – for a people conditioned by two generations of poets to view nature as a moral mirror – an unconscionable one, the development is in fact revealed most strikingly through the *inadvertent* testimony of art. Though

---

1. This paper draws heavily on *The Wacousta Syndrome*, especially chapters 1 and 12.

the effect is barely noticeable at the level of individual works, a scan of the communal oeuvre clearly demonstrates what closer scrutiny obscures, that certain peculiarities of composition and technique have been widespread and consistent enough in Canadian landscape painting from the late eighteenth right through to the twentieth century, despite its generally derivative character, to be identified as markers of a truly indigenous pattern of response. And if we go one step further and compare this body of work with American equivalents, it becomes obvious that what this pattern signifies is not merely a difference in aesthetic preferences but a divergence in communal psychology.

Take, for instance, the handling of perspective in the two countries. On the American side, landscape art characteristically comprises an unabashed celebration of man [sic] in nature. Beginning with the Hudson River school back in the early years of the Republic, the American painter has tended to combine almost illimitable recession with a sense of visual domination to assert the ascendency of the view over the vista. Not so north of the border. Far from expansive, the most notable feature of Canadian landscape painting is a tangible, almost claustrophobic foreshortening of pictorial space. Ruling out hypotheses of accident, moreover, analysis makes clear that this effect relates less to the material givens than to the peculiarities of the observer's stance. Particularly telling is the handling of sightlines. In marked contrast to the American preference for an elevated vantage, the viewpoint in most Canadian works is set oppressively close to the ground. At its most extreme this practice gives us what is virtually a worm's eye view of things. At its least, we are afoot on the field of action. In the latter case the diminished physical barriers are likely to be reinforced by psychological ones. In works dealing with open types of terrain, for instance, detail and lighting are commonly used to focus attention on the foreground. Alternately, telescoping or multiple layering of visual strata may be employed as a means of retarding visual penetration. The more the subject verges on panorama, the more blatant the attempts to deny recession. In prairie paintings, for instance, the horizon, though technically invoked, is almost always raised or obscured by atmospheric conditions. The same holds in rolling pasturelands. No matter how boundless the landscape depicted, in other words, the composition of the artifact is almost always such as to throw the viewer back upon him- or herself.

When the landscape is *not* boundless, on the other hand, the claustro-phobic effect can become even more extreme. Much of the oeuvre would seem designed to repudiate the idea that the natural world is accessible on any level whatsoever. Most striking, perhaps, is the overwhelming number of works, both early and late, which give us woods like walls: dense, diffuse, and impermeable. The fact that among the entire corpus of Canadian landscape paintings it is only in those depicting explicitly domesticated rural or urban subjects that one is likely to find any significant depth of field at all suggests that Canadian, unlike American, artists were most at ease when nature was kept cut down to a thinkable size.

The effects of this perspectival bias remain in evidence even when the subject matter is held constant. In the depiction of waterways, for instance, painters on each side of the border diverged not only along national lines but in accordance with the same pro- and anti-pan-oramic orientations revealed in their handling of the vista. In the United States, typically enough, a river was most often employed to draw the eye into and across the landscape. The view is *along* the river, in other words, not merely penetrating but laying claim to the distance. In Canada the case is quite different. Where the waterway is inviting, it leads out from, not into the picture. Where it penetrates, it is not inviting. The keynote is almost invariably reticence, not aggressiveness. In some paintings, far from eliciting even visual entry, a river or narrow lake bisects the canvas horizontally such that a raised bank of foliage radically restricts the depth of field. In other cases the *initial* view is along the river, but is quickly pinched off by high-banked, bulky curves. The most common technique, however, is to establish the viewer at ground level, looking upstream, so that the path of the water appears to terminate abruptly at the top of a small rapids or falls with a solid wall of hills or woods looming up behind it. The effect of all these compositional variations is, of course, to avoid entirely the "opening up," the suggestion of appropri-ation, that is typical of American river scenes.

A similar but even more telling distinction may be detected in the respective treatments of another popular theme, the waterfall. Again it comes down to perspective. In American variants, the viewer is usually placed above and at a considerable distance back from the falls, so that s/he gets a sense of both the vertical drop *and* the hori-zontal panorama behind it. On the Canadian side of the border, in contrast, waterfalls are typically seen from below and at relatively short range. The human figures – usually diminutive and almost always placed at or near the base of the falls – often seem to be trapped in the bottom of a deep bowl, and although the viewer usually looks *down* on these figures (diminishing them even further), we share their perspective in looking *up* at the cliff face. Whatever the specifics of style or content, in fact, there are few Canadian waterfall paintings that allow the viewer to see much beyond the rim at all.

Turning to larger geographic features we also find striking contrasts between Canadian and American mountainscapes. In the United States, painters have generally tended to focus on the valley *below* or the pass or gap *through* the mountains, usually acccentuating both the accessibility and the desirability of the space "beyond" through the use of heightened and dramatic lighting. In Canadian art, however, mountains are typically made to appear as symbolic or actual barriers to human penetraton. In some of the more extreme cases they form an unbroken palisade across the whole width of the picture plane. Even when the effect of absolute impassibility is mitigated somewhat, we note that it is more often than not the *bulk* of a mountain or group of mountains – rather than a route around or a path through – that dominates the middle of the canvas. If this weren't enough, the claustrophobic effect is exacerbated by the fact that these focal formations often shoot up with rather unnatural abruptness behind a lake or river, seemingly at no great distance, such that it is inevitably the sheer *obtrusiveness* of the geography that communicates itself to the viewer above any other feature. The obstacle posed by the mountain, in other words, is clearly implied to be much more than merely physical. Again, then, there is a subtle but important difference to be discerned between the practice of the two countries: where Americans typically emphasize the "romantic" aspects of alpine scenes, Canadian artists most often present the mountainscape in a predominantly inimical mood.

On the whole, it seems obvious from all these discrepancies in approach that even within the confines of a putatively identical range of subjects and idioms there is, as Marcia Kline says of Canadian and American writers, "some very basic cleavage in the way ... [they] see and confront the natural world."[2] The American view is perhaps not as wholly simplistic and untroubled as these comparisons may make it appear: for every moment that nature seems paradisial, there is another in which it becomes once more the Puritans' "waste and howling wilderness," full of heathens and demons. It is, however, a view in which both possibilities, if they are not reconciled, at least coexist in a kind of dynamic tension. This is not the case in Canada. Whatever one may say about individual works, when the Canadian communal oeuvre is viewed holistically, as Lévi-Strauss views his myths or Barthes his mythologies, the sense of alienation we get is so striking and so consistent – and this even among such outspoken proponents of muscular outdoorsiness as Emily Carr and the Group of Seven – that it belies the very possibility nature could ever be benevolent and maternal. It also quite pointedly militates against any ideal of assimilation. Quite apart from the question of verisimilitude, to deny depth is in effect to deny the *connection* between viewer and vista. Far from trying to appropriate the landscape, in other words, it is apparent from his/her choice of pictorial and compositional conventions that the Canadian artist is in fact attempting to dissociate from it altogether.

The question is, to be sure, why? Given the similarities in geohistorical backgrounds, why *should* the Canadian and the American have such different perceptions of the environment? Part of it, no doubt, is simply that there *is* a real if relative difference in the harshness of climate and geography. Part, too, probably relates to the fact that while the Pilgrim Fathers were well bolstered for their "errand into the wilderness" by an eminently martial theology, given that their country didn't really exist as a self-conscious entity until after the Revolution split the continent, the earliest "Canadian" immigrants were somewhat less adequately prepared for their confrontation with nature in the raw by the little books of romantic poetry that they clutched in their hands as they sailed up the St Lawrence. The real key, though, I think, is the difference between a "western" and a "northern" frontier. A western frontier is an arbitrary line denoting the limits of knowledge. A northern frontier is an existential line denoting the limits of *endurance*. A western frontier can be pushed back or jumped over or redefined, but the individual who transgresses a northern frontier simply doesn't survive. S/he is drowned or frozen to death or mauled by animals or crushed by a falling tree or knocked

---

2. *Beyond the Land Itself: Views of Nature in Canada and the United States* (Cambridge: Harvard U. Press, 1970), p. 42.

off a cliff. Canadian literature is full of such cautionary incidents. Small wonder that people who live on a northern frontier should be less impressed by nature's beauty than by nature's danger.

From one point of view, then, the recoil from nature comprises the most basic element of the Canadian experience. From another perspective, it can be seen as just a beginning. This is where Canada's youthfulness proves particularly useful to the ethnographer. Dealing with changed or disappearing cultures we can do no more than reconstruct "probabilities." If we trace the Canadian response through the last century and a half, however, we find ample hard evidence not only *that* the primal confrontation with nature was important but – far more critical for present purposes – *how* its effects were both manifested in and transformed by history. And I do mean *transformed*, Reconstructing our not-so-distant past, it becomes clear that the defensive withdrawal of affect from the landscape not only alleviates anxiety but demythicizes the erstwhile threatening object. Sufficiently distanced, in other words, the wilderness loses not only its threat but its reality. Once this happens, the centripetal impulse stimulated in the first place by the sense of external menace becomes, at least metaphorically, a prototype for responses not merely to nature but to "otherness" in general. At the same time, the "metaphor" becomes generative rather than merely reflective. By this means, the defining mental movement gradually becomes assimilated as a wholly automatic "habit" – to borrow a term from crystallography – of the communal imagination. To quote from *The Wacousta Syndrome,*

By the time the transformation runs its whole course, what started out as the specific, observable result of specific isolable causes becomes internalized as, in a sense, an ideogrammatic representation of self-in-the-world, a means of *creating* experience rather than merely responding to it. The fact is, inasmuch as a mode of vision is unconscious and spontaneous, it tends to become conventionalized; to crystallize into patterns that are fixed, simple, and self-replicating. These patterns, once generated, begin not only to subsume all functionally equivalent future experience but to impose themselves on any "free" – that is, unstructured, unsystematized – experiential phenomena which manifest themselves in the subject's perceptual set, such that these incline to express themselves in a compatible form whatever their actual content. [p. 77]

A compatible form! No wonder the preferred iconography of the Canadian oeuvre bespeaks nothing so much as a modern version of Mary Douglas's radically xenophobic "small group" type culture.[3] Enclosure images in art, house symbols in literature, an obsession with human limitations, both social and corporeal: whatever role they may play in *individual* vision, such features – improbably persistent throughout the Canadian corpus – must be taken to document a *collective* concern with and anxiety about boundaries, walls, windows, edges, thresholds; the interface between self and other, inside and outside – the numinous antithesis between figure and ground.

The next question that needs to be addressed is what effect this covert structuring has on culture-at-large apart from art. On the surface, Canada simply seems "American." More important, we *think* of ourselves as American. Judging by public rhetoric, whether we applaud or deplore the situation, as a nation we are convinced that we are little more than a cultural satellite of our southerly neighbour. If one looks just a little way *below* the surface, however, it becomes obvious that our conscious self-image is not only inaccurate but on many counts in total diametric opposition to the character we reveal *unconsciously*. Take the type protagonist who emerges from our fiction. Here is no self-created American Adam, no child of nature, no eternal pioneer – parentless, rootless, ruthless – faring forth untrammelled by tradition into a clean and fabulous future. Far from it! The Canadian is a *descendent*, fascinated by fact, obsessed with genealogy. The Canadian is a *good citizen*, preferring Law to freedom. The Canadian is a homebody, a pragmatist, a small-C *conservative*. Most telling of all, the Canadian is an individual who feels him- or herself to be irresistibly *circumscribed by history*. Long after "nature" ceases to be a fashionable subject, the sense of containment remains palpable in our modes of expression. Where the American is dynamic, extraverted, and linearly oriented, the Canadian continues to convey a sense of identity through recurrent iconic images of an isolated self, alone and static, surrounded by a diffuse, alien otherness which simply by default becomes implicated with masculine aggression. Collectively these differences in temperament and stance point to one logically inescapable if generally unrecognized conclusion. If the

---

3. *Natural Symbols: Explorations in Cosmology* (New York: Vintage, 1973), especially p. 169.

American may be seen as the archetypal male, the Canadian symbolic ego is a feminine one.

This single fact goes far to explain some of the most puzzling aspects of the Canadian national character. In particular it makes seem somewhat less mysterious those quirks of vision and practice that continue, despite our consumption of imported popular culture, to set us somehow ineffably apart from our nearest neighbours. And I'm not talking here about what Margaret Atwood and others have called, disparagingly, our "victim mentality."[4] Judging by their literature, Canadians do indeed tend to identify with saints, madmen, cripples, freaks, Indians, animals, women – the dispossessed and the powerless. Judging by their social arrangments, however – and here is where I depart quite radically from the doomsayers among us – this identification is *not* the entirely negative one it seems from an American perspective. Superheroes aside, in the kind of world we inhabit today – a world short on resources and long on hostility – there's a lot to be said for keeping a low profile. Tolerance, compromise, accommodation: when paranoids are in power, it's traits like these which are most likely to keep the *ordinary* individual out of trouble. More to the point, it's these same so-called "feminine" traits which most readily foster the kind of cooperation essential for *group* survival in marginal conditions. The "feminine" stance, in other words, may very well be the sanest stance one could possibly assume under the circumstances. So why on earth do Canadians keep castigating themselves for thinking like losers? And why is our literature so negative? *My* answer is that it's not. Contra common assumptions, the fact is that a surprising proportion of Canadian writing, despite its preoccupation with death and disaster, its gothic landscapes, imperiled artists, broken marriages, and lost children, nevertheless strikes a final note of affirmation based not on American style fantasies of omnipotence, but on an acceptance of, and – what is more important – a healthy response to, human limitations.

It's that word "response" that takes us beyond Atwood, of course. *And* beyond visions of self-defeating submission. Though convinced that no-one can choose his or her circumstances, Canadians (as written by their literature) believe that they *can and must* choose how they will react to them; what, given their undeniable finitude, they

---

4. *Survival: A Thematic Guide to Canadian Literature* (Toronto: Anansi, 1972).

will see, feel, be. It is this assumption of individual accountability that gives Canadian writing a unique, almost puritanistic flavour oddly combining tolerance with high moral purpose. It is also the feature largely responsible for the perverse cheerfulness which, repudiating definitively the institutionalized schizophrenia of the contemporary ironic stance, lies behind much that seems superficially facile or "soft" or old-fashioned in the Canadian voice. What Dennis Duffy says of Hugh Hood is true of many of our authors. "Hood is not a post modern in his sense of life – he sees it as grim, joyous, brutal, peaceful, but never as merely silly or absurd. His characters are haunted by the past, they are prone to fantasizing their way around reality, but they possess minds and bodies which struggle, at times successfully, to live really and presently. It is not that they or their creator are unaware of the Horror or the Void; it is that they do not often dwell there."[5]

This latter is the key point. Victimization is a state of mind. It is a state of mind, moreover, which is quite alien to the Canadian sense of self. Unlike the angst-obsessed anti-hero of postmodern America, Canadians (again, as written) evince the belief that it is just as self-indulgent to bemoan one's limitations, to use them as an excuse for unhappiness, as it is to pretend that they do not exist. What, then, you may ask, are we to make of all those enclosure images? Does the harping on existential constraints not comprise at least tacit negativism? Not necessarily. If you look closely at the relationship between figure and ground in many Canadian paintings, the sense of knee-jerk claustrophobia begins to dissolve. Just as the avoidance strategies of the landscape painter can be read as signifying both a source of anxiety *and* a mode of managing it, once the iconic box begins to change from *container* to *frame*, it no longer passively mirrors the plight of the isolated ego but provides both artist and auditor with a means of controlling the very element from which they have hitherto been most concerned to dissociate themselves. At this point the line around begins actually to mediate the relationship of ego *with* other. The same can be said of ritual in the social arena, of law in the political one. However manifested, Canadian life is full of mediating structures that both buffer and facilitate the act of "going between."

---

5. "Grace: The Novels of Hugh Hood" in George Woodcock, ed., *The Canadian Novel in the Twentieth Century: Essays from Canadian Literature* (Toronto: McClelland and Stewart, 1975), pp. 440-41.

This, of course, is what Canadians are really getting at with all their enclosure motifs. The thing that both fascinates and terrifies them. The lesson they have to learn if they're going to survive as social beings. Not apartness, but "managed" trans-action. It's what Canadian literature is all about, too. Notwithstanding its obvious preoccupation with isolates, the fact is that the corpus offers an enormous number of models for congregation. David Williams' Sundance; the war's-end celebration in Blondal's Mouse Bluffs; Gwendolyn MacEwan's *Breakfast for Barbarians* where, unredeemed, we are nevertheless invited (in Doug Jones' words) "to rejoice, to celebrate life in its mortal variety"; the climactic Montreal cocktail party in Hood's *White Figure, White Ground*; David Staunton's Christmas at Sorgenfrei; "the famous *'fête sauvage'* around Corriveau's coffin," where, "as the villagers pray, then slip off to eat, drink, blaspheme, eye the women and tell salacious stories, they are affirming life"; Pratt's *The Witches' Brew*, "a comic litany of the delights of rum-inspired eating, drinking and fighting"; Hoda's weddings and funerals; Hazard Lepage's wake; the dance at which Carlyle finally lets loose in *The Vanishing Point* – it is amazing how many Canadian fictions evoke, or revolve around, or climax with some form of public occasion, festivity, or celebration.[6] The meaning of these diverse types of gathering is perhaps made most explicit in Jack Hodgins' treatment of the wedding reception that ends *The Invention of the World*. "Containing" every conceivable human activity and artifact, interpreted one way this astoundingly Rabelaisian event, like the iconic enclosure of Canadian painting, could simply signify life-in-a-box. Interpreted another, it asserts unequivocally that life *is* a party.

---

6. The quotations in this section are taken from Douglas Jones, *Butterfly on Rock: A Study of Themes and Images in Canadian Literature* (Toronto: University of Toronto Press, 1970), p. 183; David Bond, "Carrier's Fiction," *Canadian Literature*, 80 (1979), 129; Sandra Djwa, *E.J. Pratt: The Evolutionary Vision* (Toronto: Copp Clark/McGill-Queen's, 1974), p. 148.

Notes on Selected
Australian Novels

James Tucker, *Ralph Rashleigh* (1845)

Interesting primarily for its documentation of the inhuman prison system and the barbarism of everyone involved, on both sides of the fence. It is significant that although his union with the aborigines enables the protagonist to survive the wilderness, the bond does not outlast his symbolic reincorporation into white society. The separation of the two worlds is evidently absolute.

Henry Kingsley, *The Recollections of Geoffrey Hamlyn* (1859)

A not-quite-standard romance. Mary is not "fine" enough to be a conventional heroine. Indeed, considering the Buckleys' invisibility, there is a gap where the "real" hero and heroine should be. The book offers multiple examples of the fragmented family theme, complete with shadow brother and brutal, destructive father. Note that part of the "happy" ending is a mass return to England.

Marcus Clarke, *For the Term of His Natural Life* (1874)

Another prison novel, but here the actors dominate the stage. The message seems to be that only the weak are capable of love, and even then the only possible consummation is oblivion. The "lovers" come together for the first time at the moment of drowning. There is a strong element of sexual disgust throughout. To be "masculine" is to be an animal. Note, though, that the wife's goodness exacerbates, perhaps triggers, her husband's brutality.

Rolf Boldrewood, *Robbery under Arms* (1888)

An early version of what was to become Australia's favourite polarity: the horse (masculine, dynamic, anti-social) versus the house/hollow (the archetypal feminine, beneficent but illusory). Other key themes include: the contest between the good and the bad woman, the emphasis on "luck." Note that although the noble bandit, with his peerless steed and mysterious past, serves throughout as a positive role model, he is ultimately a loser.

Joseph Furphy, *Such Is Life* (1903)

This book purports to offer a random selection from a pre-existing diary. Its portrait of Australian society sets up an implicit conflict between the stationary and the itinerant, with emotional laurels going to the latter. Much is made of class feeling, but the ideal of brotherhood is consistently undercut by the opportunism of the vagrants and the covert nod to station hierarchy.

Louis Stone, *Jonah* (1911)

The "natural" woman is fatally demoralized by her selfish, aggressive husband; the cultivated one turns out to be as cold, as predatory, and, ultimately, as destructive as the man. The public world in this book is very much a Darwinian jungle, where only the "bad" prosper. Note that "art" is on the negative side of the ledger. Drink is deadly but inevitable.

Miles Franklin (as Brent of Bin Bin), *Up the Country* (1928)

This book offers the standard plethora of romantic mismatches, but virtually no happy unravellings. Franklin's failure to provide suitable marriages for her characters violates the conventions of the comic genre to which the book clearly belongs. Particularly anomalous (by Anglo-American standards) is the widowed Rachel's rejection of the long-loving Bert on the practical but unromantic grounds of not wanting any more children.

M. Barnard Eldershaw, *A House Is Built* (1929)

A classic rendition of the "unattainable house" theme. Multiple cases underline the difficulty of intrafamilial communication, either horizontally or vertically. Fanny is the exemplary Australian heroine: restless, self-centred, sexually confused. Other key features: paternal obtuseness, maternal remoteness, sibling rivalry, filial betrayal – all inadvertent. Note the entrenched sexism.

K.S. Prichard, *Coonardoo (The Well in the Shadow)* (1929)

Here is the prototypical aborigine-as-anima. Hugh's rejection/destruction of the native child-woman he secretly loves clearly connotes a rejection of his own feminine nature. Note the "masculinity" of both mother and daughter; note also that the antipathetic wife is associated with the city. "Civilization" is at best an alien, and at worst a corrupting element.

H.H. Richardson, *The Fortunes of Richard Mahoney* (1930)

Another version of the "decline and fall" theme. The protagonist, haunted by dreams of "home," is unable either to assimilate or return. Torn between a restlessness rooted in self-alienation and an obsession with grand houses, he becomes increasingly isolated and eventually lapses into animal brutality. Ironically, madness brings peace by releasing him from his masculine ambition.

Brian Penton, *Landtakers: The Story of an Epoch* (1934)

A classic case of the deteriorating protagonist. The exigencies of the alien land strip away every last vestige of civilization. Cabell hates the "real" woman because she is too coarse, clinging stubbornly to images of the genteel woman left at home. The perceived contrast embitters and isolates him. In the end an uneasy equilibrium is achieved as Emma assumes the aggressive role.

Christina Stead, *Seven Poor Men of Sydney* (1934)

Michael, with his existential angst, and Catherine, with her restlessness and confused sense of sexual identity, offer particularly intense versions of key Australian psychotypes. More critical, their incestuous bonding offers a salient demonstration of the dictum that love is only possible between tabooed subjects. Note that what Michael is really in love with is death (by drowning!).

Xavier Herbert, *Capricornia* (1938)

The main theme concerns the ruthless treatment of natives, but the picture we get of the whole social scene is an extremely negative one. Almost everyone is cruel, bigoted, greedy, dishonest. The only "good" man is killed, his family dispossessed. Note that the climactic death of the anima/aborigine is temporally, perhaps causally, connected with the beginning of the "boom."

Norman Lindsay, *Age of Consent* (1938)

This book explores the relationship of the asocial artist figure with the antisocial anima figure, and of the latter with nature/naturalness. Note that Cora's "innocence" is not entirely benign, but has a distinctly predatory aspect that leads easily to destructiveness. Other key themes: the "social" man as petty criminal; the mysteriousness of the process of creation.

Eleanor Dark, *The Timeless Land* (1941)

The "hero" here is redeemed by the anima figure, but she is also ultimately the instrument of his death. Key themes include: (1) the alienness and impenetrability of the land, and (2) the way the unfamiliarity of the colonial experience works to break down conventional ideas and values. On an explicit level the book's primary message concerns the corruption of the noble savage.

Kylie Tennant, *The Battlers* (1941)

This book typifies almost every major theme examined in this study. Happy ending and token nod to mateship aside, the image we carry away is of a horde of restless and dispossessed individuals wandering aimlessly across an inimical landscape, deteriorating as they go. Particularly interesting is the apostle's philosophizing, insofar as it articulates the masculine propensity to depersonalize "love."

Leonard Mann, *The Go-Getter* (1942)
Primarily important for its portrait of a representative protagonist. Key features: (1) his early restlessness, and its causal connection with worldly failure; (2) his sense of being an outsider; (3) his concern with clothes, or "front"; (4) his moral ambivalence. Note his dream about the inaccessible anima. Note too that the "bad" wife is typified partly by her readiness to desert her children.

Eve Langley, *The Pea Pickers* (1946)
Sisters "on the road" in drag. A classic exploration of the problems of a female imbued with a "masculine" temperament. Note the implied causal connection between Steve's sexual ambivalence (her agonized vascillation between a desire for love and an obsession with "purity") and her difficulties in achieving normal heterosexual bonding. Note the mother's own restlessness; also the disabling idealization of the absent father.

Alan Marshall, *How Beautiful Are Thy Feet* (1949)
Key themes: war between the sexes; the destructiveness of the public world. The protagonist here is an interesting variant of the general psychotype insofar as his physical handicap is offset by his (emotionally disadvantageous) masculine aggressiveness. Compare the penchant for masculine women across the corpus. Clearly the masculine ideal is universal, even for types coded elsewhere as "feminine," and even when it is clearly dysfunctional.

Dymphna Cusack & Florence James, *Come in Spinner* (1951)
Despite the conventional happy ending, the overwhelming impression left by this book is of love sold out for material advantage, squandered on unworthy or inaccessible objects, or doomed by a destructive public world. The women in the forefront of the story are mostly victims; their elite customers are soulless and vulgar. Note the reluctance of the returned soldier to talk about the war.

E.V. Timms, *The Valleys Beyond* (1951)
This story develops polar types of fathers and daughters. In the first category (somewhat anomalously for the oeuvre) the "good" parent wins the day; in

the second the "natural" (child-) woman gains moral ascendency over three "unnatural" (predatory) women from different social classes. Note the affinity of the latter with sex and violence. Royd is the "natural" man as monster (clear evidence of what the land does to its habitants).

Jon Cleary, *The Sundowners* (1952)
Here is the horse versus house theme at its most explicit. For a while it seems as though the horse, as an income-earner, can be harnessed to the service of the house, but masculine weakness (drink and gambling) gets in the way. All is not bleak: Venneker, a dynamic role model, at first epitomizes restlessness and emotional incapacity, but settles down in the end. (Of course, he's an import!) Only the child relates to both house *and* horse.

T.A.G. Hungerford, *The Ridge and the River* (1952)
The key feature of this book is the improbably happy ending: war is positive here insofar as it gives men a structured context to legislate interpersonal relations. Also significant is the inverted theme of the man who must learn masculine detachment (i.e., transform to "other") in order to become a leader. The ridge/river symbolism seems obvious, but note that the feminine is associated with both the deadly jungle (inside) and the beneficent wife/anima (outside).

Ruth Park, *A Power of Roses* (1953)
Virtually all vertical relationships in this novel are destructive. The child is the only one capable of real love/motherliness. Note the inadvertent killing of the anima figure by the uninitiated male. Note too the aggressive egotism of the cripple (passiveness can never be exemplary in this oeuvre). The kind pastor is offset by the callous charlatan. The mother figure, typically, is associated with the latter.

Judah Waten, *The Unbending* (1954)
Not only does this book give us an exemplary couple, alienated by mutual misunderstanding and especially by her "unfeminine" strength, but in its portrait of the child Moses we see the making of an Australian male: violent, repelled by the feminine, isolated from society, obsessed with dreams of fortune over the next hill. With respect to ideology, it is notable that both the capitalist and the radical serve as role models for him.

Donald McLean, *No Man Is an Island* (1955)
Tensions are set up by parallels between "real" brotherhood (negative) and social solidarity (positive), and between the conflict of the bad brother with the active role model (Ted/Doug) and the more archetypal conflict between

the agitator and the madman, all being mediated through the consciousness of the artist figure. Note that responses to the aboriginal anima figure are used as a moral touchstone.

D'Arcy Niland, *Shiralee* (1955)

If the effeminate man (artist, priest, etc.) makes the only satisfactory lover, the child makes the only satisfactory "wife." This book offers an archetypal example of the restless husband versus the faithless spouse theme. Note that the latter is dangerous not just because she is "bad" (unwomanly, unmotherly), but because she represents the city (civilization, domesticity).

Patrick White, *The Tree of Man* (1955)

Danger is associated here with flood and fire. The main theme concerns the incapacity of the characters to understand themselves or communicate with others. White's pseudo-artless narrative mimics the shapelessness of life. Both the woman's inexplicit yearnings and the man's struggle to comprehend are exemplary. Note the familial breakdown, especially as epitomized by intergenerational discord; also the mad/doomed artist figure.

Ethel Anderson, *At Paramatta* (1956)

Key themes: (1) the arbitrariness of fate, especially vis-à-vis relationship; (2) the flimsiness of attachment; (3) the propensity of families to fragment. Cumulatively these convey the clear message that love is an illusion. Note the extent to which invoked convention is violated by such anti-comedic elements as Donalblain's confrontation with evil and the gratuitously violent ending.

Frank Hardy, *Power without Glory* (1956)

A conventional (though notably artless) pseudo-biography detailing the rise and fall of the self-made man, and conveying the conventional message that success does not bring happiness. The protagonist, on the other hand, is so unmitigatedly evil that he exceeds the convention. This is the psychotype at its worst: amoral, emotionally crippled, radically anti-social, destructive even (or particularly) to those closest to him.

Henrietta Drake-Brockman, *The Wicked and the Fair* (1957)

The main theme here concerns the breakdown of civilized mores. Does the killing of the albatross imply that alienation from nature is to blame? Are we to conclude that the hostility of the new land represents a kind of retribution? It's unclear. What is clear is the strong element of misogyny/sexual disgust, the lust for power, the ambiguity of religion. The loving man is neutralized early on.

Christopher Koch, *The Boys in the Island* (1958)

Fantasies of escape (fascination with "otherness," symbolized as usual by natural/unnatural females) are linked explicitly with self-destructiveness. It is interesting, though, that dis-illusionment does not trigger a healthy reorientation as convention would demand. It is also anomalous that the wishscape is a city. Note the ambivalence of the mateship theme: real mates damage each other; ideal mates exist only in dreams.

Randolphe Stow, *To the Islands* (1958)

The rather strange story of a man belatedly discovering his humanity (shared guilt) and then totally detaching himself from it. Is Heriot conquered by the land or his own proud isolation? In either case, it is his native charges who prove both his salvation and his nemesis. The aborigine survives, the book suggests, because he lives according to nature (laughing, killing: both are presented as in some sense exemplary), rather than setting himself apart from it.

H.D. Williamson, *The Sunlit Plain* (1958)

The Leo-Glory coupling represents the type marriage at its best (compare *The Sundowners*). Leo is totally irresponsible, but not vicious; Glory is the "natural" woman who is content to love him without reforming/emasculating him. Butch (the "horseman") and Regan (the policeman) are textually presented as negative and positive active role models. But note that the former is socially approved, the latter ostracized.

David Forrest, *The Last Blue Sea* (1959)

War is again presented as positive here insofar as it legitimizes man's natural isolation, eliminates any necessity for grappling with social mysteries, reduces action and morality to simple, obvious, immediate necessities, and takes away both his power and his responsibility for decision making, thus also legitimizing his impotence. Note the ambivalence of the title, invoking the feminine which is both inside and outside.

Vance Palmer, *The Passage* (1959)

Here is the conventional situation of the protagonist caught between the bad wife and the good but unattainable anima figure. Sex is opposed to art, but both women are associated with nature (one physically, the other spiritually). Note the two cases of mother-damaged sons; the discord between brothers; the ocean symbolism; the association of the anima with "away," and of the city with corruption.

Kenneth Cook, *Wake in Fright* (1961)

In this book the ambivalence of the female symbolism becomes a major thematic element. The country "inside" is hard, cruel, crude (but neigh-bourly); "outside" is the ocean and the anima, beautiful but unattainable. This duplicity perhaps accounts for the ambiguity of the denouement. What does Jack truly learn? Independence or community? Is the rifle that almost kills him a symbol of his own masculinity? Note that neither road nor rail-way is able to effect "connection" reliably.

Hal Porter, *The Tilted Cross* (1961)

Central to this story is the betrayal of a fool-saint figure by a predatory woman. Note that the former is the only character in the book capable of self-lessness. The concurrence of his death with Christmas Day has rather bleak implications for the environing society. The artist is betrayed by a woman too, but finds at least partial redemption through union with the "feminine" (innocent) man.

David Martin, *The Young Wife* (1962)

An intriguing demonstration of the dangerousness of the anima figure: Anna wreaks havoc simply because she is "out of it" (i.e., alien). The "normal" woman in the book suffers from "masculine" restlessness. Note the brutality that lurks below the surface of male camaraderie. After failing in his attempt at violence the artist bonds with the anima, but in doing so dies.

Sumner Locke Elliott, *Careful, He Might Hear You* (1963)

Here is the classic fragmented family. The house in this book represents the closedness of the unwomanly woman, her inability to bond with either man or child. Note, though, the implication of the ending that personal integrity is more important than relation. Note too that when love is possible, fate inter-venes. Note finally the climactic vignette where the storm (nature) is associ-ated with death.

G.M. Glaskin, *Flight to Landfall* (1963)

The gorge and the garden in the wilderness represent the negative and posi-tive aspects of nature/the feminine. All who confront "her" are tested. Those who are too good (Henkie) or too tainted with worldliness (Salmonson) must die, though they are changed for the better in the process. Even Fiona must be stripped to nothing before she can be reborn, and the aborigine is the "mid-wife."

D.E. Charlwood, *All the Green Year* (1965)

The main theme here relates to paternal/filial alienation (note that the obtuse and brutal fathers are simply more and less extreme versions of the same type), but more interesting is the covert implication that it is the "feminine" aspect of the son's nature (art, swimming) that comprises his greatest danger. Another theme concerns the "costs" of friendship.

George Johnston, *My Brother Jack* (1965)

This book details the role reversal of brothers, and the concurrent downfall of the active role model. There is also an ambivalent exploration of the artist's role. Davy, who starts out effeminate/victimized, manages to turn himself into the epitome of masculine success, but in the process is hardened and corrupted. Note the brutal father, the remote mother, the natural affinity of the "loser" with the anima figure.

Thomas Keneally, *The Fear* (1965)

A peculiarly formless book. The only real theme is the young protagonist's fearful identification with his persecutor. Fathers, it seems, are at best absent, at worst actively detrimental. Note the ideological ambivalence: the author's sympathy is with the working man, but not the professional agitator. Note too the explicit association of phallic imagery (a snake) with the girl-child.

George Turner, *A Waste of Shame* (1965)

Joe is the classic Australian protagonist: weak, bewildered, inadvertently brutal. His wife is the "natural" woman who loves her mate to the point of self-damage. Contrasted with them yet entirely complementary in their mutual destructiveness are the unwomanly Vera and her victim/nemesis, Arthur: a classic version of the doomed, sensitive, symbolically effeminate artist. The natural antagonism between the sexes is vividly imaged when Joe takes an axe to his wife's house.

Peter Cowan, *Seed* (1966)

Multiple cases underline the lack of communication between mates and between parents and children. Note that for both Joan/Gerald and Alan/Leonore the marital breakdown is rooted in the male's inability to live up to feminine expectations. Both men are inherently weak/incapable, while their wives – good-strong and bad-strong respectively – are lacking in "womanly" understanding.

Elizabeth Harrower, *The Watch Tower* (1966)

Here is the house as enticing trap. In a novel plotted according to Anglo-American conventions Clare would grow up to learn/find love, but in this one she learns how to be free of it, to escape, to be herself alone. Felix represents the Australian psychotype at its worst: brutal, misogynistic, emotionally crippled, devoid of inner substance. Note the absent father and the classically remote (selfish) mother.

Thea Astley, *A Descant for Gossips* (1968)

This book offer us three outsiders persecuted by society who are equally hurtful (at least by omission) to each other. Note the recurrent hints of sexual disgust, the hero's too-obvious fastidiousness that camouflages a fear of intimacy. The girl-child's suicide from fear of pregnancy only underlines the covert connections made throughout the book between love and death.

Nuri Mass, *Donna Roon* (1970)

The reincarnation motif provides an interesting demonstration of the fact that the emotional problems of the unwomanly woman are identical with those of the too manly man. Typically, the artist figure is the only character here capable of spontaneous love. Also typically, it is the woman/anima figure who imperils this love. The happy ending is anomalous, and must be paid for in pain.

David Ireland, *The Flesheaters* (1972)

The active role model in this book is admired but remote; the anima beloved but inaccessible. Only after confrontation with (crucifixion by) the father is the protagonist able to emulate the former (i.e., become cruel) and possess the latter. He does not hang on to his hard-won "masculinity," though. Brought reluctantly to accept instead the fated role of artist/castrado, he ends up mad and masochistic.

Chester Eagle, *Who Could Love the Nightingale?* (1973)

The lack of a stable viewpoint presumably echoes the search for identity in this novel, but it also intimates that the author himself has trouble "seeing" his characters, especially the woman, who is inconsistent, evasive, and in the end perhaps even hypocritical. It is possible that the confusion signals covert anxiety about the sex role reversal which is displayed by not articulated.

Donald Stuart, *Walk, Trot, Canter and Die* (1975)

Though naively written, this is a rare positive version of the prototypical Australian "life." Given the (again rare) good start of a viable paternal role model, the protagonist perfects himself by wandering, coming to terms with the land. In the end, having learned the hard way to avoid white women, he finds happiness with the aborigine who represents "true" femininity. Note that the horse is both Cole's life and his death.

Neilma Sydney, *The Return* (1976)

The house in the wilderness turns out to be a trap. Left to himself, the protagonist (a literal outsider) loses all will and direction. Quite contra his self-sufficient self-identification, it is the woman who turns out to be the dynamic as well as the emotionally stabilizing figure in the book. Note, though, that despite best intentions the pair are mutually destructive. Like nature here, "relation" is not just difficult but dangerous.

Colleen McCullough, *The Thorn Birds* (1977)

Though both sexes love the "land," the men in this novel are identified with horses, the women with the house at the heart of the homestead. A key theme concerns the male's inability to love, unless (like the priest) he has a "feminine" aspect. Note that in the first generation one son is imprisoned, one killed by nature, and one unmanned by war; in the second the only male is drowned. Here we have the decline and fall theme applied to an entire family.

Jessica Anderson, *Tirra Lirra by the River* (1978)

Having gone as a young woman to England on a quest for self, the protagonist of this novel returns in old age to the empty family home. Back on native soil she discovers that she has lost her "creativity" (can't sew any more; can't reach the river), but as she loses this feminine aspect she does manage to recapture her memory of the charismatic father. Note the cruel husband, the linking of sex and pain, the bond with homosexuals.

Roger McDonald, *1915: A Novel* (1979)

A large baggy novel too complex to summarize. Key features include: (1) the destructiveness of the unwomanly woman; (2) the association of "love" with death; (3) the downfall of the active role model (where initially his violence was constructively channelled, after he loses his fiance he turns into a monster). The protagonist himself just fades out of the scene. The idea that war is a proving ground is exposed as totally illusory.

Peter Carey, *Bliss* (1981)

This primitivistic tract puts forth the premise that modernity is a disease. The protagonist's development comprises four phases: (1) he begins oblivious and successful; (2) he "dies," recognizes reality as hell, and embraces goodness; (3) under the influence of his unwomanly wife, he sells out to evil; (4) sickened, he flees to the rainforest (home of anarchy and the anima) where he learns to live ethically as a storyteller, tree planter, and father.

Elizabeth Jolley, *Miss Peabody's Inheritance* (1983)

Created relationships replace real ones in this book (both protagonists are radical isolates), but creativity itself is shown to be dangerous. An interesting feature (inasmuch as Jolley is an English immigrant rather than a native Australian) is the anomalous association of art with (destructive) masculinity through the ambivalent intertwining of writing, riding, and sex motifs.

David Malouf, *Harland's Half Acre* (1984)

The main theme of this novel concerns the development of the artist figure, his increasing alienation from society and alignment with nature. Much is made of the transformative powers of art which neither the creating individual nor his auditors understand. A secondary theme uses multiple cases of sibling and intergenerational friction to underline the destructiveness of familial relations. Note that the artist is killed by the wilderness in the end.

Helen Wilson, *The Mulga Trees* (1985)

An aristocratic young man with naive dreams of the big strike drags his wife and children down to poverty and finally abandons them altogether, joining the army in a last desperate bid to play out his family's phallocentric myth of male glory. Even here he fails, thanks to his ultra-masculine arrogance and independence. The theme is counterpointed by the progress from better to worse houses.

BIBLIOGRAPHY

Background

Clifford, James. 1988. *The Predicament of Culture: Twentieth-Century Ethnography, Literature, and Art.* Cambridge: Harvard U. Press.

——— and Marcus, George E., eds. 1986. *Writing Culture:The Poetics and the Politics of Ethnography.* Berkeley: U. California Press.

Marcus, George E., and Fischer, Michael M.J. 1986. *Anthropology as Cultural Critique: An Experimental Moment in the Human Sciences.* Chicago: U. Chicago Press.

Gaile McGregor. 1985. *The Wacousta Syndrome: Explorations in the Canadian Langscape.* Toronto: U. Toronto Press.

———. 1986. "A View from the Fort: Erving Goffman as Canadian," *Canadian Review of Sociology and Anthropology* 23, 4: 531-43.

———. 1987a. "The 'Primal Scene' as a Culture-Specific Phenomenon: A Speculative Rereading of Freudian – or Freud's Psychology," *The Journal of Mind and Behavior* 8, 1: 133-152.

———. 1987b. "The Technomyth in Transition: Reading American Popular Culture," *Journal of American Studies* 21, 3: 387-409.

———. 1987c. Review of Trudie McNaughton, ed., *Countless Signs: The New Zealand Landscape in Literature, Landfall* 183: 363-66.

———. 1988. *The Noble Savage in the New World Garden: Notes toward a Syntactics of Place.* Bowling Green and Toronto: BGU Popular Press and U. Toronto Press.

———. 1993a. "Television in an Age of Transition: Closet Monsters and Other Double Codings," *Canadian Review of American Studies* 23, 2: 115-47.

———. 1993b. "Domestic Blitz: A Revisionist History of the Fifties," *American Studies* 34, 1: 5-34.

Australian Source Materials

Fictive

Includes poetry and drama. Note that chronological ordering is according to the original dates of publication, which are given in parentheses where appropriate.

Allyne, Kerry. 1986. *Stranger in Town*. Sydney: Mills & Boon.

Anderson, Ethel. 1956. *At Paramatta*. Melbourne: Cheshire.

Anderson, Jessica. (1978) 1984. *Tirra Lirra by the River*. Harmondsworth, UK: Penguin.

Asher, Helen. 1986. *Tilly's Fortunes*. Ringwood, Vic.: Penguin Australia.

Astley, Thea. 1968. *A Descant for Gossip*. Brisbane: Jacaranda.

Barbalet, Margaret. 1986. *Blood in the Rain*. Ringwood, Vic.: Penguin Australia.

Barnes, Rory, and Broderick, Damien. 1983. *Valencies*. St. Lucia: University of Queensland Press.

Baxter, John. 1978. *The Hermes Fall*. London: Panther.

Bedford, Jean. 1982. *Sister Kate*. Ringwood, Vic.: Penguin Australia.

——, and Creswell, Rosemary. 1986. *Colouring In: A Book of Ideologically Unsound Love Stories*. Melbourne: McPhee Gribble/Penguin Australia.

Boldrewood, Rolf. (1888) 1980. *Robbery Under Arms*. Sydney: Angus & Robertson.

Boyd, Martin. (1946) 1985. *Lucinda Brayford*. Ringwood, Vic.: Penguin Australia.

Brennan, Peter. 1982. *Razorback*. London: Fontana.

Broderick, Damien. 1981. *The Dreaming Dragons: A Time Opera*. Ringwood, Vic.: Penguin Australia.

Carey, Peter. 1981. *Bliss*. NY: Harper & Row.

——. 1985. *Illywacker*. St. Lucia: University of Queensland Press.

Chandler, A. Bertram. 1983. *Kelly Country*. Ringwood, Vic.: Penguin Australia.

Charlwood, D.E. 1965. *All the Green Year*. Sydney: Angus & Robertson.

Clarke, Marcus. 1953. *For the Term of His Natural Life*, intro. George Ivan Smith. London: Collins.

Cleary, Jon. 1952. *The Sundowners*. NY: Scribners.

——. 1954. *The Climate of Courage*. London: Collins.

——. 1985. *The Phoenix Tree*. Sydney: Fontana/Collins.

Cook, Kenneth. (1961) 1981. *Wake in Fright*. Sydney: Angus & Robertson.

————. 1980. *Chain of Darkness.* Sydney: Arkon.

Corris, Peter. 1983. *The Empty Beach.* Sydney: Unwin.

————. 1985. *The Big Drop, and Other Cliff Hardy Stories.* Sydney: Unwin.

Cusack, Dymphna, and James, Florence. (1951) 1981. *Come In Spinner.* London: Sirius.

d'Alpuget, Blanche. 1981. *Turtle Beach.* Ringwood, Vic.: Penguin Australia.

Dark, Eleanor. 1941. *The Timeless Land.* London: Macmillan.

Dowse, Sara. 1984. *Silver City.* Ringwood, Vic.: Penguin Australia.

Drake-Brockman, Henrietta. 1957. *The Wicked and the Fair.* Sydney: Angus & Robertson.

Eagle, Chester. 1973. *Who Could Love the Nightingale?* Melbourne: Wren.

Eldershaw, M. Barnard. 1929. *A House is Built.* London: Harrap.

————. (1947) 1983. *Tomorrow and Tomorrow and Tomorrow.* London: Virago.

Elliott, Sumner Locke. 1963. *Careful, He Might Hear You.* NY: Harper & Row.

Falkiner, Suzanne. 1986. *Rain in the Distance.* Ringwood, Vic.: Penguin Australia.

Farmer, Beverly. 1983. *Milk: Stories.* Ringwood, Vic.: McPhee Gribble/Penguin.

Forrest, David. (1959) 1961. *The Last Blue Sea.* London: Panther.

Frances, Helen. 1986. *The Devil's Stone.* Ringwood, Vic.: Omnibus/Penguin.

Franklin, Miles. (1901) 1974. *My Brilliant Career.* Sydney: Angus & Robertson.

———— (as Brent of Bin Bin). (1928) 1951. *Up the Country: A Tale of the Early Australian Squattocracy.* Sydney: Angus & Robertson.

Furphy, Joseph. (1903) 1962. *Such Is Life.* Sydney: Angus & Robertson.

Garner, Helen. 1978. *Monkey Grip.* Ringwood, Vic.: Penguin Australia.

————. 1985. *The Children's Bach.* Melbourne: McPhee Gribble/Penguin Australia.

Glaskin, G.M. 1963. *Flight to Landfall.* London: Barre & Rockliff.

Glassop, Lawson. (1944) 1962. *We Were the Rats.* Sydney: Horwitz.

Grant, Maxwell. 1982. *Barrier Reef.* London: Star.

Grenville, Kate. 1984. *Bearded Ladies.* St. Lucia: University of Queensland Press.

Hanrahan, Barbara. 1984. *Kewpie Doll.* London: Chatto & Windus.

Harding, Lee. 1982. *Displaced Person.* Ringwood, Vic.: Puffin/Penguin Australia.

Hardy, Frank. 1956. *Power without Glory.* Leipzig: Panther.

Harrower, Elizabeth. 1966. *The Watch Tower*. London: Macmillan.

Hazzard, Shirley. 1981. *The Transit of Venus*. Ringwood, Vic.: Penguin Australia.

Herbert, Xavier. 1938. *Capricornia*. Sydney: Angus & Robertson.

Hergenhan, Laurie. 1986. *The Australian Short Story: An Anthology from the 1890s to the 1980s*. St Lucia: U. Queensland Press.

Heseltine, Harry, ed. 1976. *The Penguin Book of Australian Short Stories*. Ringwood, Vic.: Penguin Australia.

Hooker, John. 1985. *The Bush Soldiers*. Sydney: Fontana/Collins.

Hungerford, T.A.G. (1952) 1979. *The Ridge and the River*. Sydney: Angus & Robertson.

Ireland, David. (1972) 1980. *The Flesheaters*. Ringwood, Vic.: Penguin Australia.

———. 1981. *City of Women*. Ringwood, Vic.: Penguin Australia.

Johnston, George. 1965. *My Brother Jack*. NY: Wm. Morrow.

Jolley, Elizabeth. (1983) 1984. *Miss Peabody's Inheritance*. Harmondsworth, UK: Penguin.

Jost, John. 1984. *This is Harry Flynn*. Sydney: Arkon.

Keneally, Thomas. 1965. *The Fear*. Melbourne: Cassell.

Kennett, Rick. 1982. *A Warrior's Star*. S. Caulfield, Vic.: Alternative Productions.

Kingsley, Henry. 1894. *The Recollections of Geoffrey Hamlyn*, 2 vol. NY: Scribners.

Koch, Christopher. (1958) 1974. *The Boys in the Island*, revised ed. Sydney: Angus & Robertson.

———. 1979. *The Year of Living Dangerously*. Melbourne: Nelson.

Lambert, Eric. 1951. *The Twenty Thousand Thieves*. Melbourne: Newmont.

Langley, Eve. 1946. *The Pea-Pickers*.

Lawson, Henry. 1983. *Best Stories*, ed. Cecil Mann. Sydney: Arkon.

Leakey, Carolyn. 1886. *The Broad Arrow: The Story of a Lifer*. Hobart: Walch & Sons.

Le Grand, Leon. 1986. *The Two-Ten Conspiracy*. Sydney: Fontana/Collins.

Lindsay, Norman. (1938) 1962. *Age of Consent*. Sydney: Ure Smith.

Macken, Linda. 1984. *And Brothers All*. Sydney: Fontana/Collins.

Malouf, David. 1984. *Harland's Half Acre*. NY: Knopf.

Mann, Leonard. 1942. *The Go-Getter*. Sydney: Angus & Robertson.

———. (1932) 1985. *Flesh in Armour*. Sydney: Unwin.

Marshall, Alan. (1949) 1972. *How Beautiful Are Thy Feet*. Melbourne: Goldstar.

Marshall, William Leonard. 1978. *The Fire Circle*. Melbourne: Marlin.

Martin, David. (1962) 1966. *The Young Wife*. Melbourne: Sun Books.

Mass, Nuri. 1970. *Donna Roon*. Sydney: Alpha Books.

Masters, Olga. 1982. *The Home Girls*. St. Lucia: University of Queensland Press.

Matthews, Christopher. 1985. *Aljazar*. Sydney: Unwin Paperbacks.

McCullough, Colleen. 1979. *The Thorn Birds*. NY: Avon.

———. 1986. *A Creed for the Third Millennium*. NY: Avon.

McDonald, Roger. (1979) 1980. *1915: a novel*. NY: Brazillier.

McLean, Donald. 1955. *No Man Is an Island*. Melbourne: Heinemann.

McQueen, James. 1982. *Hook's Mountain*. Melbourne: Macmillan.

Moffitt, Ian. 1983. *The Retreat of Radiance*. Sydney: Fontana/Collins.

Murnane, Gerald. 1984. *The Plains*. Ringwood, Vic.: Penguin Australia.

Napier, Susan. 1986. *The Counterfeit Secretary*. Sydney: Mills & Boon.

Niland, D'Arcy. 1955. *The Shiralee*. Sydney: Angus & Robertson.

Nixon, Marion. 1986. *The Winds of Jarah*. Sydney: Mills & Boon.

Palmer, Vance. (1959) 1965. *The Passage*. Melbourne: Cheshire.

Park, Ruth. 1953. *A Power of Roses*. Sydney: Angus & Robertson.

———. 1982. *Playing Beatie Bow*. Harmondsworth, UK: Puffin.

Parve, Valerie. 1986. *Return to Faraway*. Sydney: Mills & Boon.

Penton, Brian. (1934) 1963. *Landtakers: The Story of an Epoch*. Sydney: Angus & Robertson.

Popescu, Petru. 1977. *The Last Wave*. Sydney: Angus & Robertson.

Porter, Hal. 1961. *The Tilted Cross*. London: Faber & Faber.

Praed, Rosa. 1897. *Mrs. Tregaskiss: A Novel of Anglo-Australian Life*. London: Chatto & Windus.

Prichard, Katharine Susannah. (1929) 1964. *Coondardoo (The Well in the Shadow)*, intro. D. Stewart. Sydney: Sirius Books.

Richardson, Henry Handel. (1930) 1965. *The Fortunes of Richard Mahoney*. London: Heinemann.

Rudd, Steele. (1899, 1903) 1953. *On Our Selection, and On Our New Selection*. Sydney: Angus & Robertson

Savage, Georgia. 1983. *Slate and Me and Blanche McBride*. Melbourne: McPhee Gribble/Penguin Australia.

Smith, Vivian, and Scott, Margaret, eds. 1985. *Effects of Light: The Poetry of Tasmania*. Sandy Bay, Tas.: Twelvetrees.

Spence, Catherine Helen. (mag. serial 1881-82) 1977. *Gathered In*, intro. B.L. Waters and G.A. Wilkes. Sydney: Sydney U. Press.

Stead, Christina. (1934) 1965. *Seven Poor Men of Sydney*. Sydney: Angus & Robertson.

Stone, Louis. (1911) 1965. *Jonah*, intro. Ronald McCuaig. Sydney: Pacific Books.

Stow, Randolph. 1958. *To the Islands*. London: MacDonald.

———. 1968. *The Merry-Go-Round in the Sea*. Ringwood, Vic.: Penguin Australia.

Stuart, Donald. 1975. *Walk, Trot, Canter and Die*. Melbourne: Georgian House.

Sydney, Neilma. 1976. *The Return*. Melbourne: Thomas Nelson.

Tasma (Jessie Catherine Couvreur). (1889) 1969. *Uncle Piper of Piper's Hill*, ed. Cecil Hadgraft and Ray Beilby. Melbourne: Nelson.

Taylor, Keith. 1982. *Lances of Nengesdul*. St. Kilda, Vic.: Cory & Collins.

Tennant, Kylie. (1941) 1967. *The Battlers*. Sydney: Pacific Books.

Timms, E.V. 1951. *The Valleys Beyond*. London: Angus & Robertson.

Tomasetti, Glen. 1984. *Man of Letters: A Romance*. Melbourne: McPhee Gribble/Penguin Australia.

Tucker, James. (ms. dated 1845) 1952. *Ralph Rashleigh*, ed. Colin Roderick. Sydney: Angus& Robertson.

Turner, George. 1965. *A Waste of Shame*. Melbourne: Cassell.

———. 1984. *Yesterday's Men*. London: Sphere. Upfield, Arthur W. (1931) 1984. *The Sands of Windee*. Sydney: Arkon.

———. (1956) 1981. *Man of Two Tribes*. Sydney: Arkon.

Waten, Judah. 1954. *The Unbending*. Melbourne: Australasian Book Society.

Webb, Francis. "Leichhardt in the Theatre" and "Eyre All Alone" from *Collected Poems*, ed. Sir Herbert Reid.

Webb, Grahame. 1982. *The Numumwari*. Sydney: Fontana/Collins.

West, Morris. (1960) 1983. *The Naked Country*. London: Coronet.

White, Patrick. (1955) 1961. *The Tree of Man*. Harmondsworth, UK: Penguin.

———. (1957) 1981. *Voss*. Harmondsworth, UK: Penguin.

Williamson, H.D. 1958. *The Sunlit Plain*. Sydney: Angus & Robertson.

Wilson, Helen. 1985. *The Mulga Trees*. Melbourne: Macmillan.

Whitford, Wynne. 1985. *Thor's Hammer*. NY: Ace.

Wrightson, Patricia. 1977. *The Ice is Coming*, Vol. I of *The Book of Wirrun*. NY: Del Rey.

———. 1978. *The Dark Bright Water*, Vol. II of *The Book of Wirrun*. NY: Del Rey.

———. 1981. *Journey Behind the Wind*, Vol III of *The Book of Wirrun*. NY: Del Rey.

Factual

Due to the amount of material covered, only those texts/sources actually cited or discussed have been included in this listing.

Adam-Smith, Patsy. 1981. *The Anzacs*. Melbourne: Thomas Nelson.

Albinski, Henry S. 1985. "Australia and the United States." In Graubard, 421-38.

Alexander, George. 1985. "Australia A Prophecy," *Art & Text* 19: 34-37.

Alomes, Stephen. 1981a. "The Satellite Society," *Journal of Australian Studies* 9: 2-20.

———. 1981b. "Australian Popular Culture Revisited," *Overland* 85: 11-15.

———. 1986. "Popular Culture: From the Garden of Decency to Sensuous Surf." In Davidson, 238-46.

Andrews, Barry. 1982. "Ginger Meggs: His Story." In Dermody et al., 21-33.

Astbury, Leigh. 1985. *City Bushmen: The Heidelberg School and the Rural Mythology*. Melbourne: Oxford U. Press.

Atkinson, Hugh. 1982. *The Longest Wire*. London & Sydney: Sphere Books.

Austin, Diane J. 1984. *Australian Sociologies*. Sydney: Allen & Unwin.

Australian Literary Studies. 1985. Special Issue on War in Australian Literature, 12, 2.

Barlow, Allen R. 1985. "A Voice from the Mainstream." In Poole et al., 183-85.

Barrett, John. 1972. "Melbourne and the Bush: Russell Ward's Thesis and a La Trobe Survey," *Meanjin* 31, 4: 462-70.

Beilby, Peter, ed. 1981. *Australian TV: The First 25 Years*. Melbourne: Thomas Nelson.

Benterrek, Krim, Muecke, Stephen, and Roe, Paddy. 1984. *Reading the Country*. Fremantle: Fremantle Arts Centre Press.

Berry, Michael. 1984. "Urbanization and Social Change: Australia in the Twentieth Century." In Encel and Bryson, 12-64.

Bird, Delys. 1983. "Australian Women: A National Joke," *Australian Journal of Cultural Studies* 1, 1: 111-14.

Birrell, Tania. 1975. "Women and the Australian Media." In Mercer, 275-84.

Blainey, Geoffrey. 1966. *The Tyranny of Distance*. Melbourne: Sun Books.

———. 1985. "Australia: A Bird's-Eye View." In Graubard, 1-28.

Blonski, Annette. 1986. Review of *The Lancaster Miller Affair*, *Cinema Papers* (September), 51-2.

Bolton, Geoffrey. 1983. "Legends of Australian Identity," *Meridian* 2, 1: 47-51.

Bonnin, Margaret. 1982. "Ion Idriess: 'Rich Australiana.'" In Dermody et al., 234-49.

Bonyhady, Tim. 1985. *Images in Opposition: Australian Landscape Painting 1901-1890.* Melbourne: Oxford U. Press.

Boyd, Robin. 1963. *The Australian Ugliness,* foreword by John Betjeman. Ringwood, Vic.: Penguin Australia.

Brady, Veronica. 1981. *A Crucible of Prophets: Australians and the Question of God.* Maryborough, Vic.: Theological Explorations.

Braithwaite, John. 1980. "Women as Victims of Crime," *Australian Quarterly* 52, 3: 329-39.

Brett, Judith. 1982. Introduction to "Psychoanalysis in Australia," *Meanjin* 41, 3: 339-41.

Brophy, Vivienne. 1985. "An Australian Housewife: A Disillusioning Experience." In Mercer, 323-32.

Brown, Max. (1948) 1981. *Ned Kelly: Australian Son.* Sydney: Angus & Robertson.

Brugger, Bill, and Jaensch, Dean. 1985. *Australian Politics : Theory and practice.* Sydney: Allen & Unwin.

Bryson, John. 1986. *Evil Angels.* Ringwood, Vic.: Penguin Australia.

Bryson, Lois. 1985. "Husband and Wife Interaction in the Australian Family: A Critical Review of the Literature." In Mercer, 213-24. See also Encel and Bryson, 1984.

The Bulletin. 1986. May 27.

Burns, Ailsa. 1986. "Why do Women Continue to Marry?" In Grieve and Burns, 210-32.

Burns, D.R. 1975. *Directions of Australian Fiction 1920-1974.* North Ryde, NSW: Cassell Australia.

——. 1982. "Australian Fiction vs. Austrophobia," *Overland* 90: 44-51.

——. 1986. "The Active Passive Inversion: Sex Roles in Garner, Stead, and Harrower," *Meanjin* 3: 346-53.

Burstall, Tim. 1985. "Twelve Genres of Australian Film." In Moran and O'Regan, 215-22.

Carroll, John, ed. 1982. *Intruders in the Bush: The Australian Quest for Identity.* Melbourne: Oxford U. Press. "National Identity," 209-25.

Catalano, Gary. 1961. *The Years of Hope: Australian Art and Criticism, 1959-1968.* Melbourne: Oxford U. Press.

——. 1984. "Some Versions of Identity: Russell Drysdale, Jon Molvig, Joy Hester," *Meanjin* 43, 3: 429-40.

——. 1985. *An Intimate Australia: The landscape and recent Australian art.* Sydney: Hale & Iremonger.

Clancy, Jack. 1979. "Australian Films and Fantasies," *Meanjin* 38, 2: 193-205.

———. 1980. Review of *Breaker Morant, Cinema Papers* 7, 28: 283.

Clark, Janet, and Whitelaw, Bridget. 1985. *Golden Summers: Heidelberg and Beyond.* Melbourne: National Gallery of Victoria & International Culture Corp. of Australia.

Clark, Manning. 1985. "Heroes." In Graubard, 57-85.

Clune, Frank. (1948) 1970. *Wild Colonial Boys.* Sydney: Pacific Books.

———. 1985. *Frank Clune's Ned Kelly* (reprint of *Ned Kelly's Last Stand,* 1962; adapted from *The Kelly Hunters,* 1954). Sydney: Angus & Robertson.

Coe, Richard. 1981. "Portrait of the Poet as a Young Australian: Childhood, Literature, and Myth," *Southerly* 41, 2: 126-63.

Coleman, Peter, ed. 1962. *Australian Civilization: A Symposium.* Melbourne: Cheshire.

Colmer, John. 1984. "Australian Autobiography: Flawed and Fortunate Lives," *Meridian* 3, 2: 135-41.

Connell, R.W. 1977. *Ruling Class Ruling Culture: Studies of Conflict, Power, and Hegemony in Australian Life.* Cambridge: Cambridge U. Press.

———, and Goot, Murray. 1979. "The End of Class, Re- run," *Meanjin,* 38, 1: 3-25.

Conway, Jill. 1985. "Gender in Australia." In Graubard, 343-68.

Conway, Ronald. 1985. *The Great Australian Stupor: An Interpretation of the Australian Way of Life,* 2nd edition. Melbourne: Sun Books.

Crook, Gillian, ed. 1983. *Man in the Centre: Proceedings of a Symposium held at CSIRO, Alice Springs, April 1979.* Perth: CSIRO.

Cunneen, Chris. 1985. "Working Class Boys and Crime: Theorizing the Class/Gender Mix." In Patton and Poole, 80-86.

d'Alpuget, Blanche. 1984. *Robert J. Hawke: A Biography.* Ringwood/E. Melbourne, Vic.: Schwartz & Penguin Australia.

Daniel, Helen. 1978. "The Picaresque Mode in Contemporary Australian Fiction," *Southerly* 38, 3: 282-93.

Daniels, Kay. 1983. "Cults of Nature, Cults of History," *Island Magazine* 16 (September): 3-8.

Davidson, Jim, ed. 1986. *The Sydney-Melbourne Book.* Sydney: Allen & Unwin.

Davie, Michael. 1985. "The Fraying of the Rope." In Graubard, 369-94.

Davies, Brian. 1981. *Those Fabulous TV Years.* North Ryde, NSW: Cassell Australia.

Davies, John. 1986. "The Television Audience Revisited," *Australian Journal of Screen Theory* 17/18: 84-105.

Davison, Graeme. 1982. "Sydney and the Bush: An Urban Context for the Australian Legend." In Carroll, 109-30.

Day, Christopher. 1981. "Drama." In Beilby, 135-59.

Deacon, Desley. See Higley et al., 1979.

de Lacey, Philip. See M. Poole et al., 1985

de Serville, Paul. 1986. "Nineteenth-Century Melbourne: Ambition, Progress, Phantasmagoria." In Davidson, 64-78.

Dermody, Susan. 1982. "Two Remakes: Ideologies of Film Production 1919-1932." In Dermody et al., pp. 33-59.

Dermody, Susan, Docker, John, and Modjeska, Drusilla, eds. 1982. *Nellie Melba, Ginger Meggs, and Friends.* Malmsburg, Vic.: Kibble Books.

———. 1980. "Action and Adventure." In Murray, 79-96.

Dixon, Christine, and Smith, Terry. 1984. *Aspects of Australian Figurative Painting 1942-1962.* Sydney: Biennale of Sydney & Power Inst. of Fine Arts.

Dixon, Robert. 1986. *The Course of Empire: Neo-Classical Culture in New South Wales.* Melbourne:Oxford U. Press.

Dixson, Miriam. 1984. *The Real Matilda: Woman and Identity in Australia 1788 to the present,* revised ed. Ringwood, Vic.: Penguin Australia.

Docker, John. 1974. *Australian Cultural Elites: Intellectual traditions in Sydney and Melbourne.* Sydney: Angus & Robertson.

———. 1984. *In a Critical Condition: Reading Australian Literature.* Ringwood, Vic.: Penguin Australia. See also Dermody et al., 1982.

Dunkley, Graham. 1983. "The Economy – Performance and Prospects." In McLaren, 85-100.

Dunstan, Keith. 1973. *Knockers.* Melbourne: Cassell Australia.

Dutton, Geoffrey. 1985. *Snow on the Saltbush: The Australian Literary Experience.* Ringwood, Vic.: Penguin Australia.

Dwyer, Peter, Wilson, Bruce, and Woock, Roger. 1984. *Confronting School and Work: Youth and Class Cultures in Australia.* Sydney: Allen & Unwin.

Eagle, Mary. 1982. "Painting an Australian Identity." In Carroll, 180-91.

Elkin, P.K. 1983. "David Ireland: A Male Metropolis." In Walker, 163-77.

Ely, Richard. 1981. "Psychohistory and the Man who could not ride horses," *Journal of Australian Studies* 8: 13-34.

Emy, Hugh V. 1980a. "The Roots of Australian Politics: A Critique of a Culture." In Parkin et al., 219-35.

———. 1980b. "The Diffusion of Power." In Parkin et al., 326-39.

Encel, S., and Bryson, L., eds. 1984. *Australian Society*, 4th edition. Melbourne: Longman Cheshire.

———. 1980a. "Class, Status, and Power in Australia." In Parkin et al., 306-13.

———. 1980b. "The Bureaucratic Ascendency." In Parkin et al., 314-25.

Facey, A.B. 1985. *A Fortunate Life*. Ringwood, Vic.: Penguin Australia.

Farrar, Adam. 1985. "War: Machining Male Desire." In Patton and Poole, 59-70.

Ferrier, Carole, ed. 1986. *Gender, Politics, and Fiction: Twentieth-Century Australian Women's Novels*. St. Lucia: U. Queensland Press.

Firth, Stewart, and Hoorn, Jeanette. 1983. "From Empire Day to Cracker Night." In Spearritt and Walker, 17-38.

Fiske, John. 1983. "Surfalism and Sandiotics: The Beach in Oz Culture," *Australian Journal of Cultural Studies* 1, 2: 120-49.

———, Hedge, Bob, and Turner, Graeme. 1987. *Myths of Oz: Reading Australian Popular Culture*. Sydney: Allen & Unwin.

Fodor's Australia New Zealand and the South Pacific. NY & London: Fodor's Travel Guides, 1986.

Franklin, Margaret Ann. 1979. "Racism Australian Style," *Australian Quarterly* 51, 3: 98-109.

Freeland, J.M. 1972a. "People in the Cities." In Rapoport, 99-123.

———. 1972b. *Architecture in Australia*. Ringwood, Vic.: Penguin Australia.

Frost, Alan. 1982. "The Conditions of Early Settlement: New South Wales 1788-1840." In Carroll, 69-81.

Frost, Lucy. 1984. *No Place for a Nervous Lady: Voices from the Australian Bush*. Fitzroy/Ringwood, Vic.: McPhee Gribble & Penguin Australia.

Galbally, Ann. 1985. "Introduction." In Clark and Whitelaw, 9-10.

Gammage, Bill. 1982. "Anzac." In Carroll, 54-66.

Gardner, Susan. 1986. "*My Brilliant Career*: Portrait of the Artist as a Wild Colonial Girl." In Ferrier, 22-41.

Gerdes, Peter. 1982. "A Content Analysis of Australian TV News," *Australian Journal of Screen Theory* 11/12: 58-85.

Gibson, Ross. 1984. *The Diminishing Paradise: Changing Literary Perceptions of Australia*. Sydney: Sirius Books.

———. 1985. "Yondering: A Reading of *Mad Max Beyond Thunderdome*," *Art & Text* 19: 25-33.

Gidley, V.N., and March, B.C. 1979. "Community in Central Australia." In Crook, 209-30.

Gilbert, Alan. 1982. "The State and Nature." In Goldberg and Smith, 9-28.

Goldberg, S.L., and Smith, F.B., eds. 1982. *Australian Cultural History I: Culture and the State in Australia*. Canberra: ANU.

Goodwin, Ken. 1986. *A History of Australian Literature*. London: Macmillan.

Grant, Don. 1984. "Another Look at the Beach," *Australian Journal of Cultural Studies* 2, 2: 131-8.

Graubard, Stephen R. 1985. *Australia: The Daedelus Symposium*. North Ryde, NSW: Angus & Robertson.

Green, Dorothy. 1982. "Australian Writers as Social Critics: do they exist?" *Island Magazine* 9/10: 17-21.

Grieve, Norma, and Burns, Ailsa, eds. 1986. *Australian Women: New Feminist Perspectives*. Melbourne: Oxford U. Press.

Grove, Robin. 1984. "Transports of Mind: Literature, Establishment and Change," *Southerly* 44, 2: 154-69.

Gunew, Sneja. 1982. "Forms of Power in Recent Science Fiction," *Meanjin* 41, 2: 277-86.

Haese, Richard. 1981. *Rebels and Precursors: The Revolutionary Years of Australian Art*. Ringwood, Vic.: Allen Lane.

Hall, James. 1986. "Why No Men Writers Crowd the Best Seller List," *Bulletin* (May 27), 72-77.

Hall, Sandra. 1976. *Supertoy: 20 Years of Australian Television*. Melbourne: Sun Books.

———. 1981. *Turning On Turning Off: Australian Television in the Eighties*. North Ryde, NSW: Cassell Australia.

Hamilton, Annette. 1975. "Snugglepot and Cuddlepie: Happy Families in Australian Society," *Mankind* 10: 84-92.

Hassall, Anthony J. 1986. *Strange Country: A Study of Randolph Stow*. St. Lucia: U. Queensland Press.

Healy, J.J. 1987. "Literature, Power and the Refusals of Big Bear: Reflections on the Treatment of the Indian and the Aborigine." In Whitlock and McDougall, 68-93.

Healy, Patricia, and Ryan, Penny. 1975. "Sex Stereotyping in Children's Books." In Mercer, 247-52.

Heathcote, R.L. 1972. "The Visions of Australia 1770-1970." In Rapoport, 77-98.

Hergenhan, L.T. 1980. "Convict Legends, Australian Legends: Price Warung and the Palmers," *Australian Literary Studies* 9, 3: 337-45.

Herouvim, John. 1983. "More Questions Raised than Answered," *Journal of Australian Studies* 13: 78-88.

Heseltine, H.P. 1962. "Australian Image 1) The Literary Heritage," *Meanjin* (March): 38-49.

Hewett, Dorothy, 1979. "Western Australia: No Ratbag's Eden," *Meanjin* 38, 2: 234-45.

Higley, John, Deacon, Desley, and Smart, Don. 1979. *Elites in Australia*. London: Routledge & Kegan Paul.

Hinde, John. 1985. "*Barry McKenzie* and *Alvin*, Ten Years Later." In Moran and O'Regan, 184-87.

Hodge, Bob. See Fiske et al., 1987.

Holmes, Jonathan. 1985. "Resuming Our Journey into the Landscape . . ." In Lynn and Murray, 502-7.

Hoorn, Stewart. See Firth and Hoorn, 1979.

Horin *et al.* 1985. In Pullen, 129-42.

Horne, Donald. 1971. *The Lucky Country*. Ringwood, Vic.: Penguin Australia.

———. 1975. "Ockerism," *Meanjin* 34, 4: 462-66.

———. 1976. *Death of the Lucky Country*. Ringwood, Vic.: Penguin Australia.

———. 1985. "Who Rules Australia." In Graubard, 171-196.

Hosking, Rick. 1979. "The Usable Past: Australian War Fiction of the 1950s," *Australian Literary Studies* 12, 2: 234-47.

Hughes, Robert. 1970. *The Art of Australia*. Ringwood, Vic.: Penguin Australia.

———. 1985. *The Fatal Shore: The History of the Transportation of Convicts to Australia, 1787-1868*. London: Collins Harvill.

Idriess, Ion. (1931) 1963. *Lassiter's Last Ride*. Sydney: Pacific Books.

Inglis, K.S. 1985. "Ceremonies in a Capital Landscape: Scenes in the Making of Canberra." In Graubard, 85-126.

Ikin, Van, ed. 1982. "Introduction" to *Australian Science Fiction*. Brisbane: U. Queensland Press.

Jackson, Gordon. 1985. "The Australian Economy." In Graubard, 231-58.

James, Trevor. 1984. "From Exploration to Celebration: Writers and the Landscape in Australia's Northern Territory," *Ariel* 15, 2: 15-71.

Jayasuriya, Laksiri. 1985. "Multiculturalism: Fact, policy, and rhetoric." In M. Poole et al., 23-34.

Johnson, Dianne. 1984. "From Fairy to Witch: imagery and myth in the Azaria case," *Australian Journal of Cultural Studies* 2, 2: 90-197.

Jones, Janet. 1979. "The Amazing Women's Weekly Juggling Act," *Refractory Girl* 16: 26-30.

Jose, Nicholas. 1985. "Cultural Identity: 'I think I'm Something Else.'" In Graubard, 311-42.

Journal of Australian Studies. 1981. Symposium on Psycho-History, 8: 2-33.

Journal of Australian Studies. 1981. Symposium on Satellite Society, 9: 2-31.

Jupp, James. 1986. "Political Culture: The 'Bourgeois' and 'Proletarian' Variations." In Davidson, 79-88.

Kael, Pauline. 1985. "A Dreamlike Requiem Mass for a Nation's Lost Honour." In Moran and O'Regan, 204-9.

Kent, David. 1985a. "From the Sudan to Saigon: A Critical Review of Historical Works," *Australian Literary Studies* 12, 2: 155-65.

————. 1985b. "*The Anzac Book* and the Anzac Legend: C.E.W. Bean as Editor and Image Maker," *Historical Studies* 21, 84: 376:90.

Kent, Valerie. 1986. "Alias Miles Franklin." In Ferrier, 44-58.

Kiernan, Brian. 1971. *Images of Society and Nature: Seven Essays on Australian Novels.* Melbourne: Oxford U. Press.

————. 1980. "Sydney or the Bush: Some Literary Images." In Roe, 148-65.

Kirk, Pauline. 1971. "Colonial Literature for Colonial Readers," *Australian Literary Studies* 5, 2: 133-45.

Knight, Stephen. 1986. "Real Pulp at Last: Peter Corris's Thrillers," *Meanjin* 4: 446-52.

Koch, C.J. 1980. "Literature and Cultural Identity," *Tasmanian Review* 4: 2-5.

Kramer, Leonie. 1985. "The Media, Society, and Culture." In Graubard, 293-310.

Lawson, Sylvia. 1982. "Towards Decolonization: Film History in Australia." In Dermody et al., 19-32

Leer, Martin. 1985. "At the Edge: Geography and the Imagination in the Work of David Malouf," *Australian Literary Studies* 12, 1: 3-21.

Lewis, Glen. 1974. "Violence in Australian History: The Queensland Experience," *Meanjin* 33, 2: 313-19.

Lippman, Lorna. 1983. "A Migrant People." In McLaren, 113-26.

Lohrey, Amanda. 1982. "Gallipoli: Male Innocence as a Marketable Commodity," *Island Magazine* 9/10: 29-34.

Lynn, Elwynn, and Murray, Laura, eds. 1985. *Considering Art in Tasmania.* Sydney: Fine Arts Press.

Macdonald, Stuart. See Mandeville and Macdonald, 1980.

Mackie, Alwynne. 1979. "Fred Williams: Abstracted Landscapes," *Art and Australia* 16, 3: 248-53.

Manderson, Lenore, ed. 1985. *Australian Ways: Anthropological Studies of an Industrialized Society.* Sydney: Allen & Unwin.

Mandeville, Thomas, and Macdonald, Stuart. 1980. "Reflections on the Technological Change Debate in Australia," *Australian Quarterly* 52, 2: 213-20.

Marshall, Jock, and Drysdale, Russell. 1966. *Journey among Men.* Melbourne: Sun Books.

May, Dawn. 1983. "The Articulation of Aboriginal and Capitalist Modes on the North Queensland Pastoral Frontier," *Journal of Australian Studies* 12: 34-44.

Mayer, Henry, and Helen Wilson, eds. 1976. *Australian Politics: A Fourth Reader.* Melbourne: Cheshire.

McCaughey, Patrick. 1985. "Foreword." In Clark and Whitelaw, 3.

McColl, Margaret. 1980. "The Mass Media and Australian Politics." In Parkin et al., 250-60.

McDougall, Russell. 1987. "Sprawl and the Vertical." In Whitlock and McDougall, 205-37.

McFarlane, Brian. 1980. "Horror and Suspense." In Murray, 61-78.

———. 1981. Review of *Gallipoli, Cinema Papers* 8, 33: 285-6.

———. 1983. *Words and Images: Australian Novels into Film.* Richmond, Vic.: Heineman in assoc. w/ *Cinema Papers.*

McGregor, Craig. 1981. *The Australian People.* Sydney: Houghton & Stoughton.

McInherny, Frances. 1983. "Miles Franklin, *My Brilliant Career,* and the Female Tradition." In S. Walker, 71-83.

———. 1986. "'Deep into the Destructive Core': Elizabeth Harrower's *The Watch Tower.*" In Ferrier, 150-62.

McIntyre, Angus. 1982. "Ned Kelly: A Folk Hero." In Carroll, 38-53.

McKernan, Susan. 1986. "Crossing the Border: Regional Writing in Australia," *Meanjin* 4: 547-60.

McLaren, John. 1981. "A Satellite Society – A Commentary," *Journal of Australian Studies* 9: 26-31.

———, ed. 1983. *A Nation Apart/Essays in Honour of Andrew Fabinyi/Personal Views of Australia in the Eighties.* Melbourne: Longman Cheshire.

McNair, Ian. 1975. "A Profile of Australians – Some Characteristics and Attitudes," *Australian Quarterly* 47-4: 66-77.

McQueen, Humphrey. 1976. *A New Britannia.* Ringwood, Vic.: Penguin Australia.

———. 1979a. *The Black Swan of Trespass: The Emergence of Modernist Painting in Australia to 1944.* Sydney: Alternative Publishing Co-op.

———. 1979b. "Queensland: A State of Mind," *Meanjin* 38, 1: 41-51.

———. 1986. Review of Robert Dixon, *The Course of Empire, Meanjin* 4: 561-71.

McQuilton, John. 1981. "The Legend of Ned Kelly," *Overland* 84: 38-41.

Mercer, Jan, ed. 1975. *The Other Half: Women in Australian Society.* Ringwood, Vic.: Penguin Australia.

Millar, T.B. 1985. "The Defense of Australia." In Graubard.

Modjeska, Drusilla. 1984. *Exiles at Home: Australian Women Writers 1925-1945.* London & Sydney: Sirius Books. See also Dermody et al., 1982.

Moffitt, Ian. 1972. *The U-Jack Society: An Experience of Being Australian.* Sydney: Ure Smith.

Mol, Hans. 1985. *The Faith of Australians.* Sydney: Allen & Unwin.

Molony, John. 1982. *I Am Ned Kelly.* Ringwood, Vic.: Penguin Australia.

Moore, T. Inglis. 1971. *Social Patterns in Australian Literature.* Sydney: Angus & Robertson.

Moorehouse, Frank. 1982. "The Australian Legend and R.M. Williams – Male Costume and Accoutrement," *Island Magazine* 9/10: 24-8.

Moran, Albert. 1985. *Images and Industry: Television Drama Production in Australia.* Sydney: Currency Press. See also Rowse and Moran, 1984.

———, and O'Regan, Tom. 1984. "Two Discourses of Australian Film," *Australian Journal of Film Theory* 15/16: 163-73.

——— and ———, eds. 1985. *An Australian Film Reader.* Sydney: Currency Press.

Morgan, Patrick. 1982. "Hard Work and Idle Dissipation: The Dual Australian Personality," *Meanjin* 41, 1: 130-7.

Morris, Meaghan. 1982. "Sydney Tower," *Island Magazine* 9/10: 53-61.

Muecke, Stephen. See Benterrek et al., 1984.

Murray, Laura. See Lynn and Murray, 1985.

Murray, Scott, ed. 1980. *The New Australian Cinema.* Melbourne: Thomas Nelson.

Narasimhaiah, C.D., ed. 1982. *An Introduction to Australian Literature.* Brisbane: Wiley.

Nesbitt, Bruce. 1971. "Literary Nationalism and the 1980s," *Australian Literary Studies* 5, 1: 3-17.

Neutze, Max. 1985. "City, Country, Town: Australian Peculiarities," *Australian Cultural History* 4: 7-23.

O'Farrell, Patrick. 1982. "The Cultural Ambivalence of Australian Religion." In Goldberg and Smith, 3-8.

O'Regan, Tom. 1986. "Aspects of the Australian Film and TV Interface," *Australian Journal of Screen Theory* 17/18: 5-33. See also Moran and O'Regan, 1985.

Oxley, H.G. 1978. *Mateship in Local Organization: A Study of Egalitarianism, Stratification, Leadership, and Amenities Projects in a Semi-Industrial Community Inland New South Wales.* St. Lucia: U. Queensland Press.

———. 1979. "Ockerism: The Cultural Rabbit." In Spearritt and Walker, 190-209.

Palmer, Vance. 1963. *The Legend of the Nineties.* Melbourne: Melbourne University Press.

Parkin, Andrew. 1980. "Power in Australia: An Introduction." In Parkin et al., 263-84.

Parkin, Andrew, Summers, John, and Woodward, Dennis, eds. 1980. *Government, Politics and Power in Australia,* 2nd ed. Melbourne: Longman Cheshire.

Patton, Paul, and Poole, Ross, eds. 1985. *War/Masculinity.* Sydney: Intervention Publications.

Perkins, Elizabeth. 1983. "Living in the Deep North." In McLaren, 55-66.

Phillips, A.A. 1971. "The Cross-Eyed Clio: McQueen and the Australian Tradition," *Meanjin* 30, 1: 108-13.

———. 1980. *The Australian Tradition: Studies in a Colonial Culture,* intro. H.P. Heseltine. Melbourne: Longman Cheshire.

Phillips, Shelly. 1979. *Young Australians: The Attitudes of Our Children.* Sydney: Harper & Row, 1979.

Pike, Andrew. 1977. "Aboriginals in Australian Feature Films," *Meanjin* 36, 4: 592-99.

———. 1980. "The Past: Boom and Bust." In Murray, 11-26.

Poole, Marilyn J. 1986. "Choices and Constraints: The Education of Girls." In Grieve and Burns, 105-21.

Poole, Millicent, de Lacey, Philip, and Randhawa, Bikkar S., eds. 1985. *Australia in Transition: Culture and Life Possibilities.* Sydney: Harcourt Brace Jovanovich.

Poole, Ross. 1985. "Structures of Identity." In Patton and Poole, 71-79.

Powell, J.M. 1986. "A Broken Topography, a Monotonous Relief." In Davidson, 26-38.

Pullen, Robert, ed. 1985. *The Way We Are: A National Portrait by THE NATIONAL TIMES.* North Sydney: Unwin Paperbacks.

Randhawa, Bikkar S. See M. Poole et al., 1985.

Rapoport, Amos, ed. 1972. *Australia as Human Setting*. Sydney: Angus & Robertson.

Reid, Ian. 1980. "In Memoriam, Ned Kelly," *Meanjin* 39, 4: 595-9.

Reynolds, Henry. 1972. "Violence, the Aboriginals, and the Australian Historian," *Meanjin* 31, 4: 471-77.

Richards, Lyn. 1985. *Having Families: Marriage, Parenthood and Social Pressure in Australia*, revised ed. Ringwood, Vic.: Penguin Australia.

Rickard, John. 1979. "National Character and the 'Typical Australian': An Alternative to Russell Ward," *Journal of Australian Studies* 5: 12-21.

————. 1981. "Psychohistory in Australia: The Next Assignment," *Journal of Australian Studies* 8: 2-13.

Robson, Lloyd. 1985. "Tasmania and Its Near Neighbour to the North," *Australian Cultural History* 4: 71-8.

Roe, Jill, ed. 1980. *Twentieth-Century Sydney: Studies in Urban and Social History*. Sydney: Hale & Iremonger.

Roe, Michael. 1962. "The Australian Legend," *Meanjin* 21, 3: 363-8.

————. 1973. "The Australian Legend: A Reply to John Barrett," *Meanjin* 32, 2: 213-14.

Roe, Paddy. See Benterrek et al., 1984.

Rohdie, Sam. 1985. "*Gallipoli*, Peter Weir and Australian Art Cinema." In Moran and O'Regan, 194-97.

Rolls, Eric. 1984. *A Million Wild Acres*. Ringwood, Vic.: Penguin Australia.

Rose, A.J. 1972. "Australia as a Cultural Landscape." In Rapoport, 58-76.

Ross, Jane. 1985. *The Myth of the Digger*. Sydney: Hale & Iremonger.

Rowse, Tim. 1978. *Australian Liberalism and National Character*. Malmsbury, Vic.: Kibble Books.

————. 1978b. "Heaven and Hills Hoist: Australian Critics on Suburbia," *Meanjin* 37, 1: 3-13.

————. 1982. "The Pluralism of Frank Moorehouse." In Dermody et al., 250-67.

————, and Moran, Albert. 1984. "'Peculiarly Australian' – The Political Construction of Cultural Identity." In Encel and Bryson, 229-78.

Ryan, Penny. See Healy and Ryan, 1975.

Ryan, Tom. 1980. "Historical Films." In Murray, 113-37.

Sampson, Shirley. 1973. "The Women's Weekly: Today – Education and the Aspirations of Girls," *Refractory Girl* 3: 11-18.

Samuel, Linley. 1983. "The Making of a School-Resister: A Case Study of Australian Working-Class Secondary Schoolgirls." In R.K. Browne and L.E. Foster, *Sociology of Education*, 3rd ed. Melbourne: Macmillan.

Sandercock, Leonie. 1983. "The Cities in the Eighties." In McLaren, 67-84.

Sanders, Noel. 1983. "Crimes of Passion: TV, Popular Literature, and the Graham Thorne Kidnapping, 1960," *Australian Journal of Cultural Studies* 1, 1: 56-70.

Saunders, David. 1974. "The Sydney Opera House," *Art and Australia* 11, 3: 240-51.

Schaffer, Kay (as Kay Iseman). 1982. "Katherine Susannah Prichard: Of an End of a New Beginning." In Dermody et al., 124-61.

———. "Landscape Representation and Australian National Identity." Unpublished paper.

Schedvin, M.B. and C.B. 1982. "The Nomadic Tribes of Urban Britain: A Prelude to Botany Bay." In Carroll, 69-81.

Seal, Graham. 1980. *Ned Kelly in Popular Tradition*. Melbourne: Hyland House.

Seddon, George. 1983. "The Man-Modified Environment." In McLaren, 1-8.

Selleck, Richard. 1982. "State Education and Culture." In Goldberg and Smith, 29-42.

Serle, Geoffrey. 1973. *From Deserts the Prophets Come: The Creative Spirit in Australia 1788-1972*. Melbourne: Heinemann.

Sharkey, Michael. 1983. "Rosa Praed's Colonial Heroines." In Walker, 26-36.

Sheridan, Susan. 1982. "Ada Cambridge and the Female Literary Tradition." In Dermody et al., 162-75.

The Sixth Biennale of Sydney. 1986. *Origins Originality + Beyond*. Sydney: Art Gallery of New South Wales.

Smart, Don. See Higley et al., 1979.

Smith, Bernard. 1971. *Australian Painting 1788-1970*, 2nd ed. Melbourne: Oxford U. Press.

———. 1985. *European Vision and the South Pacific*, 2nd ed. New Haven: Yale U. Press.

Smith, F.B. See Goldberg and Smith, 1982.

Smith, Margaret. 1986. "Australian Woman Novelists of the 1970s: A Survey." In Ferrier, 211-21.

Smith, Terry. See Dixon and Smith, 1984.

Smolicz, J.J. 1985. "Multiculturalism and an Overarching Framework of Values." In Poole et al., 76-87.

Souter, Gavin. 1978. *Lion and Kangaroo: Australia 1901-1919: The Rise of a Nation*. Sydney: Fontana.

Spate, Virginia. 1984. "Introduction." In Dixon and Smith, 7.

Spearritt, Peter. 1979. "Opening the Sydney Harbour Bridge." In Spearritt and Walker, pp. 39-61.

Spearritt, Peter, and Walker, David, eds. 1979. *Australian Popular Culture*. Sydney: Allen & Unwin.

Stern, Leslie. 1982. "The Australian Cereal: Home Grown Television." In Dermody et al., 103-23.

———. 1977. "Oedipal Opera: 'The Restless Years,'" *Australian Journal of Film Theory* 4: 39-48.

Stivens, Maila. 1985. "The Private Life of the Extended Family: Family, Kinship, and Class in a Middle Class Suburb of Sydney." In Manderson, 15-32.

Stretton, Hugh. 1985. "The Quality of Leading Australians." In Graubard, 197-230.

Summers, Anne. 1975. *Damned Whores and God's Police: The Colonization of Women in Australia*. Ringwood, Vic.: Penguin Australia.

Summers, John. See Parkin et al., 1980.

Sykes, Bobbi. 1985. "Black Women in Australia: A History." In Mercer, 313-22.

Tacy, David. 1985. "Patrick White's *Voss*: The Teller and the Tale," *Southern Review* 18, 3: 251-71.

Tatz, Colin. 1980. "Aboriginality as Civilization," *Australian Quarterly* 52, 3: 352-62.

Taylor, Andrew. 1982. "Bosom of Nature or Heart of Stone: A Difference in Heritage." In Narasimhaiah, 144-56.

———. 1985. "War Poetry: Myth as De-formation and Re-formation," *Australian Literary Studies* 12, 2: 182-92.

Taylor, Paul. 1984. "A Culture of Temporary Culture," *Art & Text* 16: 94-106.

Thomson, Helen. 1983. "Catherine Helen Spence: Pragmatic Utopian." In S. Walker, 12-15.

Thwaite, Joy. 1986. "Eve Langley: Personal and Artistic Schism." In Ferrier, 118-35.

Tulloch, John. 1981. *Legends on the Screen: The Australian Narrative Cinema 1919-1929*. Sydney: Currency Press & Australian Film Institute.

Turner, Graeme. 1981. "For the Term of His Natural Life: A New View of the Self in Australian Fiction," *Overland* 86: 51-5.

———. 1986. *National Fictions*. N. Sydney: Allen & Unwin. See also Fiske et al., 1987.

Turner, Ian, ed. 1968. *The Australian Dream: A Collection of Anticipations about Australia from Captain Cook to the Present*. Melbourne: Sun Books.

———, and Sturgess, Gary. 1979. "Australia, the Myth and November 11," *Overland* 76/77: 88-95.

Uhr, John. 1981. "Australia's Political Culture and Altman's Cultural Politics," *Australian Quarterly* 53, 1: 98-108.

Vaughan, Belinda. 1983. "Woman: The Struggle to Be." In McLaren, 127-48.

Walker, Brenda. 1983. "Tea Rose and the Confetti-Dot Goddess: Images of the Woman Artist in Barbara Hanrahan's Novels." In S. Walker, 204-19.

Walker, David. 1976. *Dream and Disillusion: A Search for Australian Cultural Identity.* Canberra: ANU Press.

———. 1979. "The Getting of Manhood." In Spearritt and Walker, 121-44.

Walker, Shirley, ed. 1983. *Who Is She? Images of Woman in Australian Fiction.* St. Lucia: U. Queensland Press.

Walsh, Richard. 1985. "Australia Observed." In Graubard, 421-38.

Walter, James. 1986. "On Being Australian: Reflections on Recent Biography," *Meanjin* 4: 479-87.

Ward, Russel. (1958) 1966. *The Australian Legend.* Melbourne: Oxford U. Press.

———. 1962. "Reply to Michael Roe," *Meanjin* 21, 3: 363-8.

Watson, Don. 1982. "The War on Australia's Frontier," *Meanjin* 41, 1: 138-46.

Webby, Elizabeth. 1980. "The Aboriginal in Early Australian Literature," *Southerly* 40, 1: 45-63.

Wells, Andrew. 1986. "Business: City of Capital." In Davidson, 64-78.

White, Richard. 1981. *Inventing Australia: Images and Identity 1688-1980.* Sydney: Allen & Unwin.

Whitelaw, Bridget. See Clark, 1985.

Whitlock, Gillian, and McDougall, Russell, eds. 1987.*Australian/Canadian Literatures in English.* North Ryde, NSW: Methuen Australia.

Wilkes, G.A. 1977. "The Australian Legend: Some Notes Towards Redefinition," *Southerly* 37, 3: 318-30.

———. 1981. *The Stockyard and the Croquet Lawn: Literary Evidence for Australia's Cultural Development.* Port Melbourne: Edward Arnold.

Wilson, Bruce. See Dwyer et al., 1984.

Wilson, Paul. 1985. *Slaughter of the Innocents.*

Wilson, Sandra. 1982. "Police Work: The Role of the Police in the Kalgoorlie Community, 1897-1898," *Journal of Australian Studies* 11: 9-20.

Windshuttle, Keith. 1985. *The Media: A New Analysis of the Press, Television, Radio and Advertising in Australia.* Ringwood, Vic.: Penguin Australia.

Woodward, Dennis. See Parkin et al., 1980.

Wook, Roger. See Dwyer et al., 1984.

Zwicky, Fay. 1983. "Living in Western Australia." In McLaren, 33-42.

INDEX OF AUSTRALIAN
NAMES AND WORKS

The designation "LS" indicates that the book is part of the preliminary literature survey and as such is cited in chapter, 1, section 2 ("Marker Traits") *passim*, as well as in Appendix B. In general, secondary sources are notated only re instances when the person or item is quoted or discussed rather than simply referenced. Paintings and literary texts are listed under artist/author name, but since films, television programs, periodicals, and, occasionally, edited collections are not generally considered to be individually "authored" in the same way, these are listed separately by title. Some titles are duplicated in the case of works discussed in both book and film form